T0305034

UKRAINE
THE FORGING OF A NATION

BY THE SAME AUTHOR

A Ukrainian Christmas
(Yaroslav Hrytsak and Nadiyka Gerbish)

Ivan Franko and His Community

UKRAINE

THE FORGING OF A NATION

YAROSLAV HRYTSAK

TRANSLATED BY
DOMINIQUE HOFFMAN

SPHERE

First published in Ukraine in 2022 by Portal Books under the title
Overcoming the Past: Ukraine's Global History
This English translation first published in Great Britain in 2023 by Sphere

1 3 5 7 9 10 8 6 4 2

A CIP catalogue record for this book
is available from the British Library.

Hardback ISBN 978-1-4087-3080-5
C-format ISBN 978-1-4087-3081-2

Typeset in Garamond by M Rules
Printed and bound in Great Britain by
Clays Ltd, Elcograf S.p.A.

Papers used by Sphere are from well-managed forests
and other responsible sources.

Sphere
An imprint of
Little, Brown Book Group
Carmelite House
50 Victoria Embankment
London EC4Y 0DZ

An Hachette UK Company
www.hachette.co.uk

www.littlebrown.co.uk

CONTENTS

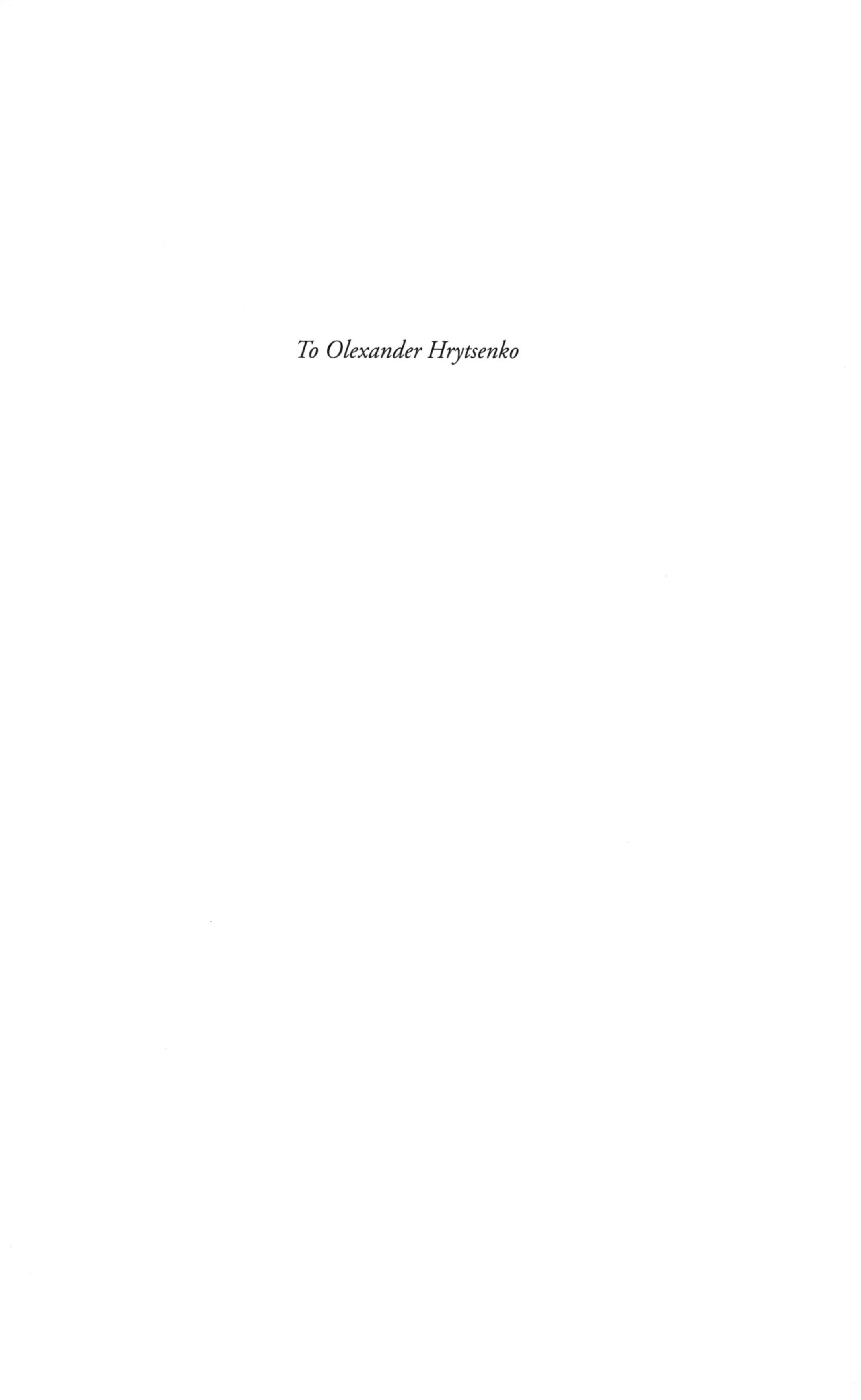

To Olexander Hrytsenko

A NOTE ON TRANSLITERATION

Personal and place names are transliterated according to a slightly simplified version of the Library of Congress systems for transliteration from the Ukrainian and Russian alphabets. Polish nomenclature is unchanged. Places are identified according to the nomenclature of the country within whose internationally recognised borders they now exist. When a well-established English spelling differs from standard transliteration (for instance Moscow or Vienna), the familiar spelling has been utilised.

INTRODUCTION

On 24 February 2022, the Russian army invaded Ukraine. The most important route of invasion came from the north, from Belarus, the shortest route from the border to Kyiv, the Ukrainian capital. The Russians travelled openly in columns, unafraid, without air cover or reconnaissance. They brought along their dress uniforms for the victory parade they planned to march through Kyiv's central square in three days' time.

There was no parade. They were stopped at the city of Bucha, twenty-four kilometres as the crow flies from Kyiv. Twenty-four kilometres is the distance from which their artillery could have reached the centre of the Ukrainian capital. The Russians were stopped by volunteers from the neighbouring city of Irpin. They occupied a hill above the bridge between the two cities and fired on the enemy from there.

The defenders held the line for an entire month until regular Ukrainian troops arrived and pushed the Russians all the way back to the Belarus-Ukraine border. Most of the defenders were civilians. Among them was a musician from an academic orchestra; a family therapist who taught Argentine tango in his free time; a lawyer who handled the radio communications, since radio was a hobby of his; several construction workers; a gas station attendant, and others. The sniper was a recreational hunter.

They fought creatively. When they came under fire from large calibre weapons, they brought in concrete mixers and bulldozers to build a barricade against shelling. When the rains and cold became too much, they ran to a nearby building that had been hit by the enemy to warm themselves by the fire and dry their clothes.

All Ukraine was seized with a spirit of initiative and self-organisation. In the early days of the war, military experts discussed what would have happened if President Volodymyr Zelensky had left Kyiv (as Western governments had suggested) or if Russian strike groups (of which there were at least three) had killed him. They reached the conclusion that while it would certainly have been a tragedy for Ukraine, it would not have radically changed the course of the war. Just look at the mayors of the largest towns and cities. Each of them took the initiative to organise their own defence without waiting for orders from the capital. This offers a striking contrast to the Russians, who lacked any initiative. President Vladimir Putin interfered in the actions of the Russian army, making decisions at the level of a colonel or brigadier general.

A comparison with the Greco-Persian Wars comes to mind. At that time, an alliance of democracies, the Greek city-states, successfully resisted and eventually defeated the much larger Persian Empire. One outcome of that victory was the birth of history. Herodotus, 'the Father of History', wanted to understand the roots of Greek resilience. He travelled to the parts of the ancient world he could reach, comparing the habits of the ancient Greeks with those of other nations.

The history of Ukraine that you hold in your hands was written with a similar goal in mind. I have tried to discover the reasons for Ukraine's resilience within a global context. Because the Russia-Ukraine war isn't just another war. This war will determine the contours of the future world. German Chancellor Olaf Scholz has called it a *Zeitenwende*, a turning point in modern history.

Historians debate what would have happened if the Greeks had lost the Greco-Persian Wars. It's not difficult to imagine what would have happened to Ukraine had it not successfully resisted in those first weeks of the war. Just look at Bucha. After the Russian retreat, the bodies of 461 residents were found here. In the broader area, there were 1,137 victims. Most had been shot and many of the bodies showed signs of torture.

Bucha now stands beside Srebrenica and Darfur as prime examples of modern genocide. The war brings more and more tragic symbols. On 6 June 2023, the Kakhovka dam, which was under the control of Russian forces, was blown up. The released water flooded vast areas of southern Ukraine all the way to the Black Sea, resulting in significant loss of life of both humans and animals and irreparable environmental damage. It has been called an ecocide. But it seems that wasn't enough for the Russians. Putin and his associates are now threatening to launch nuclear strikes against Ukraine and against the Western countries which support it. The world is facing the threat of nuclear apocalypse.

These examples raise questions that are as old as history itself: what is the nature of human evil? It is possible to limit violence in history? Is it even possible to achieve sustainable progress in the face of global threats?

The history of Ukraine and the neighbouring lands and peoples offers rich material in the search for answers to these questions. On the one hand, Ukraine's past is permeated with extreme violence. As this book attempts to show, the Ukrainian question, now and in the past, becomes particularly acute at the most critical turns of global history – the crises of the seventeenth century, the First and Second World Wars, the fall of communism. On the other hand, Ukrainian history is also exceptionally rich in examples of survival, solidarity and resilience. Thus, Ukraine's past offers both alarming warnings and grounds for optimism.

I must warn the reader up front that this book offers no

unequivocal answers. Since ancient times it has been said that history is the teacher of life. For better or worse, this pretty saying is not true. As Friedrich Hegel argued and Sting sang, history teaches us nothing. It is more like a prompter in the wings giving the actors their cues.

Alexander Gerschenkron was a historian of Eastern Europe at Harvard who was born in imperial Odessa, now Ukrainian Odesa. Gerschenkron writes that, '[t]he historian's contribution consists in pointing at *potentially* relevant factors and *potentially* significant combinations among them which could not be easily perceived within a more limited sphere of reference. These are the questions. The answers themselves, however, are a different matter. No past experience, however rich, and no historical research, however thorough, can save the living generation the creative task of finding their own answers and shaping their own future.'

Many books of Ukrainian history have been published since Ukraine gained its independence in 1991. This book is different in that it poses different and more difficult questions about Ukraine's past, questions whose answers may be critical for the future of Ukraine and the entire world.

There is no single recipe for writing history. Each historian works according to their own taste. I'll offer a few of my own criteria of 'taste'.

First, my ideal is a history without names and dates. I prefer history that attempts to see the processes behind isolated events. Such a history doesn't draw us a detailed roadmap, but it can serve as a compass and help us navigate which way to go.

Of course, it's impossible to write history entirely without names or dates. Marc Bloch, one of the great historians of our time, has compared historians to giants of the fairy tales: they know that wherever they catch the scent of human flesh, there lies the quarry. Names and dates are the muscles and blood of history. Take them away and you are left with only a desiccated skeleton. But without analysing the skeleton, we won't understand what the body of history consists of. We need a healthy compromise. This book will keep names and dates to the bare minimum.

My second criterion is that history should be global. Rudyard Kipling asked, 'And what should they know of England who only England know?' The same question could be asked about Ukraine. The central elements of its history – the appearance of Rus, the history of the Cossacks or the Holodomor – cannot be understood within only the limited frame of Ukraine itself.

The question of how far to expand the frame to the east or to the west is an open question that historians have been debating for several generations. I propose a radical resolution to the problem: expand the frame to the entire globe. Global history doesn't just mean maximising the geographic scope. First and foremost, it involves a search for the connections which made the globalised modern world possible. I will trace these connections to support one of the main theses of this book: Ukraine emerged as a result of globalisation and the rise of the West, which began with the discovery of America in 1492. In this sense, Columbus deserves to become one of the main characters of Ukrainian history.

Global history doesn't require us to abandon the nation as a unit of study and description. Theoretical historians assert that a global history can be written about anything. If so, then it is possible to write a global history of the Ukrainian nation. One important caveat here is to remember that there were periods in history when nations didn't exist, just as printed books, trains and smart phones didn't exist. Nations don't exist in nature. They are a product of historical development over the last few centuries. But if we compare nations with living organisms, they behave entirely differently from people. While most people want to appear younger, every nation tries to appear older and tries to trace its origins to ancient times – to the Old Testament or Herodotus or as some Russians try to do – the Etruscans. ('Et*rus*cans are *Rus*sians.')

We have to be able to distinguish between two things: how nations describe themselves in the mouths of politicians and intellectuals, and what actually happened. Another thing is that nations don't arise out of nothing. They are built, or rather people build them, from the building blocks of the past. Some of those blocks are imaginary and invented, sometimes to the point of absurdity. But other blocks are very real. In Ukraine, those blocks would include its fertile soil and its unique status as a geopolitically important borderland. Therefore, it will be impossible to write a convincing history of Ukraine if we limit ourselves to only the last few centuries when the Ukrainian nation was born and formed.

This brings us to our third and last criterion. Ukrainian history should be viewed in terms of the *longue durée*: long periods of time, the deep currents of the past, which can extend over centuries or millennia and continue to influence the present day.

My ambition is to present the history of Ukraine in this dual key of global history and the *longue durée*. But here, I depart not only from the path of most Ukrainian historians but most historians in general. They are likely to view my efforts with scepticism. Here I'm following in the footsteps of economists, social scientists and sociologists who use a similar approach to answer the questions posed above. For the sake of brevity, I'll mention here just a few of the best-known authors whose lead I have followed in this book: Daron Acemoglu, Ronald Inglehart, Douglass North, Robert D. Putnam, and Hernando de Soto. They belong to various disciplines but agree on one thing: history matters. In analysing and diagnosing the present, we must begin with a serious and sober analysis of the past.

Before moving on to the main story, I'd like to make a few

more subjective remarks. Writing a historical synthesis is a bit like intellectual suicide. It requires the writer to go beyond his narrow field of specialisation and make his way into realms where he has neither the relevant knowledge nor the necessary confidence. By profession, I am a historian of the nineteenth and twentieth centuries. Naturally, I can't be expected to write authoritatively about the tenth or fifteenth centuries. I'm almost certain that experts in the history of those centuries will easily find errors or inaccuracies in my writing. For this I would like to apologise in advance.

Another challenge in writing a synthesis of this kind is how to describe complex things simply, but not too simply. To facilitate the former and avoid the latter, I've relied on metaphors. Metaphors are for a historian what formulas are for a mathematician, physicist or chemist: they allow us to replace long explanations with brief formulations. I hope that intelligent readers will understand the sense and limitations of this method.

Nowhere in this book do I claim to be right. On the contrary, doubt is my intellectual homeland. As a result, I qualify almost every claim I make with words such as 'it seems', 'usually' or 'often'. Where I have not done so, readers can add the qualifications in for me.

There are no 'iron laws' of history. Therefore, no claim about the past can be absolute. But history is also not just a chaotic accumulation of facts. Between the non-existent laws of history and the chaos of past events, we can identify relevant factors – the ones that Alexander Gerschenkron urged historians to discover. This is what I've attempted to do to the best of my ability.

After long vacillations, I have chosen not to provide detailed descriptions of the exceptions to these broad tendencies – particularly when such descriptions would entail a significant expansion of the text and divert me from my central argument. The same can be said for the many people of non-Ukrainian ethnicity who have lived in these lands throughout history: Jews, Poles, Crimean

Tatars and others. Their appearances in this book are fragmentary, only in relation to the central narrative line. I'm aware of this limitation and regret it. For readers who would like to know more about the diversity of Ukraine, I can recommend Paul Magosci's *A History of Ukraine: the Land and its Peoples*. Here, I will limit myself to the observation that Ukraine has undergone a complex transformation from an ethnic to a civic nation. This transformation is one of the central themes of this book.

And one last thing. Norman Davies once wrote that 'good historians need to admit to their limitations. The worst are those who imagine themselves to be free of any bias'. In the light of this admonition, I'd like to acknowledge my own bias. I want to see Ukraine as a liberal democracy. Therefore, I've written this book in such a way as to show that this goal is not only desirable, but achievable.

I do not share the view that only some countries can have liberal democracies and the rest, due to their historical and cultural circumstances, should go their own way. This is just like saying that the people of certain countries somehow prefer to be deprived of their property, condemned to poverty, imprisoned, tortured and executed, have their women and children raped and their men sent to die in foreign wars in foreign lands just because they have their own, so-called 'traditional values'. For all its imperfections, liberal democracy is still the best safeguard against violence. A nation's history may make the path longer or more difficult, and liberal democracy won't always prevail, but I have no doubt that this path is worth following.

July 2023

CHAPTER 1

WHAT'S IN A NAME?

Almost every general history of Ukraine starts with a statement that 'Ukraine' means 'borderlands'. It is both right and wrong. As a matter of fact, Ukraine may be read both as 'borderlands' and 'a country'. The term itself comes from *kraiaty* (to cut) so it indicates a particular area that is demarcated, or cut off, from other territories. So it can mean either *kraina* (the country itself) or *okraina* (borderlands), depending on where you stand. If someone is outside this space, say in Moscow or Warsaw, it is *okraina*, or outskirts, for them. If you are within this space, in Kyiv or Lviv for instance, then it is more likely to indicate the *kraina*, the homeland.

Although there are historical texts to support both possibilities, the earliest use of the word *Ukraina* appears to reference the idea of a country. In 1187, the Kyiv Chronicle describes the heroic death of the Prince Volodymyr Hlibovych. The chronicler writes that 'all Ukraine groaned for him.' Most likely, he means 'a land (a country)' and not 'a borderland'. Another use of Ukraine as a country occurs in the Peresopnytsia Gospel of 1556, the first translation of the Scriptures from Old Church Slavonic into the vernacular. Where the Church Slavonic text reads 'he went into the land of Judea' and the Greek original reads 'ὅρια = the land', the translation into the local Slavic language reads, he 'came into the Judean ukraina'.

It is true that there are relatively few uses of the word *Ukraina* in the sense of 'country' in the oldest written sources. It has to be taken into account, however, there aren't many written sources at all from the region. The period spanning the fourteenth and fifteenth centuries in the Ukrainian lands is often called the 'long silence'. Instead of written sources, we can turn to the oral tradition of songs and proverbs and these frequently mention *Ukraina*. There we encounter expressions such as 'not far away *Ukraina*', 'he went to far *Ukraina*', 'my beloved *Ukraina*', or even the affectionate diminutive '*Ukrainonka*'.

The songs don't tell us exactly where this country is located. It could be the land in which the singer lives, or a distant land in which they'd like to live. We shouldn't be too surprised by the ambiguity. People living in the Carpathian Mountains didn't know their mountains were called the 'Carpathians'; they just called them 'the mountains'. Similarly, *Ukraina* may just have been what they called their land. It was simply the default name.

Other examples include China/Zhong guo as 'the central states', the region of Slovenia called *Krajina* or Germany's name for itself, *Deutschland*. *Deutsch* comes from the Old German *diutisc*, which means 'people.' Accordingly, *Deutschland* literally means 'the land of the people' – 'the country in which we live'. This roughly corresponds to the name *Ukraina* in the sense of 'country'.

Ukraina in the second sense, i.e., as a 'borderland', dominates in documents written after 1569, when the Ukrainian lands entered the Polish-Lithuanian Commonwealth. That's how it appears on a map drawn by the French engineer and cartographer Guillaume Le Vasseur de Beauplan in 1651. The Polish king hired Beauplan to construct the Kodak fortress, which was intended to control the Ukrainian Cossacks. Beauplan's map is one of the earliest and most detailed maps to come from Eastern Europe. The territory depicted coincides with the borders of later Ukrainian ethnic territory, from Lviv in the west to the Don in the east. But in Beauplan's conception, Ukraine, as the map's title and the preface to his *Description of Ukraine* suggest, is actually only the steppe, the Wild Field (*camporum desertorum*), 'a great frontier between Muscovy and Transylvania'.

The word *Ukraina* means different things. At various times it may reference specific provinces (Volhynia-Ukraine, Podolia-Ukraine, Kyiv-Ukraine, Bratslav-Ukraine); the general borderlands at the edge of the Polish-Lithuanian Commonwealth (the Bratslav and Kyiv principalities); the territory at the 'edge of Europe' (the point where the Christian world bordered with the Muslim world); or it could also be named as a 'country' on a par with the Polish and Russian states of the time (the 'Polish-Lithuanian Commonwealth', 'Muscovy' and 'Ukraine'). 'Ukraine' during this period is a wandering term that can't be firmly pinned to one and only one territory.

The word 'Ukrainian' emerged around the turn of the seventeenth century. In 1619, the Zaporozhian Cossack Oleshka Zakhariv identified himself as Ukrainian when he was captured during the Polish-Muscovite War. In his *History of the Russian Empire* (1759), Voltaire was the first non-Ukrainian writer to use the term 'Ukrainian'. However, he only identified the Cossacks as Ukrainians and 'forgot' about all the Ukrainian peasants, townspeople and clergy.

The Cossack uprising (1648–1657) led by Bohdan Khmelnytsky represents a turning point in Ukrainian history that marks the formation of the Cossack state. For the next several decades, 'Ukraine' was one of the names of this state. There were also references to the 'Ukrainian people' and 'the united brotherhood of the Ukrainian Commonwealth'. The leaders of the Cossack state, the hetmans, referred to 'our fatherland Ukraine' and 'glorious Ukraine' (*Slavna Ukraina*). At the same time, the name 'Ukraine' referred not only to the Cossack state within specific borders, but also to the lands beyond it, all the way to the Polish-Ukrainian ethnic border to the west.

The fate of the word 'Ukraine' mirrors the fate of the Cossack state itself after its absorption into Muscovy in 1654. For as long as the state retained its autonomy, the name 'Ukraine' regularly appeared in written documents. When the state was absorbed into the body of the later Russian Empire (from 1721) and eventually disappeared, the names 'Ukraine' and 'Ukrainians' also disappeared. Although they were lost, they didn't disappear entirely. They seemed to be playing hide-and-seek: now you see me, now you don't. 'Ukraine' begins to appear more frequently again in the nineteenth century, during the rise of nationalism throughout Europe. Along with Ukraine, the word Ukrainians also becomes more common. For instance, the writer Nikolai Gogol (born as Mikola Hohol to a Ukrainian family) appears in the Carlsbad spa register as: *Mr. Nicolas de Gogol, Ukrainien, établi à Moscou.* In 1884, the young poet Larysa Kosach adopted the pseudonym 'Ukrainka' (the female form of Ukrainian), most likely influenced by her uncle, Mykhailo Drahomanov, who signed his articles with the pseudonym 'Ukrainets', aka Ukrainian in the male form. She has been known ever since as Lesia Ukrainka.

The examples of Mykola Hohol, Mykhailo Drahomanov and Lesia Ukrainka are just some of the most prominent historical figures. We know of at least twenty-five other less famous individuals, nineteenth-century writers, politicians and public figures, who used the pseudonyms 'Ukrainka' or 'Ukrainets'. Obviously, this isn't an exhaustive list of everyone who considered themselves Ukrainians, nor does it suggest that *everyone* considered themselves Ukrainians. It only shows that the word was in broad circulation at the time. 'Ukrainians' is also used as an ethnic marker to distinguish Ukrainians from Poles, Jews, Muscovites, Swedes, Tatars and Turks.

We must bear in mind, though, that the word Ukrainian did not strictly carry any sense of Ukrainian ethnicity. When the Ukrainian literary scholar Mykhailo Rudnytsky was studying at the Sorbonne in the early twentieth century, people viewed him as a curiosity: he was the first 'Ukrainian' who wasn't Polish! Up to that time, the only Ukrainians they'd seen were Poles who came from the eastern Polish regions of present-day Volhynia and Central Ukraine.

Taras Shevchenko's *Kobzar* (1840), the book that serves as a kind of Ukrainian national Bible, is another curious example. Although the entire book is about Ukraine, the word 'Ukrainian' never appears. That doesn't mean Ukrainians did not exist in Shevchenko's time. The Bible doesn't use the words 'religion' or 'religious' either. Nonetheless, no one denies that the Bible is a religious book.

Shakespeare presented this thesis in a poetic way:

What's in a name? That which we call a rose
By any other name would smell as sweet;

The main theme of Ukrainian history can be summarised in one sentence: The history of Ukraine is about dropping the 'the'. In English, *the* is used to refer to specific geographical regions (or outlying areas), not countries. Geographical areas, as opposed to legal jurisdictions, are frequently referred to with 'the'. For instance, 'the Scottish Highlands', 'the Mississippi Delta', or 'the Donbas' (Donetsk Coal Basin). The exceptions are generally when the country name is plural (*the United States, the Netherlands,* or *the Bahamas*). There is one curious exception – *the Gambia.* In 1964, when *the* Gambia gained independence, its prime minister asked the Standing Committee on Geographical Names to add the article *the* to the country's name so that it would not be confused with the better-known Zambia.

For a long time, Ukraine was written in English with the article: *the* Ukraine. This reflected its formal status: it was not a separate state, but a part (outskirts) of the Russian Empire and the USSR. This all changed when Ukraine declared its independence in 1991. Since then, the proper name has been *Ukraine,* without the article. If someone continues to write or say, 'the Ukraine', it is either due to a slip of the tongue, ignorance, or ill will. When Barack Obama said 'the Ukraine' in an interview during the 2014 Ukraine crisis, he became the target of journalistic ridicule.

In Slavic languages, the difference between *Ukraine* and *the Ukraine* is represented by a preposition: '*on* Ukraine' vs '*in* Ukraine'. 'On Ukraine' references the sense of borderland: *on* the outskirts. Not *in* a country. This difference is particularly significant in Russia: a significant portion of the Russian elite, if not the majority, continues to believe that Ukraine is part of the 'Russian World' and that Ukrainians and Russians are one people. In 2011, then-President Dmitry Medvedev held a meeting with a group of Russian historians. When one of them said, 'in Ukraine', Medvedev immediately corrected him, 'on Ukraine.' Medvedev continued, 'That's what *they* say, "in Ukraine". *We* say "on Ukraine".' Putin, however, said 'in Ukraine' up until the summer of 2013. He began to say 'on Ukraine' at the very moment when he declared his strategic goal of uniting Russians and Ukrainians into one state. In other words, his military aggression in 2014 was preceded by linguistic aggression. In 2014, Putin's former advisor and later opponent Andrei Illarionov advised his fellow liberal Russians: if you want to help Ukraine in any way, stop saying 'on Ukraine', say 'in Ukraine'.

This brief introduction illustrates a dominant feature of Ukrainian history: everything, or almost everything, related to it immediately becomes the subject of heated ideological debate, starting with something as basic as the name of the country itself.

Rus and Others: A Tangle of Terminology

Two other names for Ukrainians were 'Cherkasy' and 'Cossacks'. The origin of the word 'Cherkasy' is unclear. According to one version, it is of Turkic origin and means 'warrior'. Russian texts use the word Cherkasy as one of the names for the Ukrainian Cossacks, who became a central symbol of Ukrainian identity. 'Cossack' is of Turkic origin and meant 'free person', as well as 'nomad' and 'robber' (the name of Kazakhstan comes from the same Turkic root).

The Turkic origins of the names 'Cossacks' and, most likely, 'Cherkasy' once again demonstrate how Ukraine emerged from the intersections of several worlds. An integral element of this synthesis is reflected in the derogatory Russian term for Ukrainians, 'khokhols'. A khokhol is a single lock of hair on an otherwise clean-shaven scalp. This hairstyle was common for men among steppe peoples. The earliest mention appears in texts describing tribes in Manchuria in the fourth century. In the early years of the Polish republic, the khokhol was popular among the local gentry and Cossacks. The khokhol on the head was paired with a shaved chin. This differentiated the Ukrainian Cossacks from the Muscovites, who wore beards. (This may be the origin of the Ukrainian insult for Russians, goats or 'katsapy' because they wore long beards, like goats.) In the eyes of Orthodox Muscovites (future Russians), the khokhol became a symbol of Catholicism. They wrote that the Ukrainian Cossacks walked around like Poles, with khokhols, shaved their beards like those of the Roman faith and were overall 'heretical khokhols, satanic beggars and unruly grandchildren'. They eventually learned that the Cossacks were Orthodox like themselves, despite the fact that they came from the Polish-Lithuanian Commonwealth. Nevertheless, the distaste remained: the 'khokhols' are part of us and yet not of us, with their own uncouth habits and sly 'khokhol' nature. The existence of the 'khokhol/katsap' word pair shows that future Ukrainians and Russians were different long before they became 'Ukrainians' and 'Russians'.

Most often Ukraine and Ukrainians were known by the name 'Rus' and later its derivatives: 'Rosiya', 'Rus', 'Rusyns', 'Ruthenians', 'Russians', 'Little Russians', and so on. But if the story of Ukraine and Ukrainians is complicated, the story of Rus and Russians is even more complicated. It is total terminological chaos.

It's impossible to determine exactly where the name 'Rus' came from or what it meant. There are various versions of its origin: it could be a local, East Slavic word, or maybe it's Gothic, Celtic, Iranian, Serbian, or Scandinavian.

The claim for a local origin posits that 'Rus' is derived from the name of an East Slavic tribe that lived near the Ros River, a tributary of the Dnipro. This region became the centre of the large medieval state called Rus, with its capital in Kyiv.

The problem with this version is that there is no mention of such a tribe in historical sources. It appears to be an invention of patriotic historians who wanted to prove that the ancient Rus state had local origins. This theory was established as state ideology during the Soviet era, but it originated in the mid-eighteenth century. On 6 January 1749, Gerhard Friedrich Müller (1705–1783), a member of the Russian Imperial Academy of Sciences, was to give a lecture in St Petersburg entitled 'On the Origin of the Russian People and their Name'. Basing his claim on Frankish and Byzantine sources, he attempted to show that Kyivan Rus was founded by Scandinavians. Müller never finished giving his lecture. One of the Russian academics interrupted his speech with the words: 'You, worthy author, are insulting our people!' A special commission was assembled and Müller was forbidden to address the topic further. They advised him to study a safer, less hazardous topic: the history of Siberia. (He was lucky not to get sent there.)

This story shows the level of passion in the debate over the origins of Rus. But long before this debate, in the twelfth century, the Scandinavian origins of Rus were recorded by the anonymous author of *The Tale of Bygone Years*, the most important local medieval chronicle. The earliest example of the term Rus also supports the Viking origin: the Annals of St Bertin, under the date 839, refer to 'Swedes who call themselves Rhos'. In modern Estonian and Finnish, ruotsi still means Swedish. According to this version, 'Rus' most likely referenced a military grouping, like Cossacks or Cherkasy, based on the Proto-Germanic or Old Norse verb 'to row'. So 'Rus' referred to military units that travelled along rivers and seas in large boats.

Most likely the term 'Rus' was an exonym, that is, a name utilised by outsiders. They did not call themselves that, just as Indians did not call themselves Indians – either in India or North America. The closest analogy to 'Rus' may be the word 'Spaniards'. The inhabitants of the Iberian Peninsula did not call themselves that; they considered themselves Aragonese, Castilians, Catalans and Basques. But outside their peninsula, in military service, they became Hispanici to strangers, because their peninsula had been called *Hispania* in Latin since ancient times.

From the beginning, 'Rus' was used in two senses: narrow and broad. In the broad sense, 'Rus' meant all the possessions of the 'Rus' dynasty. In the narrow sense, it meant only the core of their possessions, i.e. the Central Dnipro region centred on Kyiv. 'Rus' in this sense went out of usage after the Mongols conquered the local state in the second half of the thirteenth century. For almost a hundred years after that, only the rulers of the southwestern lands, territory within the borders of modern Ukraine, used the title of rulers of Rus. They titled themselves *dux totius terrae Russiae* (prince of all Rus – called Russia in Latin), *dux et dominus Russiae* (prince and ruler of Rus), *rex Russiae* (king of Rus). After that princely line died out, these lands passed to their closest relatives – the rulers of Poland, Hungary and the Grand Duchy of Lithuania.

The northern, Muscovite rulers began using 'Rus' significantly later. The title of 'Sovereign of All Rus' was first used by Tsar Ivan III of Moscow in 1478. Over time, Muscovy began to identify as the only true 'Rus'. So did the Grand Duchy of Lithuania. As a result, two 'Rus' emerged: Lithuanian and Muscovite. The rulers of each claimed that they alone ruled 'All of Rus' and denied that right to the other side. That is why the Lithuanian-Polish tradition called the northeastern lands not Rus, but the Muscovite state, the Moscow kingdom, or simply Muscovy, while Moscow called the Polish-Lithuanian Commonwealth the Lithuanian state, Lithuania, or the Lithuanian lands.

Separate from its geographical political meaning, 'Rus' also had a religious meaning. It could mean the Orthodox Church ('Rus Church') and the Orthodox faith ('Rus faith'). But the Orthodox were not the only 'Rus'. The Greek Catholic (Uniate) Church, which emerged in 1596, was also called Rus. It was subordinate to the Vatican, but retained the Orthodox rite and so was 'Rus'. On the other hand, both churches were also called 'Greek' as a sign that they had adopted Christianity from the 'Greeks', i.e., the Byzantine Empire.

'Rus' could also refer to ethnic identity. The Rus scribe Meletii Smotrytsky (1577–1623) stated: 'It is not faith that makes a Rus a Rus, a Pole a Pole, a Lithuanian a Lithuanian, but birth and blood as Rus, Polish, or Lithuanian.' Rus was particularly common among people who lived side by side with those of other faiths, particularly in Galicia and Transcarpathia. There, religious identities coincided with ethnic ones. To say 'I am Rus' was equivalent to saying 'I am not Catholic' (i.e., not Polish or Hungarian), 'not Muslim' (a Tatar) and 'not Jewish'. But a 'Rus' of that time might well be what we would call a 'Belarusian' today. Although the name 'Belarusian' first appears at the same time as 'Ukrainian' (in the early seventeenth century), there was no clear division between Belarusians and Ukrainians at the time. They were united by a common 'Rus faith' and 'Rus blood' and their language was perceived as one. Future Belarusians and Ukrainians could be distinguished by their place of origin: Belarusians came from the Lithuanian part of the Polish-Lithuanian Commonwealth and were also called 'Lithuanians'.

These names were neither fixed nor mutually exclusive. If, for example, a member of the Rus gentry from Lithuania was asked who he was, his answer would depend on the circumstances of who asked him and where. In church, he would identify himself as Rus, at the gentry Sejm (noble parliament) he was Lithuanian and in a conversation with a foreigner he was a Polish nobleman.

The matter is further complicated by the fact that the term 'Rus' was used in two forms – Latin and Greek. In Latin, it was written *Russia*. This was the form used in areas neighbouring the Catholic world, for example, in the titles of Galician princes. We should not be surprised that on Beauplan's map, the only area labelled *Russia* is the territory of modern Ukrainian-speaking Galicia. At that time the official name for the Galician lands was the Rus Voivodeship, or in Latin *Palatinatus russiae*.

The Greek form is 'Rosiya'/'Rossiya'. Initially, this term was only used in Byzantium. It first appears in a local Slavic text from 1387. Metropolitan Cyprian called himself Metropolitan of Kyiv and all Rosiya. In the northeastern regions of Rus lands, 'Rossiya' (with the double 's') has been used since the time of Peter I. This is the name he adopted for the empire he founded in 1721 on the foundations of the old Muscovite Kingdom. This form appears to have originated with Ukrainian churchmen, who knew Greek well and used this form to describe their home. They helped Peter I build his empire and brought the name 'Rossiya' with them. The fact that the name was imported from Kyiv should not be surprising, given that at the time Kyiv was superior to Moscow in terms of education and the Ukrainian elite had a powerful influence on the political and cultural life of the Kingdom of Muscovy and the later Russian Empire. In Slavic languages, adjectives are often formed by the addition of a -ky or -kii ending. Thus, Rus becomes russkii as an adjective. The Slavic form of 'russkii' has not disappeared from the Russian language; it exists in parallel with the Greek 'rossiiski' with an 'o'. The former is used mainly for people of Russian ethnic origin, while the latter is used for citizens of the Russian state. For example, world chess champion Garry Kasparov is a 'Rossiyanin' (Russian citizen), but not a 'russkii' because he is of Armenian-Jewish descent. On the other hand, a citizen of the Russian Federation who is of Ukrainian or Belarusian descent would be considered both 'russkii' (ethnically descended from the Rus) and a 'Rossiyanin'. The centres of Old Rus (Holy Rus) were the old Orthodox centres of Kyiv and Moscow, but not modern cosmopolitan Petersburg.

And the difficulties don't end there. Adjectives were frequently added to 'Rus' and so the number of possible combinations increased. One of the earliest maps of the world, a map by the Venetian monk Fra Mauro (1450), lists as many as five lands called variations of *Rossi*: a 'White Rossia', 'Black Rossia', 'Red Rossia', 'Rossia or Sarmatia in Europe' and 'Rossia or Sarmatia in Asia'.

In addition to the 'White', 'Black' and 'Red' Rus, there was also 'Little' and 'Great' Rus. Ukraine was called 'Little Russia' and Russia was called 'Great Russia'. In more recent times, 'Little' and 'Russia' have been read as signs of status: Russia is bigger and older and Ukraine is smaller and younger. This is anachronistic. Originally, 'Little' Russia was older and higher in status. This corresponds to the Greek (Byzantine) tradition of calling the original core of a church or state 'lesser' (minor) and the lands to which that church or state later spread 'greater' (major). Accordingly, Little Russia referred to the core of the ancient Rus lands centred in Kyiv, while Great Russia referred to the northern Rus lands centred in Moscow. We find the first mention of 'Little Russia' in Byzantine documents from 1303 referring to the Metropolis of Galicia. The title of the last prince of Galicia, Yuri II Boleslav, included 'King of Little Russia'. The words 'Great Russia' appear in the title of the Moscow tsar only in the sixteenth century and didn't immediately take root: the first Romanovs didn't adopt the title.

'Little' and 'Great' Russia, as well as 'White' Russia, became fixed political terms only after these separate Rus polities finally 'met'. This took place when the Ukrainian Cossack state voluntarily accepted the protection of the Muscovite tsar in 1654. The Cossacks insisted on the equal dignity of Little and Great Russia. For instance, in his 1762 poem 'A Conversation between Great Russia and Little Russia', the Cossack scribe Semen Divovich puts the following words into the mouth of his Little Russian homeland:

I know that you are Russia. That's what I call myself, too.
Why are you threatening me? I'm perfectly brave.
It wasn't to you I swore loyalty, but to your sovereign,
To whom you and your forefathers were born.
Don't imagine that you rule over me,
We just have the same sovereign.

By the nineteenth century, the usage of 'Little' and 'Great' Russia with implied reference to status and size was fully established. In the Russian Empire, the term 'Little Russian' was the official term. In the western Ukrainian lands that were under Austrian rule, the norm was 'Ruthenian' or 'Rusyn'. These terms were gradually replaced by the names 'Ukraine' and 'Ukrainians' in the twentieth century. After the Second World War, when the Soviet government completed the unification of all Ukrainian lands into a single state, these names were used for the entire territory. However, 'Little Russians', 'khokhols' and 'Rusyns' don't disappear entirely. The first two appear whenever the Russian elite wants to assert its monopoly on the past and present of Ukraine and all of Eastern Europe. The term 'Rusyns' remains alive in Transcarpathia and ethnically Ukrainian areas that were never part of Soviet Ukraine (like the Prešov region of Slovakia).

This brief history of the word 'Rus' and its derivatives reflects the long and sometimes confusing evolution from peoples or nations to modern states. From the time of the formation of the Russian

Empire to Putin in the present day, the Russian elite has been offering a straightforward path: 'Russia has always been Russia!' In this way, it claims a monopoly on Ukraine's past and present: Russians and Ukrainians ('Great Russians' and 'Little Russians') are one people. Until recently, many people in the West believed this. One reason for this is that modern English, German and French, have used identical terms for 'Rus' and 'Rossiya'. They are both called 'Russia'. Even in the works of eminent Western historians, one can find such clumsy terms for the local medieval state as *Kievan Russia*, though more recent works tend to consistently use the more accurate term Kyivan Rus. More cognisant historians try to spell 'Rus' and 'Ruskii' as *Rus*, *Rusian* (with one 's'), or *Ruthenian* to distinguish it from Russian. In this text, Rus and Rus'ke (for adjectives) will generally be rendered as '*Rus*'. Various kinds of Rus existed at various times and sometimes at the same time. There was Muscovite Rus, Ukraine Rus, Lithuanian Rus. The Russian Empire will be called Russia, the Russian Empire or the Russian Federation. Ukrainian lands will be used to describe areas that later became part of the modern Ukrainian state.

It is important to understand that 'Russky' was not identical to 'Rossisky'. They were like two dice that could produce different combinations and, accordingly, different meanings. Separately, they might refer to what we would now call Ukraine and Ukrainian.

Tradition and Modernity

Most of the examples above illustrate the golden rule of historians: 'The past is a foreign country: they do things differently there.' One of the main differences is that in the past, ethnicity and nationality did not play the central role that we ascribe to them today. In the past, if you asked the inhabitants of any territory who they were, the first three answers would have been: 'we are local', 'we belong to such and such a religion' and 'we belong to such and such a group' (peasants, tradesmen, or artisans). If they were slaves or serfs, they might also name their owner or master.

To us, it's incomprehensible. We live in a world of documents. Our height is measured and our eye colour described. We are identified by the language we speak, our income, etc. and then this information is entered into official documents. Or collected by Google. This information is then used to determine our suitability for a job, loyalty to the government, purchasing power, etc. The Stalinist-era saying 'no documents, no person' conveys this feature of modernity quite precisely.

In the pre-modern world, it was possible to spend your entire life without any documents. Identity depended less on relationships between people and more on the relationship between people and God. Therefore, one could safely do without Google, because God knew everything – not Google.

For instance, just three or four generations ago, most people in Ukraine lived in villages and few knew their date of birth. Instead, everyone knew their name day: the day dedicated to the Christian saint they were named after. If a girl was born in early January, the second half of August, early September, or mid-October, a time when the Christian calendar celebrated the feasts of the Virgin Mary, she was named Maria. The man's name that appears most often in the Christian calendar is St John, or Ivan. Therefore, 'Ivans' became a collective name for Ukrainians and Russians (a nation of Ivans).

All of these names indicated that the villagers belonged to the Christian faith – unlike, say, Jews, who gave their children names from the Old Testament (Abraham, Moses, Sarah, etc.). Christians and Jews had one thing in common: their identification was, so to speak, vertical. It flowed from their relationship with God.

In the modern world, we have almost stopped celebrating name days based on the religious calendar. Instead, we celebrate the birthdays recorded in our passports. The church is separated from the state. Therefore, official documents rarely, if ever, mention religious affiliation. An Orthodox Christian, a Greek Catholic, a Jew, a Crimean Tatar, or an atheist can have a Ukrainian passport. In the modern world, our identities are recorded in many different documents. And among all possible identities, nationality is often first: the identity of the state that grants you a passport.

The transition from *religious* vertical identification (person–God) to *national* horizontal identification (person-person) meant a radical rewriting of old identities. In modern society, children can be given names that don't appear in Christian texts, such as the 'pagan' names of the Kyivan princes. These names only became popular in the mid-nineteenth century. It was then that the first Volodymyrs, Yaroslavs, Ihors and Olha's appeared – first in the families of nationally conscious intellectuals and later among the townspeople and peasants.

It is not only the names of people which change, but also the names of nations as they transform from traditional religious communities into modern secular nations. Prussians and Bavarians become Germans, Samogitians become Lithuanians, some Lithuanians became Belarusians, Muscovites become Russians, Vlachs become Romanians, Jews became Israelis, and the Rusyns of Austria-Hungary along with the Little Russians of the Russian Empire become Ukrainians.

These changes have provoked and continue to provoke disputes. For example, Belarusians and Lithuanians argue about who has more right to the historical name 'Litvins'; Ukrainians claim that Russians 'stole' their name because Moscow has no greater relationship to Rus than modern Romania has to ancient Rome; Russians claim that Ukrainians are an artificial nation invented in the twentieth century by the German General Staff, Poles, Bolsheviks, Jewish Freemasons, etc. because they used to be called 'Little Russians'.

If we set aside the political overtones of these disputes for a moment, it is worth noting that they are based on the mistaken belief that names, like the nations they describe, are fixed and unchangeable. This is not the case. Everything in the world is subject to change. Without these changes, we would continue to live, as American sociologist Rodney William Stark has suggested, in a world where most infants do not live to the age of five and many women die in childbirth; a world with many astrologers and alchemists but no scientists; a world of despots, lacking universities, banks, factories, eyeglasses, chimneys and pianos. And, I would add, without passports or fixed national identities.

Different peoples on different continents experienced these changes with different intensities and at different times. In some places, they emerged locally, in others, they were imported as a result of globalisation and colonisation. The general nature of these changes can be described by the basic term modernisation. But even this term requires us to explain what modernity is and how it differs from the pre-modern world.

In the pre-modern world, the majority of the population lived in villages and worked the land; in the modern world, the majority live in cities and work in industry or service. In the pre-modern world, few people could read; in the modern world, few people *cannot* read. The pre-modern world was characterised by low social and geographic mobility: a person born a peasant would die a peasant, most likely in the same village. In the modern world, the children or grandchildren of those who work the land may leave their ancestral lands and eventually become professors, poets, commanders-in-chief and even the leaders of superpowers (like Mikhail Gorbachev or Barack Obama).

Dichotomies like these help us organise our thinking, but they're not particularly good at describing reality. For example, the rural/urban opposition is a key contrast in identifying the transition from the pre-modern to the modern world. A society is considered modern when 50 per cent or more of its population live in cities. If we stick to this criterion, then Ukraine became modern only in the 1960s and the world as a whole only in the early 2000s. We will thus reach a conclusion that is formally correct, but in fact, meaningless: modernity began only a few decades ago!

Another challenge lies in the fact that these criteria differ from one society to another. For example, if we are talking about the share of the population living in urban areas, we must take into account that the size of a city is defined differently in different places at different times. In nineteenth-century Ireland, Germany or France, a city was defined as any populated area with more than two thousand inhabitants. In the Netherlands, that number was twenty thousand. Thus, an urban population of 50 per cent in Ireland is not at all equivalent to an urban population of 50 per cent in the Netherlands.

The criteria that we often use as if they were universal, actually belong to a specific society. In terms of modernity, that society can be described by the term 'WASP' – white, Anglo-Saxon, Protestant. In fact, English society is considered the birthplace of modernity. The question becomes whether these same criteria can be applied to societies where the majority of people are neither white, Anglo-Saxon nor Protestant?

To escape this narrow track of dichotomies and criteria, it may help to shift the emphasis from objective features (those that can be touched and counted) to subjective features (those that exist only in our heads). The term 'modern' comes from the Latin word *modo*, meaning recent. It first appeared only after the fall of ancient Rome, in the sixth century, and belonged to what was called Vulgar Latin. The very origin of the word offers a clue to its semantic load. Vulgar Latin was considered inferior to ancient Latin and 'modern' meant something that was obviously of inferior quality. Everything new (moderne) was inferior to the 'good old days'. *Homines novi* (new people) meant roughly the same thing as *nouveaux riches* in French or 'new Russians' in Russian and 'new Ukrainians' in Ukrainian: people with bad manners. The modern had the right to exist only insofar as it attempted to imitate the ancient. As Petrarch rhetorically asked: 'What is all history, but the praise of Rome?'

'Modern' has radically changed its meaning from negative to positive over the past three to four centuries. The beginnings of this change can be seen in the so-called 'Quarrel of the Ancients and Moderns' waged by French and British writers in the seventeenth and eighteenth centuries. The 'Ancients' such as La Fontaine, Jonathan Swift and others, argued that ancient Greece and Rome represented the peak of human civilisation; everything that came later was of lesser value. The 'Moderns', on the other hand, drew attention to scientific discoveries. They acknowledged that Homer, Plato, or Virgil may remain unsurpassed, but you can't compare Archimedes and Ptolemy to Copernicus or Newton.

Since the nineteenth century, the value placed on 'modern' and 'ancient' has completely swapped. In the imagination of educated people, modernity carries the promise of change for the better. To be modern, you don't have to live in an industrial, urbanised, educated society; you just have to *want* your society to become industrial, urbanised and educated. If traditionalists base their legitimacy on loyalty to traditions, modernists justify themselves by faith in a better future. Modernity begins when people start to believe in change and strive towards it.

The fact that the modern world contrasts itself with traditional societies does not indicate that modern societies lack traditions. In reality, no society can exist without traditions. Where tradition is lacking, new ones are invented, such as the idea of naming children after ancient rulers of Rus that I mentioned earlier. This is why the nineteenth century can be called the century of 'invented tradition'. The main feature of modernity is not the presence or absence of traditions, but the way in which these traditions are passed down from generation to generation. In a traditional society, a son learns to plough by working in the field with his father; a daughter learns to run a household by helping her mother; an apprentice craftsman learns the craft in his master's workshop. Traditional knowledge is transmitted orally from person to person. A father knows his son, a mother knows her daughter, a master knows his apprentice and they can be taught without the need for textbooks or even the ability to read.

In contrast, modern society requires education. If factory workers are to master complex operations, they need at least a minimal level of education. Industrial production cannot function without mass education and children can only be taught en masse using textbooks in a language they understand. Various dialects and vernaculars must be reduced to a single unified and standardised language, what we call the literary or standard language.

The modern elite has to pay attention to the language, because the strength of the economy and, consequently, its power depend on it. The nation itself is a child born of the marriage between the modern state and folk culture. Traditional society managed without nations, modern society cannot. This does not exclude the possibility that proto-national communities existed in the pre-modern world. But if they did exist, they were nations 'in themselves' rather than nations 'for themselves'. They knew who they were *not*, but could not yet say who they *were*. For a nation 'in-itself' to become a nation 'for-itself', it needs books, passports, maps, schools and so on – all those elements of the modern world that *fix* national identities and make them into *mass* identities.

The difference between a nation 'in-itself' and a nation 'for-itself' can be conveyed through another contrast: 'a people' and 'a nation'. A people simply exists in itself, just as grasses or trees grow. Nations, on the other hand, do not exist in nature. They have to be cultivated, like lawns or gardens. And a new product needs a new name. You could hardly call the primordial forests they replaced by the names of the Luxembourg Gardens or Central and Hyde Parks!

The key figures in the transformation of peoples into nations are 'gardeners' of a special variety – poets, writers, literary critics, historians, geographers, philologists and other 'highbrow' representatives of the elites. They glorify the nation's past and predict its even greater future, define its borders and draw maps, write national history, create a grammar of the national language and above all, choose or invent a name for the nation. Until they agree on what to call it, terminological chaos will reign.

We can say with a fair degree of precision when this chaos ended for Ukraine: during the last decades of the nineteenth century. Before the last decades of the nineteenth century, there was no agreement on what most Slavic peoples should be called, with the exception of Poles and Russians. In Ukraine, the terms 'Rus', 'Little Russian', and 'Ukrainian' could be viewed as interchangeable or could be viewed as mutually exclusive. In the first half of the nineteenth century, an anonymous 'History of the Rus' was popular among the descendants of Ukrainian Cossacks. The patriotic author of that text disagreed with the change from the name 'Rus' to 'Ukraine': in his perception, the name 'Ukraine' was the invention of 'shameless and malicious Polish and Lithuanian fabulists'.

In the mid-nineteenth century, a compromise emerged: 'Rus' and 'Ukraine' began to be used as two parts of the same name. The term 'Rus-Ukrainian' was first coined by Galician poet Ivan Hushalevych during the 'Spring of Nations' (revolutions of 1848–49). He did it to emphasise the unity between the parts of Ukraine under Austrian control and those under Russian control. In 1890, the term appeared in the name of the first Ukrainian political party, the Rus-Ukrainian Radical Party (commonly translated to English as the Ruthenian-Ukrainian Radical Party). In 1898,

Mykhailo Hrushevsky called his magisterial text, *The History of Ukraine-Rus*. In the early twentieth century, the first half of the term 'Rus-Ukrainian' disappeared. At the end of the First World War, on the ruins of the Austro-Hungarian and Russian empires, the first states with the words 'Ukraine' or 'Ukrainian' in their names appeared. The Ukrainian People's Republic, the Ukrainian State, the Western Ukrainian People's Republic, the Ukrainian SSR, or the Reich Commissariat 'Ukraine'. During the interwar period, the terms 'Ukrainian and Ukrainians' gradually replaced 'Rus or Rusyns' and after the Second World War, following the Soviet unification of all Ukrainian territories, 'Ukraine' became the commonly accepted name.

In a nutshell, 'Rus' is primarily the name of a traditional, historical community and 'Ukraine' is primarily the name of a modern society. In this sense, the creation of Ukraine was threefold: from a people to a nation, from a traditional to a modern society, from Rus to Ukraine. Although this formulation is somewhat oversimplified, it does permit us to construct meaning from terminological nonsense.

By paying so much attention to names, we are pushing aside questions that are no less significant: what makes up the societies whose names we are discussing? What is the social capital passed from generation to generation: the social values, interpersonal relations, relations between people and government? Does this social capital change with each such transfer and to what extent?

The author of these lines is of the opinion that there are more connections between the traditional and modern worlds than we realise. In particular, these links to the past explain the specific character of modern Ukraine, including why it resists Russian aggression so intensely and why it is so drawn to unite with Europe.

That is the subject of the rest of this book.

CHAPTER 2

RUS

ANCIENT RUS, ca 1000

'Who can be happy in Russia?' asked the Russian poet Nikolai Nekrasov in the 1870s. He didn't provide a clear answer and even if he had, it would have been self-referential: 'not poets'. In Russia, the vocation of poet is both highly respected and dangerous. As Osip Mandelstam stated, 'Only in Russia is poetry respected – it gets people killed.' The poet's fate confirmed his words: he died in the Gulag in 1938.

No one has attempted to estimate how many other poets, writers and literary critics of Russian, Ukrainian, Georgian, Kazakh and other nationalities were repressed in the Russian Empire and the USSR. In Soviet Ukraine, an estimated 85 per cent of poets, writers and literary critics fell victim to Stalinist repression in the 1930s. This period is known as the 'Executed Renaissance'. After Stalin's death in 1953, mass repressions were no longer as widespread, but they didn't cease entirely. From 1960–80, poets and writers were overrepresented among those targeted for persecution.

Ukrainian poet Vasyl Stus was first arrested in 1972. He returned to Kyiv in the autumn of 1979, after serving time in prison and exile, but he was not free for long. Soon he joined the Ukrainian Helsinki Human Rights Protection Group and 'earned' a second arrest, this time for fifteen years of prison and exile. While he was in transit to the camp, labour strikes broke out in neighbouring communist Poland. Solidarity, the anti-communist trade union, took shape.

Although communism existed in both Ukraine and neighbouring Poland it was much milder in Poland: poets were not repressed by the dozens; books and magazines banned in the USSR could be read in local libraries; Warsaw was the only communist capital to host a Rolling Stones concert; the Catholic Church in communist Poland had more influence than the Polish communists did; and in 1978 Cardinal Karol Wojtyła of Krakow became the first Slavic pope as John Paul II.

Stus admired Poland. He wrote that, 'There is no other nation in the totalitarian communist world that has so passionately defended its human and national rights.' He predicted that Poland would lead the way for the collapse of communism and regretted that he wasn't Polish himself. He particularly wondered whether Ukraine would 'follow the Polish example'. He believed that Ukrainians were psychologically closest to Poles, but that they lacked the most important thing: national pride.

At that time, the Soviet government in Ukraine was preparing for the fifteen hundredth anniversary of Kyiv. This date was invented: no one knows when Kyiv was actually founded. The atheist Soviet authorities invented this anniversary to counter the celebration in the West of the millennium of the baptism of Rus (988). All this led Stus to think about the influence of Orthodox Christianity on Ukraine. He wrote, 'I believe that the first mistake was the adoption of the Byzantine-Moscow rite, which brought us, the easternmost part of the West, into the East. Our individualistic Western spirit, stamped by despotic Byzantine Orthodoxy, could not free itself from this duality of spirit, a duality that eventually became hypocrisy.'

Stus's words resembled the conclusions of the famous Russian Byzantinist Alexander Kazhdan. As a Jew, Kazhdan was allowed to leave the USSR in 1978. He settled in the United States and worked at Harvard University. There, summarising his academic career, he wrote: 'When I think of the history of Byzantium and its significance for the twentieth century, I always come back to the same idea: Byzantium has left us a unique experience of European totalitarianism. For me, Byzantium is not so much the cradle of Orthodoxy or the storehouse of the treasures of ancient Hellas, as a thousand-year-long experiment in totalitarian practice, without whose understanding we are, it seems, unable to see our own place in the historical process.'

Vasyl Stus died in a prison camp in Russia on 4 September 1985. According to the official version, he died of cardiac arrest. Others believe that his death was arranged by the prison guards. Almost four years later, as he had predicted, the collapse of communism began in Poland. In June 1989, Solidarity won the first democratic elections and formed an anti-communist government. The revolutionary wave moved further east. In September 1989, Kyiv hosted the founding congress of the People's Movement of Ukraine, which modelled itself after Solidarity.

After years of communist isolation, Soviet Ukraine began opening to the outside world. In the summer of 1990, Harvard professor of Byzantine studies Ihor Ševčenko came to Kyiv for an international academic conference. Observing the changes in the Ukrainian capital, he concluded: 'The Byzantine legacy ... along with later long-term trends ... may, in the midst of rapid change, recede into the background, but their effects will not fade overnight.'

The twentieth century is called the 'age of extremes'. Vasyl Stus, Alexander Kazhdan and Ihor Ševčenko had very different fates in this century, but they all reached a common conclusion: Prince Volodymyr's decision to adopt Christianity from Byzantium in 988, rather than from Rome, had a profound impact on the people who would live in the shadow of Russian Orthodox civilisation for the next thousand years.

Between the Civilised and Barbarian Worlds

The history of every country is linked to its geography. People rarely consider the fact that Ukraine is among those countries whose climate and soil permit the cultivation of grapevines. It is one of the world's few brandy-producing regions. Before the 2014 Russian annexation of Crimea it was one of the twenty-five largest wine producers in the world.

The Mediterranean and Black Sea regions have long provided for grapevines. Viniculture originated in the southeastern part, now known as West Asia and the Middle East. The 'fertile crescent' of this region – the lands between the Mediterranean Sea and the Persian Gulf, that are irrigated by the Tigris, Euphrates and Nile – was the birthplace of the earliest writing systems. Much earlier, about ten thousand years ago, the people in these lands initiated the cultivation of wheat, rye and other cereals during the earliest revolution in human history – the transition to agriculture.

Bread and wine are symbols of Christianity. In the Middle Ages, Christianity defined the borders of Europe. Christianity itself arose in the environment of Jewish, Greek and Roman cultures. Therefore, whatever history we choose-economic, political, or cultural – the Mediterranean region remains the cradle of European civilisation. It stretched from Egypt in the south to the Black Sea in the north, from Gibraltar in the west to the Caucasus in the east. Barbarians lived to the north. In ancient times, the main line of division between civilisation and the world of barbarians ran along the North-South axis. The Mediterranean was the civilised 'South', where all the riches of the world were found: gold and silver, luxurious fabrics and good wines. And, of course, books and libraries.

The latter, however, were of little interest to the barbarians. Their lives were based on working the land where conditions permitted and nomadism everywhere else. Both groups came into contact with the civilised South through trade and warfare. In the end, robbery and trade were often different sides of the same coin, as they were part of a general economic scheme that was largely based on violence. It is noteworthy that for a long time one of the main commodities on Mediterranean markets was slaves brought from the North.

The riches of the South were like a magnet for the northern barbarians, who constantly raided the civilised lands. During the Roman Empire, the South tried to protect itself from the barbarians by building a line of fortifications (limes) which stretched from the Atlantic coast of northern Britain across the entire European continent to the Black Sea. In the Roman imagination, the limes were more than just a fortification. They represented an almost sacred boundary that no civilised person would cross without a very good reason.

The Peloponnesian Peninsula, inhabited by the ancient Greeks, was a centre of Mediterranean civilisation starting from the middle of the first millennium BC. Its lands were poor in natural resources, as only 25 per cent of the territory was available for agriculture and the rest was mountainous. This lack of arable land and other resources forced the population to colonise neighbouring territories. From the Peloponnese, Greek colonisers moved throughout the Mediterranean, accessing neighbouring seas and coasts through the straits. Greek colonisation linked these coastlines into a single Mediterranean world. The later campaigns of Alexander the Great and Roman generals united them into a single political body.

Sea travel was dangerous. According to the ancient Greeks, the distance between life and death is measured by the thickness of a ship's plank. The Black Sea was especially perilous. Unlike the Mediterranean or the Adriatic, there were no islands where you could dock along the way and warlike tribes inhabited the shore. The ancient Greeks originally called this sea 'inhospitable' (Pontus Axenus). And then, with the cunning of the ancient Greeks, they renamed it the 'hospitable sea' (Pontus Euxinus) to deceive both fate and the gods.

For the Greeks and later the Romans, the Black Sea region was a distant, little-known land inhabited by strange creatures and tribes. The Amazons, a warlike tribe of women known from the *Iliad* and the exploits of Hercules, were said to live here. Tacitus wrote that these lands were inhabited by creatures with human faces but animal bodies. The idea of the Black Sea region as the 'homeland of barbarians' outlived ancient Greece and Rome, entering later European culture. Robert Howard placed his hero Conan the Barbarian here. The name of the Amazon River (and, later, amazon.com) is also associated with Black Sea mythology. When Pizarro's warriors were searching for El Dorado in the South American jungle, they reached a river. There they encountered a bellicose tribe led by women who would beat their men to death if they tried to retreat. Pizarro's men named the South American river after the female warriors of the Black Sea.

We know about the Black Sea region as part of the ancient world primarily thanks to Herodotus, the father of history. He travelled throughout the Mediterranean world and described what he encountered. Therefore, his work can be considered the first global history, within the limits, of course, of what the Greeks knew of the world. Like any good history, the book was built on the elucidation of causes, effects and connections – all the things that make history a science. In the case of the inhabitants of the Black Sea region, the departure point for comparison was obvious: the local barbarian tribe of Scythians had achieved the same thing as the Greeks by defeating a Persian army several times their size.

But comparing the Scythians and the Greeks is like comparing fire and water. The Scythians wore cloaks made from the scalps of their dead enemies. They had no settlements; men spent their lives on horseback, women and children in carts. They were distinguished by their drunkenness ('drinks like a Scythian,' meaning they drank undiluted wine, while the Greeks diluted wine with water), talkativeness ('jabber like a Scythian') and lack of taste (the Greeks considered modesty a virtue, while the Scythians loved to drape themselves in gold). The Greeks looked at the Scythians as if in a distorted mirror. The Scythians were everything they were not and did not want to be. In short, barbarians.

Of course, Herodotus lacked the level of objectivity that we demand of modern historians. Fascinated by ancient civilisations, we often forget how chauvinistic (to use a modern term) the ancient Greeks could be towards other peoples. Their stories often fail to mention the mutual nature of the Greco-Scythian ties. Not only did the Greeks reach the Black Sea region; the Scythians also reached Asia Minor. Scythian warriors were the guardians of order in Athens. One of the seven great Greek sages was a Scythian – Anacharsis, who is credited with the invention of the anchor. On his return, he was killed by the Scythians for becoming Hellenised and even the mention of his name was forbidden. The same fate befell the Scythian king Scyles, who tried to lead a double life as a barbarian Scythian and a civilised Greek until his tribesmen discovered his secret and beheaded him.

In any case, the written history of the Ukrainian lands should begin with Herodotus' *History*. The Black Sea region had a particular role in the Roman Empire: it was the 'Roman Siberia', a place of exile for criminals and undesirables. It was here that Ovid (43 BC–17 AD) was exiled, having fallen out of favour with Emperor Augustus for corrupting Roman youth with erotic poetry, although speculation suggested more personal reasons. Ovid bewailed his exile in the 'Sarmatian land' or Scythia, where he suffered from storms, the sea and (allegedly) the severe winter. This is a classic example of poetic licence, whereby the poet did not consider it a sin to exaggerate or even lie for the sake of a good story. And really, the poets weren't the only ones with the habit. Herodotus himself reported that in the lands north of Scythia, so many feathers fall from the sky that it's impossible to see.

In the second half of the eighteenth century, the Russian Empire won the Black Sea steppes. Russian Empress Catherine II undertook the project of creating a 'New Greece' and gave Greek names to the newly founded cities there. She also changed the name of the Tatar city Hacıdere to Ovidiopol, literally 'the city of Ovid'. This new city stood near one of the most ancient cities in the region, Ophiusa, meaning 'city of snakes' in Greek. Later, under the Romans, it was called Tyras and was the northern outpost of the empire. Today it is Bilhorod-Dnistrovskyi in Ukraine.

Another famous exile was Clement (35–99), one of the early popes. Christianity was outlawed in the Roman Empire at that time and Christians were persecuted and killed. Clement was exiled to the Crimean quarries near Chersonesus Taurica (Korsun in the Slavic tradition). Labour in quarries in those days was tantamount to execution, due to the slow and painful death from exhaustion. According to legend, Clement not only survived but also converted several prisoners and guards to Christianity. For this, he was drowned with an anchor around his neck so that his followers would not find his relics and worship them. The sea, however, gave up his tortured body.

The miraculous relics of Pope Clement were kept in Chersonesus. In the ninth century, the Slavic enlightener Cyril found them there and took some to Rome. The rest were taken to Kyiv by Prince Volodymyr (960/963–1015) after he conquered the city. He built the Church of the Tithes in Kyiv to store the relics and he was later buried there with his wife, the Byzantine princess Anna. Volodymyr's son Prince Yaroslav (983/987–1054) showed the head of St Clement as his most precious relic to the envoy of King Henry I who was sent to woo Yaroslav's daughter Anna. The cult of St Clement spread throughout the Rus lands. Clement became one of the first saints in the local Christian tradition and his legend is firmly entrenched in local folklore.

If we track the movements of this legend, along with written and material artifacts (such as white stone architecture), we can follow the path of civilisation through Eastern Europe. It moved from south to north through the ancient Black Sea region to Kyiv and then from Kyiv to all the Rus lands. The oldest Rus historical chronicle, *The Tale of Bygone Years*, tells us that the apostle Andrew travelled all the way to the site where Kyiv would later arise and blessed the future 'mother of Rus cities'.

The term 'mother of Rus cities' is actually just a literal translation from the Greek for 'capital of Rus' ('metropolis' means 'mother of cities'). Greek was the language of the Byzantine Empire. But although the Byzantines spoke Greek, they called themselves Romans. They traced their roots to the city on the Tiber and the twins Romulus and Remus. This empire was not just a direct successor to the Roman Empire – in the minds of the Byzantine writers, it was the *same* Roman Empire. They believed that a state continues to exist for as long as there is government in a capital and precisely where this capital was and what it was called were matters of secondary importance.

The capital moved from Rome under Emperor Constantine (ruled 306-337). To escape the threat of barbarian attacks, he transferred the centre of the empire from Rome to the Black Sea colony of Byzantium, which was ideally defended from all sides by the sea and mountains. Initially, this capital was to be called 'New Rome', but it went down in history as the city of Constantine – Constantinople. Constantine is also associated with another great transformation of the Roman Empire. Before him, the Roman Empire was pagan and polytheistic; after him, it was monotheistic and Christian. Constantine stopped the persecution of Christians, declared himself their protector and on his deathbed, he converted to Christianity.

The Byzantine Empire lasted just over a thousand years, until the Turkish conquest of Constantinople in 1453. By destroying Byzantium, the Ottoman Turks completed the process that had begun with the Arab conquests of the seventh and eighth centuries AD: the transformation of the eastern and northern Mediterranean into a Muslim world. Since that time, the South-North line as the *main* marker of civilisational divide has gradually transformed into the East-West line. But the old division did not die. It lived on into the nineteenth century. The Russian Empire was called the Northern Empire and travellers who set out from St Petersburg or Moscow to Little Russia (Ukrainian lands) were sure that they were going to the South, to look for the roots of the old civilisation.

Between the Vikings and the Greeks

The first great state on this territory emerged on this South-North axis, a state that textbooks call Kyivan Rus. But a state with that name never actually existed. The name was coined in the nineteenth century by Ukrainian and Russian historians to distinguish the Rus centred in Kyiv, from the later Rus (Russia), centred in Moscow and St Petersburg.

The Byzantine Empire didn't exist either. German historians invented the name in the sixteenth century to distinguish the empire centred in Rome from the later empire centred in Constantinople. There is, however, a fundamental difference between the history of the Byzantine Empire and the history of Kyivan Rus. While the former is rich in texts, the latter was rather 'silent'. We know much less about it than, say, ancient Egypt. The history of old Rus can be compared to an Egyptian pyramid turned upside down: it is based on a small number of definite facts above which rise a mass of hypotheses, interpretations, guesses, speculations or simply manipulations. The further you move up from the bottom, the more unbridled the fantasy.

One of these fantasies is reflected in the dispute between Ukrainian and Russian historians: who can lay claim to the nation-state of Rus – Russia or Ukraine? This debate is meaningless. Rus was neither a Russian nor a Ukrainian state. In fact, you could have hardly called it a state for quite some time. For the first hundred years, it was more like the East India Trading Company that helped found the British Empire. Established in 1600, this company, with the help of its own army, conquered a vast territory from western India to eastern China over the next two hundred and fifty years. Later, the British crown took over control of these lands in the mid-nineteenth century. Similarly, Rus emerged and operated as a trading company, which then turned into a state at the end of the tenth century.

Calling Rus a nation-state is like calling a wooden abacus the first computer. Nation-states didn't appear until much later, almost a thousand years later, in the nineteenth century and were broadly recognised as the basis of international politics only after the First World War. It makes about as much sense to fight over claims to the legacy of Rus as it would to debate whether the Carolingian Empire was French or German.

A comparison with the Carolingian Empire, another large empire of the early Middle Ages, at the western end of the European continent, will help us better understand the nature of Rus. Both states were empires of the North, founded by barbarian conquerors – the Franks in the first case, the Rus (Varangians) in the second. Ibn Khaldun, the fourteenth-century Arab author known as the 'father of sociology', described a general scheme of relations between conquerors and conquered. He asserted that in a military confrontation between barbaric and civilised peoples, the former will defeat the latter due to their greater military prowess and tribal solidarity. However, within a few generations, the conquerors succumb to the temptations of civilisation, dissolve among the conquered majority, lose internal solidarity and lapse into internal strife – at which point their state falls victim to the next barbarians.

This scheme of Ibn Khaldun's conveys the history of Rus in general terms. The first two generations of rulers had Scandinavian names: Hrorekr (Rurik), his voivode Hélgi (Oleh), his son Ingvar (Ihor), and his daughter-in-law Hélga, feminine form of Hélgi (Olha). By the third generation, they have Slavic names: Sviatoslav (938–972), Volodymyr, Yaroslav. The reigns of Volodymyr (980–1015) and Yaroslav (1019–54) mark the high point in the political power of Rus. During the twelfth century, Rus breaks up into smaller principalities ruled by numerous Rurikids (members of Rurik's dynasty). They spent their time waging incessant and brutal internecine wars until they fell victim to new conquerors, the Mongols and Tatars, in 1237–41.

Rus was a multi-ethnic entity. The conquerors were the Rus (most likely Scandinavians); the peoples of the north belonged to the Ugro-Finnish tribes (called the Chud, Vsev and Meria in the ancient chronicles); the southern peoples were Turkic nomads (Pechenegs and Cumans). The core was made up of Slavic tribes. Where they originated is a matter of scholarly debate. Two of the three established theories of the origins of the Slavs, place the Slavic ancestral homeland on the territory of modern Ukraine. Recent genetic studies offer some support for this version. According to one study, the 'Slavic' gene appeared about fifteen thousand years ago on the territory of Ukraine, from where it spread west, north and south after the Ice Age, probably under pressure from migration by the steppe peoples.

Linguistic analysis suggests that early Slavs lived on the banks of rivers and lakes, or near swamps. This is supported by the argument of 'three trees': the beech, larch and yew. These are the only local trees whose names are borrowed from other languages rather than having Slavic roots. Most significantly, these particular trees do not grow near swamps. The Pripet Marshes on the border between modern Belarus and Ukraine may have been the Slavic ancestral homeland. The linguistic records also suggest that the early Slavs did not live by the sea: words related to navigation, sea fishing and maritime trade are of foreign origin in Slavic languages. The fact that the rivers Daugava and Neman (Nemanas) have Baltic names suggests that they mark the northern boundary between Slavic and Baltic tribes, who were probably once part of a common Balto-Slavic group.

In the south, the ancient Slav settlements reached as far as the Wild Field – the Black Sea steppe inhabited by nomadic peoples. The Scythians and neighbouring steppe tribes described by Herodotus were most likely proto-Iranian and inhabited these territories long before the Slavs appeared. Strong evidence for this theory is provided by the fact that the largest rivers on Slavic territory have proto-Iranian names, such as the Danube, Dniester, Dnipro and Don (from the common root *d-n*, meaning river). The history of these tribes and later nomadic peoples is the history of the great Eurasian steppe. It stretched in a wide swath from Manchuria and Mongolia through Northern China and Kazakhstan, Southern Siberia, the Volga and Black Sea regions, present-day Moldovan and Romanian lands and part of the Balkans, ending on the Pannonian Plain (in present-day Hungary).

The Eurasian steppe was a kind of broad highway along which nomadic tribes – Avars, Ugrians, Bulgarians, Tauri, Goths, Visigoths, Vandals, Franks and others – passed from east to west during great migrations of peoples. It is assumed that their appearance in the western part of the Eurasian continent was associated with two periods of prolonged drought in Western and Central Asia around 300 and then 800 AD.

The climate of the Wild Field differed from that of the rest of the Eurasian steppe. It had particularly fertile soil, which had been washed in the warm Black Sea. Simply put, the steppe grass was juicier here. It is believed that the origins of horsebreeding can be traced to this area. Sometime between 4000 and 3500 BC, horses were domesticated and then horsebreeding culture spread all the way into China and as far south as Egypt. For most nomads, the Black Sea steppes were a kind of throughway: they passed through the Wild Field and continued further. This is evidenced by the names of some European countries and regions where they finally stopped: Andalusia (from the Vandals), Bulgaria (from the Bulgars), Hungary (from the Huns) and, most likely, Catalonia (originally Gothalonia, i.e., the land of the Goths). Some nomads settled in the Volga and Black Sea regions. Huge Hun and Avar empires emerged and disappeared here. In the early period of Rus, directly to their east lay the Khazar Khaganate, a large Turkic state whose elite adopted Judaism. Some Slavic tribes also fell under the governance of the Khagans. One legend holds that the Khazar Khagans were the actual founders of Kyiv. In 969, Rurik's grandson Sviatoslav defeated the Khazar Khaganate. Sviatoslav himself was killed three years later by the Pechenegs, another nomadic tribe who were later ousted by the Cumans in the early eleventh century.

The proximity of the steppe made Eastern Europe a region of intense contacts between peoples – both military and peaceful. High degrees of multiethnicity and multiculturalism have always characterised its history. No single ethnic group here can claim ethnic purity or autochthonous rights. Any such claims are dangerous political fantasies. We can only roughly determine who was here earlier and who arrived later. We don't know when Slavs appeared in these lands. Their existence as a separate group can be affirmed more or less definitely only from the sixth century onward. The first culture that archaeologists consider undoubtedly Slavic is the Prague-Korchak culture. It existed in the years 500–700 between the Elbe and Dnipro rivers. The first written references to the Slavs appear in Byzantine sources of the sixth century. There, the Slavs appear as Anti, Slaveni and (probably) Veneti. By the end of the ninth century, they had settled Eastern, Central and Southern Europe, displacing Germanic tribes in the West and Illyrian tribes in the Balkans.

The speed with which the Slavs settled Eastern, Central and Southern Europe is another great mystery. The Slavs were an agricultural civilisation and such civilisations typically spread at an average of one kilometre per year. The Slavs spread almost six times faster than that! One possibility is that Slavic culture was not an ethnic culture, but rather a mode of existence. On the one hand, this way of life was associated with a more sophisticated economic structure that lifted local tribes above the level of mere survival. On the other hand, Byzantine sources speak of the warlike nature of the Slavs. They also note a unique characteristic: unlike other tribes, the Slavs did not keep their captives in permanent slavery, but after a period of time gave them the option of returning home or remaining with them as free people. The combination of these two traits – a better way of managing the economy and an egalitarian ethos – made the Slavic way of life as attractive to other tribes as, say, the hippie communities of the 1960s and '70s. Over time, this spirit evaporated and the Slavs became a hierarchical community, but it may explain the rapid pace of Slavicisation in Eastern, Central and Southern Europe.

In the ninth century, new barbarians appeared in this vast contact zone: Scandinavians. Like the much earlier ancient Greek colonisation, Scandinavian colonisation was carried out along waterways. In the eastern part of the European continent, the Scandinavian colonisers moved from North to South along the river system connecting the Baltic with the Black Sea. Here, their appearance is plausibly linked to the restoration of trade links between Northern Europe and the Mediterranean in 750–900. This restoration was based, on the one hand, on the rise of the Carolingian Empire, which stabilised the political situation in Western Europe and thus made long-distance trade possible. On the other hand, the Arab conquests in the South intensified the slave trade in the Mediterranean and the barbaric North was one of the main suppliers of slaves.

Whatever you call them, between 850 and 1050 these Northern tribes were attacking all the coasts of Europe and in England, northern France (Normandy) and southern Italy they even established local governments. Those who appeared on the Slavic lands were called the Rus.

The Tale of Bygone Years claims that there was no agreement among the local Slavic tribes and they were constantly fighting each other. To stop the strife,

> ... they went overseas to the Varangians, to the Rus. These particular Varangians were known as Rus, just as some are called Swedes and others Normans and Angles and still others Gotlanders, for they were thus named. The Chuds, the Slavs, the Krivichians and the Ves then said to the Rus, 'Our land is great and rich, but there is no order in it. Come reign as princes, rule over us'. Three brothers, with their kinfolk, were selected. They brought with them all the Rus and migrated. The oldest, Rurik, located himself in Novgorod; the second, Sineus, in Beloozero; and the third, Truvor, in Izborsk. From these Varangians, the Rus land received its name.

This story is too good to be true. No one invited the Vikings – they came on their own. They came looking for silver, the main precious metal of the Middle Ages (gold coins were more expensive and rarer). Silver was plentiful in the South. The main deposits were in the vicinity of Baghdad, the capital of the Islamic

Abbasid dynasty. Baghdad was one of the largest and richest cities in the world at the time and the Arab drachma played a role like that of the American dollar today. The Vikings travelled along the Volga to reach the Abbasid Caliphate. Thus, the Arabs called them the 'Volga Varangians'. But starting in the second half of the ninth century, the flow of Arab silver coins gradually started to dry up and in search of new sources of wealth, the Varangians reoriented themselves from Baghdad to Constantinople. They moved from the Baltic to the Black Sea like an avalanche, absorbing other nations on their way. In the 830s they opened the route to Constantinople and in 860 they attacked the city with a large fleet of two hundred ships and, after plundering its surroundings, returned North unhindered. They repeated this move several times later in the tenth century.

By that time, they controlled the entire trade route 'from the Varangians to the Greeks'. Of all the Rus princes, Sviatoslav was the most successful in military terms. His main goal was to get as close to Byzantium as possible. His ambitions are best evidenced by his intention to move his capital to the Danube, to the Bulgarian city of Pereiaslavets. We can't know how his plans would have turned out had he not died near the rapids of the Dnipro at the hands of a steppe prince. But it's certainly possible that modern historians would be speaking of Pereiaslavan Rus rather than Kyivan Rus.

Ancient Rus State

The southward movement of the Rus stopped when Sviatoslav's son Volodymyr converted to Christianity in 988. There may be no other event that has had such a profound impact on the history of Eastern Europe in general and Ukraine in particular, as the baptism of Rus. It was a civilisational leap from a pagan society to a Christian society – with consequences in almost every area of public life: politics, economics and culture. In *The Tale of Bygone Years*, the chronicler describes this story as 'choosing a faith'. Supposedly, Prince Volodymyr first listened to the stories of envoys from different lands about their religion and then sent his own envoys to those lands to determine which faith was better. He allegedly rejected Islam because of the complete ban on alcohol, because 'the joy of the Rus is drinking, we cannot do without it'. Fascinated by their description of the Hagia Sophia in Constantinople, where his ambassadors felt as though they were in heaven, Volodymyr decided to convert to Byzantine Christianity.

The story of 'choosing a faith' is not unique. It wanders from one folklore to another. We find similar stories among the closest neighbours of Rus, the Khazars, Lithuanians and Volga Bulgarians. We should assume that the choice of Christianity from Constantinople was rather a 'choice without a choice'. Living in the shadow of the largest and richest civilisation of the time, Volodymyr had limited options.

This choice was advantageous for Constantinople, as well. Arabs were approaching from the south and east and Bulgarians were moving down from the Balkans. Just before the Rus adopted Christianity, Basil II, the Byzantine emperor, was fighting for the throne with the commander-in-chief of his army. Volodymyr promised the emperor military support and with his help the pretender to the throne was defeated.

The price for his assistance was Volodymyr's marriage to Princess Anna, Basil's sister. This was a great achievement for the barbarian ruler from Kyiv: now he was related to the family of the Byzantine emperor himself. In those days, the Byzantine emperor was considered the father of a great European dynastic family, in which the Bulgarian king was symbolically his son, the English king was just a friend, and so on. Charlemagne, who in 800 made the pope grant him the title of emperor of the Roman Empire, was, from the perspective of Constantinople, just an insolent barbarian impostor. Volodymyr rose in the European dynastic hierarchy in another way – through marriage. Anna, the sister of the Byzantine emperor, had a special status. She was 'born in the purple', that is to say, during her father's reign, and thus she had imperial blood in her veins. Every European monarch dreamed of marrying such a princess. Both the French King Hugo Capet and the German King Otto I sought her hand in marriage for their sons, but Volodymyr won her.

Volodymyr's son Yaroslav became a successful European matchmaker: all of his children were married to European kings and queens. The children of Rus princes left their mark on the life of Europe's royal courts. One was the appearance of new names: among the French rulers, Philippe (in honour of the apostle who allegedly reached Scythia); among the Hungarian rulers András (a Hungarian form of the name of the apostle Andrew); and among the Danish rulers, Valdemar (in honour of Volodymyr). These were the names of children born of the marriages of local rulers with the daughters of Kyivan princes. Since some of these children, such as Philippe or András, became rulers themselves, their names took root in Western courts and became widespread.

According to Metropolitan Ilarion of Kyiv, the Kyivan princes 'did not rule in some poor and unknown land, but in Rus, which is known and heard in all four corners of the earth'. The statistics on the relations of Kyivan princes with monarchs of the time show one important thing: out of fifty-two such marriages concluded over two hundred years, forty were with Catholic states (Scandinavia, Poland, the Holy Roman Empire and Hungary) and only five with the Orthodox Byzantine Empire. These statistics show that the idea of the unity of Rus and Byzantium is greatly exaggerated – the unity was more religious than political. Religious commonality with Orthodox Byzantium did not prevent Kyivan princes from marrying their children to the children of Catholic monarchs. Although in 1054 the spiritual rulers of Constantinople and Rome excommunicated each other, the spirit of this great schism was not felt for a long time either in Catholic Europe or in Orthodox Rus.

Constantinople considered itself immeasurably superior to others in matters of faith as well as politics. It was the capital of the first Christian empire, which was to exist until the second coming of Christ, or in earthly terms, forever. According to the Byzantine rulers, God had chosen their state to serve as a new Israel among the pagans and convert them to Christianity. The Gospels were written in the language spoken in the Byzantine Empire. Among the rulers of Europe, the ability to pray in Greek was considered an exceptional accomplishment. The Polish prince Mieszko was praised for praying in Greek. He owed his knowledge of Greek prayers to his connections with Kyiv. On the scale of civilisation, Rus, which was closer to Byzantium, was higher than early medieval Poland.

A Byzantine diplomat in a discussion at the Arab court proudly asserted: 'All the arts come from us!' This diplomat was the future St Cyril. Together with his older brother Methodius, he translated the main Christian texts from Greek into Old Bulgarian in 860–80. Most likely this was their native language. Later it was called Church Slavonic and, along with Greek and Latin, was considered one of the sacred Christian languages.

There were certain benefits to the fact that the scriptures and prayers were translated into Slavonic. Orthodox Christians understood the liturgy better than, say, Polish Catholics, for whom the liturgy was celebrated in Latin. But there was also a significant drawback. Having received the sacred texts in Church Slavonic rather than Greek, Rus was thus cut off from the 'Greek wisdom' that Cyril was so proud of.

The Greek cultural tradition was richer than the Roman, but Rus could not take advantage of this. Unlike Rome, which gave the converted tribes both religion and language, Constantinople gave the southern and eastern Slavs religion, but not language. This imposed inevitable limitations on the cultural tradition of Rus. Whereas Polish chroniclers of the time could freely quote Virgil, Horace, or any other Latin author, the Rus chronicler in *The Tale of Bygone Years* does not quote Homer, Plato or other wise Greeks.

The lack of Aristotle is especially significant. His translation into Arabic and then into Latin gave a strong impetus to the development of the sciences in the Muslim and Catholic worlds. At the risk of oversimplification, we can say that Muslim civilisation experienced its 'golden age' of the eighth to thirteenth centuries precisely from the time Aristotle was translated and integrated until the time his works fell into disfavour because they allegedly contradicted the Qur'an. But as soon as Aristotle was 'expelled' from the Muslim world, he 'migrated' to the Catholic world. Thomas Aquinas (1225–74) incorporated him into the foundations of the Catholic faith and Thomism became official Vatican doctrine for many centuries.

Aristotle's strength lay in his logic and rationalism. He believed in God. Aristotle's God was not like the gods of Olympus or the God of the Judeo-Christian tradition. His God was a metaphysical construct, the prime mover and the primary cause of everything on earth. Aristotle followed in the footsteps of his great teacher, Plato. The latter divided the world into 'the cave' – the world of shadows in which we live – and 'the light' – an immense truth beyond the bounds of earth that can be known only after death. Unlike Plato, Aristotle believed that we can experience this truth during life. God endowed us with reason for a reason and that reason was to allow us to recognise Him. And since our world was created by God, by coming to know the world, we come to know God Himself. Nature is like another great book of revelation that God provided humanity along with the Bible. Therefore, the understanding of nature is pleasing to God: it is simultaneously an understanding of God Himself.

The inclusion of Aristotle in Catholic doctrine radically distinguished Western Christianity from other faiths. In no other confession will we find what Thomas Aquinas did: attempts to prove the existence of God through the evidence of reason. Over time, the strong rational stream of Western Christianity led to the technological superiority of 'old Europe' over the rest of the world. This synthesis of Western Christianity and rationalism was to some degree fortuitous. It could never have happened. At first, Aquinas' views were considered possibly heretical and Thomism became church doctrine only after his death. It is hard to imagine Descartes' analytical geometry or Newton's laws without the influence of Aristotle.

Figures like Aquinas, Descartes or Newton are unimaginable in the Orthodox world of the time. According to theologians, the church was more Platonic than Aristotelian. Aristotle was known in Rus only from fragments and second-hand reports. He remained largely unknown until the teachers of the Kyiv–Mohyla Academy began studying his works in the seventeenth century. The poverty of the Rus intellectual tradition is striking. Between the tenth and seventeenth centuries, we don't find a single scholarly work in the Church Slavonic tradition, not even a theological treatise. Nor will we find Rus equivalents of Omar Khayyam, Abelard, Cervantes, Machiavelli or Shakespeare. The only thing we can offer as Rus secular literature is *The Tale of Igor's Campaign*. Yet, there are serious reasons to suspect that the *Tale* is not an original work but a forgery of the eighteenth century.

If we were to collect all the Church Slavonic books that were in circulation in the Rus lands from the adoption of Christianity until the beginning of the sixteenth century, the list would have no more volumes than the library of an average Byzantine monastery. Intellectually, Rus was 'slavishly dependent' on Byzantium (to quote the Russian theologian Georgy Fedotov). At the start of the seventeenth century, an educated person in Rus would read almost the same Church Slavonic books that were available to his Rus ancestor in the eleventh and thirteenth centuries.

The differences between the book cultures of Western and Eastern Christianity became even more pronounced following the advent of the printing press. Historians estimate that from the time of its invention in the middle of the fifteenth century until the end of the sixteenth century, 200 million books were printed in the Western Christian world, while in the Eastern Christian world, no more than forty to sixty thousand. This difference of almost three thousand times is more than just a quantitative difference. It is a qualitative difference.

Printed literature is one of the main prerequisites for the formation of nations. A contemporary historian formulated this theory succinctly: 'Nations are book-reading tribes.' Take away books and tribes remain tribes. They will lack an important tool for perceiving themselves as a nation.

From the perspective of nation-building, the world of Rus was like the proverbial 'suitcase without a handle': difficult to carry, too valuable to abandon. The inhabitants of its vast expanses had some idea of the origin of their civilisation from Kyiv. They spoke mutually intelligible dialects and prayed to God in the same Church Slavonic language. However, this did not make them one great nation, nor did it make them multiple smaller nations. Their world was largely an *anational* world.

It is impossible to say precisely what caused the 'great silence' of Rus. One explanation attributes it to the proximity of the steppe. The constant threat of invasion by nomadic steppe peoples forced them to invest considerable resources and energy in the defence of their lands. There was a lack of resources for the development of intellectual life. This factor played a particularly disastrous role during the Mongol invasion of 1237–40. Kyiv, Pereiaslav, Ryazan and other once great cities were reduced to the status of provincial towns. The Mongol conquest is said to be one of the greatest massacres in world history: nearly 30 million people died as a result.

But for every argument there is a counterargument. The Mongol invasion did not touch churches and monasteries. The Mongols treated every religion with respect; it is said that the Orthodox Church never enjoyed such privileged status either before or after Mongol rule. In medieval Europe, monasteries and churches were the main centres of intellectual life. However, we see no such activity in Orthodox Eastern Europe.

Most likely, the main reason lies hidden in the earliest days of the Slavic Orthodox tradition formed at the court of the Bulgarian king Simeon (893–927). Simeon was a brilliant scholar of the ancient philosophers, including Aristotle, but not a follower of Aristotle. Simeon advocated the 'monastic style of education', which later spread throughout the Eastern Christian lands. The main features of this approach include a deliberate rejection of classical heritage, the primacy of church literature over secular, and a personalised transmission of knowledge from teacher to student, which essentially meant abandoning the school tradition of studying philosophy and theology. This type of education has no need for universities. No one forbade them in Rus, but no one tried to establish them either. All the well-known universities of the time emerged and operated in the context of Catholic culture. One of the latest, Jagiellonian University in Krakow, was founded in 1364, practically on the border between the Western and Eastern Christian worlds. But university education only arrived in the Eastern Christian world in the seventeenth and eighteenth centuries with the establishment of the Kyiv-Mohyla Academy (1632) and, later, Moscow University (1755).

Although Orthodoxy – like all of Christianity, Islam and Judaism – was a religion of the book, it did not require intensive study of the book itself. Until the sixteenth century there was no complete Church Slavonic translation of the Holy Scriptures – only the New Testament and those parts of the Old Testament used in the liturgy were translated. You could say that for a long time the Orthodox Church was a church without a Bible. Not because it did not want such a translation, but because it did not need it. This way of transmitting information – oral and personal – is the most relevant feature of what we call traditional society. It can function without the written word and therefore is characterised by a high level of illiteracy. In Central and Eastern Europe, Eastern Christian and Muslim communities held to traditional values for a longer period of time. This is shown, in particular, by the first censuses of the local population at the turn of the twentieth century: in the literacy statistics of the peoples of the Austro-Hungarian and Russian empires at the time, the highest rates of literacy were seen among Protestants (Protestantism requires its faithful to read religious books) and Jews (among Jews this requirement applies only to men), followed by Catholics. The lowest rates of literacy were reported among Eastern Christians (both Orthodox and Greek Catholics) and Muslims.

Scholars call this East Slavic cultural zone *Slavia Orthodoxa*. The term is not entirely accurate, because, in addition to the Slavic peoples, it also includes the present-day Moldovans and Romanians, whose liturgy was also in Church Slavonic. Modern Kremlin propaganda proudly proclaims this environment to be the 'Russian world', a separate civilisation that, with its unspoiled traditional values, stands above Western Europe and follows its own path. But if we free historical reality from its patriotic gilding, it becomes clear that belonging to this world could only serve as a basis for arrogance, not justified pride. Rus monks may have been closer to God with their culture of spiritual asceticism, but when it comes to rational thought, their work looks rather poor, even in the field of theology.

Over time, the proximity of Rus to Byzantine civilisation

became a disadvantage instead of an advantage. After the light of Byzantium was extinguished – the fall of the Byzantine Empire in 1453 as a result of the Turkish conquest – the Rus lands fell into a darkness from which they started to emerge only at the end of the sixteenth century. But they were emerging into a new world, one in which the division between the *civilised* South and the *barbaric* North would gradually be replaced by the division between the *developed* West and the *backward* East.

Rus emerged on the old North-South axis. Ukraine, on the other hand, was formed mainly on the later East-West axis. It would be difficult to understand the emergence of Ukraine without understanding this reformatting of the world. Although there is a certain continuity between Rus and Ukraine, *the formation of Ukraine inevitably meant the destruction of Rus.* The same is true for Belarus and Russia.

This was not a complete destruction. All three nations have adopted certain parts of the heritage of Old Rus. Ukraine is heir to the oldest core of the ancient Rus state, along with the capital city of Kyiv. Russia emerged on the peripheries of ancient Rus much later. Although Russians claim to be the older brothers of Ukrainians, these statements don't correspond to reality: in fact, this 'older brother' is historically the younger. But the main thing that Ukrainians have inherited is the idea that Europe is not alien to them, let alone hostile. This idea relates directly to the fact that ancient Rus was an integral part of Europe, if we accept the medieval definition of Europe as a shared Christian civilisation.

History is not mathematics or chemistry, so it speaks in metaphors rather than formulas. In the language of metaphors, the transformation of Rus into Ukraine can be compared to the transformation of a caterpillar into a butterfly. There is certainly a connection between the caterpillar and the butterfly. But that connection becomes irrelevant following the transition from the 'crawling' state to the 'flying' state.

The Long Shadow of Rus

When did Rus collapse? Its end is typically associated with the Mongol–Tatar conquest. In reality, it had ceased to exist as a political union almost a hundred years earlier. After the deaths of the sons of Volodymyr Monomakh, the last great Kyivan prince (1113–25), an intense internecine war began in Rus, in which the Rus princes fought among themselves with no less passion than against external enemies. Suffice it to say that over the course of one hundred years (1146–1246), power in Kyiv changed hands forty-seven times. Thirty-five reigns lasted less than a year.

The political history of the Rus lands can be described as alternating periods of integration and disintegration. These cycles generally coincided with those that took place on the Eurasian continent as a whole, from southeast Asia to the North Atlantic coast. The Rus political system was distinguished, however, by the fact that it contained a special virus of self-destruction. This virus was the local principle of succession. In Western Europe, power was passed from father to eldest son. Power belonged to a royal dynasty and, as long as the king could ensure a healthy heir to the throne, power remained with that family. In Rus, it was not a single princely family who ruled: the entire extended family ruled. The eldest brother sat on the throne of Kyiv. After his death, his younger brother inherited the throne and so on, until this line was completely exhausted. Then it was the turn of the elder brother's sons and then the sons of the next brothers. Those sons whose fathers did not have time to take the Kyiv throne became outcasts: they fell out of the line of succession and were granted fiefs from the senior princes in the system of kormlenie or 'feeding'. In particular, this is how the domain of Halych emerged, from which the great Galicia-Volhynia principality later developed.

Such a scheme is called lateral succession and has a distinctly 'steppe' origin – it existed in the Khazar Khaganate and the early Hungarian state. It exists to this day in the Saudi monarchy. Under these circumstances, the struggle for power in Kyiv was fratricidal in the truest sense of the word. Suffice it to say that in order for the Kyivan throne to pass from Volodymyr to Yaroslav, ten brothers had to die 'along the way'.

In recording this history of fraternal strife, Russian and Ukrainian historians point to a particular event: the sacking of Kyiv by the army of Prince Andrei Bogoliubskii of Vladimir-Suzdal in 1169. According to the chronicler, 'there was no mercy for anyone from anywhere' during the sacking of Kyiv. Many view this event as a historical precedent for the Russian-Ukrainian war. It has been presented as a major turning point in Rus history: the royal capital was dethroned. However, this is actually a story created by Russian imperial historians to 'prove' that the centre of Rus was then transferred from Kyiv to Muscovy, later to be called Russia. In reality, it was nothing of the sort. Historical sources show that the 1169 invasion, unlike the sack by the Mongols in 1240, did not devastate Kyiv. The city continued to grow and retained its position as the political and cultural centre: there was no 'transfer of power'. However, it did become possible to rule Kyiv without living in Kyiv. When Prince Danylo Halytskyi of Galicia-Volhynia conquered Kyiv just before the Mongol invasion, he appointed his boyar Dmytro as voivode. Dmytro led the city's defence and died along with its defenders.

After the Mongol victory, the Rus 'migrated' to separate fiefdoms. The Rus princes became vassals of the Mongol Khan, but continued to rule their own lands. The very geography of the Golden Horde, the great Mongol empire, divided the Russian lands into two large zones: those that were closer to its centre and most zealously followed its orders (the Vladimir-Suzdal, later Moscow principality) and those that, due to their remoteness from the Mongol centre and proximity to Catholic Europe, could manage a certain degree of autonomy (the Novgorod Republic in the north and the Galicia-Volhynia principality with a new centre in Lviv in the west). Danylo Halytskyi even tried to work with Catholic rulers to form an anti-Tatar coalition. For this effort, he was awarded the title 'King of Rus' along with a crown from the hands of the Pope's envoy, who had similar plans.

However, neither the Novgorod Republic nor the Principality of Galicia-Volhynia lasted long. In 1478, the Muscovite Tsar Ivan III conquered and destroyed Novgorod. The reign of the Galician princes was even shorter, lasting only until the death of the childless Yuriy-Boleslav Troidenovych (1340), who was poisoned by his own boyars. The death of the last Galician prince led to an almost fifty-year struggle for his lands between his closest relatives, the Polish and Hungarian kings. In 1387, the Polish king won the final victory and Polish rule was established which lasted, with some interruptions and mutations, until the Second World War.

Lithuanian princes seized the rest of southwestern Rus from the Mongols from 1350–60. The Lithuanian principality had emerged in the early twelfth century in the lands around Vilnius. It later extended its possessions to the Rus lands of modern Belarus, eastern Poland and northern Ukraine, including Kyiv and became the Grand Duchy of Lithuania.

The general outlines of Lithuanian rule over the East Slavic peoples, the future Belarusians and Ukrainians, resemble the history of Rus itself. The Lithuanians were the 'last pagans of Europe': they did not accept Christianity until the late fourteenth century. Lithuanians were a minority in the state. For every Lithuanian, there were seven or eight non-Lithuanians, mostly Rus. Like the Varangians, the Lithuanians adopted Rus culture. Rus was the language of chancellery and law. The Lithuanian Statutes, the main code of law in the Grand Duchy of Lithuania, which was in effect on Belarusian and Ukrainian lands until the nineteenth century, was written in this language. For a time, the full name of the state was the Grand Duchy of Lithuania, Rus and Samogitia. Like the Kyivan rulers, the Lithuanian princes also faced the question of choosing a faith and the choice was between Western and Eastern Christianity. In the first centuries, the Orthodox orientation prevailed, but in the end, the Catholic line won out. In 1385, the Lithuanian prince Jagiello married the Polish queen Jadwiga. This marriage laid the foundations for the unification of the two states, which resulted in the formation of the Polish-Lithuanian Commonwealth in 1569. However, Rus culture remained influential in the Lithuanian part of the country.

The Polish-Lithuanian Commonwealth emerged as an alliance between two rulers: a Lithuanian prince and a Polish king. Rus does not appear in this formulation, probably because there was no Rus prince or king. The closest candidate for such a title (if there had been a Rus state) was Prince Vasyl Kostiantyn Ostrozkyi (1526–1608), the 'uncrowned king of Rus'. He was one of the last local Orthodox nobles in whose veins the blood of Rurik flowed, although according to another version he was descended from the ruling Lithuanian family. The death of his grandson Janusz in 1620 coincides with the extinction in the late sixteenth and early seventeenth centuries of almost forty local princely families. This demographic catastrophe happened suddenly and without obvious reasons. But it can be considered another end of Rus in the Ukrainian and Belarusian lands.

The male Rurikid line died out at almost the same time in the Russian lands. In 1610, the last Rurikid prince, Tsar Vasily Shuisky, died in Moscow in 1612. His death, coupled with the preceding devastating reign of Ivan the Terrible (1547–84), gave rise to a major and protracted crisis in Muscovy – the Time of Troubles. The Polish-Lithuanian elite attempted to place an impostor on the Moscow throne – False Dmitry, who claimed to be the son of Ivan the Terrible. The Rus elite and Ukrainian

Cossacks also took part in this attempt. The Polish-Cossack army was defeated. The Romanovs, distant and indirect relatives of the Ruriks, became the tsars of Moscow. During the reign of the second Romanov, Alexei Mikhailovich (1645–76), Muscovy gained part of the Belarusian and Ukrainian lands from the Polish crown following Khmelnytsky's Cossack uprising and the war with the Polish-Lithuanian Commonwealth. At that time, his official title became 'Grand Duke, Tsar and Grand Duke of All Great and Little and White Russia'. His son, the gifted and adventurous Peter I instituted radical reforms and transformed Muscovy into the Russian Empire in 1721. This date is yet another candidate for the end of Old Rus.

The Russian Empire viewed itself as the sole heir to Rus and pursued expansion under the slogan of 'gathering the Russian lands'. From 1772–95, the Russian, Austrian and Prussian empires partitioned the Polish-Lithuanian Commonwealth and Russia took over the remaining Belarusian and Ukrainian lands. The exception was the lands of Galician Rus. The Austrian Habsburgs annexed them to their possessions as the allegedly restored 'Kingdom of Galicia-Volhynia'. This annexation was justified by the fact that the Rus princes were related to the Hungarian kings and since the Habsburgs controlled the Hungarian crown, they had a legitimate right to its 'Rus inheritance'. This right extended to Bukovina and Transcarpathia. At the very beginning of the First World War, in the autumn of 1914, Russia conquered Galicia and Bukovina. The Russian army remained there only until spring 1915 and two years later, after the outbreak of the Russian Revolution in March 1917, it ceased to exist altogether.

Where the Russian Empire failed, the Soviet Union succeeded. During the Second World War, Stalin annexed the last fragments of the former Rus lands – Western Belarus, Western Ukraine, Bukovina and Transcarpathia. Russia was reborn, now in the form of the USSR. This is referenced in the words of the Soviet anthem written in 1944:

Great Rus has bound forever
The unbreakable union of free republics

The theory of a direct historical link between Rus and the USSR lasted until the end of Soviet rule. One might have thought that Rus had fully died with the fall of the USSR in 1991, if not for Putin's rhetoric and attempts to revive a 'Russian world'.

Regardless of the date we choose for the 'end of Rus' – 1146, 1169, 1340, 1440, 1569, 1620, 1721, 1917 or 1991 – we still come to the conclusion that Rus never really disappeared. Its long shadow is still with us. As one Ukrainian socialist wrote in the late nineteenth century, in addition to the three Russian tribes – the Great and Little Russians and the Belarusians – there is a fourth, 'pan-Russian', 'bleak something-or-other' that buries the folk Rus, national Rus and tribal Rus in a thick layer of dust.

These comparisons inevitably raise the question: What is it about the Rus heritage that dooms its successors to economic backwardness and chronic bouts of authoritarianism? The most common answer is the influence of Byzantium. And this idea isn't solely the domain of kitchen philosophers or armchair political scientists, but also of professional Byzantine specialists like Alexander Kazhdan, quoted at the beginning of this chapter.

There is, however, another perspective that claims this is a 'black legend' that emerged in the West after Byzantium's fall. We can see the weaknesses of this legend by comparing the Byzantine Empire with the Japanese Empire. For many centuries, Japan had no great achievements in science, philosophy, or political theory and remained a generally poor country until it began to modernise in the late nineteenth century. It is not known what would have happened to Byzantium if it had existed as long as Japan.

The main problem with our perception of Byzantium is that we approach it with modern standards. And we often believe that wealth and democracy are norms by which we can measure the development of other countries. In reality, despotism and poverty were the norms in the past.

If we were to reduce world history to a single common denominator, one option would be as follows: it is the history of a ruling elite, which collects and distributes among itself rents from the broad population either for the promise of protection from neighbouring elites, or even without any obligations at all, relying on the rights of conquest. The key condition is 'access to the body' of the ruler, no matter who it is: a Kyivan prince, a Byzantine emperor, a Mongol khan, a Muscovite tsar, the general secretary of the CPSU Central Committee, or the president of Russia. This organisation of power is called a 'limited access order'. It is characteristic of the Intermarium of Hammurabi's time, Tudor Britain and Putin's Russia. The differences between these countries are more in the details than in the broad outlines.

The 'open access order' is the exact opposite. Instead of rents, it is based on profits and the ability to earn them is regulated not by privileges for a minority, but by rights for all. Such a system might well sound like a utopia, if not for one circumstance: it works. Approximately 25 per cent of contemporary nations operate on a basis of open access. They have entered this state over the past two hundred years. Almost all of these states belong to the formerly Catholic (Western) Europe and its 'offspring': North America, Australia and New Zealand. The only exceptions are the 'Asian tigers' which moved to open access after the Second World War. After the fall of communism, the former communist countries of Central Europe and the Baltic states, are approaching this 'gold standard'. So far, however, there is no such state in the 'Russian world'.

Various factors can explain why Western Europe succeeded

and others did not: climate, geography, scientific and technological advantages of the West, conquests, etc. These circumstances seem to be necessary but not sufficient. The key condition is that the ruling elite give up its monopoly on the economy. The elite did not generally do so voluntarily. It gave in under external pressure – wars, revolutions, coups d'état. In other words, open access is not given – it is taken. But the chances of success depend on whether the society has someone to take it – that is, viable institutions that exist independent of the state.

In this respect, old Europe did have certain advantages. They were related to religion. A first and almost unerring impression of a country's political system and well-being can be based on the appearance of its main religious buildings: whether they are soaring Catholic cathedrals, simple and restrained Protestant churches, Jewish synagogues, Muslim mosques with tall minaret towers, or Orthodox churches with onion domes.

These differences did not emerge recently; they are rooted in the past. By way of example, Charlemagne's coronation as emperor in Rome was a challenge not just for the Byzantine emperor but also for the pope. Two more or less equal rulers had appeared in the Western Christian world: the Holy Roman Emperor and the Pope. Whose power was superior? From the perspective of the church, the pope was Christ's vicar on earth, so his power was higher than that of the emperor. From the secular perspective, the Catholic Church lived according to Roman law, where the emperor was the centre of power. Accordingly, the pope was subordinate to the emperor. This theoretical dispute had a practical dimension: who had the right to appoint bishops? On the one hand, bishops were part of the church hierarchy and thus fell under the authority of the pope. On the other hand, they often took on secular responsibilities of leadership in a society with few educated people, so they were appointed by the emperor.

This conflict, called the investiture controversy, emerged

as a power struggle between Pope Gregory VII and Emperor Henry IV. It ended rather dramatically in 1076, when the pope excommunicated the emperor. This was the greatest punishment of the time: the emperor could now be killed with impunity, he lost the right to pass the throne to his son and worst of all, he would go to hell after his death. Henry IV had no choice but to remove his imperial robes and set off on a difficult trek through the winter Alps to the northern Italian castle of Canossa, where the pope was hiding, to beg forgiveness.

Where two struggle, a third will take advantage. These third parties were institutions with independent resources and (relatively) independent power: city-states, autonomous universities, artisan guilds and spiritual brotherhoods – all those elements we call 'civil society' in modern parlance. Whenever the pope tried to establish absolute control over them, they could escape to the protection of the emperor – and vice versa. Manoeuvring between two poles of power, they created space for a third. British political scientist George Schöpflin writes that,

> The peculiarity of the Western pattern of development lay in the separation of religious and secular legitimation ... The symbolic drama of Canossa illustrated this vividly. In no other historical tradition was it conceivable that a powerful secular ruler like Emperor Henry IV would undertake a penitent's pilgrimage, in a hair shirt with a rope around his neck, to expiate his politico-religious sins or, in power terms, to recognise the religious authority of Pope Gregory VII, whom he had unsuccessfully challenged. The idea of the tsar of Muscovy or the Byzantine emperor or the Ottoman sultan performing an analogous penance is an inherent absurdity.

In contrast, the Byzantine Empire was dominated by the principle of caesaropapism – the ruler of the country was also the informal head of the church. It is believed that this type of relationship was adopted by Rus and that it forms the core of the Byzantine heritage. This assumption is based on the same logical fallacy as the assumptions about poverty and despotism: in the pre-modern world, the combination of religious and secular power was not the exception, it was the rule. The separation of secular and religious power was the exception. And it does not appear to have stemmed from theological differences between Eastern and Western Christianity or between Christianity and Islam. It was the product of a confluence of circumstances. This confluence happened to occur in the Western Christian world and later, as Western Europe began to pave the way for global dominance in modern times, it became a kind of imaginary norm. The dynamics of its spread is the same as that of many other things and concepts that have changed the course of history: first no one has it, then someone has it, then a few and eventually, almost everyone wants it. The exception becomes the rule.

What does the Rus inheritance look like from this perspective? Time and again, examples remind us that the Rus princes did not exercise absolute power. It was limited in Novgorod by the city assembly, in Halych by the power of the boyars. The leaders who had the most absolute power were in Kyiv. But even here, the townspeople could drive away or kill an unpopular prince, as happened to Ihor Olhovych in 1147.

An illustrative example in this context is the crowning of Iziaslav (1024–78), son of Yaroslav. In his struggle for the Kyivan throne, he tried to enlist the support of both figures in the drama of Canossa. When his brothers Sviatoslav and Vsevolod expelled him from Kyiv, he fled to the Holy Roman Empire to ask Henry IV for help. He sent his son Iaropolk to Rome at the same time to ask for the pope's help. Gregory VII promised to help Iziaslav regain the Kyivan principality in Rus' and crowned his son 'King of Rus'. In return, Iziaslav swore allegiance to the pope. In 1077, he regained the throne in Kyiv, but his rule did not last long. Iziaslav was killed in battle a year later.

Which all goes to show that it is impossible to draw a straight line linking the political model from the Kyivan princes to the Muscovite tsars and later Russian emperors. There are alternative political models such as the Novgorod Republic or the Principality of Galicia-Volhynia. Ultimately, the Muscovite model, which was the most distant from Western Christian Europe politically, culturally and geographically, prevailed.

In summary, the heritage of Rus was deeply heterogeneous. Various factors contributed to its emergence and development as a state: Scandinavian expansion from the North, Byzantine cultural influences from the South, an East Slavic core in the centre, nomadic peoples on the periphery and dynastic ties with Western Christian Europe. These factors not only shaped Rus, but also survived it. Ukraine has Orthodox and Greek Catholic churches, Catholic churches, Protestant churches, Jewish synagogues and Muslim mosques. Each of these denominations behind these churches has roots stretching back to the time of Rus. This does not make the Ukrainian situation unique. Similar diversity can be seen in the Balkans and North America. On the one hand, it is pregnant with conflicts and a significant instability, but on the other hand, it increases the chances of overcoming that part of its historical heritage that is associated with the 'Russian world'.

INTERLUDE A Brief History of Ukrainian Bread

One geographical factor in Ukrainian history is the exceptional fertility of the soil. About 40 per cent of Ukrainian territory is black soil. The proportion of arable land composed of black soil is even higher – 58 per cent. There are some regions of America and Canada that may rival Ukraine in terms of the area of black soil, but the depth of Ukrainian black soil (up to one and a half metres) is unmatched anywhere else.

The fertility of the land explains the historical roots of agriculture in Ukraine. In prehistoric times, there was a developed agricultural civilisation here and in the neighbouring Romanian and Moldovan lands, which archaeologists have dubbed the Cucuteni-Trypillia civilisation. The first written references appear in Herodotus. He described the agricultural tribes of 'Scythian ploughers' who lived to the north of the Scythians. Medieval Arab geographers claimed that the Slavs harvested not one but two crops a year, which likely reflects the fact that at some point in ancient Rus, the local tribes adopted the three-field system. In Renaissance and Baroque poetry, local writers imagined the Ukrainian lands as the biblical Palestine, a land flowing with milk and honey.

This rich breadbasket was both a blessing and a curse. The blessing was the high standard of living of the local population. At a time when people depended on the mercies of nature, it was easier to survive on fertile land. The curse was the desire of both near and distant neighbours to conquer and control these lands for economic and political gain. The idea, constantly repeated in the writings of travellers, that even a stick stuck in the local soil would invariably sprout the following year, created a foundation for colonial fantasies about this land and became almost an invitation to exploit it. It is enough to read Hitler's statements before the attack on the USSR in June 1941 to understand the importance of Ukrainian black soil in his plans for world domination. At the 1936 Nazi party conference in Nuremberg, he declared that if the unending fields of Ukraine lay within Germany, the Germans 'would swim in plenty'. On the other hand, Red Army soldiers sang:

We'll smash the fascists,
And go live in Ukraine.
Life is good in Ukraine,
We'll eat and drink our fill.

For the most part, these fantasies were unfounded. Ukraine as the breadbasket of Europe was more a matter of imagination than reality. Foreign powers never managed to take as much bread from Ukraine as they had hoped. One challenge to the full exploitation of local natural resources was purely logistical: there were no good land or river routes connecting Ukrainian land with world markets. Until the late eighteenth century, Ukrainian black earth regions were separated from the Black Sea by the Wild Field and there were no direct river routes to allow the export of grain via the Baltic Sea.

An additional issue was social rather than logistical: how to extract grain from its producers, the local peasants, particularly since the lack of connection with world markets kept agricultural production at a subsistence level. A local proverb provides the answer: 'You've got to kill the bees if you want to eat the honey.' In other words, force was the main method for obtaining the grain. From the mid-sixteenth to the mid-nineteenth centuries, serfdom was the type of force required. The peasants were the lowest link in a food chain that stretched from the soil to gentry dining rooms. Only the peasants' livestock, their horses, oxen, cows and pigs, were lower. In fact, the peasants were often compared to their livestock and given nicknames that emphasised their inferior, bestial character: a peasant (or khokol) is 'a bull, a snake, a pig'. He lives and dies like cattle and no one knows whether he has a soul. Theological justifications were provided for the power the aristocracy held over them. Even the behaviour of the peasant was described in beastly terms: they were dark, dirty, stinking, predatory, treacherous, violent and, above all, lazy. The only language they understood was the language of the stick and the whip. The theological explanation for their servitude claimed that they were the descendants of Ham, the son of Noah who sinned gravely before his father by his unworthy behaviour and thus was punished by God. Peasants in Central and Eastern Europe were called Ham or 'kham', which is still used as an insult in Polish, Russian, Ukrainian and Czech, but not in English, Spanish, Italian and French, the languages of countries where serfdom was less prevalent.

Today serfdom is rarely mentioned, as if it had never existed. But the very fact that generations of Ukrainians, like neighbouring Poles, Russians and Belarusians, lived under a form of de facto slavery inevitably shaped their history.

Areas rich in natural resources tend to have histories shaped by violence. This is very evident in the short twentieth century (1914–91), which was dominated by wars and revolutions. The hunger for Ukraine's grain, oil, coal and iron ore provides a partial explanation for the fact that Ukraine was one of the main military theatres during both World Wars. The Holodomor of 1932–33 is the most eloquent proof of the existential threat that natural wealth can pose.

Another risk of abundant natural resources is known as the resource curse. Countries rich in natural resources tend to focus on exploiting those resources rather than developing human resources and technologies. Why focus on efficiency if nature already generously provides everything you need? The black soil allowed Ukrainians to harvest five to six times more grain than was sown. This is a much higher yield than was seen in neighbouring regions. According to agricultural historians, Ukrainian farming methods changed very little from the ninth century until the end of the nineteenth century. As a result, by the late nineteenth century, the much poorer lands of Moravia enjoyed grain yields three to four times higher than those in Ukraine due to the use of modern agricultural technology and fertilisers.

The central significance of rural agricultural life is reflected in Ukrainian national culture. The national flag depicts a rye field under a blue sky. Modern Ukrainian culture has consciously defined itself an agricultural society. This corresponded to reality to a significant degree: after losing most of its elite to Polish or Russian assimilation and acculturation, the Ukrainian nation became a peasant nation.

At the turn of the twentieth century about 90 per cent of Ukrainians were peasants and among the peasants approximately 90 per cent were ethnically Ukrainian. Most public figures in modern Ukraine were either born under the thatched roof of a peasant house or were just one or two generations removed from it. They celebrated peasant virtues: hard work, sociability and hospitality. And they had good reasons. Traditional society provided a sense of family warmth and protection in difficult circumstances – unlike the modern world with its individualism and cold rationality.

However, what was an advantage in traditional societies has become a hindrance in the transition to a modern one. Education is the foundation of modern society. And education was not a priority in agrarian society. On the contrary, school took rural children away from working on the farm, so formal education was perceived as a waste of time. Farm work tied entire generations of talented children to the land more firmly than gravity. They were expected to farm the land just as their parents, grandparents and great-grandparents had.

Another element of modern society is industrialisation. At the start of the twentieth century, a Ukrainian peasant was often faced with a choice: either go to the city to work in a factory or mine, or else emigrate with the entire family to distant lands, to America or the Far East, to settle new territories without changing his traditional way of life. He often chose the latter. Other ethnic groups went to the cities and factories in the Ukrainian parts of the Russian Empire – mostly Russian peasants. A person's previous way of life shaped these decisions around migration. Peasants from the black earth regions tended to move to similar land. To this day, all over the world, areas with large numbers of Ukrainians are often located in areas similar to the areas of Ukrainian black soil – in the Northern Caucasus and Kazakhstan, in the Russian Far East, the Canadian Far West and the Brazilian province of Paraná. In contrast, Russian peasants had lived on poorer soils and were accustomed to seeking additional earnings: they were more often attracted to work in industry.

As a result, a certain pattern developed: the larger the settlement, the less Ukrainian-speaking it was. This is particularly true of large cities. The converse is true as well: the smaller the town, the more Ukrainian could be heard there. This pattern persisted even when Ukrainians ceased to be a rural nation in the mid-1960s and became a predominantly urban nation.

Peasants were at the very bottom of the social ladder. Hence the habit of looking down on them with disdain and contempt. In the eyes of city dwellers, Ukrainian peasants were backward and cunning, or, on the contrary, 'stupid buckwheat growers' and 'salo lovers'. (Salo is a form of cured pork fat.) This stereotype of Ukrainians is still widespread in contemporary Russian culture. The peasants reciprocated this hostility. They viewed the city as an external power filled with hostile government officials, incomprehensible laws and freeloaders living off the labour of the countryside.

The opposition between urban and rural was not absolute, however. In the twentieth century, a third, intermediate group emerged between the Ukrainian-speaking peasants and Russian-speaking city dwellers: these were assimilated Russian-speaking Ukrainians, who had moved to the large cities out of need or poverty. Although they lost the main characteristics of traditional village culture, they retained an emotional attachment to their peasant childhoods or, for the next generation, an attachment to the Ukrainian-speaking grandparents with whom they spent summer vacations in the village.

The struggle for the souls of these Russian-speaking Ukrainians has been at the heart of many political processes since Ukraine became an independent state in 1991. Russia's military aggression against Ukraine in 2014 became their 'moment of truth'. According to the Kremlin's plans, the entire urbanised Russian-speaking region of southern and eastern Ukraine was to secede into a separate republic called Novorossiya. That did not happen: most of the Russian-speaking population preferred to remain with Ukraine and not to bring war into their homes.

In rural areas, Jews tended to be more literate than the local population. An analysis of nineteenth-century statistics shows a clear correlation: the lower the literacy rate was among the local non-Jewish population in a given area, the more Jews there were. This makes sense, so it can probably be extended to previous centuries. No society can exist without crafts, trade and money. In societies that are 'tied to the land', ethnic minorities often fill non-land-based economic niches, like Armenians in the Ottoman Empire or Chinese in Southeast Asia. Jews played this role in Ukraine. In Christian Europe, Jews were forbidden to own land. Therefore, the main occupations available to them were often those related to the market economy, rather than subsistence farming.

Written sources show the presence of Jews on these lands since the time of ancient Rus. They came from neighbouring states: from the Khazar Khaganate, a Jewish state to the east and from Bohemia and Moravia in the west. The largest influx of Jews was associated with the mass expulsions from Catholic Europe in the fifteenth and sixteenth centuries. The Polish-Lithuanian Commonwealth was known for its religious tolerance and many Jews from Central Europe found refuge there. They were under the protection of the Polish king, who along with other priorities engaged them in the colonisation of the rich lands of the Wild Field.

In Hebrew, Poland (Polin) sounds like 'rest here'. A Polish proverb in Latin, the lingua franca of Medieval Europe, calls the Commonwealth a *paradisus judaeorum* (a paradise for Jews). It was home to the majority (80 per cent) of all Jews in the world, most of whom lived in the eastern parts of the Commonwealth (present-day Lithuania, Belarus and Ukraine). Ukrainian lands became Palestine not only as the 'land of milk and honey', but also as a homeland for the Jews.

However, the same proverb identifies these lands as an *infernus rusticorum* – hell for the peasants. While life for the Jews was hard, they remained free people, whereas most of the peasants were enserfed. Mass Jewish immigration began about the same time as the mass enserfment of peasants, as the gentry and greater magnates aimed to maximise profits from the production and sale of bread on European markets. Local peasants rarely saw their lord, who lived far away in a palace in Warsaw, Krakow, or Lviv. Instead, they regularly saw a Jewish rent collector, a Jewish estate manager, or a Jewish tavern keeper, who had received a license from the gentry to manage their land or to use the lord's monopoly on the production and sale of alcohol. Therefore, peasant hatred, driven by social-economic problems, focused on Jews.

The painful irony of Jewish-Ukrainian relations was that groups at the very bottom of the social pyramid were at war with each other. They lived together, but separately. They were competing for the few resources that remained after the ruling elites had already taken for themselves most of what was produced.

The social-economic foundations for distrust were amplified by religious factors. In the Christian imagination, Jews were reviled as the 'killers of Christ'. These two sets of motives combined to make Jews complete outsiders to peasant communities. They were even more distrusted than the 'masters'.

Stereotypes led to violence. In the early modern and modern periods, there were multiple large-scale pogroms including during Khmelnytsky's Cossack revolution in 1648; the 1768 Cossack uprising known as the Koliivshchyna; after the assassination of Tsar Alexander II in 1881; during the revolutions of 1905–07 and 1917–20; in the summer of 1941 in Western Ukraine; and throughout Ukraine during the Holocaust. Ukrainians were not the only perpetrators of pogroms. For example, in 1881 the main pogromists, industrial workers, were mostly non-Ukrainians. But in Jewish historical memory, Ukraine is closely associated with pogroms and Ukrainians with anti-Semitism.

The modern era set in motion the end of traditional Jewish society. Increasing numbers of young Jews, often influenced by the ideas of the Haskalah, the Jewish enlightenment, left their traditional communities in search of the opportunities and possibilities offered by the world of modernity. Often they assimilated into secular, urban society. Many famous Jews, from Freud to Nobel laureates and Hollywood actors, had ancestors from the territory of Ukraine. They identified themselves as Poles, Russians and Americans, but not as Ukrainians. There are a number of reasons to explain the fact there were so many Jews in Ukraine, but no Ukrainian Jews. First, when assimilating, ethnic minorities prefer to adopt the identity of the ruling elite. This provided at least some protection from popular anti-Semitism. Second, in the case of Ukrainians and other peasant peoples, Jews had no one to assimilate with, because for a long time there was neither a ruling elite nor a middle class among these peoples – lawyers, doctors, journalists, etc. If they were to assimilate, they would have to become peasants or priests and this choice, to put it mildly, hardly corresponded to their life ambitions. And third, they were repelled by the image of Ukraine as the homeland of anti-Semitism.

Of course, Jewish-Ukrainian relationships were not always antagonistic. Studies of the language and culture of both peoples reveal numerous mutual borrowings. There were also many examples of cooperation and solidarity. For example, Ukrainian politicians were the first in the Austro-Hungarian Empire to demand the recognition of Jews as a separate nation with all the associated rights. The Ukrainian People's Republic in 1917 was characterised by inclusive legislation regarding Jews. Ukrainians also constitute one of the largest groups among the Righteous Among the Nations, people who risked their own lives and those of their families to save Jews during the Holocaust. For a long time, the two peoples managed to live together more or less peacefully. Anti-Jewish violence erupted in times of great crisis-wars, uprisings, revolutions, or, as in 1881, the assassination of the monarch, which in the imagination of traditional peasants and workers was tantamount to the end of the world. There were many reasons for the violence, but one of the main ones was the economic conflict.

An indirect proof of the latter point is the fact that Jewish-Ukrainian antagonism weakened as soon as the Ukrainian peasant-land connection was broken. In Soviet times, this occurred in two stages: in the 1930s and '40s, when peasants lost their land as a result of forced collectivisation and in the 1960s, when Ukrainians were already a predominantly urban people.

In the twentieth century, there were some Jews who broke with the imperial paradigm, built solidarity with Ukrainians and came to consider themselves Ukrainians. A breakthrough took place in the Soviet camps and prisons, where Jewish and Ukrainian dissidents met in the 1970s and '80s. There they had ample time and opportunity to build relationships and form an alliance against their common enemy: the Soviet regime. The final chord in their convergence can be traced to the Euromaidan (2013–14), when a new group emerged: the 'zhidobanderovtsi'. This satirical name was adopted by Ukrainian Jews who supported the 2014 revolution and combines two Russian slurs: the age-old Russian slur for Jews as Zhids combined with the modern denigration of Ukrainians as Banderites (used by the Kremlin as a synonym for Nazis). Ukrainian Jews use the term to mock Russia's claim that Ukraine's government and everyone who defends its freedom is a Nazi. In 2019, Ukraine and Israel were the only countries with both a president and prime minister of Jewish descent. A 2018 Pew opinion poll showed Ukraine as the least anti-Semitic of the post-communist countries.

The postmodern and late modern eras tend to blur clear distinctions and problematise previous divisions. These changes have affected our perception of agriculture as well. It has gone from being a symbol of outdated tradition and backwardness to become one of the most advanced and profitable post-industrial sectors.

In a world suffering from environmental crises, Ukraine's black soil is once again immensely important. This became particularly clear after the start of Russia's large-scale war against Ukraine. As David Beasley, director of the UN World Food Programme, warned in the third month of the war, if the supply of Ukrainian crops through the Black Sea ports occupied by Russia is not resumed, the world faces 'hell on earth'.

Ukrainian bread is one reason for the fact that at the most critical moments in modern history, the fate of the world has largely depended on what was happening in and around Ukraine. This was true during two world wars and it is true today.

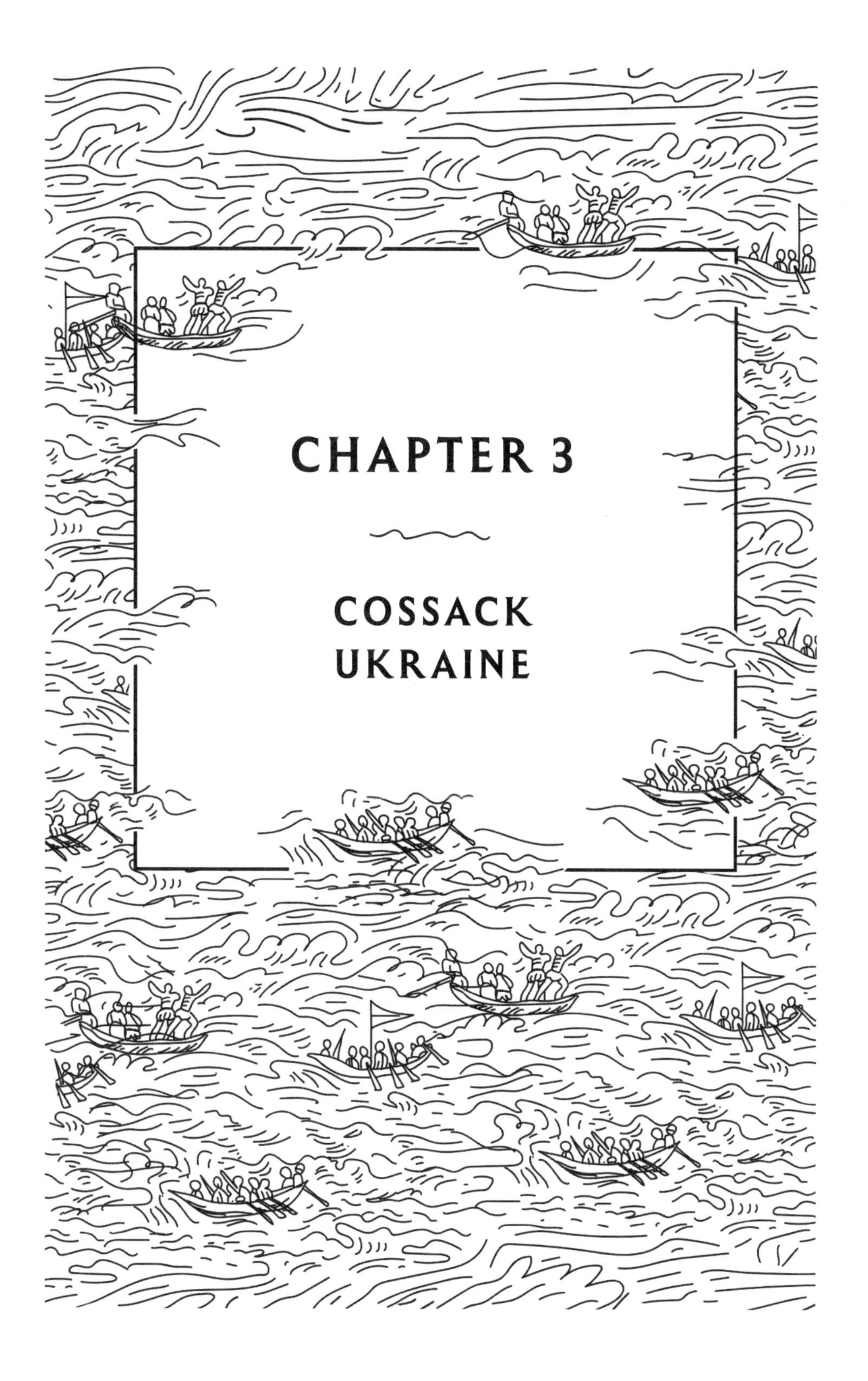

CHAPTER 3

COSSACK UKRAINE

UKRAINIAN COSSACK STATE, ca 1700

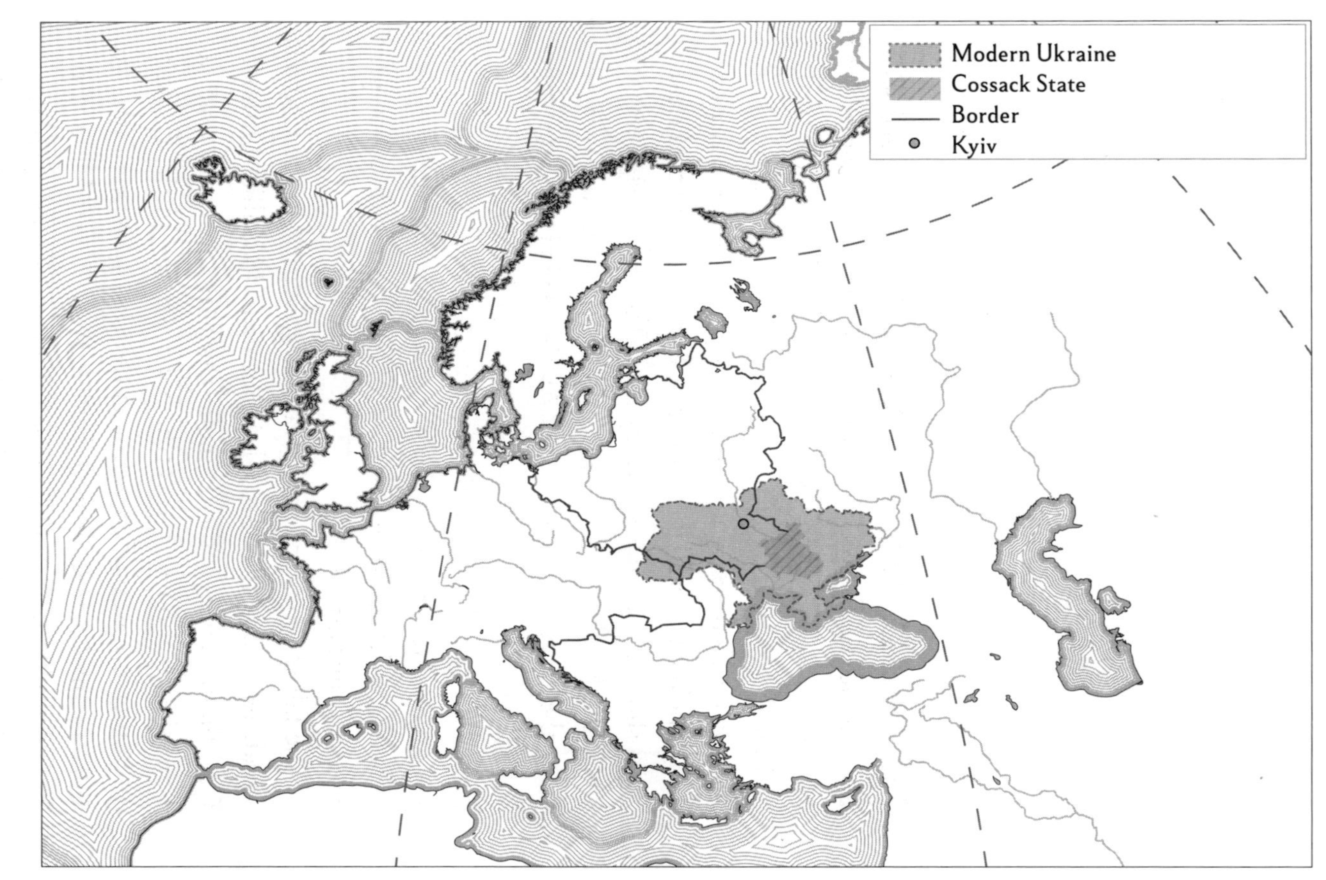

It was the end. The End of the World, which was created seven thousand years ago. The fullness of time had come. God Himself chose the number seven. He created the world in six days and on the seventh day, He decided to rest after His work. But one day for God was a thousand years for people on the earth.

Just before the end, the Antichrist would descend to the earth. Signs showed that he was already here. The clearest sign was seen when the Muslims conquered Constantinople in the year 6961 from the creation of the world. As the capital of Christianity, Constantinople was supposed to stand until the end of time, so its fall showed that the end was very near. The Orthodox world saw no need to extend the church calendar beyond the year 7000 because, as the scribes wrote, it would be filled with 'terror, grief and great misfortune'.

The fall of Constantinople was also mourned in the Catholic world, as it was the first Christian capital. Unlike Orthodox Christians, however, the Catholic calendar calculated time not from the creation of the earth, but from the birth of Christ. The difference was 5,508 years. So the Orthodox year 7000 was 1492 in the Catholic world. That year Alexander VI ascended to the papal throne. His name (Borgia) became synonymous with debauchery and corruption. Many believed that Alexander

VI's papacy proved that the Antichrist had seized not only Constantinople but the second Christian capital, Rome, as well.

But there was also good news. At the start of 1492, the troops of King Ferdinand and Queen Isabel captured Granada, the capital of the Muslim state on the Iberian Peninsula. This victory marked the final stage of the Reconquista, the expulsion of the Arabs from Spain. The struggle against the 'infidels' had been going on here since the eighth century, but only Ferdinand and Isabel successfully brought it to a victorious conclusion.

Up to that point, the Muslim world had been victorious in its military confrontations with the Christian world. Continuing into the sixteenth and seventeenth centuries, the Ottoman Empire, with its capital in Istanbul (formerly Constantinople), conquered the Balkans and Hungary and tried to reach the heart of Christian Europe, the Holy Roman Empire. The confrontation between the Muslim and Christian worlds came to a head in 1683 in the Battle of Vienna, where Ottoman troops were defeated by a united Christian coalition. The tide of military dominance then swung in the other direction. The Muslim world never recovered from the defeat.

But that was two hundred years in the future. Another important event took place in 1492. A few months after the Reconquista, the royal couple, Ferdinand and Isabel, kitted out an expedition led by the Italian captain Christopher Columbus. He promised to find a new sea route to India to end the Muslim blockade of Christian Europe.

Instead of the sea route to India, Columbus discovered America, although he never realised his mistake. This mistake was of global significance. It laid the foundations of the New World. Until 1492, the continents were cut off from each other by vast expanses and their inhabitants knew little or nothing about each other. The discovery of the Americas marked the beginning of their connections, linking the distant continents politically, economically and culturally. In brief: the world became global.

At approximately the same time, an event occurred in the eastern part of the European continent that was also destined to redraw the map of the world, albeit in a more modest way. In the lower reaches of the Dnipro River, a local tribe of Cossacks from Kyiv and Cherkasy captured and destroyed a Turkish ship. The Crimean khan's complaint to the grand duke of Lithuania marks the first historical mention of the Zaporozhian Cossacks. A couple of centuries later, the name of the land they occupied, Ukraine, the Cossack land, would become the name for an entire nation and state.

Ukraine emerged from the encounter between two worlds: the world of Columbus and the world of the Cossacks. At the time of this first mention of the Cossacks, they knew nothing about Columbus and he knew nothing about them. In the coming centuries, these two worlds would come so close together that Khmelnytsky's Cossack uprising would be discussed in Spain and products brought from America, especially tobacco, would become commonplace among the Cossacks: a folk song praised the Cossack hetman Sahaidachny, 'who traded his wife for tobacco and a pipe'.

The Commonwealth: The West in Polish Garb

The world of Columbus and the world of the Cossacks met within a single state. That state was the Polish-Lithuanian Commonwealth, formed in 1569. Within its borders, Catholics and Orthodox coexisted in approximately equal proportions. In no other country did Eastern and Western Christians coexist in such numbers.

We often view Ukrainian history in the shadow of Russia and we forget that the Polish influence was actually longer and stronger than the Russian one until at least the end of the eighteenth century. Rus princes and Polish kings had been fighting each other and forming alliances against a common enemy since the time of

Volodymyr. However, the significant Polish presence began with their annexation of Galicia in 1349. After the union of Poland and Lithuania in 1569, the Polish influence expanded to cover almost the entire territory of 'old Ukraine'. Even after the fall of the Polish-Lithuanian state (1772–95), the Polish influence remained strong in Central Ukraine until the First World War and in Western Ukraine until the Second World War. The Polish factor is still relevant today. If we draw zones marking the intensity of Poland's 'drive towards the East' onto a map of modern Ukraine, it becomes obvious that those lines correspond to the intensity of Ukrainian language use and Ukrainian identity.

The fact that the Polish-Lithuanian Commonwealth was part of Western Christian civilisation is important for the emergence of Ukrainian identity. There are good reasons to believe that the concept of nation originated in the bowels of this civilisation. England is considered the prototype of the nation. As with other English 'inventions' such as parliament, political parties and the Industrial Revolution, it spread across the European continent and became one of the phenomena that shaped the modern global world. By the end of the fifteenth century, we can talk about the *beginnings* of modern Western European nations – Italians, Germans, French and Spaniards. Other peoples of Europe found themselves between these nations rather than in them: they were neither entirely distinct nor fully integrated. Accordingly, the transformation of the Orthodox Rus into a Ukrainian nation was a consequence of the spread of Western Christian ideas to the East, through the mediation of the Polish-Lithuanian Commonwealth. In the words of Ihor Ševčenko, in Ukraine, 'this West was, for the most part, clad in the kontusz (Polish garb).'

The Polish-Lithuanian Commonwealth was one of the largest states in Europe at the time. It was formed by a union of the Kingdom of Poland and the Grand Duchy of Lithuania. As a result of this union, most Ukrainian ethnic territory, with the exception of the later colonised steppe, now lay within the borders of a single state. This fact in itself laid the foundations of Ukraine as a distinct national community.

There are two opposing perspectives regarding the nature of the Rzeczpospolita's rule on Belarusian and Ukrainian lands. According to one, it was an exploitative and colonising power, much like British rule in India or French rule in Algeria. Another emphasises the tolerance of the Polish government and its democratic character. Each of these points of view is correct depending on the timeframe or groups in question. But regardless of who is talking about what, we must consider the fact that, compared to other states, the Polish-Lithuanian Commonwealth was largely a historical anomaly. Its anomalousness can be summarised in three features.

First, the Polish-Lithuanian Commonwealth was famous for its religious tolerance. Although religious wars were raging to the west of its borders, the Polish-Lithuanian Commonwealth was an oasis of stability and peace from the earliest years of its existence. It was no accident that Jews who had been expelled from other Catholic countries found refuge here. Catholics, Orthodox believers and Jews lived alongside Protestants, Muslims, Armenian Apostolic Christians and Judaic Karaites.

Overall, the population of the Rus lands was more ethnically and religiously diverse than the population of central Poland. This diversity was embodied in Lviv, which was the largest city of Rus from the fall of Kyiv in 1240 until the mid-nineteenth century. At the turn of the sixteenth and seventeenth centuries, Lviv was home to at least five sizeable distinct ethnic and religious groups: Rus, Germans, Poles, Jews and Armenians, each of whom accounted for more than 5 per cent of the local population. It has been said that no other city in the Polish-Lithuanian Commonwealth and perhaps in all of Europe at the time, could match Lviv in terms of population diversity.

Diversity is a core trait of the borderland. Since the nineteenth century, the eastern borderlands, the *kresy* in Polish, have been central to Polish national mythology. Józef Piłsudski compared the Polish-Lithuanian Commonwealth to a bagel: a big hole in the middle with all the good stuff around the outside. He knew what he was talking about – Piłsudski came from the kresy himself. Many scientists, poets and artists hailed from the kresy. It reflects an important reality: peripheries are zones of increased creativity. Their multiethnic and multicultural character is a key reason for that fact. The borderland was a land of fugitive peasants, adventurers of various stripes, religious dissidents and rebellious Cossacks. Due to the coexistence of different cultures, both peaceful and non-peaceful, the boiling point was much higher here than in the 'cold' monocultural centre. Therefore, the likelihood of a new identity emerging was much higher here than anywhere else.

A second anomalous feature of the Polish-Lithuanian Commonwealth was its political system. It was an elective monarchy. The practice of electing a monarch ('free elections') was established after the death of the last king of the Jagiellonian dynasty, Sigismund II Augustus (1520–72), and continued until the very end of the Commonwealth. The idea itself of electing a king was not especially unusual. The Holy Roman Empire, Hungary, Sweden and Denmark were elective monarchies at different times and to varying degrees. In other states, such as Britain or Muscovy, the 'one-time' election of a monarch took place in moments of political crisis. What made the Polish-Lithuanian Commonwealth a real anomaly was that it was simultaneously both a monarchy and a republic (its very name in Polish, the Rzeczpospolita, is a literal translation from Latin of *res publica* aka republic). Other republics of the time included Switzerland, some city-states in Italy, later the Netherlands and, for a short time, England under Cromwell. In most of the European republics, power belonged to the urban aristocracy. In the Polish-Lithuanian Commonwealth, the petty gentry were the main source of power. The gentry elected the monarch and limited his power. In the words of one contemporary, the Polish king 'governed, but did not rule'.

The third anomalous feature of the Polish-Lithuanian Commonwealth is the very size of its gentry class, along with their unique status. In most European countries, the nobility accounted for approximately 1–2 per cent of the population. Spain and Hungary were exceptions, where this proportion reached 5 per cent. In contrast, the share of nobility in the Polish-Lithuanian Commonwealth was 8–10 per cent and in some areas, it was as high as 20 per cent. Most of the gentry scarcely differed from peasants in terms of their wealth. Many came from commoner backgrounds and achieved noble status through money or favourable marriages, which, of course, they preferred to keep quiet. The thing that united them all, rich and poor, was 'noble honour', a sense of superiority to others.

Although some claim that the Polish gentry based their sense of superiority on a myth of descent from the royal Sarmatians who once inhabited the steppes of the Black Sea region, recent research refutes this view. The 'Sarmatian myth' is a late invention of Polish national mythology. It is true that 'Sarmatian style' was widespread among the nobility and that the nobility of the Polish-Lithuanian Commonwealth looked to Istanbul rather than Paris for the latest fashions. But Sarmatian style in dress did not indicate adherence to any particular Sarmatian myth. In reality, each gentry family cared primarily about its own genealogy, not the genealogy of the entire noble class. Noble identity was not based on the past, but on the idea of serving the Polish-Lithuanian Commonwealth with the sword. Military valour was as important as ancestry.

In fact, their privileged status was based on this valour: if they constantly put their lives at risk for the sake of the Polish-Lithuanian Commonwealth, they deserved special privileges. The privileges of the Polish gentry were genuinely unprecedented. They chose the king and the king, with a few exceptions, had no right to judge or punish them. Only a gentry court of their peers could do so. Their motto was: 'Nothing about us without us'. The unprecedented nature of the nobility's privileges was also reflected in the right of 'veto': any nobleman could overturn the decisions of the entire Sejm with a single vote of dissent, 'I do not allow it!'

Of course, noble democracy was far from modern democracy. It was a democracy for 10 per cent of the population. But those who criticise the democracy of the Polish-Lithuanian Commonwealth should be reminded that in the cradle of democracy, ancient Greece, full citizens were also a distinct minority. The majority – women, slaves and foreigners – did not have the right to vote. In any case, regarding the formation of an open access order, it can be argued that the Polish-Lithuanian Commonwealth, with its limitations on the power of the monarch and exceptionally privileged gentry, probably went the furthest in this direction for its time. However, there is one significant caveat: the free will of a large part of the nobility was a fiction. Due to their economic weakness, many of them depended on the favour of large landowners. That is to say, they functioned as clients of the more powerful nobles and carried out their political will. In fact, the magnates, not the gentry as a whole, chose the king and limited his power and the noble democracy was largely a democratic oligarchy.

Too little central power is as harmful as too much. Over time, the Commonwealth of gentry became a symbol of unsustainability. Its 'golden age' lasted fifty years, ending in the early seventeenth century. By the mid-seventeenth century, the Polish-Lithuanian Commonwealth entered a period of protracted crisis, from which it never truly recovered. The noble democracy degenerated into anarchy. Attempts at reform in the eighteenth century did not save the situation. And eventually, in the years 1772–95, the Polish-Lithuanian Commonwealth disappeared from the map. It was divided by three powerful neighbours: the Austrian and Russian Empires and the Kingdom of Prussia. Political decline went hand in hand with economic decline. The Polish economy stood as a symbol of disorder and low standards.

A bad example is contagious. The rights and privileges of the Rzeczpospolita gentry served as a model to which the Orthodox elite also aspired. The Polish-Lithuanian Commonwealth was a state composed of Poland and Lithuania. It's not entirely clear why Rus did not appear in this formulation. It is likely because the Union of Lublin was a union between the rulers of two states: the Polish king and the Lithuanian prince (in this case, the same person) and since there was no separate Rus prince or king at that time, there was no place for Rus in it. However, the Rus nobility managed to defend their rights to the maximum extent possible: they could freely practise Orthodoxy, use the Rus language in local administration and preserve the judicial system based on the Lithuanian Statutes. By default, these rights were extended to the rest of the Rus population as well. Over time, some of the Rus nobility in the Commonwealth followed the same path as the Lithuanian nobility: they converted to Catholicism and became Polish. In 1610 the Rus polemist Meletii Smotrytksy lamented the conversion of the most 'noble, glorious, benevolent, strong and ancient houses that resound with the glory, power and courage of the Rus'. The most telling case was the story of the Vyshnevetsky/Wiśniowiecki family: a descendant of Dmytro Baida Vyshnevetsky (1510?–63), immortalised in Cossack ballads as the founder of the Zaporozhnia Sich, became the king of Poland under the name of Michał Korybut Wiśniowiecki (1640–73). Still, much of the Rus elite remained Orthodox. And those who left Orthodoxy often chose Protestantism rather than Catholicism.

It is true that the Rus gentry participated in the political life of the Polish-Lithuanian Commonwealth and even switched to the Polish language. But at the same time, the gentry families often remained Rus patriots and supported plans to add Rus to the two-state Polish-Lithuanian state. There is no contradiction here. Regional or even national patriotism could coexist peacefully with loyal service to the Polish-Lithuanian Commonwealth. The Rus and Polish gentry shared a common ethos. Service lay at the core of this ethos and the Rus gentry served their fatherland, the Polish-Lithuanian Commonwealth. Orthodox nobleman Adam Kysil (1600–53) rose to the position of voivode in the Commonwealth and, at the same time, supported the addition of a third constituent nation, Rus, to the composition of the Commonwealth.

It was among this Rus gentry that understanding of a distinct 'Rus people' first appeared in the early seventeenth century. Over time, however, the right to represent this people passed to the Ukrainian Cossacks. Not only did the Cossacks take over this primary role, they also changed the very contours of the Rus nation. The Orthodox in the Lithuanian part of the Commonwealth (the future Belarusians) were no longer considered part of Rus and Rus itself was no longer part of the Polish-Lithuanian Commonwealth. So thanks to the Cossacks, Rus became Ukraine.

The transformation of the Cossacks into the primary symbol of Ukrainian identity was associated with radical changes on the European continent that were initiated in one way or another in 1492. They can be briefly described as two parallel processes: the Price Revolution and confessionalisation. Both of these processes impacted the Polish-Lithuanian Commonwealth and the Rus lands. They accelerated the collapse of Rus and, accordingly, the emergence of Ukraine. Simplifying somewhat, we can say that the Price Revolution created the Cossacks and confessionalisation made them Ukrainians.

From Columbus to the Cossacks

The discovery of America marked the beginning of the exchange of food, goods and diseases between the New and Old Worlds. It had tragic outcomes for the peoples of the New World: about 90 per cent of the local population died as a result of the violence and diseases brought by the Europeans. The Old World, however, benefited from this 'Columbian exchange'. We can just note that out of the 640 agricultural plants known on the European continent, about a hundred originated in the New World. Potatoes and corn are the best known. People believe that the appearance of these products in Europe was one of the reasons for the constant growth of the European population in the modern era, but their spread across the European continent actually took several centuries. The potato did not become widespread until the eighteenth century. Silver imported from South America had a more immediate and radical impact on Europe in the sixteenth and seventeenth centuries.

The shortage of precious metals was a chronic problem for the European economy. Many of the Europeans who went to the New World were drawn there by rumours that somewhere in the American jungles, lay a 'golden city' (El Dorado) where the streets were paved with gold. They didn't find gold: the California 'gold rush' didn't begin until centuries later in 1848. However, they did find silver. In 1545, the Spaniards discovered rich silver deposits at the foot of the Cerro de Potosí (present-day Bolivia). They ruthlessly set about exploiting these deposits, demanding gruelling unpaid labour from the local populations. The colonisers shipped the silver to Spain, from where it was distributed throughout Europe. By 1600, the total weight of silver on the European market had increased eightfold.

Silver was the most important metal for coinage. Massive imports of South American silver led to an increase in the mass of money and, consequently, to its rapid depreciation. A situation in which more and more people had more and more money to buy fewer and fewer goods resulted in sharp price increases. First the prices of the most universal commodity, food, rose. In some places, the cost of grain increased by a factor of eight to ten.

One man's misfortune is another man's gain. The Price Revolution in the West opened opportunities for the gentry and other residents of the Commonwealth to get rich quickly. The Polish-Lithuanian state was seen as the breadbasket of Europe and the source for shipbuilding materials. The black soil of Ukraine was especially fertile, but it remains unclear whether (and how) Ukrainian grain was transported to Western markets. Ukraine's fertile lands were cut off from the Black Sea by the Wild Field. The closest seaport from which local grain could be shipped was the city of Gdańsk on the Baltic Sea, which is where Western merchants came to buy agricultural products. But transporting grain from most Ukrainian lands to Gdańsk was exceedingly difficult, as only Galicia and Volhynia had direct river routes to the Baltic coast. However, there were other locally profitable commodities, such as timber and potash in the northern forested regions and cattle in Central Ukraine. The cost to transport cattle was particularly low as they could simply be driven across open land.

In any case, Ukrainian lands became a sort of El Dorado of the Polish-Lithuanian Commonwealth. During the early seventeenth century, Ukrainian lands had the highest population growth rate on the European continent. People flocked there in search of wealth, adventure and freedom. One factor behind the economic boom was that the creation of the Polish-Lithuanian Commonwealth led to a strengthening of the southern borders and thus better protection of local settlements. This provided the necessary stability to support economic development. In addition, rapid population growth and the need to feed an army led to an increase in the demand for bread and other agricultural products.

In a brief span of time, the local noble families became extremely wealthy. They received new land grants from the king and expanded their estates. That wealth was converted into political influence. Their estates became a kind of state within a state, with their own courts, clients and army, with which they fought against the Tatars and Cossacks. In fact, they became real rulers on the border and competed with the king in the centre. Unlike the king, their power on their own lands was virtually unlimited.

In addition to local magnates, the petty gentry also actively participated in the colonisation of Ukrainian lands. We don't know what the ratio of Polish to Rus gentry was in that process. What we do know is that the colonisation of Ukraine resembled the colonisation of America in many ways. Both were dominated by a cult of violence and quick profit and both disguised this cult as a civilising mission towards local populations. There was a belief that just as Spain was looking for gold in India (i.e., in the newly discovered Americas), the Polish nobility was looking for money in the Rus provinces. In order to make the cultivation of grain and other products even cheaper, the gentry enserfed the peasants to gain a source of free labour. In the sixteenth century, Europe east of the Elbe experienced what historians came to call the 'second serfdom'. Where serfdom no longer existed, it was revived and where it still existed, it expanded.

It should be noted here that there is no clear and unambiguous connection between the 'Price Revolution' and the 'second serfdom'. Peasants in Muscovy were also enserfed, despite its lack of the close relationships with Western European markets that characterised the Polish-Lithuanian Commonwealth. Muscovy grew rich from the fur trade and the consequent colonisation of Siberia and the Volga region. In the history of the Polish-Lithuanian Commonwealth itself, the causes and regional characteristics of the 'second serfdom' remain a subject of scholarly debate. But whatever the reasons, economic processes now divided the

European continent into Western and Eastern Europe. In this division, Eastern Europe became an agrarian colony of the West, situated on the periphery of the capitalist system that was emerging on the Atlantic coast of Western Europe.

Serfdom was taking on more extreme and disturbing forms. In his *Description of Ukraine*, Guillaume Levasseur de Beauplan claimed that the situation of local peasants was worse than that of Turkish galley slaves. Oppression led to resistance. The easiest way to protest was with your feet – escape to the Wild Field. Significant parts of the borderlands of the Kyiv voivodeship were under the direct authority of the king. The nobility could not demand the return of fugitives from the king's lands and royal authorities and local magnates actually encouraged peasant resettlement there. The fugitive peasants either joined newly founded settlements or moved to the lands of the Zaporozhian Sich. Meanwhile, those who remained on the lords' lands often joined the rebellion during Cossack uprisings. As the gentry complained, 'the whole of Ukraine has gone Cossack'.

In the 1590s and again from 1620–30, Ukraine was rocked by Cossack uprisings sparked by the Cossacks' dissatisfaction with their status in the Polish-Lithuanian Commonwealth. Cossack elites wanted the same rights and privileges as the gentry: self-governance, rights to land, hunting, fishing, trade, alcohol production and tax exemptions. They had clear justification for these demands. Like the gentry, the Cossacks defended the borders of the Polish-Lithuanian Commonwealth from Tatar attacks and fought in its military campaigns. In particular, Cossack troops under the leadership of Hetman Petro Konashevych-Sahaidachny (1575–1622) played a major role in the war against Muscovy in 1617–18. Their participation was also decisive in the 1621 Battle of Khotyn against the Turkish army.

The Cossacks were especially known for their naval campaigns. They would sail down the Dnipro River to the Black Sea and attack coastal Tatar and Turkish cities, including the capital, Istanbul, plundering, destroying ships and fortifications and liberating slaves. Thanks to these naval campaigns, the Cossacks gained international renown and drew the attention of states seeking allies in the fight against the Ottoman Empire, particularly after the naval battle of Lepanto (1574). In 1594, the Austrian emperor sent an ambassador to the Sich for talks. Muscovy also approached them wanting support. The Cossacks were gaining in significance and therefore demanded attention and respect.

The Cossack elite sought, with some success, an ally in the Polish king, who hoped to strengthen his power in the confrontation with the magnates and their gentry clients. But the Polish-Lithuanian Commonwealth was still controlled by the gentry, who jealously guarded their privileges. The gentry viewed the Cossacks as commoners, a rebellious rabble who, by definition, could not claim equal dignity with them. The Christian society of the Commonwealth was divided into clearly defined estates: nobility, clergy, townspeople and peasants. There was no place for the Cossacks in this structure.

The Polish gentry failed to recognise the fact that the Cossacks had become a fully fledged de facto estate of their own. To understand these changes, we must return to the story of globalisation.

As secular, modern people, we tend to emphasise the secular elements of history and ignore the role of religion. Surviving fragments of Columbus's diary show that his desire to find a new way to India was motivated at least in part by religion. He hoped to use the wealth he would bring from India to finance a new crusade to liberate Jerusalem from Muslim rule before the second coming of Christ. It was this argument that won him the hearts and minds of Ferdinand and Isabel. After their victory over the Arabs, the royal couple believed they had a special mission in Christian history. Among the Spanish ruler's many titles ('King of Aragon, Count of Barcelona' etc.), there was one that corresponded to Columbus's plans: Ferdinand was the 'King of Jerusalem'. It was believed that the 'last emperor' would conquer Jerusalem, unite the whole world and stand at Christ's side in the final battle against the antichrist. In preparation for this role, Ferdinand hurried to turn his kingdom into a purely Christian state. After expelling the Arabs, he expelled Jews from his realm in 1492. In doing so, he established a significant precedent: a religiously homogeneous state.

Such a thing was virtually unheard of at the time, but with the advent of Protestantism it became the norm. In 1517, the German monk Martin Luther published his *95 Theses*, which challenged the authority of the pope. Luther had no intention of creating a new Church. He wanted to reform it, to return it to the times of the original, unspoiled Church of the early Christians. But, as often happens, calls to return to the past led to changes in the future.

The Reformation split the Western Christian world into Catholics and Protestants; the latter then separated into Lutherans, Calvinists and other denominations. These splits led to long and extremely brutal religious wars. Since Protestantism was originally a German phenomenon, the wars were fought almost exclusively on the lands of the German states that were part of the Holy Roman Empire. The first such war between the Catholic Emperor and Luther's supporters began in 1547. The war ended with no clear winner and this stalemate was enshrined in the Peace of Augsburg in 1555. The main point of this peace was the principle of *cuius regio, eius religio*, or 'whose realm, his religion'. Accordingly, the subjects of Catholic rulers were to be Catholics and those of Lutheran rulers were to be Lutherans. Those who did not fall under this principle – Catholics in Protestant states and Lutherans in Catholic states – faced a choice: convert to the ruler's faith or give up their homes.

The Peace of Augsburg established peace, but not for long. In

1618, a new religious war began that lasted for three decades. The Thirty Years' War was one of the bloodiest in European history and could be compared to the two world wars in terms of destruction and loss of life. In the German lands of the Holy Roman Empire at the centre of the conflict, nearly a third of the population died. Thirty years of bloodshed, however, still failed to deliver victory to either side. The Peace of Westphalia in 1648 confirmed the original principle of 'whose realm, his religion' and introduced two new ones: borders between states are inviolable and no state has the right to interfere in the affairs of another.

The Peace of 1648 gave its name to the Westphalian system, which is considered a draft of the modern geopolitical system. However, this was a formula for a state based on religious rather than ethnic identity. Nonetheless, this formula laid the foundations for a 'marriage' between religion and nationalism: the transition from a religious to an ethnic national concept of the state was at hand.

The Polish-Lithuanian Commonwealth successfully stayed out of the Thirty Years' War. Ironically, the very year that war ended in Western Europe, a new one began in the Commonwealth. It lasted almost continuously for the next forty years. And it began with a Cossack revolution led by Bohdan Khmelnytsky.

How Cossacks Became Ukrainians

The Ukrainian Cossacks are a central symbol of Ukrainian identity. Just as many Poles view themselves as descendants of the Polish gentry, many Ukrainians consider themselves descendants of the Cossacks. The Ukrainian national anthem identifies Ukrainians as part of the 'Cossack family'. Contemporary Ukrainian author Anatolii Strelianyi has described the significance of the Cossacks as the core of Ukrainian identity in a different way. He notes that the phenomenon of Cossacks exists in both Russian and

Ukrainian history. The difference is that Russian history can be written without the Cossacks – Ukrainian history cannot.

Initially, the Cossacks didn't have any clear connection to nationality. They seemed to be a typical borderland phenomenon: groups of hunters living on the border between settled agricultural lands and the Eurasian steppe in the Urals, the Don, Kuban and the lower reaches of the Dnipro. The Cossacks were a unique social entity.

The closest analogies are the Balkan haiduks, Hungarian betyars, American cowboys, or even pirates. The Cossacks could be considered the pirates of the steppe or, considering their raids along the Turkish coast of the Black Sea, simply pirates. Historians might prefer the more accurate and inclusive term 'social bandits'. It's not an insult: the English Robin Hood, the Slovak/Polish Jánošík and the American Billy the Kid were all social bandits. Those outcasts were also known by nicknames – just like the Zaporozhian Cossacks. They primarily robbed the nobility who were often viewed as 'outsiders' by the commoners (Robin Hood was Anglo-Saxon, while the nobility were Normans) and so, in the popular imagination, these outlaws were often seen as heroes in the struggle against social and national oppression.

The stories of outlaws were celebrated in ballads and adventure novels. Indeed, their lives held ample adventure. But there was also quite a lot of violence, which the folk songs and romanticised stories tend to leave out. It is worth remembering that the violence of the 'outlaws' was a mirror image of the culture of violence that prevailed among the ruling elites.

The Cossacks lived free but dangerous lives. Danger was the price they paid for freedom. Their stronghold was the Zaporozhian Sich, a hidden wooden fortress which we know from Byzantine descriptions lay beyond the rapids of the Dnipro, along the former route 'from the Varangians to the Greeks'. It is believed that the first Sich was built in the 1550s. From that time until 1775, when it was destroyed by Russian troops, the location of the Sich changed at least eight times. But each time it was built according to the same plan, in places well defended by nature: river islands hidden among the floodplains. This is the place where Cossacks lived, from which they departed for military campaigns and to which they returned.

Most Cossacks lived in the surrounding areas rather than inside the actual Sich. They would gather at the Sich when military mobilisation was declared, but they didn't spend all their time at war. They also participated in the same occupations as the non-Cossack population: farming, crafts, fishing and trade. However, a life of constant danger dictated its own rules. Women were strictly forbidden from staying in the Sich. The Cossacks were known for their strict discipline during campaigns. Alcohol was entirely prohibited during sea campaigns and violations were punishable by death. The Cossacks were also distinguished by a strong sense of solidarity and an egalitarian ethos (when the Cossacks chose their military leader at the Sich, they would throw garbage on him so that he didn't get too full of himself).

Their survival necessitated that they master the art of war. Until the end of the sixteenth century, the best warriors came from the steppe. Accordingly, the weapons, clothing and hairstyles of the Cossacks were modelled on those of nomadic peoples. Western ambassadors who visited the Zaporozhian Sich, seeing the clothes and weapons of the Cossacks, could not immediately understand whether they were dealing with Christians or Muslims.

The Cossacks honed their military skills in raids and campaigns against the Crimean Khanate, Moldova and the Ottoman Empire. The Polish king Stefan Batory (1576–86) decided to create a permanent standing army from them: the 'registered Cossacks'. The irony was that the registered Cossacks were supposed to both defend the borders of the Polish-Lithuanian Commonwealth from the Tatars and Turks and also to deter the Cossacks themselves from attacking the Crimeans and Ottomans without orders. The Cossack raids provoked conflict with the Ottoman Empire and were a constant headache for Warsaw. Accordingly, there was friction between the registered Cossacks and other Zaporozhian Cossacks. The situation was further complicated by the fact that not only did peasants and gentry 'go Cossack', many Zaporozhian Cossacks also sought to become registered Cossacks, because registered status offered a steady salary and certain advantages, such as the right to be paid while recovering from an injury or illness. The royal quota was much lower than the number of applicants. It increased in times of war or military threat and decreased in peacetime: despite the military service of the Cossack army, the government tried to economise on its maintenance. This caused outrage among the Cossacks. Those who weren't on the register were at risk of enserfment. If we add in the conflict between the king and the magnates, in which the registered Cossacks could also play their card, the number of possible combinations of 'who with whom against whom' was considerable.

However, the number of registered Cossacks did increase over time: from an initial count of 530 up to six thousand on the eve of Khmelnytsky's uprising. Most of the registered Cossacks (80 per cent in the mid-seventeenth century) came from the Rus lands of the Commonwealth. However, they came from much further afield as well, from all over the European continent, from Scandinavia in the north to the Peloponnesian Peninsula in the south, from the German lands in the west to the Urals in the east. In other words, by origin, the Cossacks were a pan-European or even more broadly a Euro-Asian phenomenon.

The European religious conflicts served as the reagent that, when added to the supersaturated solution of borderland society, accelerated the crystallisation of the Cossacks into the nucleus of a new, Ukrainian nation. The confessionalisation of Europe forced Protestants to leave Catholic countries. Many of them found refuge in the Polish-Lithuanian Commonwealth thanks to its religious tolerance. They were often members of the most radical Protestant movements – Calvinists, Arians/Unitarians and others. Protestant ideas were also brought back by the children of nobles and merchants who had studied at Western universities. The extent of the spread of Protestantism is evidenced by the fact that at the time of the formation of the Polish-Lithuanian Commonwealth, only half of its senators were Catholic, and in the lands of the Grand Duchy of Lithuania, Protestants even constituted the majority among senators, including among the Rus. The Commonwealth could have followed the same path as England, Holland, northern Germany, Denmark and Sweden and become a Protestant country.

That didn't happen. Unlike in other European lands, Protestantism in the Polish-Lithuanian Commonwealth did not take root with the monarchs or the peasantry. The arrival of the Jesuits introduced an additional factor. The Jesuit movement started in 1534 and in 1540 was officially recognised as a religious order. They carried the Catholic faith beyond the borders of the Old World and within just a few decades had reached North and South America, India and Japan. Still, Europe remained the centre of their activity. Here they focused their efforts on stopping Protestantism. The Jesuits followed the Protestants like hunting dogs following game. They appeared in the Commonwealth almost from the beginning and they served as confessors and advisors to the richest families in the coming decades.

The Jesuits became the subject of a 'black legend' whose echoes are still felt in Ukrainian culture. This legend presents the Jesuit as a treacherous Catholic, honey-tongued, but with a knife at hand. In reality, the Jesuits defeated their opponents not so much by brute force as by soft power. They emphasised preaching, confession and education. Education was their most effective weapon. A network of Jesuit educational institutions (collegiums) covered the entire country, including the Rus lands. When relatively wealthy families were choosing where to send their sons to study, Jesuit institutions were often the only option. This was true for Rus families as well. The Jesuits did not explicitly demand that students convert to Catholicism: they hoped that a few years of study at a Jesuit college could implicitly turn non-Catholic children into devout Catholics. In any case, Rus children were able to study with the Jesuits and keep the faith of their parents. Bohdan Khmelnytsky very likely graduated from a Jesuit college in Lviv. Ivan Mazepa, Feofan Prokopovych and many other Ukrainian leaders were graduates of Jesuit colleges, both in the Polish-Lithuanian Commonwealth and in Western Europe.

Thanks to their schools and educational efforts, the Jesuits managed the Protestant influences in the centre of Poland with relative ease. The situation in Rus proved to be more difficult. According to one Jesuit account, the Rus regions were not only 'infested with heretics' (i.e. Protestants), but also 'poisoned by Jews' and 'overflowing with schismatics' (i.e. Orthodox believers). Although the Orthodox were theoretically Christians, the Jesuits considered their faith flawed or, as they said, lacking in dignity. Piotr Skarga, one of the leading Jesuit intellectuals of the time, wrote that 'it is impossible to be educated in the Slavonic tongue'. He considered the Rus a deceived and lost people.

There was a bit of bitter truth in these words. There were no Orthodox seminaries and priests had little understanding of the intricacies of the faith. Orthodox religious books were full of errors because the scribes who had copied them did not know Greek, the language of the original. According to the Jesuits, Orthodox Christians were baptised, married and buried 'wrong,' and thus were condemned to the eternal torments of hell. Their souls were in need of 'saving' no less than the souls of Protestants.

The decisions of the Council of Trent (1545–63) and the activities of the Jesuits upset the religious balance between Catholics and Protestants that had been established in Central Europe after the Peace of Augsburg. These changes put an end to the Polish-Lithuanian Commonwealth as a religiously tolerant state. The fact that a zealous Catholic, Sigismund III, sat on the throne in 1587–1632 played a role in this transition. He worked with the Jesuits to create a plan to convert the Orthodox to Catholicism.

Talks of unification of the Catholic and Orthodox Churches had already begun in the early fifteenth century. The talks were initiated in Constantinople, where church leaders sought the support of Rome against the Turkish threat. In 1437, the Greek monk Isidore was appointed Metropolitan of Kyiv and all Rus. In 1439, Metropolitan Isidore signed an act of unification of the two Churches at the Council of Florence. But the union never took place. At the end of the sixteenth century, the matter resumed. Only now, after Catholicism had become the de facto state religion of the Polish-Lithuanian Commonwealth, the position of the Orthodox Church was considerably weaker. We should note that there were Catholic bishops in the Senate, but no Orthodox bishops. In order to protect their status, some of the Orthodox hierarchy accepted the authority of the pope, while successfully demanding the right to retain Orthodox rites. Thus, in 1596, a new church emerged, the Greek Catholic Church or, as it was then called, the Uniate Church. This led to a religious split in the Orthodox world similar to that which occurred in the Catholic world in the early sixteenth century. After the establishment of the Uniate church, Orthodox church activity essentially became illegal in the Commonwealth. The Kyiv Metropolitanate was subordinated to Rome and Orthodox churches either joined the new church or were forcibly closed.

Most Orthodox Christians rejected these innovations. They saw joining the Uniate church as a betrayal of the faith of their ancestors. In Volhynia, resistance to Catholicisation was led by Prince Kostiantyn Ostrozkyi, who was considered 'the richest and most influential lord in the entire kingdom'. In Lviv and Kyiv, Orthodox church brotherhoods took up the cause of defending Orthodoxy. The Kyiv and Lviv brothers succeeded in gaining the patronage of the Patriarch of Constantinople and thus achieved independence from the 'traitorous' Uniate hierarchy.

The Orthodox Rus elite accepted the challenge of Catholics and Protestants and adopted their methods in battle. Catholics say that our priests are uneducated? Well, we'll build our own schools to form an educated clergy. They complain that we have no books? We'll establish our own printing houses. Are our church books full of mistakes? Then we'll retranslate them and, to do so, we'll teach our priests and monks ancient Greek.

Under the influence of Catholic pressure, local Orthodoxy experienced a genuine revival in the late sixteenth and early seventeenth centuries. Polemical theological literature and book printing flourished and the first Rus grammar and primer appeared. Protestants infected the Orthodox with the desire to give the Word of God to ordinary people in the language they understood. In 1561, the handwritten Peresopnytsia Gospel appeared. This was the first translation of the New Testament from Church Slavonic into the contemporary Rus language. (This is the bible on which modern Ukrainian presidents take their oath of office.) The pinnacle achievement of the Rus Renaissance was the Ostroh Bible (1580–81), the first complete printed edition of the Bible in Church Slavonic with the previous errors corrected. The translation was made by a group of Rus and Greek scholars at the court of Prince Ostrozkyi. None of these achievements had been imaginable just a few decades earlier.

The Rus Orthodox revival resembled the European Renaissance in certain ways and with a certain delay. However, it had different foundations. The Rus elite was not so much concerned with reviving an ancient, pre-Christian heritage as they were with returning to the purity and simplicity of early Christianity. Ivan Fedorov, one of the first Rus printers, wrote: 'And everything that befell me along the way, I considered as nothing, if only to comprehend my Christ.' 'Seeking Christ' was the general spirit of the new Christian Europe.

This ferment even reached the Kingdom of Muscovy. In the 1550s, the Muscovite tsar Ivan IV (the Terrible, 1547–84), learned that church books were being printed 'among the Greeks and in Venice and in Phrygia and in other languages'. He ordered the establishment of a printing house in Moscow, which is where Fedorov began his printing activities. However, after the publication of just two books, he was forced to run for his life from angry clergymen who accused him of heresy and burned down his printing house. He moved to the Rus lands of the Polish-Lithuanian Commonwealth, first to the Lithuanian part and then to Lviv, where the printing trade was in great demand.

By translating the Holy Scriptures into the local language and establishing schools and printing houses, the Rus elite were seeking Christ. What they actually found were a people and eventually a nation. We should keep in mind that reading books in an understandable language is a key element in the transformation of a community into a nation. In distinguishing themselves from Western Christianity, the Rus elite also involuntarily drew a line between themselves and the unreformed Orthodox world of Muscovy. One example of the differences that emerged can be seen in the popularity of Christmas nativity scenes and carols in the non-Russian (i.e. Belarusian and Ukrainian) Rus Orthodox world. These Christmas traditions have Catholic roots and originated with Francis of Assisi. They could convey the Word of God through oral tradition to those who could not read. There were no such Christmas traditions in Russian Orthodoxy. Further, in the new Rus icons, the traditional golden background of the Byzantine tradition that symbolised eternity is replaced by secular subjects like those in Catholic icons. These examples demonstrate how the reformed Orthodox Rus culture gradually trickled down from the elites into popular culture.

The Orthodox revival was not supported 'from above' by the state but started 'from below' with the initiative of local nobility and a strong network of public institutions. The Ostroh, Lviv and Kyiv schools were founded with donations from Kostiantyn Ostrozkyi and funds from the cities' church brotherhoods. Graduates of these schools formed the backbone of the Kyiv-Mohyla Collegium (1632), the first Orthodox institution of higher education in the Ukrainian lands. Within a relatively short time, a network of fraternal schools covered the Rus lands offering an alternative to the Jesuit colleges. It is characteristic that these schools and the Kyiv-Mohyla Academy copied the Jesuit educational programme: in order to defeat a stronger enemy, one had to master his weapons.

The Rus bourgeoisie was characterised by soft power: self-organisation, donations, agility and the ability to survive. But you couldn't really rely on them for hard power: the Cossacks became the mainstay of reformed Orthodoxy. In 1620, the Cossack hetman Petro Konashevych-Sahaidachny, along with the entire Zaporozhian Host, joined the Kyiv Orthodox Brotherhood. That same year, Patriarch Theophanes III of Jerusalem ordained the Kyivan abbot Iov Boretsky as Metropolitan of Kyiv, Galicia and all Rus. This meant the restoration of an Orthodox metropolitanate in Kyiv, the spiritual capital of Rus Orthodoxy. All of these acts testified to the emergence of a new alliance between the reformed Rus Church and the local Cossacks. As a later historian wrote, the monk shook hands with the warrior and the warrior with the monk. While the Cossacks offered support and protection to the Church, the Church offered the Cossacks a sense of a national mission.

Khmelnytsky's 1648 revolution should be viewed within the context of this alliance between church and Cossacks. It was different from previous Cossack rebellions. It went beyond the revolt of one class for its rights and privileges and becomes a national struggle for the reorganisation of the entire world. The key element is the presence of a revolutionary ideology, which can provide a vision of a future just and more perfect world. In early modern Western Christian Europe, anti-Catholic doctrines played the role of such a revolutionary ideology. This was the case during the Hussite wars of 1419–34, the Dutch Revolt (1568–1648) and the Great Rebellion in England (1642–51). Khmelnytsky's revolution was the first to emerge outside the borders of the Western Christian world, but it followed the same outline.

Great revolutions begin from small events. In Khmelnytsky's case, it started with an armed raid on his estate by a neighbouring nobleman. Unable to get justice from the king, Khmelnytsky turned to the Sich. In the spring of 1648, he raised a large Cossack army and that summer and autumn he won victory after victory over the Polish army. It was once said that Khmelnytsky had intended to leap into the saddle, but instead jumped all the way over the horse. In early 1649, Khmelnytsky told a group of Polish ambassadors that, 'Up to now, I have fought to address the injuries and harms against me. Now I will fight for our Orthodox faith.' A few weeks earlier, on Christmas Day 1648, Khmelnytsky had entered Kyiv at the head of a victorious Cossack army. He was welcomed by the Kyivan Metropolitan, Sylvester Kosiv, and the Jerusalem Patriarch, Paisius, who was visiting at the time. Kosiv greeted him as 'Moses, the saviour, redeemer and liberator of the Rus from Polish bondage, the radiant ruler of the kingdom of Rus'. Let's note the ways in which these words clearly point towards the union of religion and the state, a formula already established in the Western Christian world of the time. And just as in Western Europe's religious wars, the Cossacks mercilessly killed representatives of other faiths: Poles, Jews and Uniate Christians.

Khmelnytsky's revolution marks the founding of the Cossack-Orthodox state. It is hard to overestimate its significance for

Ukrainian nation-building as it gave birth to the concept of Ukraine as a separate political entity. To better understand what happened and how, let's compare the Ukrainian and Russian Cossacks. Khmelnytsky's revolt tore part of the Rus lands away from the Polish-Lithuanian Commonwealth and, in 1654, transferred them to the rule of Muscovy. At that time, Nikon, the Patriarch of Moscow, was reforming the local Orthodox Church. Nikon's reforms provoked a new split in the Orthodox world. Old Believers who did not accept the innovations broke away from the church and declared Nikon to be the Antichrist.

In its broad outlines, this split in the Orthodox lands resembled the conflict between Catholics and Protestants in the Western Christian world. Like Protestants in the Catholic part of Europe, Old Believers of Muscovy fled to the outskirts, to Siberia and the region of the Don River, which was part of the Cossack patrimony. The situation seemed similar to that in Ukraine: an alliance between the Old Believers and the Don Cossacks could have emerged on the Don and resulted in a separate Don nation.

That didn't happen. The Don Cossacks lacked everything that was present in the Ukrainian case: an educated Cossack elite, an organised and autonomous burgher class and a network of schools and publishing houses – all the things that make up the backbone without which no national body can emerge. This foundation could only have emerged in the Orthodox lands of the Polish-Lithuanian Commonwealth, where there was no tradition of the autocracy that characterised Muscovy. Instead, thanks to the challenges brought by the Western Christian world, there was a tradition of separation of powers and autonomous institutions.

Ukrainian liberal historians have conveyed this difference as follows: the biggest national difference between Russia and Ukraine is not religion or even language but differing political cultures. Due to Polish mediation, historical processes in the Ukrainian lands were intimately tied to the processes taking place in Western Christian Europe, where different political traditions of leadership and a different relationship between state and society emerged.

The Cossack State

What was only a possibility for the Don Cossacks became reality for the Ukrainian Cossacks – the emergence of a Cossack state. It was known by various names: Ukraine, the Zaporozhian Host, the Hetmanate, Little Russia and even the Ukrainian state. It existed with certain interruptions for just over a hundred years, from Khmelnytsky's uprising until 1764, when it was dissolved by the Russian Empress Catherine II. (It could also be argued that it existed even longer, until 1782 when the lands of the Cossack state were officially organised into Russian provinces.)

It is difficult to tell the story of its first decades, as it is so complicated, dramatic and often tragic. Khmelnytsky died in 1657. In terms of power, he left behind shoes that were too big to fill. Khmelnytsky's son Yurii, to whom his father bequeathed the hetman's power, could not equal him either in military talent or charisma. The succession crisis led to a struggle between various Cossack groups. As a result, in 1663 the territory of Cossack Ukraine was split along the Dnipro into two parts: the Left Bank and the Right Bank. Each had its own hetman and army. The Zaporozhian Sich was a third force, supporting one side or the other at various times. The warring factions called on help from Muscovy, the Polish-Lithuanian Commonwealth, the Ottoman Empire and the Crimean Khanate at various times. Accordingly, the civil conflict acquired a geopolitical dimension. It was literally a 'war of all against all', resulting in huge losses and destruction. The Right Bank, the main theatre of hostilities, lost up to between 65 and 70 per cent of its population. The former 'land of milk and honey' was turned into a wasteland. Its Cossack elite was destroyed and the surviving Cossack units and part of the population moved to the Left Bank and settled on the Russian-Ukrainian border in the area called Sloboda Ukraine (literally: free land).

This extended military conflict ended with the 'Perpetual Peace' between Warsaw and Moscow in 1686. According to its terms, the territory of the Cossack state was reduced to the Left Bank and Kyiv and remained under Moscow's rule. The Right Bank was ceded to Poland. The Zaporozhian Host became a separate semi-independent military organisation under the protection of Moscow. Sloboda Ukraine, despite its Cossack administrative system, lay outside the control of the Cossack hetmans.

Ukrainian historians call the events in Ukraine in 1663–87 the Ruin. A similar, though shorter, period (1655–60) in the Polish-Lithuanian Commonwealth was provoked by Khmelnytsky's uprising and the invasion of Swedish troops. Poles call this period the Deluge. Although neither name is entirely accurate from a scholarly perspective, they do convey the spirit of the times. Together, the Polish and Ukrainian events, like the Thirty Years' War before them, were part of the 'General Crisis' of the seventeenth century – a wave of political instability and war that swept the entire European continent. In the eastern part of the continent, the Ukrainian lands were a kind of 'golden share': whoever controlled them had the best chance of dominating the entire region between the Baltic and the Black Sea. In the end, Muscovy won. In fact, Russia's ascent to the status of a great European power began from that moment. It also initiated the gradual decline and eventual disappearance of the Polish-Lithuanian Commonwealth. Of course, the Cossack factor was not the only or even the decisive reason for its fall. However, the Cossacks and their descendants could boast that they 'destroyed Poland'. In reality, as Shevchenko said, 'Poland fell and took us down, as well.'

One question repeatedly arises when we discuss the Cossack state: what kind of state was it, if its borders and status were constantly changing and it was liquidated with a single stroke of a pen? Can we even call it a state? These doubts make sense to us, modern readers. But they did not make sense at the time. State structures then were very different from today. Formally, modern states enjoy equal status; that was not the case at the time of the Hetmanate. Then, states operated within a hierarchical system. At the top were the states that had full sovereignty. Eighteenth-century cartographers identified sixteen such states on the European continent: Portugal, Spain, France, Germany (the Holy Roman Empire), Switzerland, Italy, the Netherlands, Great Britain, Norway, Denmark, Sweden, Muscovy (the Russian Empire), Poland (the Commonwealth), Hungary, Turkey and Prussia. Most of them were 'composite states'. Like a desk with many drawers, they were composed of smaller states with varying levels of sovereignty or no sovereignty at all. The Polish-Lithuanian Commonwealth was composed of two states (Poland and Lithuania); the Spanish monarchy was composed of three (Aragon, Castile and Catalonia). The British monarchy consisted of four states (England, Wales, Ireland and Scotland, which retained some elements of autonomy). The Holy Roman Empire was the champion. It included 1,610 different principalities, bishoprics, duchies and cities. All were subordinated to the central authority to varying degrees. Some enjoyed autonomy and could even participate in selecting the supreme ruler. Others were sovereign only on paper and were actually ruled by officials sent from the centre.

The main criterion regarding autonomy was the status of the local ruler. The title of 'hetman of the Zaporozhian Host' roughly corresponded to the title of 'duke'. It allowed for a certain degree of sovereignty and this degree varied depending on the circumstances. Initially, the Cossack state enjoyed the maximum amount of independence that could be achieved within the framework of a semi-sovereign status. The Hetmanate entered the

Tsardom of Muscovy on the basis of the widest possible autonomy, including its own customs service and the right to conclude international agreements. Until the beginning of the eighteenth century, Cossack hetmans made broad use of this right, concluding bilateral and trilateral agreements with the Polish-Lithuanian Commonwealth, the Kingdom of Sweden, the Ottoman Empire, the Crimean Khanate and even with Rome and Venice.

But the Hetmanate was not and could not be a fully sovereign state. It could have become one if Khmelnytsky or any of his Cossack colonels had had royal blood in their veins. But by the middle of the seventeenth century, all of the princely Rus families had either died out or converted to Catholicism.

In the Christian world of the time, there were very few examples of anyone without royal blood becoming head of state. One of them was Cromwell, the Lord Protector in revolutionary England who came to power in 1649 and executed the 'anointed' king, Charles I. As ambitious and strong revolutionary leaders, Cromwell and Khmelnytsky were similar. In his contemporaneous account, Pierre Chevalier, the French author of the *History of the Cossack War Against Poland*, called Khmelnytsky 'the Cromwell of Rus'. A legend even arose that the two of them had exchanged correspondence. But Cromwell went much further than Khmelnytsky. He was a Puritan, a radical Calvinist and believed that there should be no intermediary between the faithful and God, regardless of whether it was a pope or a monarch. Therefore, Cromwell felt neither fear nor remorse when it came to executing the English king. Khmelnytsky, on the other hand, was an Orthodox Christian and rebelled against the power of the nobility, not the king. Perhaps he could have claimed to be a sovereign ruler if he had been of a magnate family, like the Vyshnevetsky/Wiśniowiecki family, one of whom became king of Poland. But Khmelnytsky was from the minor gentry. He tried to 'acquire' noble blood by marrying his eldest son Tymish

(1632–53) to the daughter of the Moldavian ruler, but the plan was never brought to fruition. Tymish died young on a military campaign before he could inherit his father's power.

Khmelnytsky's other son, Yurii, was granted the title of prince by the Ottoman sultan. This elevation in rank was intended to legitimise Istanbul's power over Central Ukraine and Podolia. In reality, Yurii was a toy in the sultan's hands and when their plans didn't work out, the Turks disposed of him. According to one version, they killed him in Kamianets-Podilskyi, while another version claims that they exiled him to a monastery on an island in the Aegean Sea.

Their weak claims to legitimacy led Khmelnytsky and his successors to be haunted by the nightmare of coalitions. The Cossack hetmans were looking for a sovereign under whose rule they could preserve their rights and privileges. They negotiated at different times with the kings of Poland, Sweden and Prussia and with the Ottoman sultan. Their alliance with Muscovy lasted the longest. In Pereiaslav in 1654, the Cossack officers swore allegiance to the Muscovite tsar. This agreement decided the fate of Ukrainian lands for the next several centuries.

Russian and Soviet historians attributed great significance to the Pereiaslav Agreement as a historical and strategic choice that supposedly united the two brotherly nations forever. In reality, the Pereiaslav Agreement had no exceptional status. It was a military-political alliance of the sort which were concluded left and right at the time and which were just as readily broken. Khmelnytsky concluded a similar agreement with the Polish king in 1649 in Zboriv. His successor, Ivan Vyhovsky, concluded another in 1658 in Hadiach. Under the terms of the latter, the Polish gentry granted broad autonomy to the Ukrainian lands and the Polish-Lithuanian Commonwealth was to be transformed from a state of two to a state of three nations: Rus would be added to Poland and Lithuania. The agreement didn't suit either the majority of the

Polish gentry or the majority of the Cossacks: reconciliation after years of war felt tantamount to betrayal. Moreover, an agreement with the Muscovite tsar had one chief advantage for the Cossacks: they shared a faith with the tsar.

But what looked like a good deal to Khmelnytsky and his successors, eventually proved to be a fatal weakness for the Hetmanate. Like boiling a frog in water, the tsarist (later imperial) authorities gradually turned up the temperature on the Hetmanate: with each new turn of events, they slowly but surely curtailed Cossack rights and freedoms. When they felt betrayed, the Cossack hetmans tried to break free from the grip of the Moscow authorities. The first attempt came just two years after the Pereiaslav Agreement. When Khmelnytsky learned in 1656 that Muscovy had signed an armistice with the Polish-Lithuanian Commonwealth behind his back, he formed an alliance with Transylvania and Sweden. Then Khmelnytsky's death in 1657 disrupted all plans.

Fifty years later, Ivan Mazepa picked up where Khmelnytsky left off. A popular saying telescopes time to place him beside Khmelnytsky: 'There was no hetman between Bohdan and Ivan.' Mazepa came to power in 1687, a year after the conclusion of the 'Perpetual Peace', and his reign until 1708 can be considered the golden age of the Hetmanate. It was a time of political stability, economic activity and cultural flourishing in literature, music and architecture (the Cossack Baroque).

Mazepa began as a super-loyal vassal to Peter I, which is why the Cossacks initially called him 'not the father, but the stepfather of Ukraine'. Peter I is associated with a turning point in Russian history: the transformation of the Tsardom of Muscovy into the Russian Empire based on European models. Peter I's intention to 'cut a window to Europe' strained his forces and resources to their limits. These efforts were all directed towards the strategic goal of defeating Peter's main rival, King Charles XII of Sweden, in the Great Northern War (1700–21). The Hetmanate paid a disproportionate cost for this war. The Cossacks were sent to the military theatre in the far north and required to build fortifications. Their forces suffered losses of 50–70 per cent. Meanwhile, Malorossia itself suffered from harbouring the outposts of Russian troops, who behaved like an occupying army: they abused and sometimes killed local residents, raped women and commandeered livestock. In response to numerous complaints, Peter I forbade his troops, under penalty of death, to 'plunder and harm the Little Russian people'. But when word spread that the troops of Polish king Stanisław Leszczyński, an ally of Sweden, were moving into Ukraine, Mazepa asked Peter I for help. Peter refused, saying: 'I can't give you ten thousand men, I can't even give you ten; you'll have to defend yourselves as best you can.'

Mazepa decided to leave Peter's service and go over to the side of Charles XII. This ended in complete disaster: the Swedish troops and Cossack regiments were defeated at the Battle of Poltava in 1709. The name of this battle became synonymous with a crushing defeat (which led to the local idiom for complete and utter failure: 'to lose like a Swede at Poltava'). For Ukrainian patriots, the Battle of Poltava became a symbol of national catastrophe, like the Battle of Mohács in 1526 for Hungarians, the Battle of White Mountain in 1620 for Czechs, the Battle of Waterloo for Napoleon in 1815 and the Battle of Caporetto in 1917 for the Italians. Mazepa and the remnants of his Cossack troops barely survived by fleeing. The capital of the Hetmanate, Baturyn, was destroyed by Russian troops and awash in blood. And Peter I was strengthened in his belief that 'since the time of the first hetman, Bohdan Khmelnytsky ... all hetmans have turned out to be traitors'.

From then on, the Hetmanate was entirely under the control of the Russian tsars. It was liquidated twice and restored twice. The last time it was restored for the sake of Alexei Razumovsky, a descendant of the Cossack elite and the Russian Empress

Elizabeth's favourite lover, whom she secretly married. Aleksei's brother Kirill was appointed President of the Russian Academy at the age of eighteen and Ukrainian hetman at the age of twenty. Razumovsky seems to have tried to further modernise the Hetmanate. In particular, he hatched plans to establish the first university in the Russian Empire there. Nothing came of this plan: the first university was established in Moscow. Elizabeth's successor, Catherine II, forced Razumovsky to 'voluntarily' step down as hetman. Catherine II ordered the elites of the Cossacks, along with the elites of Livonia and Finland, two other autonomous provinces of the Russian Empire, to be 'gently Russified so they would stop looking to run into the woods like wolves'.

The Cossack state ceased to exist. Ukrainian patriots blamed Bohdan Khmelnytsky, believing that his short-sighted decision to accept the patronage of the Russian tsar had doomed the Hetmanate to failure and Ukraine to captivity. They contrasted him with Ivan Mazepa as a champion of Ukrainian independence. Russian patriots, including those of Ukrainian descent, thought exactly the opposite: they considered Khmelnytsky a role model and Mazepa a disgusting traitor. The division between 'Bohdanists' and 'Mazepists' was particularly strong on the eve of and during the Ukrainian Revolution of 1917. The 'Bohdanists' wanted Ukraine to remain part of Russia, while the 'Mazepists' favoured its formation as an independent state.

The contrast between Mazepa and Khmelnytsky is yet another example of historical anachronism. Both Khmelnytsky and Mazepa pursued the same goal and were guided by the same logic. Both were students of the Polish and, in fact, European political school. In this school of thought, relations within the ruling elite were regulated by mutual rights and obligations: of the sovereign towards the vassal and of the vassal towards the sovereign. The vassal was obliged to serve the lord faithfully and the lord was obliged to protect the vassal in return for his faithful service. If the lord violated these rights or failed to protect them, the vassal had the right to rebel. This 'right to rebel' was enshrined in the English Magna Carta and the Hungarian Golden Bull. Thomas Aquinas laid the foundation and John Locke updated it. In the Polish-Lithuanian Commonwealth, where the gentry had expansive rights, it was a self-evident norm. Khmelnytsky was following this principle when he left the service of the Polish king to serve the Muscovite tsar; Mazepa did the same when he left the service of the Russian tsar to join the Swedish king. But what the Cosssacks viewed as an exercise of their natural rights, was viewed as a flagrant betrayal by the Russian tsar. The church pronounced anathema against Mazepa, which the Russian Orthodox Church has not lifted to this day.

Mazepa was not the only leader to rebel against his suzerain during this period. In the second half of the seventeenth and first half of the eighteenth centuries, we can observe similar examples in Portugal, England, the Netherlands, Catalonia, Naples, France, Livonia, Hungary, Poland and Moldova. All were attempts by local nobility to retain their rights and privileges in the face of an encroaching centralised royal power. All followed a similar pattern: as a rule, they were not mass uprisings but small group conspiracies which relied on foreign assistance. Few were successful. Most were defeated and the fate of their leaders resembled that of Mazepa and his associates: they saved their lives and titles by emigrating elsewhere, dependent on the mercy of foreign rulers. None of the others, however, were subjected to church anathema. Thus, in the case of Mazepa, Peter I clearly overreacted.

The cause of this severity can be identified in their different political cultures. The Russian ruler was an autocrat, that is, an absolute sovereign who had total control over the lives and property of his subjects. This was radically different from the political system of the Polish-Lithuanian Commonwealth, where the power of the king was limited by the nobility. A characteristic episode was seen when Khmelnytsky and the Cossack elites swore allegiance to the Moscow tsar at the signing of the Pereiaslav Agreement and demanded that the Russian ambassador swear on behalf of the tsar that he would not violate Cossack rights and freedoms. The tsar's envoys refused: the tsar does not swear oaths to his subjects.

The Cossack elites viewed themselves as the Rus version of the Polish gentry and their state as a copy of the Polish-Lithuanian Commonwealth. They demanded 'noble dignity' for themselves. This meant, among other things, exemption from state duties and the right to be tried only in a noble court. Khmelnytsky's revolution opened social elevators: initially, Cossacks made up 30–50 per cent of the population and could achieve noble status in one or two generations. But over time, the Cossack elites became a closed estate. While elite status was initially obtained through military prowess, now the title was inherited by sons along with their estates. In the words of Zenon Kohut, one of the best experts on the Cossack state, only a few moved upward, while thousands sank down. Formally, the Cossacks were equated to the nobility. In reality, most of them, like the petty gentry in Poland, differed little from the peasantry in their economic status. At the same time, the peasants themselves became dependent on the elites and the Cossack elite treated them as serfs. An aristocracy emerged from the Cossack elites, a few families of 'newly rich' who fought for power among themselves and didn't hesitate to inform on each other to the Russian authorities. Corruption and nepotism flourished in the Hetmanate. In short, it was turning from a military democracy into an oligarchic state. Its history, like that of the Polish-Lithuanian Commonwealth, can serve as another illustration of the 'iron law of oligarchy': democracy tends to turn into an oligarchic system. This will sound familiar to many people in modern democracies.

Another estate open to people from below was the clergy. A

commoner gifted with innate intelligence, perseverance and talent, could make a career in the Orthodox Church. One religious ideologist of Peter I's reforms was Feofan Prokopovych, the son of a simple shopkeeper from the Hetmanate, but such examples were rare. Most people in the Orthodox hierarchy in Ukraine came from gentry and Cossack families.

The thing that distinguished the church elite from the secular elite was that the secular elite tried to maintain some degree of autonomy from Russia, while the local Orthodox elite rapidly integrated into the Russian Orthodox Church. While the Ukrainian lands were part of the Polish-Lithuanian Commonwealth, the local Orthodox Church maintained only a loose connection with Moscow. When the Cossack state was integrated into Muscovy, the situation changed radically. And the local Orthodox Church became the first Ukrainian institution to lose its autonomy. In 1686, utilising a mix of blackmail and bribery, Moscow persuaded the Patriarch of Constantinople to transfer the Kyiv Metropolis from Constantinople's purview to that of the Moscow Patriarchate.

At first, the Moscow clergy treated Ukrainian monks and priests with the suspicion that they had been 'Catholicised'. They demanded that they cross themselves according to the Moscow rite and after their deaths they were buried in a separate cemetery so as not to desecrate Orthodox land. But the Ukrainian clergymen not only mastered the new rules of the game, they rewrote them. They shaped the idea of Russia as a Slavic empire. A Kyivan monk, Innocent Giese, wrote the Synopsis of Eastern European History (1674), in which they emphasised the ecclesiastical unity of Kyiv and Moscow. Furthermore, they affirmed the existence of a single 'Slavo-Rus people'. The Synopsis has very little to say about the Ukrainian Cossacks and does not mention the Khmelnytsky era at all. In contrast, Cossack chronicles emphasised the role of the Cossacks in the history of the lands that had recently been Rus and were now Ukraine. Differences between those two narratives may indicate the split among the Ukrainian elite that became more obvious later between those who helped to build the Russian empire and those who wished to destroy it.

The Hetmanate had many problems and weak spots. A negative image has generally been painted in broad brushstrokes both by populist Ukrainian historians and Russian imperial ones. Although there are elements of truth in this image, it becomes pure caricature if the historical context is not taken into account. Any state of that time could be characterised in the same negative way, including the Russian Empire (perhaps most of all). What distinguished the Hetmanate from the rest of Russia, however, was its sense of freedom and liberty. In the mid-seventeenth century Paul of Aleppo, the son of the Patriarch of Antioch, travelled with his father through the Cossack lands. His travel notes capture that sense of freedom. Paul was equally fascinated by the exotic Ukrainian and Russian lands, but he describes a culture of prying and denunciation in Moscow that is entirely absent in his description of Cossack Ukraine. Reading his travel notes, one comes to the conclusion that in Moscow one could find power and money, but in Ukraine, one could breathe the air of freedom.

This sense of freedom was lost as the Hetmanate was absorbed into the body of the Russian Empire, but it did not disappear completely. Whereas in Russia most peasants were serfs, in the Hetmanate peasants could leave their lord for one of the few villages that remained free or move to the steppe beyond its borders. In addition, while in Russian society peasants made up approximately 90 per cent of the population, in the Hetmanate they made up only half. The other half was made up of free Cossacks, townspeople and clergy. Accordingly, the level of education was higher. This, in particular, surprised Paul of Aleppo when he travelled through the Cossack lands: he wrote that even women and children could read there.

Just as we notice air only when we don't have enough, the true significance of the Hetmanate was felt when it was gone. One of the first steps Catherine II took after the liquidation of the Cossack state was to introduce serfdom on its territory. Life for Ukrainian peasants was difficult under the Hetmanate; it became even worse afterwards.

To a certain degree, the Cossack state – in the form it had at the time – was doomed to fade away and die. Other states that disappeared in the following decades included the Polish-Lithuanian Commonwealth (1772–95), the Crimean Khanate (1783) and even the Holy Roman Empire (1806). Their disappearance reflected the general Zeitgeist: the decline of the composite monarchy model. It was replaced by an absolute monarchy with a strong ruler and centralised power, in the spirit of Louis XIV of France. In the late eighteenth century, this model seemed to presage the future of all of Europe.

Enlightenment philosophers supported and promoted the model of a strong central ruler and Catherine the Great enthusiastically supported them in turn. She corresponded with Voltaire and Diderot and in justifying the liquidation of the Zaporozhian Sich, she called the Ukrainian Cossacks 'a misfit rabble of people speaking different languages, with different faiths ... living in total idleness, vile drunkenness and contemptible *ignorance*' – that is, everything that the enlighteners condemned and intended to correct by turning 'ignorant' people into useful subjects through reform.

One cause of the new Zeitgeist was the military revolution, which ended the military dominance of the Muslim world and opened the way for Europe to become a world power. Between 1550 and 1650, the nature of military affairs on the European continent changed radically. Gunpowder weapons came into wide use, particularly artillery. This led to the need for stronger fortifications and larger armies. As the cost of war increased dramatically, only large states with strong centralised power could afford it.

The hetmans and Cossack elites recognised the need for modernisation. Mazepa was the hetman who went furthest in his efforts to reform the Cossack state. He regulated the status of the Cossack elite landholdings, stopped the transformation of rank-and-file Cossacks into peasants, limited work on the lords' estates to two days a week and protected the interests of tradespeople. His fiscal plans supported economic development, including the industrial production of textiles and metal. His rule was also marked by advances in education and culture. He tried to create a standing army. On the foreign policy front, he focused on returning Right Bank Ukraine to the Hetmanate and protecting its southern borders.

We can see the outlines of a strategic plan in Mazepa's actions: to transform the amorphous Hetmanate into a stable, consolidated, rich and educated state. His ultimate goal was the same as that of Peter I and later Catherine the Great: to create what later historians called a 'well-regulated society'.

Mazepa was a moderniser. Had his plan succeeded, the Hetmanate could have become an autonomous state that exerted an inordinate influence on the empire and paved the way for it to become a world power. Indeed, at the beginning of the eighteenth century, the influence of the Little Russians on the Russian Empire was so great that this empire could de facto have become the *Little Russian* Empire. Mazepa's defeat at Poltava put an end to his plans. Any modernisation that was carried out on the lands of the former Cossack state would follow the Russian imperial formula. All reforms were intended to lead to the homogeneity of the entire Russian Empire, first administratively, later socially and in the long term, culturally. There was no place in this formula for an autonomous Cossack state or for autonomous Cossack institutions in Zaporizhia or Sloboda Ukraine.

A year after the liquidation of the Hetmanate, the Cossack system was abolished in the neighbouring Sloboda region and in 1775 the Zaporozhian Sich was destroyed. What did not disappear, however, was the image of Ukraine. In the Cossack chronicles of the eighteenth century, Ukraine is not just an 'outskirts' or Cossack territory. It wasn't even just the Hetmanate. The Cossack chroniclers saw Ukraine as much larger than that. It included both left bank and right bank Ukraine, stretching from the Polish-Ukrainian ethnic border in the west to the Ukrainian-Russian ethnic border in the east. The Cossack elite had a clear sense of what distinguished their land from Poland, Muscovy, Lithuania and the Tatar lands.

When the Cossack chroniclers wrote about Ukraine, they called it 'our fatherland'. There is a particular sense of dignity in the image. There is a sacred duty to defend the borders of one's 'fatherland' and, if necessary, to give one's life for it. This concept was definitely new. Earlier, 'fatherland' had been understood as the land inherited from your father and the highest object of loyalty was the 'anointed' monarch. This new understanding appeared in the West during the Renaissance and was derived from ancient tradition. Horace's words *dulce et decorum pro patria mori est* – it is sweet and fitting to die for one's country – appeared in the code of honour of the Polish nobility in the mid-sixteenth century. Up till 1648, the Cossacks viewed the Polish-Lithuanian Commonwealth as their fatherland. After Khmelnytsky, the Cossack elites transferred this understanding to their own state.

The Ukrainian Cossacks existed for three hundred years, the last hundred of which were with the Cossack state. In its own way, the history of the Cossacks was connected to the early stages of globalisation. The Cossacks 'rode' its early wave but vanished when they could not meet the challenges of the later one. What they left behind, however, was the image of Ukraine as a rebellious but free and rich land.

INTERLUDE A Brief History of Ukrainian Song

One of the long-running debates in the academic world is the dispute over when nations emerge. One school argues that nations are a concept as old as the world. The other claims that nations emerged rather late, in the nineteenth century. Benedict Anderson, one of the most influential contemporary theorists of the histories of nations and national movements has proposed an elegant compromise. Modernists, he argued, have the power of theory behind them, while primordialists have the power of facts. Anderson's compromise is that he proposed and argued for an intermediate date. Nations, in his view, are born at the boundary between the medieval and modern worlds, in the sixteenth and seventeenth centuries. The interaction of three fundamental factors led to the emergence of nations: printing, Protestantism and capitalism. The printing press simplified the production of books, lowering their cost and making them accessible to the general public. Protestantism introduced the new tradition of printing books in the languages of the lower classes. Capitalism created a global market where those books became a mass commodity.

Benedict Anderson's scheme seems to accurately describe the emergence of Ukraine. Although we might debate the extent to which the processes he describes applied to Ukrainian lands, it can readily be shown that the Ukrainian (or rather, Rus-Ukrainian) nation emerged in the early modern period.

Of course, that nation isn't identical to the one that emerged later, in the nineteenth and twentieth centuries. The connection between the two is not direct or exclusive. As the history of the nineteenth century shows, the Rus-Ukrainian nation could have easily been integrated into either the Polish or Russian nations. Such attempts were made with limited successes. But without the early modern Rus-Ukrainian nation, the modern Ukrainian nation would not exist.

Anderson's formulation recalls the ideas of Ernest Renan, another early theorist of nations and nationalism. In his famous Sorbonne lecture 'What is a Nation?' (1882), Renan argued that a nation is not about a common language, a common religion, or common economic interests. First and foremost, a nation is a spiritual principle. It is the result of sacrifice and self-denial – for we love in proportion to the sacrifices we make.

And here again, Ukrainian history provides immense resources – particularly for explaining how the Cossack concept of Ukraine survived after Cossack Ukraine itself disappeared. It survived in oral folklore.

The word 'folk' is not quite accurate here. The folk themselves do not write songs. Each song has a specific author or authors. We are lucky enough to know some of their names such as Marusia Churai (1625–53) from the times of Khmelnytsky and the Cossack poet Semen Klymovsky (1705–85). Nevertheless, most of the songwriters' names have been lost.

In any case, folk culture is not a spontaneous creation of the people. It is created by representatives of what we like to call high culture. Folklore emerges as this high culture 'sinks' to the lower strata of society. Anthropologists offer the following image: the old high culture is like a large ship that has sunk to the bottom of folk culture. Although it has crashed and been transformed, its general outlines are still recognisable.

This image is helpful for describing the situation after the liquidation of the Hetmanate. Although the Hetmanate disappeared as a state, the people still remembered it. The presence of 'Ukraine' in folk songs is undeniable: researchers have counted about 1,200 songs which reference Ukraine. These songs were found well beyond the borders of the Cossack state, extending not only to Right Bank and Sloboda Ukraine but also to Austrian Galicia. In his preface to an 1836 St Petersburg edition of *Ukrainian Folk Songs*, Platon Lukashevych wrote:

> Who would have believed that a Galician shepherd knows far more epics about the heroes of Ukraine and its history than a settled Little Russian Cossack? He takes pride in the exploits of Little Russians as if they were his own. He rejoices in their good fortune and successes and in his beautiful songs, he yearns 'for the adventures of the Cossacks'.

Lukashevych was a romantic and therefore we might suspect him of patriotic exaggeration. Ukrainian poet and activist Ivan Franko, however, was a positivist, meaning that he believed only in what could be verified by facts. The songs and rhymes he took down in his native Galician village of Nahuyevychi, near Drohobych, in the 1860s and '70s, confirm Lukashevych's point. In these songs, Ukraine appears as a distant and free land defended by Cossacks from its enemies (Turks, Tatars and Poles). Its heroes, Cossack hetmans and colonels, are often mentioned by name:

> *'Oh, like in glorious Ukraine . . . '*
> *'What's happening in your glorious Ukraine?'*
> *'Come to glorious Ukraine . . . '*
> *'Ukraine is empty under Khmelnytsky's Yuri . . . '*
> *'All Ukraine cries for you, Morozenko.'*

This cumulative image of Ukraine from folk songs provides the foundations of the Ukrainian national myth. Myth doesn't mean a lie or a deliberate distortion here, but a much deeper concept. It is something like a biblical truth and therefore more powerful than the smaller truths and lies of daily life.

This myth was propagated by blind wandering musicians (lyre players, elders, or *kobzars*). Kobzars earned their living by singing near churches after Sunday services, at weddings, markets and wherever people gathered. There was a special genre in their repertoire: Cossack *dumas*, which were heroic and often tragic stories about the Cossack past. The dumas made up a relatively small part of the kobzar repertoire: they mostly sang religious songs. However, they created an oral tradition that was passed from generation to generation along with folk tunes, long after the last people who could personally remember the Ukrainian Cossacks were gone.

As with any historical myth, we cannot demand historical accuracy from the folk myth of 'Cossack Ukraine'. In song, the Zaporozhian commander Sirko can fight Napoleon. But if you boil away the layers of this Cossack myth, you will be left with the essence of a folk utopia: Ukraine as a rich and free land without social and ethnic oppression.

We can see this image in a song from Sahaidachny's time:

There is nothing greater, no nothing better,
Than life in Ukraine!
No Poles, no Jews,
No Greek Catholics either.

In these words, one can hear a distant echo of the Reconquista, the Peace of Augsburg and the Peace of Westphalia, i.e., a homogeneous religious state. This is not yet a nation-state in the modern sense of the word. It lacks several fundamental things.

In particular, a clear spatial identification. In most folk songs, Ukraine is not tied to recognisable geographical names. An example is the image of the Danube. The name of this river is often repeated in folk songs: to get to Ukraine, one must go 'across the Danube'. If we consider where these songs were sung (Austrian Galicia and the Ukrainian provinces of the Russian Empire) in relation to the Danube we come to a clear and entirely implausible conclusion: the Ukraine of the songs is not located in the lower reaches of the Dnipro, but somewhere in the lands of modern Austria or Hungary or in the Balkans.

There is a simple answer for this paradox. In Ukrainian folklore, the Danube is not a specific river, but any large body of water. In traditional mythology, 'big water' has a sacred meaning. To cross it means to make a radical change, to reach a qualitatively new state. (Recall the river Styx in ancient mythology, which separates the world of the living from the world of the dead.) To cross the Danube means not only to find yourself in a distant and foreign land, but also to change radically, to abruptly cut off ties with your old life, to become a new person.

The transformation of this 'transcendental Ukraine' into a modern one, one that would appear on geographical maps and in school textbooks, would require the work of writers, historians, geographers and politicians. For many of them, beloved Ukrainian songs connected them to what they had heard as children from their mothers, nannies, or peasants in their own homes.

There was the telling case of Mykola Kostomarov (1817–85), one of the early researchers of Cossack history. Kostomarov was raised in a Russian-speaking environment and didn't know Ukrainian. When he began his studies at Kharkiv University in 1837, he could not read Ukrainian literature without a dictionary. Since no Russian-Ukrainian dictionary existed at the time, a Ukrainian servant fulfilled that role instead. When Kostomarov read the collection of Little Russian songs published in 1827 by Mykhailo Maksymovych everything changed for him:

> I was amazed and delighted by the genuine charm of Little Russian folk poetry. I never suspected that such elegance, such depth and freshness of feeling could be found in the works of a people so close to me and about whom I actually knew nothing. The Little Russian songs captured my feelings and imagination so powerfully that within a month I knew Maksymovych's collection by heart.

His fascination with Ukrainian music led him to learn the language. Within a few years, Kostomarov had become a leader in the Ukrainian national movement and the author of its first programmatic documents.

In addition to the collections by the Little Russians Lukashevych and Maksymovych, early collections of Ukrainian song were also compiled and published by the Georgian Nikolai Tseretelev (1790–1869) and the Poles Zorian Dołęga-Chodakowski (1784–1825) and Wacław Zaleski (1799–1849). A fascination with Ukrainian folklore was one factor in the emergence of the 'Ukrainian school' in nineteenth-century Polish literature.

A fondness for Ukrainian songs did not necessarily make one a Ukrainian nationalist. Alexander Pushkin also admired them, but he remained a Russian poet. Joseph Stalin's favourite songs were Georgian and Ukrainian, but he could hardly be called a Ukrainian nationalist.

Just as 'Ukraine' was not the only name for the region, it was not the only concept in folk songs. The 'Rus land' also appears and it seems to have a different significance from that of Ukraine: it is often paired with the word 'holy'. In folk music, this understanding of land frequently has a sacred character. For example, in 'The Captive's Lament', a Ukrainian duma from the fifteenth or sixteenth century, a Cossack in Turkish captivity prays to God:

Deliver, O Lord, this poor captive
To the shore of Holy Rus,
To the happy land, among the christened people!

Another Ukrainian folk work, a baroque psalm, opens with the words 'Holy Virgin, Mother of the Rus Land ... ' One story tells of the power of this musical image: when the great-great-grandfather of the Ukrainian poet Maksym Rylsky (1895–1964), a Pole named Romuald Rylski, was captured by the Haidamaks, he saved his life and the lives of other prisoners by singing this psalm.

Both 'Rus' and 'Ukraine' had a sacral element. We can't know how these concepts coexisted in the minds of those who listened to these songs. Were they the same or different concepts? Where did Uniates, Belarusians, Old Believers and Little Russian landowners, the descendants of the Cossack elites, fit into these concepts? In any case, Ukrainian nation-builders had ample material for their efforts to transform 'Cossack Ukraine' and 'Rus' into the concept of the 'Ukrainian nation'. Although the path was not straightforward or automatic, they weren't starting from scratch.

When we discuss the foundations of this concept, we should consider its sacred dimension separately. Thinking in terms of dichotomies – either/or, tradition/modernity, people/nation, myth/reality – is rarely productive. The most effective formulations will combine tradition with modernity, the secular with the sacred and reality with myth. The mythical worldview is inherent in every person, modern or not – we simply cannot live without it. It manifests itself especially powerfully in times of crisis and upheaval.

More recently, in the early 1990s, during the renovation of a house in the German city of Freiburg, workers found a cardboard box filled with almost 1,300 letters written by Ostarbeiters. These were people, primarily young women, taken prisoner from occupied Belarus and Ukraine for forced labour in Nazi Germany. Most of them came from the countryside and were carriers of the oral folklore tradition, who scarcely knew the modern literary language. Many of their letters included poems they had written. In artistic terms, they're not masterpieces. But a researcher notes 'an undeniable energy of self-identification, an affirmation of one's own human dignity'. For example, the author of the poem 'Memory of Ukraine' does not write about the hardships of camp life or complain about her situation. All her thoughts are about her 'dear Ukraine', where her parents and beloved live and where she hopes against hope to one day return ... She asks her family and her homeland not to forget her.

Folk songs also played an important role in shaping the identity of the Ukrainian 'sixtiers', the generation of Soviet Ukrainian intellectuals who emerged in the 1960s. They were a product of the Soviet system, they considered themselves Soviet patriots and some spoke primarily Russian. But many of them remembered the folk songs their parents had sung them when they were small and the songs they heard at village weddings. When they heard these songs again as adults, something shifted inside them. Leonid Plyushch (1938–2015), a mathematician by training and a cyberneticist by profession, a Ukrainian dissident who lived in Soviet Ukraine but spoke Russian until he discovered Ukrainian culture, described it thus:

> Ukrainian songs and dumas are perhaps the most profoundly Ukrainian aspects of culture. A Ukrainian may call himself a Russian, despise his people or even torture them. He may not even know his own language, but if he lived in Ukraine

as a child, he becomes Ukrainian once more when he hears these songs.

The young poet Leonid Kyselov (1946–68) beautifully conveyed the transcendental dimension of Ukrainian song. Kyselov was born in Kyiv right after the war, to a Russian-Jewish family and was diagnosed with leukemia as a young man. In his hospital room, shortly before his death, he wrote:

I will stand at the edge of the abyss,
And suddenly realise, overwhelmed with yearning,
That the whole entire world . . . is no more than
A Ukrainian song.

You can't say it any better than that.

CHAPTER 4

THE LONG NINETEENTH CENTURY

UKRAINIAN ETHNIC TERRITORIES AND SETTLEMENTS, ca 1900

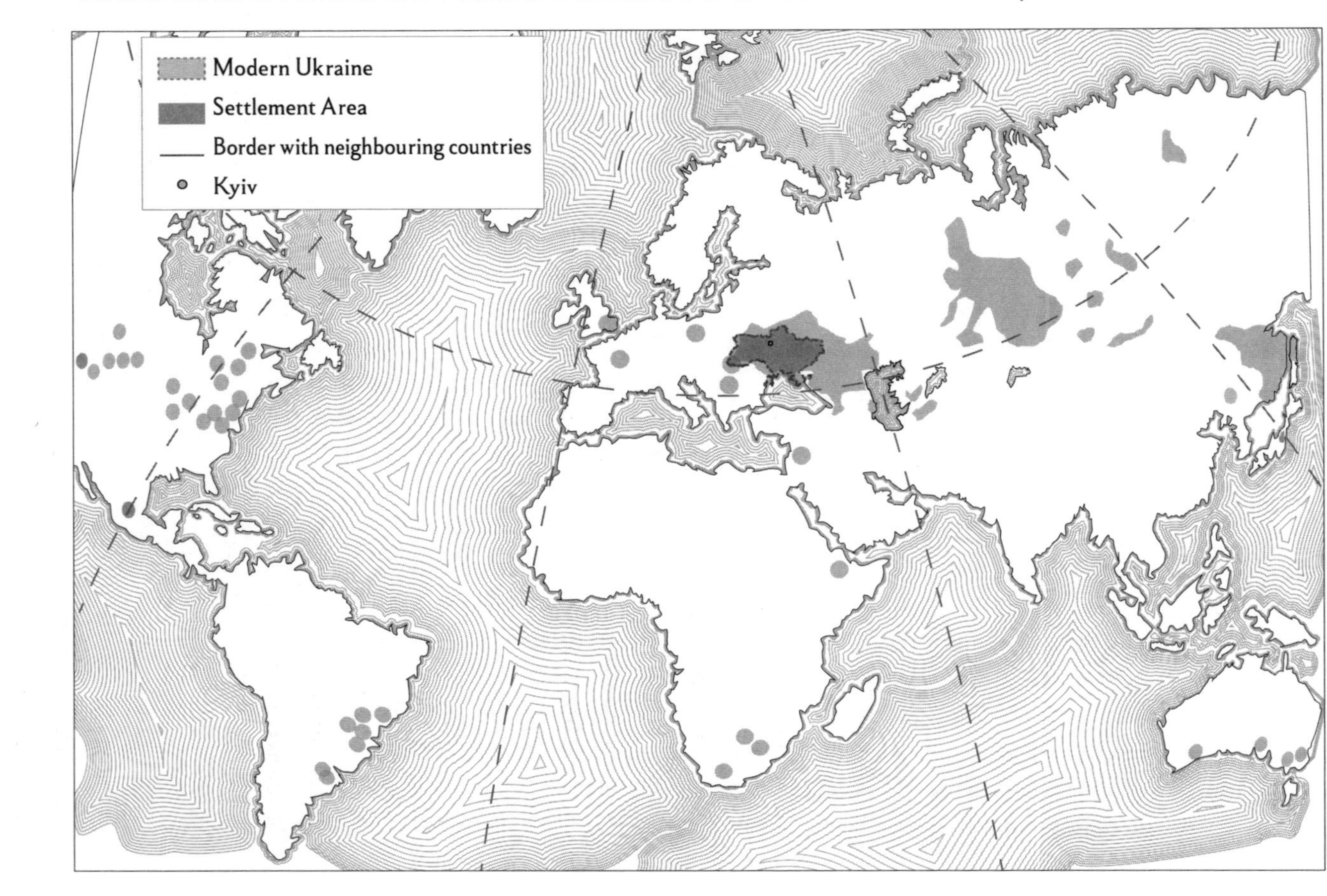

At the beginning of the eighteenth century, in the Austrian province of Styria, an unknown artist painted a 'Table of Nations' with brief descriptions of European peoples and their characteristics. We might call it the first European public survey as it contains a list of stereotypes about various European nations. There are ten peoples depicted: a Spaniard, Frenchman, Italian, German, Englishman, Swede, Pole, Hungarian, Muscovite and a strange breed called the 'Turk or Greek'. The list of traits consists of seventeen categories, ranging from 'reason', 'dress' and 'knowledge' right up to 'end of life'.

The first thing that jumps out is that Westerners are depicted far more positively than Easterners on this chart. When it comes to intellect, the Spaniards are regarded as 'wise and intelligent', the French are 'cautious', Italians 'sharp'. The Germans are considered 'witty', the English are 'charming', Swedes 'stubborn'. Poles are viewed as 'inattentive', while Hungarians are even less attentive. Muscovites have no intellect at all and the Turk-Greeks are 'arrogant'. As for character, the Spaniards are 'wonderful', the French are 'friendly' and 'talkative', Italians 'jealous', Germans 'quite good', the English are 'good-natured', the Swedes are 'vicious', while the Poles are even worse; the Hungarians are the most 'vicious', while the Muscovites are really Hungarian and the Turk-Greeks are 'lying devils'.

This scale of stereotypes clearly shows that the East-West divide, so familiar to us today, already existed in the imagination of educated Europeans at the beginning of the eighteenth century. There is, however, one thing that differentiates our perception from that of the Europeans of the eighteenth century: for them, these 'national' traits were permanent. Anyone who had the misfortune to be born Hungarian, Polish, Muscovite, Turkish or Greek would die with that misfortune. They would always be inferior to an Englishman, a Frenchman, or a German in their essential traits. It was as God and nature had decreed and nothing could be done about it.

Modern people think differently. Karl Marx summarised this way of thinking best: 'The country that is more developed industrially only shows a less developed country an image of its own future.' Industrial development will lead to a reality in which Hungarians, Poles, Muscovites and even Turk-Greeks will live and act like Spaniards, Germans, French, or the English.

In other words, this chart of nations depicts the modern East-West divide, but without the modern idea of progress. Progress breaks and changes everything: it's like an avalanche or hurricane – impossible to stop. But unlike a natural disaster, it brings change for the better, including the opportunity for people in the East to 'westernise'.

The idea of progress is one of the main ideas of the nineteenth century. The concept of progress had existed before. It meant gradual changes. In contrast, in the nineteenth century progress came to mean, above all, changes according to the formula: 'More, more, and more and up, up, and up.'

This reflected a new reality. The nineteenth century experienced one of the most radical transformations that humanity has ever experienced. It can be briefly characterised as the transition from an agrarian to an industrial society. This was a quantum leap in human history. The nineteenth century defined the contours of the modern world, in which most people live in cities rather than villages; where people can read and write and go hungry just for their diet; where they are cured of diseases that used to be fatal; where they travel tens or hundreds of times faster than their ancestors; and where the time it takes for a message from the capital to reach the suburbs has been reduced from several weeks to a fraction of a second.

We call these changes modernisation. Historians suggest that the modernisation of the nineteenth century was the result of a double revolution: an industrial revolution that began in the 1770s and '80s in Britain and a political revolution that was launched by the American (1775) and French (1789) revolutions. The end of this century is generally considered to be the first major catastrophe of modernity, the First World War. This periodisation aligns closely with the Ukrainian nineteenth century. Its beginning is traditionally associated with the appearance in 1798 of the first work written in the modern Ukrainian language and it ends with the First World War, in which the Ukrainian factor played a significant role.

The period between 1789 and 1914 is called the 'long nineteenth century'. It lasted twenty-five years longer than the calendar nineteenth century (1801–1900). This 'long' nineteenth century stands in contrast to the 'short twentieth century', which is generally considered to have begun with the First World War and ended with the fall of communism (1914–1989/91). These centuries differed in many ways. But there was a connection between them: the nineteenth century wrote the scenarios which became realities in the twentieth century. These scenarios can be briefly characterised as 'isms' (aka ideologies): socialism, liberalism, conservatism, feminism, etc. All of these are products of the nineteenth century, but they created the blueprints for the 'brave new world' of the twentieth century.

One of these 'isms' was nationalism. In Western thought it is a negative word, especially after the nightmares of the two world wars. However, we must account for two things. First, nationalism is too broad a phenomenon to be reduced only to its most xenophobic and violent expressions. Like any other 'isms' – liberalism, Marxism, feminism and others – it can take various forms: there is conservative, leftist and even liberal nationalism. In a nutshell, nationalism stands for both the ideology and the political movements based on it, whose main demand is the following: political borders should coincide with the borders of ethnic nations. Or, as the Italian nationalist Giuseppe Mazzini demanded: 'To each nation, its own state!'

Second, in the nineteenth century nationalism was predominantly a revolutionary movement. It opposed the old regime, based on monarchies, empires and aristocratic rule. What the nationalist revolutionaries demanded in the nineteenth century became the norm of the geopolitical order in the twentieth. This is why the main international organisation of the twentieth century is called the United Nations, not the United Empires.

Ukraine is a founding member of the United Nations. It didn't appear in that eighteenth century Table of Nations but became a reality in the twentieth century. The main features for Ukraine's eventual independence were developed between the eighteenth and twentieth centuries, that is, in the long nineteenth century.

The Long Nineteenth Century in Ukraine

If we look at Ukraine's long nineteenth century as a drama, then we can see that it is not only the script that changes: the actors and the scene change as well. The beginning of the long nineteenth century marks a great divide between 'old' and 'new' Ukraine. Three of the old actors of Ukrainian history were first to leave the stage: the Ukrainian Cossacks, the Polish-Lithuanian Commonwealth and the Crimean Khanate. After the three partitions of Poland (1772–95), the majority of Ukrainian lands (85 per cent) fell under the rule of the Russian Empire, while the remaining 15 per cent (Galicia, Bukovyna and Transcarpathia) were ruled by the Austrian Empire (after 1867, the Austro-Hungarian Empire). This system remained in place without major changes until 1914.

The 'old' Ukraine and the 'new' Ukraine also differed in size. After the Russian Empire eliminated the Crimean Khanate and annexed the Wild Field, these lands became a zone of intensive economic colonisation. The scale of change was comparable to the development of the American West. Attracted by opportunity and encouraged by Russian authorities, immigrants from German lands, Orthodox Christians from the Balkans and individuals from various corners of Europe arrived here in search of adventure and wealth. But the greatest migration was that of Ukrainian peasants from adjacent regions. By the end of the nineteenth century, Ukrainians had become the largest group among the population of what was once the Wild Field.

Peasant colonisation of the Black Sea steppes led to the area of Ukrainian ethnic territory almost doubling during this time period. What the Russian authorities planned to call 'Novorossiya' or 'New Russia' became de facto a 'New Ukraine'. The only area where Ukrainians did not constitute a majority was Crimea. The peasants were settling the fertile lands of the Black Sea region; they weren't especially interested in the craggy Crimean Peninsula.

But there were even more transformations of the traditional 'stage' on which Ukrainian history unfolded. The next act began with the abolition of serfdom (in 1848 in the Austrian Empire and 1861 in the Russian) along with developments in transportation, particularly railroads and steamships. Both of these factors enabled the mass migration of Ukrainian peasants to new, hitherto unknown territories. At the turn of the twentieth century, Ukrainian settlements popped up from Edmonton in the Canadian Far West to Vladivostok in the Russian Far East. This peasant migration was part of the first wave of economic globalisation from 1870–1914. As a result, Ukrainians became a globalised people.

Another factor connects Ukrainian and global history in the nineteenth century: a change in mentality. The old, agrarian society was afraid of change. Any change – a bad harvest, bad weather, a new lord, or a new government – represented a threat to people who were already scratching out a minimal subsistence. In their minds, everything good was in the past, in the 'golden age', and the present was just a worse copy of the past. Mykhailo Kovbasiuk, the peasant ambassador to the Galician Sejm, expressed this very clearly: 'Let it stay as it was.' In contrast, a modern person is not afraid of change. On the contrary, they seek out change because change offers the promise of a better life. In the words of Ukrainian rock star Slava Vakarchuk, 'everything will be fine'.

As a result, a new line of conflict emerged on Ukrainian soil: between those who feared modernisation and tried to avoid it and those who welcomed it and spared no effort to promote it. The latter considered the challenge to be a matter of life and death: 'Modernise or die!' The conflict between supporters and opponents of progress became one of the main plotlines of nineteenth-century Ukrainian history.

And one last thing. When we talk about the main features of the nineteenth century, it is worth mentioning that it was one of the most peaceful centuries in European history. For a hundred years – from Napoleon's defeat in 1815 until 1914 – there were no large-scale wars on the European continent. There were local wars, such as the Austro-Prussian and Franco-Prussian wars, but they cannot be compared to Europe's wars before or after the nineteenth century in terms of the scale of casualties and destruction. This is also true of the Ukrainian lands. The only major war here, the Crimean War of 1853–56, barely impacted 'mainland' Ukraine.

In short: for those who crave a life of peace and tranquillity, nineteenth-century Ukraine could seem ideal. Nikolai Gogol (1809–52) conveyed this atmosphere in his stories of Old-World landowners who, unlike their Cossack ancestors, lived peaceful, placid lives. Panteleimon Kulish (1819–97), one of the leaders of the Ukrainian movement, wrote that during his childhood in the lands of the former Hetmanate, the social order established after Khmelnytsky continued unchanged and his relatives lived as they had in Mazepa's time.

Time seemed to stand still in Ukraine. The educated public saw Ukraine as the personification of peace and prosperity. In reality, Ukraine could look like a peaceful and fortunate land only to those who knew little about it. It was like a sleeping volcano: restless flows bubbled below the surface, breaking out again and again. Between 1793 and 1914, there was one Russian uprising and four Polish revolts, three mass peasant rebellions, two major anti-Jewish pogroms and two revolutions – one in the Austrian Empire (1848) and one in the Russian (1905–07).

And there was one more troublemaker on these lands: Ukrainian nationalism.

National Revival

To tell the story of Ukrainian nationalism in the nineteenth century, it is worth going back to the Table of Nations to see who else is missing besides Ukrainians. It's a long list: Albanians, Basques, Belarusians, Bulgarians, Walloons, Armenians (there were a lot of them in Eastern Europe), Estonians, Jews, Irish, Catalans, Latvians, Lithuanians, Sorbs, Norwegians, Provençals, Roma, Serbs, Croats, Silesians, Slovaks, Slovenes,

Czechs, Tatars, Ukrainians, Finns and Flemings. They all had one thing in common: they did not have their own state. That is why these peoples were called 'stateless' in the nineteenth century.

Stateless nations had three features in common:

1. Their ethnic borders did not coincide with state borders; some peoples, such as Jews or Ukrainians, were divided among several states.
2. They had an incomplete social structure – there was no aristocracy and almost no middle class – bankers, entrepreneurs, lawyers, professors, etc. In the Ukrainian case, the former Rus nobility and Cossack officers had assimilated and become either Russian nobles or Polish gentry. And so the former 'Cossack nation' became a 'peasant people'.
3. There are large gaps in the development of culture. A nineteenth-century Englishman could easily read and understand Shakespeare and a modern German can comprehend Martin Luther's translation of the Bible. In contrast, the languages of modern Jewry – Yiddish or Ladino – are entirely different from the Hebrew of the Old Testament. Similarly, there is a significant difference between the language of the poets of old and new Ukraine, Hryhorii Skovoroda and Taras Shevchenko respectively.

These aspects can make stateless nations difficult to notice. Somehow they are both there and not there. In any case, they are easy to ignore. In the eyes of a 'civilised' European, they haven't contributed to the development of European civilisation and therefore do not deserve any other future than to dissolve into the larger nations.

In the nineteenth century, individuals appeared in those stateless nations who rejected that perspective. They believed that history had treated their people cruelly and unfairly: they once had a state, but it had been destroyed by violent attackers. Only the ordinary peasants remained, but, against all odds, they had preserved their language and the memory of their glorious past. And so the nation hadn't disappeared. It had fallen asleep, it was buried alive, and it was time to bring it back to life, like the prince who woke the sleeping beauty in the fairy tale, overcoming all obstacles, often risking life and limb.

The national movements of stateless nations are called national revivals. This name is imprecise: the ideologists of these movements didn't so much revive the old nation as give birth to a new one. However, the term 'national revival' is established in historical science and it continues to be used, despite its imprecision.

Comparative studies of stateless nations have shown that national revival follows a certain pattern. It goes through three stages:

1. Stage A (academic or collecting). This stage is characterised by the appearance of scholars and writers, often young, who collect local folklore and create a new national language and literature on its basis and, more broadly, a national ideology.
2. Stage B (institutional or organisational). At this stage, institutions or organisations emerge that spread national consciousness among the local population, primarily among villagers, who make up the majority of the nation.
3. Stage C (political or mass). This is the final stage, at which parties and mass political movements emerge to demand the formation of an independent nation-state.

If we continue to speak in the language of metaphors, national revival can be imagined as a long-distance race. Not everyone finishes the race. Some people drop out and disappear into the past. One of the main conditions for success is to make it through

Stage B. Once a national movement is embedded in the backbone of institutions, it becomes irreversible.

What does this model look like in the Ukrainian case? In the Russian Empire, Ukrainians entered Stage A in the early decades of the nineteenth century. It began with the activities of a group of teachers and students at the newly founded universities of Kharkiv (1804) and Kyiv (1834). The culmination of their efforts can be seen in the 1840 publication of *Kobzar* by Taras Shevchenko (1814–61). In the Austrian Empire, Stage A began in 1810–20 in Przemyśl and continued in Lviv in the 1830s, with the work of the 'Rus Triad' – Markiyan Shashkevych (1811–43), Yakiv Holovatsky (1814–88) and Ivan Vahylevych (1811–66). In 1837, they published the first work in vernacular Ukrainian, the almanac *Rusalka Dnistrova* or *Nymph of the Dniester.*

Stage B began almost simultaneously in the Russian and Austrian empires. In 1840, the first cultural-political organisations appeared: in 1845, the Cyril and Methodius Brotherhood was founded in Kyiv and in Lviv, the Supreme Rus Council was established during the revolution of 1848. These organisations made two critical statements: the Cyril and Methodius Brotherhood declared the great future of the Ukrainian nation among all the Slavs and the Supreme Rus Council affirmed that Austrian 'Rusyns' and Russian 'Little Russians' were one and the same people. However, this optimistic beginning proved to be a false start. In 1847, members of the Cyril and Methodius Brotherhood were arrested and punished and the Supreme Rus Council ceased to exist in 1851 after the defeat of the revolution.

After the counter-revolutionary decade of the 1850s, the political climate in the two empires liberalised – not out of choice, but out of necessity. Both empires had suffered humiliating military defeats: Russia in the Crimean War (1854–55) and Austria in both Italy and the war with Prussia (1866). To prevent further defeats, the empires had to modernise. The 1860s and '70s were characterised by the most systematic and consistent reforms in the history of the Russian Empire. Taking advantage of the liberalisation of the political climate, former members of the Cyril and Methodius Society published the journal *Osnova* (1861–62) in St Petersburg. In Kyiv, a group of students and young teachers formed the first Hromada (Commune) – an organisation to spread education in Ukrainian. The Russian government dealt a severe blow to their activities with two laws – the Valuev and Ems Decrees (1863 and 1876 respectively) that banned the printing of books in the Ukrainian language. In 1881, the assassination of Tsar Alexander II brought an end to reforms in the Russian Empire and ushered in a period of almost thirty years of reaction.

Events in Austria followed a different scenario: the reforms were not curtailed. In 1867, the Austrian Empire became the dual Austro-Hungarian Empire and the provinces were granted broad political autonomy. In Galicia, the Polish elite were the primary beneficiaries of this autonomy. They took local power into their own hands. They envisioned Galicia as the territory around which the revival of a unified Polish state would take place, much as Piedmont had been in the Italian Risorgimento. The Galician Ukrainians also took advantage of the reforms. They shared a vision of Galicia as a 'Piedmont', but for the future Ukrainian state, not a Polish one. They began developing mass movements in the region, including the 1868 establishment of the Prosvita Society (Enlightenment Society), whose activities were aimed primarily at the peasantry. By the end of the 1880s, there was no doubt that the Galician Rusyns, unlike the Little Russians, had passed Stage B.

The gap between the Ukrainian movements in the Austro-Hungarian and Russian empires reached its widest point at the turn of the century. In the 1890s, the first Ukrainian parties emerged in Lviv: the Rus-Ukrainian Radical Party (1890), the Ukrainian Social Democratic Party (1899) and the Ukrainian

National Democratic Party (1899). These parties relied on an extensive network of cultural and political organisations. The strength of the Ukrainian movement was already so evident that even their Polish opponents spoke of the 'Ukrainian conquest of Galicia' as a very plausible scenario.

Ukrainian parties emerged in the Russian Empire also: there was the Ukrainian People's Party (1902) as well as the Ukrainian Democratic Party and Ukrainian Radical Party (1904), the latter two of which merged into the Democratic-Radical Party the following year. However, unlike the Galician parties, these were parties in name only. They did not have mass membership. Most of them were in fact just groupings that were still trying to move to Stage B, to create a network of organisations modelled after the Galician Prosvita. The Russian Revolution of 1905–07 opened opportunities for this when, under pressure from below, a constitution with civil rights was finally introduced in Russia and bans on the Ukrainian language were lifted. But this brief thaw ended with the period of reaction from 1907–14 which was marked by a ban on the registration of societies and publishing houses of 'alien nations', including Ukrainians. The Ukrainian movement in the Russian Empire was stuck at Stage A, while in the Austro-Hungarian Empire it had reached Stage C and was ready to proclaim its own state.

The difference was so marked that the Ukrainian activists feared that it would come to the formation of not one but two nations, similar to the Serbo-Croatian situation: one (Little Russian and Orthodox) in the Russian empire and another in the Austro-Hungarian Empire. This challenge was overcome when the Ukrainian patriots from the Russian Empire moved their centre of activity to Galicia. To a large extent, patriots from 'Greater Ukraine' were responsible for the Ukrainisation of Galicia. Young Galician Rus in the 1860s became Ukrainianised under the influence of the *Kobzar* brought from Kyiv. Mykhailo

Drahomanov (1841–95), leader of the Kyivan 'Hromada' converted an entire generation to Ukrainianism in the 1870s, including the exceptionally gifted Ivan Franko (1856–1916), who became the greatest national poet after Taras Shevchenko. The Taras Shevchenko Society, founded in Lviv in 1873, played a key role in uniting Galicians and the new arrivals from central Ukraine. In 1892, the society changed its name to the Taras Shevchenko Scientific Society and took on the role of an unofficial Ukrainian Academy of Sciences. A young Kyivan historian, Mykhailo Hrushevsky (1866–1934), served as the chair of the society. Hrushevsky had moved to Lviv to head the Ukrainian history department at the local university where he published his monumental work, the multi-volume *History of Ukraine-Rus*. Thanks to the activities of political parties and scientific and cultural organisations, the Ukrainian movement in Galicia developed into a massive dynamic force.

In contrast, the Ukrainian movement in the Russian Empire suffered from arrested development. The situation can be understood by an anecdote related to the unveiling of a monument to writer Ivan Kotliarevsky in Poltava in 1903. All the Ukrainian leaders travelled together to the unveiling in just two train cars. They joked that if the train derailed, the Ukrainian movement would be finished.

Like every joke, this one also had an element of truth. It conveyed the difficulties the Ukrainian movement would face when, after the fall of two empires in 1917–18, it attempted to create an independent state. In the lands of the former Russian Empire, these efforts were almost doomed to failure: how can you build your own state when you don't even have your own schools? To a certain extent, the defeat of the Ukrainian national liberation struggle of 1914–20 was preordained by the events of the nineteenth century.

Geopolitical Dimension

The ABC schema serves as a primer for anyone studying national movements of stateless nations. But, like any model, it cannot explain everything. Comparative studies suggest that during the 1917–20 revolution, the Ukrainian movement was stronger than the Lithuanian one. Yet the Lithuanians won their own state and Ukrainians did not.

The reason Ukrainians failed lies in geopolitical circumstances. Ukraine was especially significant to the Russian Empire – much more so than Lithuania. First, control over Ukraine's rich human and natural resources was critically important to the Russian imperial authorities: Ukrainians were the second largest ethnic group in the empire after Russians and the Ukrainian lands were a 'land of milk and honey' compared to poorer Belarus or Lithuania. Second, the symbolic dimension was no less important. The Russian Empire traced its origins to ancient Rus and saw Little Russia as its historical cradle. Third, Ukrainians (Little Russians) were linguistically and religiously close to Russians (Great Russians) and could act as partners in maintaining this empire. The Russian authorities were very sensitive to 'Mazepism' – any threat of tearing Ukrainian lands away from Russia. Thus, Ukrainian was systematically banned by the authorities. Ukrainian patriots complained that the ban on the Ukrainian language made about as much sense as banning matches due to the threat of fire. Nonetheless, Petersburg saw an ironclad logic here: any recognition of the Ukrainian language as a separate language would mean opening the gates to political separatism. The Russian Empire could certainly exist without the Baltic States or even the Caucasus, but the loss of Ukraine would be the beginning of the end.

The Russian government wasn't the only group to think so: the Russian revolutionary opposition believed the same thing. Before the First World War, Lenin and the Bolsheviks rejected out of hand any possibility of a separate Ukrainian Marxist Party. They might have agreed to the creation of a Lithuanian party, but the Bolsheviks considered it 'political suicide' to allow Ukrainians to have their own party.

The Ukrainian question was not purely an internal issue of the Russian Empire. Control over Ukrainian lands was also critically important to Polish nationalists. The 'Kresy' had the same significance for the Polish elites as the Little Russian 'borderlands' did for the Russian authorities. In 1795, the Polish-Lithuanian Commonwealth completely disappeared from the world map. Nevertheless, the Poles did not become a stateless nation. There was still a large Polish elite and they did not need to go through stages A, B and C: the Polish movement was political from the very beginning. From the moment of the partitions of Poland until 1863, almost every generation of the Polish elite had its own national uprising against the Habsburgs (1846, 1848) and against the Romanovs (1793, 1830, 1863). No wonder the Austrian Chancellor Metternich considered Poland to be synonymous with revolution. A Ukrainian proverb conveyed this Polish revolutionary spirit with straightforward simplicity: 'What kind of a Pole am I? I haven't fought the Muscovites!'

The Polish gentry was suppressed and discriminated against. In Austrian Galicia, Poles were not allowed to hold high office until sometime in the mid-nineteenth century. In the Russian Empire, a significant portion of the nobility were punished for the uprisings through loss of their land and rank. Nonetheless, Polish landowners still made up the majority of the nobility on Ukrainian lands until the First World War.

In addition to the quantitative advantage, the Polish elite had a qualitative advantage. The Polish gentry and the Baltic Germans were two of the most educated groups in the empire. In the early nineteenth century, the education system in Vilnius, ruled by the

Polish elite, had more students in schools than all other districts of the empire combined. The Russian Minister of the Interior, Pyotr Valuev, the author of the anti-Ukrainian law of 1863, doubted that it would be possible to end the dominance of the Polish gentry by replacing local Polish families with imported Russian ones. In his opinion, this would accomplish nothing, because Russian landowners and officials lacked that intangible power, the civilisational advantage that could have backed up the use of brute force.

Polish patriots saw the future Polish state within its historical borders, i.e., the borders of the old Polish-Lithuanian Commonwealth, 'from sea to sea' (the Baltic Sea to the Black). It was not an ethnic view of the nation but a political one. Polish rebels went in to battle under the slogan: 'For your freedom and ours.' In addition to ethnic Poles, the Polish political nation was to include Belarusians, Jews, Lithuanians and Ukrainians.

Similar to the French Revolution in the West, the Polish national movement in Eastern Europe made local populations into nationalists. Just as Napoleon's campaigns awakened nationalist aspirations among the conquered Italians, Spaniards and Germans, the Polish uprisings broadened the idea of nationalism among Belarusians, Lithuanians, Ukrainians and Jews. Suffice it to say that the original first line of the Ukrainian anthem, 'Ukraine has not perished,' and the words in the Israeli anthem, 'Our hope is not yet lost,' repeat almost verbatim the beginning of the Polish anthem, 'Poland has not perished.' The reason for this 'coincidence' becomes clear if we consider the fact that the author of the Ukrainian anthem, Pavlo Chubynsky, was born in Right-Bank Ukraine and Naphtali Herz Imber, the author of the Israeli anthem, was from Galicia, that is to say – both came from historically Polish lands.

Right up to the late nineteenth century, Polish leaders particularly singled out Ukrainians among all the 'kresy' peoples because of their freedom-loving Cossack past. Polish officers tried to convince Napoleon that in Ukraine, the descendants of Ukrainian Cossacks were eagerly awaiting his arrival, ready to rebel against Russia. The 'Ukrainian question' occupied an important place in the politics of Prince Adam Czartoryski, the 'uncrowned king' of the Polish emigration. Franciszek Duchinski, a nobleman from Kyiv who was close to Czartoryski in Paris, wrote in an appeal to the peoples of Europe: 'To the Dnipro! To the Dnipro! To Kyiv! Oh, peoples of Europe! There is your unity, for there it is that the Little Russians are fighting against Moscow in defence of their European civilisation.'

It is difficult to say to what extent these views were based on sincere faith and to what extent on pragmatic calculation. We can assume, however, that at least some of the Polish revolutionaries believed in the revolutionary nature of Ukrainians. Their faith was not unfounded. Russian General Mikhailovsky-Danilevsky, who was stationed in Kremenchuk in the 1820s, wrote: 'Not a single person I spoke with in Malorossia was favourably disposed towards Russia; a clear spirit of opposition prevailed in all . . . '

In the 1830s, a German traveller named Johann Kohl travelled from St Petersburg to Lviv and reported similar impressions: 'The disgust that the people of Little Russia feel for the people of Great Russia is so strong that it can be fairly characterised as national hatred . . . If the day ever comes when the colossal empire of Russia falls to pieces, there is no doubt that the Little Russians will form a breakaway state.'

The Little Russian nobility was dissatisfied with the Russian government. But, unlike the Polish rebels, they never rebelled against it. To understand why, we should start by recognising that the choice they faced was not a choice of 'to rebel or not to rebel': it was broader. The attitude of provincial elites towards the imperial centre can be summarised in three different categories:

loyalty, autonomy and separatism. These categories were not mutually exclusive and no elite adhered to only one. Even a significant portion of the Polish nobility chose loyalty and 'served the Muscovite'. A single person might be a loyal government official at work, favour autonomy in private conversation and become a separatist during an uprising. These categories should not be presented as permanent decisions, but rather as shifting points along a wide range of political positions. The Baltic Germans occupied the extreme point in the 'loyalty' category. They were the most loyal elite and held the highest government positions. In fact, the Russian Empire was sometimes called a 'German state'. At the opposite pole of 'separatism', you could find a part of the Polish nobility and the Muslim elite of the Caucasus and Crimea. Many of the latter 'voted with their feet', abandoning Russian Crimea en masse for the Ottoman Empire.

The Little Russian gentry occupied a position somewhere in the middle of this scale, balancing between 'loyalty' and 'autonomy', but rarely reaching 'separatism'. And for at least two reasons. First, the Russian Empire was a large but backward empire. It desperately needed an educated elite to govern its vast expanses and that elite was most abundant on its western margins. The Little Russian nobility, although not as educated as the Baltic German barons and not as numerous as the Polish gentry, had one advantage: they were of the same faith as the Great Russians. In the eighteenth century, Little Russians made up almost half of the Russian imperial intelligentsia. In the capital itself, they created something like a bureaucratic mafia – the 'Little Russian colony', without whose support one could not hope for a high position. They paved the way for the Russian Empire to become a global power because they considered it their empire as well. The Russian Chancellor, Viktor Kochubey (1768–1834), once wrote to a fellow Ukrainian:

> Although I was born a khokhol, I am more of a Great Russian than anyone else ... My position elevates me above all petty concerns. I view the problems of your provinces with respect to the common interests of our entire state. Microscopic views are of no interest to me ...

Little Russian influences on the Russian state in the nineteenth century become increasingly difficult to trace, as they assimilated into the society over several generations and are not easily distinguished from the general stream. What is certain is that, just as the first generations of Cossack officers and the Orthodox Little Russian hierarchy transformed Russia into a world-class empire, their descendants transformed Russian culture from provincial to world-class. Many of those who embodied the highest achievements of this culture, such as Nikolai Gogol, Pyotr Tchaikovsky and Anton Chekhov, had Ukrainian roots. A significant number of them could easily have subscribed to Kochubey's words, preferring not to mention their 'Little Russian roots'. Or consider the case of Anton Chekhov, who called himself a 'lazy khokhol' during fits of depression.

The second reason the Little Russian nobility did not rebel was the very concept of nobility. To be a nobleman meant to serve the monarch. Without service to the emperor, noble status lost its meaning and significance. When the Little Russian nobility spoke of their historical rights, they emphasised that they had sworn an oath to the Russian tsar, not to Russia. Since a separate Ukrainian monarch did not exist, separatism from the perspective of the nobility meant the search for an emperor other than the Romanovs. Such attempts were made. In 1791, the Cossack elite secretly sent the poet Vasyl Kapnist as an envoy to the royal court in Berlin to find out whether the Little Russian nobility could count on the support of the Prussian emperor if they tried to 'throw off the Russian yoke'. The Prussian emperor did not grant him an audience.

In the early nineteenth century, some Little Russian nobles spoke highly of Mazepa and Napoleon. Still, during the invasion of 1812, most of them sided with the Russian emperor against France, unlike the Polish nobility. The descendants of the Cossack officers might not like Russians and occasionally express anti-Russian feelings, but they did not consider Russians to be their main enemies. That role was still played by Poles, Tatars and Turks.

The Russian writer Nikolai Leskov (1831–95) accurately described the worldview of the Little Russian gentry. He lived in Kyiv for about ten years (between 1849 and 1861) and came to know the habits of the local population. Leskov describes a Little Russian landowner whose patriotism was manifested primarily in his fondness for the Little Russian cloak and Little Russian language and his contempt for outsiders. This contempt, however, had a religious basis. He honoured Orthodoxy as the only true Christianity. He considered everyone else heretics – most significantly the Germans because they 'do not honour the saints' (a reference to Protestantism), followed by the Jews and 'the rest of the scum'.

But in his Orthodoxy, 'Muscovite' and 'Rus' were two entirely different concepts, in heaven as it is on earth. He placed the 'Little Russian' St George (Yurko) far higher than the 'Muscovite' St Nicholas. He greeted his guests with the question of which of these two saints was more important. If the guest failed the test, he would feel the hardness of the master's chairs and even the flexibility of his canes. He did not like Poles, but he showed arrogance when it came to Russian nobles: 'What kind of nobility do they have! All of their grandparents were whipped.' He put the Baltic Germans above all others. But if they went to war against Russia, he would go to 'beat them with zeal'.

Leskov compared the head of this Little Russian patriot to 'a pantry where everything is piled up and everything . . . is there, but no one can find anything useful'. We see here a deep ambivalence in which mutually exclusive ideas peacefully coexist in a single person's mind. Which idea prevails depends on circumstances. It's not hard to imagine that if Napoleon had won the war, the Little Russian nobility would have been ready to serve him just as they had served the Russian tsar.

However, there was one imaginary bar that the Little Russian nobility could not jump over – the old concept of the nation. According to this concept, the nation consisted of a single class: the nobility. Most of the Ukrainian nobility did not pursue careers at the imperial court, remaining instead on their family estates. Their numbers were small (25–30,000 in 1790), their estates were small and they could barely make ends meet. With the abolition of serfdom in 1861, they lost the economic basis for their existence altogether. One alternative was the civil service. However, the share of Little Russians in the state apparatus of the Little Russian provinces was steadily falling: from 50 per cent in 1800 to 10–15 per cent in 1914. This was not due to discrimination; in fact, there was never any discrimination against Little Russians. But the governors sent from the centre did not come alone. Instead, they would bring a whole host of employees and relatives whom they would give government positions, thus pushing locals out of the civil service.

The clan system of the Russian Empire could provoke feelings of nationalism in the Little Russian nobility – nationalism often begins from the slogan: 'Outsiders shall not rule us!' But as long as their understanding of the 'nation' was limited to their own class, they had no source of allies. The only option available was to invoke their historical rights and demand that the Russian government restore them. In fact, the 'History of the Rus', the most revealing example of the political thought of those supporting Ukrainian autonomy, was written with those motives in mind. The Little Russian nobility would surely have taken advantage of the collapse of the Russian Empire, but they didn't have the strength, need or desire to destroy the empire themselves. They could work for the benefit of their small homeland, mourn its glorious past and resent the new order, but they were certain that their Cossack nation was going to the grave with them. They were convinced that no radical political changes could be expected in the world in general or in their corner of it.

Such sentiments were not uniquely Ukrainian. After the defeat of the 1863 uprising, the Polish nobility felt the same. They gave up the struggle. In relation to the Russian authorities, the Polish nobility professed a 'sober pragmatic attitude to life'. They wouldn't lick the hand clenched into a fist, but nor would they bite the hand extended in solidarity. An independent Poland no longer existed on the horizon of their ambitions and fighting for it was equated to tilting at windmills.

One reason for this situation was the disappearance of the Polish question from the concerns of European politics. After Prussia's victory in the war with France in 1870–71 and the formation of the German Empire, the German question took centre stage in European geopolitics. And the Ukrainian question disappeared along with the Polish one. It became an internal issue for both empires. It required a great deal of imagination to believe that Ukraine had not only a past but also a future.

Literary Ukraine

Poets have always been granted the freedom to fantasise. Of course, this poetic licence also led people to view them condescendingly, without particular confidence. Then in the nineteenth century, the status of the poet changes radically. He is now elevated to almost celestial heights in the public imagination. Poets come to occupy the place that had once belonged to the Christian saints. They become the voice of the nation and the heralds of its future – national poets become national prophets. And just as for saints, the poet's path to acclaim lay through martyrdom. To become national poets, they had to suffer for their ideals, be arrested, imprisoned, exiled and then die tragically, often in their youth. The emotional turmoil they experienced during their torment revealed truths inaccessible to others. God Himself spoke in the voice of national poets and therefore they could foresee the future.

Anyone who has studied the history of Central and Eastern European literature will recognise the names of the Germans Johann Wolfgang Goethe and Friedrich Schiller, the Russian Alexander Pushkin and the Hungarian Sándor Petőfi. There are also three Poles in this pantheon of national poets: Adam Mickiewicz, Juliusz Słowacki and Zygmunt Krasiński.

In Ukraine, the creator of the new Ukraine was Taras Shevchenko. His lowly birth distinguishes him from the other national poets. Shevchenko was born a serf, but eventually was able to purchase his freedom thanks to the efforts of Great and Little Russian patrons of his painting and with the participation of the imperial family itself (1838). His manumission took place in St Petersburg, where he was a talented but unfree young artist. In 1840, his collection of poems *Kobzar* was published, at which point his poetic talent came to overshadow his skill as a painter. Shevchenko spent the years 1845–47 in Ukraine. His best poems were written during this period, the ones that cemented his status as a national prophet. In Kyiv, he joined the circle of young people who created the Cyril and Methodius Brotherhood. It is not entirely clear whether he belonged to the Brotherhood or whether there was actually any formal membership in the Brotherhood at all. In any case, in 1847 several of the 'brothers' were arrested following a denunciation and he was arrested with them. Moreover, he suffered the most severe punishment: he was sent to serve as a private in the army without the right to draw or write. Shevchenko served ten years in exile and returned to St Petersburg in poor health, where he died in 1861.

This is certainly a dramatic story that perfectly embodies the canonical biography of a national poet. To achieve the status of prophet one must endure a difficult fate filled with trials and suffering. However, to understand the Shevchenko phenomenon, we must take the broader context into account. We can think of the emergence of Shevchenko and the associated myth of Ukraine as a complex chess problem. The first move is the French Revolution of 1789–93. It introduced a new model of the nation. The French revolutionaries struck at all three pillars of the old regime: the monarch (executed by guillotine), the Church (separated from the state and deprived of property) and the nobility (lost their privileges and often their lives). The third estate, the commoners, took over. Before the revolution, they were 'nothing'; afterwards they were 'everything'. Accordingly, the concept of 'nation' was no longer limited to the nobility but included all citizens.

Napoleon carried this revolutionary concept of the nation across Europe on the bayonets of his army. Wherever Napoleon set foot, a new political and intellectual climate was created. After his defeat, the European monarchs formed the Holy Alliance (1815) to stop the spread of the revolutionary spirit. But they weren't entirely successful. By the 1820s, two new waves of revolutions swept through the Mediterranean (Spain, Naples, Greece) and South America (all of Spain's American colonies won their independence within a short period of time). France remained the main centre of the revolutionary virus. As Metternich said, 'when France sneezes, the whole of Europe catches a cold'. A new revolution began in Paris in July 1830. It was followed by revolutionary uprisings in Belgium, Italy and Switzerland and the Polish armed uprising began in the Russian Empire.

The Polish rebellion undermined the old model of imperial identity. Until then, loyalty to the person of the tsar was enough to make you a loyal subject of the Russian Empire. Ethnic or religious identities weren't especially significant. After the Polish revolt, loyalty was not enough; one also had to have the 'right' faith and the 'right' nationality, i.e., you needed to be 'Russian'.

The Russian Minister of Education, Sergei Uvarov, proposed a new formula for identity: 'Orthodoxy, Autocracy, Nationality'. Uvarov's triad was counterposed to the slogan of the French Revolution: 'Liberty, Equality, Fraternity'. Uvarov was inspired by the works of the French counterrevolutionaries and German conservative romantics. According to Uvarov's logic, in order to fend off European nationalism, the Russian Empire would have to strategically adopt some of its language and logic without allowing them to threaten the empire itself. Hence, the appearance of 'nationality' in Uvarov's triad.

There was one major problem with this model: where would they get so many Russians when the Orthodox were actually a minority among the elite? Uvarov's answer was simple: if the necessary elite does not exist, it must be created. The universities would become factories for the production of a Russian elite. Since most university professors were not actually of Russian ethnicity, in order to ensure the Russianness of the universities, Uvarov would promote the most capable young Russians to leadership positions.

According to the court in St Petersburg, Little Russians were considered Russians and the southwestern region of the empire (the Ukrainian lands) became the main battlefield against Polish nationalism. The Kremenchuk Lyceum had been the main centre of education for the local Polish elite. Following the Polish uprising, all of its holdings, including the library, were taken to Kyiv, where they formed the foundations for Kyiv University, which opened in 1834. On the direct order of Uvarov, thirty-year-old Mykhailo Maksymovych (1804–73), a young botany professor and collector of Ukrainian folklore, became the first rector of Kyiv University. Another of Uvarov's protégés was Izmail Sreznevsky (1812–80), a professor at Kharkiv University and another collector of Ukrainian folklore. Two prominent figures of the Cyril and Methodius Brotherhood, Mykhailo Kostomarov (1817–85) and Panteleïmon Kulish, became pupils of Maksymovych and Sreznevsky. Taras Shevchenko, the third and most important member of the 'Ukrainian Trio' also arrived in Kyiv as a result of Uvarov's reforms. He was hired as an artist at the Kyiv Archeographic Commission, which was tasked with collecting and publishing historical documents to prove the 'Russianness' of the southwestern region.

Thus it was thanks to Uvarov that the fathers of Ukrainian nationalism, Shevchenko, Kostomarov and Kulish, found themselves in the same place at the same time. Caught 'between a Russian hammer and the Polish anvil,' they developed their own national programme. They benefited from Russian hard power (imperial resources) but imitated Polish soft power (intellectual models). Suffice it to say that the programmatic work of the Cyril and Methodius Society, *The Books of the Genesis of the Ukrainian People*, was directly inspired by Adam Mickiewicz's *Books of the Polish Nation and Polish Pilgrimage* (Paris, 1832).

A distinct 'Ukrainian school' emerged in Polish literature at this time. Its main theme was admiration for Ukraine and its heroic past and one of its central figures was the Cossack Musii Wernyhora, the 'spiritual hetman of Ukraine'. According to the legend, Wernyhora killed his own mother and brother and then, in a state of profound shock and repentance, he began to have prophetic visions. He became something of a Cossack Nostradamus. In apocalyptic visions before his death, Wernyhora allegedly predicted the partition of Poland, the French Revolution, Napoleon's military campaigns and subsequent defeat (including exile to an island) and most importantly, the restoration of Poland and great changes in Ukraine that would bring it happiness. Wernyhora became a symbol of Polish-Ukrainian unity against Russia as the Polish revolutionaries envisioned it.

Wernyhora's prophecies were fictitious, but they were fictitious in the spirit of European romanticism. The founder of Romanticism, Johann Herder, prophesied that 'Ukraine will become a new Greece: the beautiful sky of this people, their cheerful disposition, their musicality and their fertile land ... one day they will awaken and its many wild peoples will merge to form a cultured nation, just as Greece once did and its borders will reach to the Black Sea and from thence to the entire world'.

Romanticism created a fashion for everything Ukrainian. We could also note the popularity of Mazepa's image among European romantics. While in Russia his name was cursed, in the works of Byron, Victor Hugo and other European romantics he was cast as a romantic hero. For them, the main event in Mazepa's life was not his 'betrayal' of the Russian tsar Peter I, but another, entirely invented episode. It concerns the young Mazepa's stay at the Polish court. One of the nobles allegedly discovered his wife's affair with Mazepa and took revenge by tying him to a horse and releasing him into the steppe to certain death. However, the horse brought Mazepa to the Cossack Sich, where he became hetman and a fighter for the freedom of his people. The parallel with the image of Wernyhora is obvious here: the spiritual transformation of a hero under the influence of sin and personal tragedy was a favourite Romantic trope.

The influence of European Romanticism also played a decisive role in the life of Nikolai Gogol, another descendant of Cossacks, who moved to St Petersburg in the hopes of making a career for himself. St Petersburg was a cosmopolitan metropolis and the most European city in Russia. Gogol's earliest works were written in the style of Goethe and his debut was not a success. However, there was a fashion for all things Ukrainian in the Russian capital at the time. In his next work, *Evenings on a Farm Near Dikanka*,

Gogol depicted life on an imagined Ukrainian farmstead with affectionate humour (and a touch of the macabre). This collection brought him the fame he craved.

After he had achieved that fame, Gogol switched to Russian subjects. Literary critics note a fundamental difference between his Little Russian and Great Russian figures. The former are natural and genuine, rosy-cheeked, while the latter are inferior and damaged, their identities replaced by external features (*The Nose*, *The Overcoat*, *Dead Souls*). One of Gogol's most famous images is striking in its implicit anti-Russianism. In *Dead Souls*, he describes Russia as the 'Russian troika', the three-horse carriage that sweeps across the world, 'flying past everything that exists on earth, as the other nations look on askance, then step aside and yield the road'. But the person riding in that three-horse carriage is none other than Chichikov, an opportunist and a rogue!

It's no surprise that Gogol was accused of being anti-Russian. Russian philosopher Vasily Rozanov compared Gogol's influence to the Mongol yoke. And in 1918, having witnessed the death of the Russian Empire, Rozanov wrote: 'You've beat me, you awful khokhol.'

Although Gogol's biography includes many actions and statements that suggest support for Ukraine, he can hardly be moulded into a Ukrainian nationalist. He himself wrote, 'I don't know whether I have the soul of a khokhol or a Russian. I only know that I would never give preference to a Little Russian over a Russian, or a Russian over a Little Russian.'

He believed that the differences between the two peoples showed that they could each complete the other and together 'constitute something perfect in humanity'.

Gogol appears to have suffered from the same mental chaos as the characters depicted in Leskov. His example shows the limited extent to which the Little Russian intelligentsia could have constructed their identity if Little Russia had remained only an internal issue of the Russian Empire.

In contrast, Shevchenko had no such duality. Before he ever saw the imperial capital, he spent two years in Vilnius, one of the largest centres of Polish culture, just as the Polish uprising was taking place there. Later in St Petersburg, Shevchenko spent his time with the 'Little Russian colony' which was his university. His main 'nationalist' poems were written later, in Ukraine, during his work as a member of the Archeographic Commission, when he and the other members were collecting and documenting evidence of the glorious Cossack past. The synthesis of these three elements – the folk memory of the Cossacks, the Polish influence and the environment of educated Little Russians in the imperial capital – helped Shevchenko to forge a new Ukrainian identity. In short, Shevchenko replaced the old Cossack model of the nation as consisting of members of a single estate with a new vision based on the French model. To the monarchs, he sounds just like a Jacobin: 'Ready the guillotines/For those tsars, the executioners of men.' For him, Peter I and Catherine II are the enemies of the Ukrainian people: 'He the first, who crucified/Our Ukraine,/And she the second, who finished off/The poor orphaned widow'. In Shevchenko's view here, the Cossack officers are no more than 'slaves, lackeys, Moscow dirt, Warsaw scum'. His hero is the Ukrainian common people: 'I will raise up/Those silent downtrodden slaves/I will set my word/To protect them.' Shevchenko united Ukraine's Cossack past with its current present of serfdom seen as a temporary state and he predicted a great future for it. One of his most famous works is entitled: 'My friendly message to my fellow countrymen, both in Ukraine and not in Ukraine, dead, living and not yet born.' This concept is powerfully reminiscent of Edmund Burke's formulation of the nation as a spiritual connection between generations. It is unlikely that Shevchenko ever read Burke. Rather, they both drew from the same source: the new European Zeitgeist.

The phenomenon of Shevchenko cannot be explained by rational arguments. There is always something that escapes our explanations. That 'something' is the transcendental dimension of his poetry. As Kostomarov said, 'Shevchenko's muse ripped the veil from our national life. It was horrifying, fascinating, painful and tempting to look.' We can suppose that this dimension arose from the Bible, which, along with the 'History of the Rus', became the main source of his inspiration. But this hypothesis is rational in nature and so certainly insufficient to explain the phenomenon of Shevchenko.

We can simply acknowledge the fact that Shevchenko's biography and works show that the Ukrainian idea emerged out of the export of Western ideologies to Eastern Europe. The Western aspect of Ukrainian identity was recognised even by the opponents of the Ukrainian movement, who generally tried to portray it as uninteresting and provincial. According to one of them, 'Ukrainianism is a consequence of a new tendency in Europe's spiritual life that began in the late eighteenth century, gradually spreading from West to East. When these new ideas reached Russia, they created a complete transformation in the views of the educated classes of the Russian people. In the field of science, they created empiricism; in the field of fiction – romanticism; in the field of art – realism; in political and social terms, it gave rise to the ideas of individual freedom and the equality of all people.'

Among all the 'isms' that influenced the ideology of the Ukrainian national movement, socialism played a significant role. The leaders of the Kyiv 'Hromada' were said to carry Shevchenko's *Kobzar* in one pocket and Marx's *Das Kapital* in the other. The chief theoretician of the Ukrainian movement, Mykhailo Drahomanov, invented a new formula for Ukrainian identity: since Ukrainian peasants formed the majority on Ukrainian lands, then, under local conditions, every Ukrainian should be a socialist and every socialist a Ukrainian. His pupil Ivan Franko embodied this formula: he became both a Ukrainian and a socialist. And although he was born into a semi-gentry family, after his conversion to socialism he even took to calling himself a peasant son. By becoming a peasant, Franko seemed to echo the destiny of Shevchenko, the peasant poet. This move strengthened the image of Ukraine as a 'peasant nation': two of its leading poets were peasants.

Another thing that made Franko attractive to young people was his personal fate. Like Shevchenko, he didn't just preach new ideas; he also suffered for them. He was arrested three times and almost died twice during these detentions. For a long time he barely scratched out a living by the labour of his pen.

While Franko's generation was simply interested in Marxism, the younger generation of the Ukrainian intelligentsia became dedicated Marxists. Between the years 1870 to 1917, Marx and Engels' *Communist Manifesto* was translated into Ukrainian no fewer than five times. One of the translations is attributed to Lesia Ukrainka (1871–1913), Drahomanov's niece and a Ukrainian poet who is considered on a par with Shevchenko and Franko.

The popularity of Marxism in Eastern Europe is explained by the fact that here it was not so much a theory of the class struggle between workers and the bourgeoisie as a theory of modernisation. Marxists even surpassed poets in their modernising utopias. In the Ukrainian case, Marxism is associated with that most utopian of ideas for the time: an independent Ukrainian state. In his 1895 work *Ukraina Irredenta*, the Galician 'young radical' (Marxist) Julian Baczyński presented Ukrainian independence as an essential precondition for the victory of the world proletarian revolution!

Marxism was never the central ideology in the Ukrainian movement. It did, however, play the role of an important intellectual enzyme. By the start of the twentieth century, the demand for Ukraine's political independence, put forward by

Ukrainian Marxists, had been adopted by all the major Galician-Ukrainian parties.

Other radical changes in Galicia followed. In 1901 Andrei Sheptytsky became the head of the Greek Catholic Church. Under his leadership, the Church finally came to support pro-Ukrainian positions. Another major change concerned the hierarchy of national enemies. Previously, the Poles had been considered the main enemy, while the Russians were seen as natural allies. At the end of the nineteenth century, Russia became the main enemy, although the conflict with Polish nationalism did not stop, but rather escalated and turned violent. In 1908, the Ukrainian Social Democrat Myroslav Sichynsky shot and killed the viceroy of Galicia, the Polish Count Andrzej Potocki. Later, Polish-Ukrainian clashes broke out at Lviv University, killing a Ukrainian student, Adam Kotsko. Nonetheless, Poland 'fell' to second place in the list of adversaries in the drive for Ukrainian independence.

This radical anti-Russian turn was in keeping with the spirit of Shevchenko's poetry, but Little Russians living under the tsar did not accept it. Most of them did not envision a future separate from Russia and they were annoyed by the 'Ukraine of Galician manufacture'. However, this Galician Ukraine was actually largely a product of the 'Russian Ukrainians', first and foremost Mykhailo Drahomanov, who also hadn't previously imagined Ukraine independent of Russia. Sometimes an idea will change beyond recognition when transferred to new soil.

At the turn of the twentieth century, the Ukrainian movement united the national question and socioeconomic issues, attracting more and more educated young people to its side. But every victory has its price. In the case of the Ukrainian movement, the price was the powerful linkage of Ukrainian literature with politics and politics with literature. In the last decades of the long nineteenth century, literary images and metaphors sometimes replaced sober political analysis. Not only did Ukrainian politics suffer from this fact, so did Ukrainian literature. Many literary works read like disguised political programmes. Attempts by young writers in the late 1890s and early 1900s to separate literature from politics and create 'art for art's sake' were unsuccessful: the older Ukrainian activists 'crushed' them.

In the nineteenth century, Ukrainian literature produced a remarkable trio: Taras Shevchenko, Ivan Franko and Lesia Ukrainka. Their biographies were equal to their poetry, each of them a model of uncompromising sacrifice and devotion to a great cause. And yet they were less influential than the Russian trio of Dostoevsky, Chekhov and Tolstoy. The difference, I propose, was not in the level of raw talent. The difference lay primarily in the circumstances in which Ukrainian and Russian literature functioned. The readership of Ukrainian authors was many times smaller than that of Russian authors, they were paid meagre royalties and in order to survive, they had to do dozens of things, which inevitably affected the quality of their works. Most of them could not afford the luxury of focusing purely on literature.

The status of Ukrainian literature could not equal that of Russian literature, which gained world renown in the nineteenth century. Hence the arrogance and disdain of the educated Russian public. For many Russians, putting Shevchenko next to Pushkin is tantamount to sacrilege. Nobel laureate Joseph Brodsky wrote in 1991, when Ukraine gained its independence:

> *Go with God, you eagles, Cossacks, hetmans, ne'er do wells!*
> *You can be sure, you mighty oxen, that when it comes*
> *your time to die,*
> *And you lie there grasping the edge of the bed, you'll*
> *be gasping*
> *Lines from Alexander [Pushkin] and not Taras' lies.*

And so, you can see that in our part of the world, the struggle between national literatures never ended.

Urbanisation and Industrialisation

In 1857, Shevchenko was returning from exile on a steamship. In his diary, he described steam power as 'a young child who is growing not by the day, but by the hour, who will soon devour all the whips and crowns and thrones, and will just snack on diplomats and landowners, playing with them like a schoolboy with a lollipop'.

Shevchenko meant that the Industrial Revolution would do what politics had failed to deliver – to destroy the old regime. While the revolution in politics merely proclaimed the contours of a 'brave new world', the Industrial Revolution created this new world 'here and now', dragging political changes in its wake.

Great Britain was the birthplace of the Industrial Revolution. There, the revolution began in the 1770s and '80s and by the end of the 1840s, the UK had become the world's industrial workshop. From the British Isles, the Industrial Revolution gradually spread across the European continent. In the 1850s, it reached the Atlantic coast of Europe, in the 1860s it spread to German and French lands and in the 1870s and '80s it reached Southern, Northern and Eastern Europe.

Ukrainian lands were caught up in the last wave of industrialisation. This lateness was not entirely negative; it offered certain advantages. First, it freed 'delayed' countries from the need to develop new technologies – they could adopt ready-made technological innovations. Second, 'backward' countries in the early stages of industrialisation can achieve impressive results: the lower the starting point, the more dizzying the leap appears.

The Ukrainian provinces of the Russian Empire demonstrated these benefits of lag. Although almost all industrial technology was imported from Europe between 1870 and 1914, the local economy was one of the most dynamic in Europe and at the forefront of modernisation. Ekaterinoslav and Hughesovka (present-day Dnipro and Donetsk) became centres of iron production and coal mining, respectively; Kharkiv, Kyiv, Kherson and Odesa – of metalworking and machine-building industries; and Right-Bank Ukraine – of sugar production. Along with industrial centres in Moscow, Lodz and oil basins in Baku and Grozny, the Ukrainian provinces became the economic base of the Russian Empire in its competition for great power status.

This advantage of 'backwardness' was not felt in the Austro-Hungarian regions of the Ukrainian lands. In the Habsburg Empire, industry was concentrated in the centre. The peripheries of Galicia, Bukovyna and Transcarpathia remained poor agrarian provinces. The Boryslav-Drohobych oil basin in Galicia was the only exception. So, if we want to discuss Ukraine in the context of colonised status, this characterisation is more suitable for describing the state of affairs in the Austro-Hungarian Empire. On the other side of the Austrian-Russian border, the Ukrainian lands were not a colony, but an integral part of the political and economic life of the Russian Empire.

One thing that was consistent across both parts of the Ukrainian lands was the fact that local industry was more concentrated on the extraction and primary processing of raw materials than on complex manufacturing. The Ukrainian provinces supplied about 75 per cent of the coal and metal and 80 per cent of the sugar in the Russian Empire and the Boryslav oil fields made Austria-Hungary the third largest producer of oil in the world after the United States and the Russian Empire.

Another feature of industrialisation in the Ukrainian lands was that it took place outside the large cities. In Great Britain, the historical birthplace of the Industrial Revolution, industrialisation went hand in hand with urbanisation. By the middle of the nineteenth century, most of the English lived in cities rather than the countryside. Outside of Britain, the link between industrialisation and urbanisation was weaker. In the Ukrainian lands, cities served as administrative and commercial centres, not industrial ones. It is noteworthy that both Boryslav and Hughesovka were still officially classified as villages up to 1914. Conversely, neither Kyiv, Lviv, Odesa, nor Kharkiv – four of the five largest cities on the Ukrainian lands – could be called industrial cities. The industrial sector was not the mainstay of the economy for any of them and industrial workers made up no more than 10 per cent of the population in each.

Ekaterinoslav was the sole exception among the large cities. At the turn of the twentieth century, it looked much like industrial Moscow, St Petersburg, Łódź, Manchester, or Berlin. Among smaller cities, the exceptions were Luhansk (originally built around a foundry and cannon factory) and Mykolaiv, a shipbuilding centre.

The fact that urbanisation in the Ukrainian provinces was only weakly linked to industrialisation does not suggest that urbanisation itself was weak. On the contrary, the Ukrainian lands did experience a true urban revolution in the nineteenth century. But rather than being connected to industrialisation, it resulted from colonisation of the Wild Field. A clear tendency can be observed in Europe: most of its large cities were founded before 1300. In modern Ukrainian lands, that rule applies only to 'old' Ukraine. Otherwise, most cities emerged much later, after the Russian annexation of the Black Sea steppe.

The urbanisation revolution on these lands dramatically changed the hierarchy between cities in Ukraine. Until the 1840s, Lviv was the largest city of Ukraine, but newly founded Odesa surpassed it mid-century. It wasn't until just before the First World War, after a gap of almost seven hundred years, that Kyiv regained its position as the largest city. Ever since that time, there has been a significant difference in urbanisation levels between 'old' Ukraine and 'new' Ukraine. Old Ukraine is less urbanised than new Ukraine.

If we want to talk about quality rather than quantity, the situation looks rather different. A modern city is not only characterised by size. Modernity is determined primarily by the presence of a modern urban infrastructure, paved streets, sewage systems, public transportation, parks, coffee shops, etc – and the degree to which these conveniences are accessible to the population. In the nineteenth century, only one city on the Ukrainian lands met these criteria: Lviv. In the early 1880s, Lviv outpaced not only Kyiv, Odesa and Kharkiv, but even Moscow in terms of the number of periodicals per capita. Lviv basked in its renown as the 'Vienna of the East' and provided a comfortable life for its residents. Paradoxically, this comfort was primarily due to the absence of large factories in the city. This 'saved' the city from excessive demographic pressure (primarily from the poor) on the city's infrastructure. Lviv was a bureaucratic city. It represented a particular type of modernisation – modernisation through bureaucratisation – where the main agents of change were not entrepreneurs or financiers, but bureaucrats. The Austrian officials who were exiled from the centre of the empire to this backward periphery compensated by creating a city with a high quality of life.

These amenities were much less common in other cities. All the way up to 1914, only 60 per cent of Kyiv's residents had access to running water and city schools had to close from time to time due to a lack of water. The first thing a tourist would notice when arriving in Odesa or the resort towns of the Black Sea region in the summer was the stench of untreated sewage. With the exception of Ekaterinoslav, the industrial cities looked extremely monotonous. The names of the suburbs – Nakhalivka (Boorsville), Sobachivka (Dogville), etc. – speak for themselves.

When it rained in Boryslav or Hughesovka, the roads would turn into impassable swamps where horses could drown along with their wagons. The pigs, cows, horses and stray dogs roaming the streets made the towns look more like farms.

Another striking feature of Ukrainian urbanisation was the degree to which it did not involve Ukrainians. As historian Patricia Herlihy put it, the cities were in Ukraine, but they were not Ukrainian. Throughout Europe, industrialisation created a need for mass labour and the main source of that labour was the countryside. The massive influx of rural populations transformed Prague from a German city into a Czech city, Tallinn into an Estonian city and Riga into a Latvian city. This did not happen on Ukrainian lands. Ukrainian peasants largely avoided working in factories, plants and mines. Peasants from neighbouring Russian provinces made up most of the industrial labour force in the 'new' Ukraine. As a result, ethnic differences between the countryside and the city became more pronounced rather than disappearing. The only major city with a Ukrainian majority was Poltava, but this is simply the exception that confirms the rule.

The urban-rural and industrial-agricultural axes are two of the main axes of modernity. In the case of Ukrainians, they coincided and not always in a beneficial way. According to historian Orest Subtelny, an unfortunate dichotomy had emerged on Ukrainian lands by the start of the First World War: whatever was considered modern, was not Ukrainian; whatever was Ukrainian, was not modern.

Dichotomies rarely provide an adequate reflection of reality, because real life is better characterised by various shades of grey than simple black and white. This is certainly true for the history of industrialisation in Ukraine. In 1911, the Russian Marxist political economist Peter Struve was convinced that in the Ukrainian lands 'capitalism speaks and will continue to speak Russian, not Little Russian'. The truth, however, was that in the Russian Empire, big capital was mostly not Russian, but foreign. That is why the largest entrepreneurs spoke German, English, French and, in the central provinces, Yiddish or Polish, but rarely Russian. The example of John Hughes, the founder of Hughesovka and the industrial Donbas, is typical. He was a Welshman by birth and never learned to speak Russian. Instead of using the Cyrillic alphabet, he signed his name with the numerals, '103', connecting the first and second with a slash, which was supposed to read as the Cyrillic letters for Ю3, aka Hughes.

A similar degree of deciphering is required to understand the participation of Ukrainians in industrialisation. They appear infrequently as workers, more often as entrepreneurs. Some people were not ethnic Ukrainians by birth, but adopted a Ukrainian perspective. Many Ukrainian cultural and scientific initiatives were supported by entrepreneurs. In particular, the noted industrialist and philanthropist Platon Symyrenko provided the loan for the publication of *Kobzar* in 1860. His brother Vasyl was one of the founders of the Shevchenko Scientific Society in Lviv.

As for the dichotomy of Ukrainian villages vs Russian cities, that dividing line was less solid outside southern Ukraine. On the Left Bank, in the lands of the former Cossack Ukraine, Ukrainians made up the largest group of the urban population, while on the Right Bank Jews were the largest group. Most Jews lived in small towns. Small towns were also one of the main bases of the Ukrainian movement: many of its leaders came from medium-sized towns with mixed features of cities and villages. In general, in the portion of the Ukrainian lands under the Russian Empire, the urban population was divided into three more or less equal groups – Ukrainians, Russians and Jews – none of which dominated.

But even the conclusion about three equal groups requires a significant correction. It assumes that these groups had a national identity, which was not the case. National identities have to take root. Their roots are in urban public spaces: newspapers, magazines and coffee shops, where intense discussions and the exchange of ideas take place. For these identities to take root, it is also important that they be free, that they grow from below, rather than being planted from above. These conditions were present in Austrian Galicia, where conceptions of nationality had grown deep roots in the cities by the turn of the twentieth centuries.

In contrast, in the Russian-controlled cities, identities remained amorphous and unstable. Odesa was a Russian-speaking city, but not a Russian city. Russian surnames coexisted with Polish, Greek, Armenian, German and, most of all, Jewish surnames. The Odesan language was comprehensible, but only Odesans could speak it. Historian Volodymyr Antonovych joked that Kyivans spoke neither Great Russian nor Little Russian, but a *little* Russian. Kyiv looked Russian, but linguistically and culturally it was not anything like Moscow, a fact which Muscovites would notice immediately upon arriving. In 1916, a critic from Petrograd wrote that Kharkiv was an 'indeterminate' city because it had borrowed its entire costume from someone else.

Most large cities on the Ukrainian lands resembled New York more than Prague or Tallinn: different ethnic and religious groups walked the same streets but spoke different languages and sometimes even lived in separate neighbourhoods. The social structure of such cities resembled that of medieval towns, where each ethnic group occupied a specific niche: Ukrainians were domestic servants and lived on the outskirts; Russians were officers, engineers and workers; the British, Belgians and French were entrepreneurs or the most skilled workers who lived in the most expensive neighbourhoods; Poles were landowners who spent winters in the city and so on.

The most socially diverse group were the Jews. The range of their social roles and occupations was wide: from traditional Jews who firmly adhered to the Old Testament commandments to representatives of the most modern professions – lawyers, doctors, professors and entrepreneurs. Jews modernised and penetrated all sectors of modern life, except for one: they had no access to political power. They weren't the only group for whom this was the case, but they were the most obvious. Modernisation created entire groups of people with high expectations and ambitions which eventually came up against the glass ceiling of the old regime. All of which created an explosive situation: the pot was boiling and the authorities were doing all they could to keep the lid on.

In any case, Ukrainian cities under Russian control did not become a melting pot that melted different ethnic groups into a single nation – Russian or other. The same can be said of industry. Lenin argued that in southern Ukraine, 'Capitalism is replacing the ignorant, conservative, sedentary muzhik of the Great-Russian or Ukrainian backwoods with a mobile proletarian whose life circumstances break down all narrowly national biases, either Great-Russian or Ukrainian.'

These words were as far from the truth as Struve's prophecy. The workers of Ekaterinoslav and Hughesova were divided into three groups: skilled manufacturers, Jewish artisans and unskilled labourers. Each of these groups kept to themselves and looked down on the others. The unskilled labourers were 80 per cent 'peasant labourers'. They were hired to work in the mines during breaks from the agricultural seasons and were divided into communities according to native regions. Drunken fistfights between fellow countrymen were a standard worker's pastime on Sundays. If anything did unite the workers, it was anti-Semitism. Workers' demonstrations often took on the character of anti-Jewish pogroms. Workers in the southern provinces were the main perpetrators of the 1881 pogrom.

Historians of the nineteenth century are amazed by the

rapid and unprecedented nature of industrialisation but forget to consider the impact of these changes on the majority of the population. In the Ukrainian lands, you could go just a couple of kilometres from a large steel mill and find that the local households didn't possess even an atom of iron. Their inhabitants still lived in thatched-roofed houses, with dishes made of clay and doors and fittings hung from wooden hinges.

Until 1914, European modernity existed only in isolated islands and the example of the Ukrainian lands reflected this general trend. Of the six superpowers that entered the First World War – Austro-Hungary, Britain, Italy, Germany, Russia and France – only England was dominated by the industrial sector and only France was a republic. The industrial bourgeoisie and middle class didn't wield political power in any of these places and the major industrial centres were surrounded by an ocean of agriculture and traditional workshops.

Another characteristic of European modernity was the gap between economic and political modernisation. Political modernisation lagged behind economic development almost everywhere, but nowhere did it take on such tragic forms as in the Russian Empire. In the 1900s and 1910s, the annual rate of industrial development (8 to 16 per cent) was the highest in Europe. At the same time, until the first Russian Revolution of 1905–07, corporal punishment was standard and trade unions were banned.

The life of most industrial workers in the nineteenth century was difficult, marked by heavy, monotonous labour; long, gruelling work hours; earnings that barely ensured survival; and a lack of any insurance for accidents or pensions. In industrialised countries, the improvement of the workers' lot was the result of labour movements organised by trade unions, often under the leadership of social democratic parties. The labour movement in the West developed in an evolutionary way. In the Russian Empire, excluding a brief period of the 1905–07 revolution, trade unions either did not exist at all or existed illegally and the Russian Social Democratic Party was predominantly a party of the intelligentsia with little influence on workers. The labour movement here tended towards violence. It is not surprising that one of the local labour leaders, Lazar Kaganovich, later became one of the main organisers of the Ukrainian famine of 1932–33.

Industrialisation took different forms and achieved different results depending on local historical and cultural conditions. It originated in Britain under truly unique circumstances: the agricultural question had been resolved before industrialisation began, rule of law had been fully established and there was a large reservoir of cheap, non-enslaved labour. These circumstances did not exist anywhere else on the European continent. Max Weber doubted whether the German nation would be able to repeat the British success because it had not gone through the rigorous school of Protestant asceticism. He blamed everything he hated in his country and in himself on this historical difference. In the Russian Empire, these problems were even more acute than in Germany in Max Weber's time: most of the population still belonged to the peasantry, there was no rule of law or political rights and the bourgeoisie lacked political power. In these circumstances, the state took the lead in modernisation. After the collapse of the 'Great Reforms' in the early 1880s, the Russian government rejected the European model of constitutional reforms and proposed its own: reforming the economy without reforming politics.

Another element in the Western model was nations: without the nation, there is no modernisation. German economist Friedrich List put forward this concept, inspired by American and British successes. In Russia, Finance Minister Nikolai von Bunge, mentor of the last two Russian tsars, adopted List's ideas. He wrote: 'Hungary is Magyarising the Slavs, Germans and Romanians; Germany is Germanising the French in Lorraine, the Danes in Schleswig and the Poles in Poznan; the Poles are Polonising the Little Russians in Galicia; we must Russify our borderlands.'

One of Bunge's pupils was Sergei Witte, the architect of the pre-war reforms that helped the Russian economy develop at an impressive pace. The trouble was that these reforms came too late and there were no political foundations to support them. The Russian Empire had neither a large middle class nor a politically influential bourgeoisie and most importantly, there was no clearly defined Russian nation.

To a large extent, the model of authoritarian modernisation from the top failed, even from a military perspective: the Russian Empire fought four major wars during this period – the Crimean, Balkan, Japanese and the First World War – and lost three of them.

The pre-war economic success of the Russian Empire and the interwar success of the Stalinist regime still impress today's apologists for authoritarianism. They are mesmerised by the rapid pace of development and fail to notice that rapid development doesn't translate into sustainable development. After the fall of communism Andranik Migranyan proposed an authoritarian model of modernisation. According to his logic, an authoritarian government conducts economic reforms while restricting political freedoms; the reforms lead to the formation of a middle class that then becomes the basis of a stable democracy. This model was tested in Russia in the late 2000s, but the results were very limited. The example of Russia shows once again that those who undertake economic reforms without reforming politics will be left in the long run without either a competitive economy or a functional democracy.

A Sea of Peasants

Even if most peasants did not go to work in factories, plants and mines, modernisation was catching up with them in one way or another. It manifested itself most clearly in what is called the demographic transformation. Until the nineteenth century, demographic processes around the world fluctuated around a certain balance called the 'Malthusian trap': high mortality rates were offset by high birth rates. And vice versa, an increase in the birth rate led to an increase in mortality, because the availability of resources for sustaining life remained essentially unchanged. In the Ukrainian lands, women gave birth to an average of ten to twelve children, one-third of whom did not live to be five years old. Natural disasters sometimes forced peasants to leave their farms to look for additional means of subsistence. Accordingly, the formula for reproduction in traditional peasant society was based on three pillars: high mortality – high birth rate – occasional short-distance migrations.

This system broke down in the nineteenth century. First, the mortality rate decreased. One reason for this is assumed to be the spread of medicine and hygiene, including vaccinations and the habit of washing hands with soap. However, these changes had little effect on peasant households, so it is believed that the widespread adoption of potatoes as a core crop could explain the decrease in mortality. The potato was less vulnerable to weather fluctuations than grain crops and offered more calories and vitamins. Potatoes were also more filling and boosted immunity. Consequently, mortality rates fell, but the birth rate remained high for a long time due to inertia, which led to an increase in population. Only now, the 'extra mouths' were not doomed to die, because the Industrial Revolution created new resources: work in the cities and opportunities to develop previously inaccessible lands. The result was the emergence of a new type of migration: regular and over long distances. The new reproduction scheme also consisted of three pillars, but different from the traditional ones: low mortality – lower fertility – regular long-distance migration.

As with industrialisation, the demographic transformation began in Western Europe. In the last third of the nineteenth century, its wave swept through the Austro-Hungarian and Russian empires. Some of the highest population growth rates were observed among Jews and Ukrainians (both Austrian Rus and Russian Little Russians). In 1848, the Supreme Rus Council in Lviv claimed to speak for 15 million of the Rus. Censuses in the late 1890s showed that this number had doubled in fifty years to 30 million. One Ukrainian patriot wrote enthusiastically at the time: if this rate of growth continues, in a hundred years, in 1998, at the bicentennial of Ukrainian literature, one of the speakers in Lviv will say, 'We, the Austrian Rus, are part of a nation of 120 million!'

These words reveal how little Ukrainian patriots knew and understood their 'own' people. What the patriots in the city viewed as cause for celebration was actually a disaster for the countryside. The sharp increase in population meant that from half to two-thirds of peasant farms suffered from land hunger, in which households didn't have enough land to support the size of their growing families.

The situation was complicated by the manner in which serfdom was abolished. As the peasants ironically said, in abolition they gained their freedom but lost their shoes. The conditions of emancipation required large repayments by the peasants to their former lords. Repayment periods extended into decades: some of the payoffs were scheduled to last until the 1940s! This requirement to pay for their freedom sapped peasant households of needed resources. In addition, the peasants lost legal access to the forests and pastures without which their farms could not function.

The introduction of intensive farming methods such as new machinery and fertilisers, could have saved the day. These methods were implemented by colonising settlers (Jews and Germans in the southern steppe regions and Czechs in Volhynia) and those Ukrainian peasants who lived nearby could see firsthand the advantages of new farming methods. However, the other peasants were unaccustomed to taking risks. And even if they had decided to make changes, there was another problem: the lack of cheap loans to buy equipment.

Ukrainian patriots were interested in what language the peasants spoke; the peasants were primarily interested in the land they worked. There was a fundamental mismatch between the two. The difference between their ways of thinking can be seen in a study from the period of how local peasants perceived Shevchenko's poetry. The most popular poem was 'Kateryna', which told the story of a village girl seduced and abandoned by a Russian officer. It began with words that could be read as a national manifesto: 'Fall in love, dark-browed beauties/ But not with Muscovites,/For Muscovites aren't our people,/ And they'll do you harm.' The villagers listened with interest when Shevchenko was recited to them and were surprised that something like this could be written in their language. But they perceived the poem differently from Ukrainian intellectuals. Girls and young women cried over Kateryna's fate. They set the beginning of the poem to music and sang it as a sad folk song. Young men, on the other hand, mocked her and older people complained that the poem promoted debauchery: 'Why did he write such a thing? It's a bad book.' Even educated peasants couldn't understand many of the words: 'harem' was thought to be some kind of Turkish house, 'Byzantium' must be a Turkish ship and the island of Khortytsia in the Sich was mistaken for a Cossack ship. Borys Hrinchenko, who conducted this research in Central and Southern Ukraine, summarised: 'Shevchenko may be a great peasant poet, but in a peasant's house he is little understood.'

The peasant mentality was fundamentally different from that of educated people. It was deeply rooted in hard physical labour on the land. They believed that though the work was hard, it was pleasing to God and that those who suffered in this world would be rewarded in the next. The peasant world was imbued with religion, but it was a folk religion, more Manichaean than Orthodox. In the peasant imagination, the world was divided into two parts: God's and the devil's. On the side of God are 'we' the honest Christians who feed themselves and the whole world with hard work. On the side of the devil are 'they', the 'lords', who do not work and live as parasites on the peasant body. The peasants did not view intellectual work as work at all; in their eyes, it was a waste of time. That is why peasants considered not only landowners, but also teachers and even priests, to be 'masters'. In the peasants' minds, the 'masters' were trying to deceive, exploit and even destroy them in every possible way. And the 'lords' would succeed if not for the monarch. The monarch stands in defence of the peasants because God himself has anointed him to power. Faith in the 'good monarch' lay at the core of peasant consciousness right next to faith in God. From the peasants' point of view, the 'lords' could not be trusted. Especially when they dressed like peasants or spoke their language. That was just another trick to undermine their vigilance.

The peasants were the object of constant attention and a source of constant disappointment – practically a nightmare for those educated strata of society who placed special hopes on the peasants as allies in the struggle against the monarchy or the empire. As a social group, the peasants did not have a stable, distinct identity. One could even say that peasants did not exist as a separate social group. They were more like a projection of the hopes and aspirations of urban intellectuals. Socialists saw them as potential socialists and nationalists as potential nationalists. Meanwhile, most peasants were indifferent to both socialism and nationalism. Among all social groups, they were the last to join modern social formations. Even in France, the birthplace of the modern nation, local peasants mostly did not know that they were French; they were more connected to regional identities. The transformation of 'peasants into Frenchmen' began only at the end of the nineteenth century and was largely complete by the start of the First World War. It resulted from a deliberate process of nationalisation conducted by the state through two modern institutions: the army and the school.

In Central and Eastern Europe, neither the army nor the school could fulfil this role, as they had very limited contact with the peasants. Only 25 to 30 per cent of the male population passed through the Russian imperial army, while in France this figure was closer to 80 per cent. Only 15 per cent of the population of Western Europe was illiterate at the start of the twentieth century. That number was reversed in the Russian Empire: only 15 per cent of the population was literate! The situation in the Austro-Hungarian Empire was better with a 77 per cent literacy rate. The further east you went in the Austro-Hungarian Empire, the lower this figure became, dropping down to 50 per cent in the eastern ('Rus') part of Galicia.

The authorities were primarily responsible for this state of affairs. But the characteristic features of peasant life also played a role. Free child labour was an important condition for survival in the peasant economy. School only took children away from working, so the peasants were not interested in education. Even if peasant children did attend primary school intermittently, they had little cause to read after graduation. Without consistent practise, their school skills deteriorated. After completing her schooling, a peasant child became effectively illiterate within just a few years. In the Ukrainian provinces of the Russian Empire, this sad situation was compounded by another factor: the absence of Ukrainian-language schools. Children were taught in a foreign language and so forgot how to read and write even faster.

The local peasants had very little education and so had little sense of national or class identity. That does not mean that they had no sense of identity; peasant identity just depended on the situation. During times of stability, it was imperceptible, but grew significantly in times of crisis. The situation at the turn of the twentieth century can be described as one big, continuous crisis. The crises could not eliminate the essential features of the agricultural economy: the peasant's efforts to survive and avoid risk under any circumstances. However, the ways in which peasants responded to external threats changed.

One consequence of these changes was mass economic migration over long distances – to Siberia, the Far East, Brazil and North America. Finding themselves in a new, often sharply different environment in terms of language, ethnicity and religion, peasants inevitably had to define themselves. Moreover, labour migration undermined the foundations of the traditional way of life. The appearance of money in peasant households was one of the changes and the penetration of the money economy into the village awakened consumer desires. Young men and women who returned from working away from the land would buy themselves 'lordly' clothes. Ethnographic studies of those times recorded the appearance of new furniture in rural houses, including bookshelves. Paintings and portraits appeared on the walls beside the icons. Another change was that as young peasants returned home from paid work elsewhere, they demanded independence from parental control. They could refuse to contribute the money they earned to the general family budget, demand their share of the farm and make their own decisions on who to marry rather than allowing their parents to control the process.

The most radical change was the willingness of the more

prosperous peasants to invest in their children's education. It is said that by the time of the First World War, an average Ukrainian peasant from Galicia could afford to send one or even two sons to high school. This may be an exaggeration. Still, statistics of the time show a significant increase in the number of peasants attending high schools, seminaries and universities in both the Austro-Hungarian and Russian empires. They mostly chose professions with direct utility for the village: agronomist, veterinarian, or priest. During the last decades before the First World War, a new intelligentsia of peasant origin was emerging.

Due to these changes, the peasant world in the Ukrainian lands was becoming younger, full of social energy and ready to overcome any obstacles standing in its way. Many prominent political leaders of the twentieth century were products of this transformation. Volodymyr Vynnychenko (1880–1951), the prime minister of the first independent Ukrainian government, was the son of a labourer who graduated from high school and went on to Kyiv University, becoming a famous writer and one of the leaders of the Ukrainian Social Democrats. Andriy Melnyk (1890–1964), the leader of the Organisation of Ukrainian Nationalists, was the son of a peasant. Two General Secretaries of the Soviet Union, Nikita Khrushchev (1894–1971) and Leonid Brezhnev (1906–82) were the children of peasants. Khrushchev's parents had emigrated from the village to Donbas in search of work and Brezhnev's to Ekaterinoslav. There were many others as well. Some became nationalist leaders, some became communist leaders and still others, like Ivan Maistrenko (1899–1984), combined communism with nationalism.

The emergence of the first generation of rural intellectuals altered political configurations. The last decades before the war were a time of mass political action on the part of the peasants. When peasants went on strike or elected deputies to represent their interests in parliament, they turned to various parties for help and support. They most often chose the parties with representatives from the peasantry, because they spoke the same language and understood their demands.

Since a majority of the population worked the land, Ukraine's fate depended not so much on industrial or national questions as on the agricultural question. It had not been resolved in either the Austro-Hungarian or Russian empires and it is impossible to say whether any satisfactory resolution of the problem was even possible. Nonetheless, the two empires took significantly different approaches to the issue. In Austria-Hungary, the peasants frequently utilised the legal system. They sued their lords for access to 'forests and pastures'. They took part in demonstrations and rallies organised by urban patriots and voted in elections for the candidates these patriots proposed. There was occasional violence, but legal practices and institutions helped to mitigate this threat, serving as lightning rods to divert the current.

There were almost no such lightning rods in the Russian Empire. There, we see the situation we saw earlier regarding issues of industrial development and national identity: increasing modernisation increased the threat of mass violence. It seems that the greatest skill of Russian autocracy was the production of discontent and radical opposition. On the eve of the First World War, there was widespread discontent in the Ukrainian provinces. Liberals were unhappy about the lack of political rights, nationalists resented oppression of their distinct identities, the industrial proletariat struggled against difficult living and working conditions, social democrats spoke on behalf of the workers, peasants demanded land and Jews were dissatisfied with the imperial government's inability or unwillingness to curb anti-Jewish violence.

They were all united by a common enemy. The big question, however, was whether they would be allies once that enemy disappeared.

We have seen that modernisation in the Ukrainian lands took

many forms during the long nineteenth century, which makes it difficult to conclude with a single, broad generalisation. The Ukrainian historical experience of this century serves as a good illustration of what sociologists and historians call 'multiple modernities'. In the Russian-controlled areas, there was significant economic modernisation but minimal political modernisation; in the Austrian part, the situation was reversed.

The same can be said of the process of creating the modern Ukrainian nation. It was contradictory, incomplete and the degree of success varied dramatically from one region to another. It had some success in literature, less in politics and virtually none in economics. It was more successful under Austrian rule than Russian; more in cities than in villages; and, among cities, more in those with universities and developed public spaces. However, if we imagine the history of the long Ukrainian century as a scale, then despite a certain amount of chaotic noise, the degree of 'Ukrainianness' increases the further we move towards the endpoint.

At the same time, measures of violence are increasing as well. When we evaluate the Ukrainian nineteenth century from the perspective of today, we can clearly see what this century passed on to the next: the embryo of the modern Ukrainian nation and the seeds of modern violence.

INTERLUDE A Brief History of the Ukrainian Borderland

Ivan Mazepa is credited with a song about a seagull. It begins with the words:

> *Oh the poor seagull, the poor lost soul,*
> *Who brought her chicks to the busy road.*

The song describes chumaks, the travelling merchants of early modern Ukraine, who were travelling along the road and took away the seagull's children. The seagull wants her children back, but the chumaks have eaten them and reply that 'the children made good porridge'.

Some people say the image of the seagull here is that of a despairing mother whose children were taken by the Tatars. The 'History of Rus' says the song refers to 'suffering and oppressed Little Russia'.

The song about the seagull dates to the late seventeenth century. At that time, wars had been raging on Ukrainian lands for almost forty years (1648–86). As one Cossack chronicler wrote, blood 'flowed like a river and rare was the person who had not dipped their hands in that blood'.

Blood flowed like a river through the Ukrainian lands once more from 1914–45. According to one estimate, 50 per cent of the men in Ukraine and 25 per cent of the women, died of some form of violence between the beginning of the First World War and the end of the Second World War. According to other, more conservative estimates, the demographic losses on Ukrainian lands between 1914 and 1945 amounted to about 15 million people.

It is impossible to confirm these estimates: no one kept accurate records of casualties during the world wars and censuses taken between the wars are unreliable. There is, however, another indicator that allows us to imagine the scale of the catastrophe. This is life expectancy, one of the most reliable indicators of social welfare. It is like a thermometer that can be used to measure a society's temperature. A comparison of life expectancy in Ukraine and in 'old Europe' (the European Union before its eastward expansion in 2004) throughout the twentieth century can provide some indication. Ukrainian life expectancy was six to twelve years shorter than that of other Europeans. However, twice – in 1932–33 and in 1942–43 – this difference reached a catastrophic gap of thirty to forty years shorter.

No matter how immense and tragic the human losses in 1942 were, they are not entirely unexpected: a war was taking place on Ukrainian territory. However, there was no war in 1932–33. Those years were supposedly peacetime. Which could lead us to conclude that in the Ukrainian history of the short twentieth century, it makes little sense to separate the 'peaceful' interwar decades from the two world wars. The interwar period can only nominally be called peaceful. It was a 'war by other means'. Therefore, it makes sense to speak of the years 1914–45 as one great Thirty Years' War of the twentieth century.

Recent research shows that this concept does not apply only to Ukraine. With the exception of Britain, France and a few neutral countries, the end of the First World War in 1918 did not end mass violence on the European continent. Almost everywhere, the two decades between the wars were marked by revolutions, coups d'état, civil wars, terror and pogroms.

But even against this background of the pan-European catastrophe of 1914–45, Ukraine was exceptional. Just consider the number of times power changed hands during this period. Each change opened the doors to a new wave of terror. Between 1914 and 1945, the government in London did not fundamentally change (except for changes in the ruling party). In Berlin, Moscow, Petrograd and Paris the government changed two or three times each. In Warsaw and Prague five times. In Lviv – eight. In Kyiv, the government changed hands eleven times and at one railway station in Donbas up to twenty-seven times during the first half of 1919 alone.

The area that went through the greatest number of these changes was between Berlin and Moscow. These are the lands of present-day Belarus, the three Baltic states, Poland and Ukraine. Historian Timothy Snyder called this area 'the bloodlands' and Ukraine was at the very centre. In just fifteen years (1932–47), there were multiple genocides on Ukrainian lands. (I use genocide here in the broad sense proposed by the creator of the term, Raphael Lemkin: acts of mass violence that threatened the existence of entire groups either by physical destruction or by creating conditions under which they could not reproduce as a group with their own culture and identity.) Such genocidal acts included: the liquidation of the 'kulaks' as a class in 1930–31; the Holodomor of 1932–33; the 'Polish' and 'Greek' operations of the NKVD; the Holocaust against the Jews; the elimination of the Roma; the Nazi destruction of Soviet prisoners of war (1941–44); attacks against the Polish population by Ukrainian nationalists (the Volyn massacre of 1943); attacks on Ukrainians by the Polish underground. Also three mass deportations: of Crimean Tatars from Crimea (1944); of the Polish population from the western lands of the Ukrainian SSR and of the Ukrainian population from the southeastern lands of communist Poland. In addition, the list of mass violence includes state-sponsored violence that, although not genocidal, nevertheless resulted in large numbers of victims: Stalin's Great Terror of 1937–38, Soviet deportations of the population of Western Ukraine in 1939–41 and the terror the Soviet authorities wielded in the fight against the anti-communist nationalist underground in the same Western Ukrainian lands in 1944–50.

Such a list could be compiled for the other 'bloodlands' as well, but the Ukrainian list is always longer. For example, Belarus did not have a large, local nationalist underground and Lithuania and Poland did not experience the Holodomor.

Timothy Snyder begins his history of the bloodlands with the famine of 1932–33. The famine, however, was not the first act of mass violence. It was an echo of the Bolshevik-peasant war of 1918–20. This war, in turn, was an outgrowth of the 1917 revolution and the 1917 revolution was an outgrowth of the First World War. In other words, acts of mass violence did not occur by themselves – they were connected by a long chain of causal and other relationships.

How can we explain the intensity of violence on Ukrainian lands in 1914–45? We can hardly speak of specific *national* causes, although such explanations do exist. Ukrainians were predominantly a peasant people and peasants are sometimes credited with a special propensity for violence. In particular, the Ukrainian peasantry 'achieved' an almost mythical reputation as rabid anti-Semites. Indeed, Ukrainian folklore contains proverbs and sayings that sound like direct calls for the extermination of Jews and Poles. However, researchers of peasant society argue that, contrary to the idea that peasants are particularly cruel, it is difficult to provoke them to mass violence. For peasants to take up arms and start killing landlords or their neighbours, the Jews, Poles or German colonists, something extraordinary must happen, something that threatens their way of life and their very existence: war, epidemic, the murder of 'the good tsar'. None of these root causes were local.

The mass violence on Ukrainian lands in 1914–45 was largely initiated by external agents. This is clear from the chronology. Extreme violence began with the First World War and ended mainly with the conclusion of the Second, with its last waves lasting until Stalin's death in 1953. All of these events – the outbreak of the two world wars and the death of Stalin – began outside of Ukraine with causes only tangentially related to Ukrainian circumstances.

There were certainly local factors, though, that intensified the violence. One of the most significant factors is the topic of that seagull song: an 'unlucky' geography.

This becomes clear if you look at a physical map of Europe. You can immediately see a significant difference between the western and eastern parts of the European continent. Western Europe has lots of mountains. This is why the Western Front was largely limited to the French-Belgian-German border and Italy in both the First and Second World Wars. The largest battles were fought here because large-scale military operations were virtually impossible on the rest of the western part of the continent. Eastern Europe is completely different. It looks like one big plain stretching from the Carpathian Mountains to the Urals without any significant geographical barriers. Eastern Europe is like a 'generals' paradise'.

The only major barrier is the Pripet Marshes of Polesia on the modern Belarusian-Ukrainian border. Invaders were forced to either go around them on one side, leaving an uncontrolled rear, or divide the army into two wings, the northern and southern, posing a threat to the coordination of joint actions. The 'Pripet problem' is considered one of the causes of Hitler's defeat. He allegedly underestimated the significance of the problem and it slowed down the advance of German troops in the summer of 1941, hampering the planned blitzkrieg. The Pripet problem was, however, of a relative nature: swamps can't halt an advance if massive troop losses aren't a concern. For instance, for the Russian military during the Brusilov Offensive in 1916 or the Red Army in the Polish-Soviet War in 1920 and the Second World War in 1943–44.

The geographical factor is one reason (among others) that the largest battles of both world wars took place in these territories. Some of those battles, such as the aforementioned Brusilov Offensive or the Battle of Kyiv in the summer of 1941, were fought on Ukrainian lands. These battles were great, but not decisive; the decisive battles, such as the Western Front in 1918 or the Battle of Stalingrad in 1942–43, were fought outside of Ukraine. Ukraine, however, served as a wide corridor through which troops moved back and forth, each time leaving large-scale destruction and casualties among the local population.

Another long-term geographic factor is that almost half of Ukrainian ethnic territory is steppe. Historians compare Ukraine's Wild Field to the American frontier. American historian Frederick Jackson Turner theorised that the frontier played a critical role in the formation of American identity. Similarly, Ukrainian identity was born on the Ukrainian frontier and the Cossacks became its symbol. The difference was that the Ukrainian frontier emerged much earlier and lasted much longer. Its presence was a constant source of destabilisation. Kyiv became both symbol and victim of this geopolitical instability. Kyiv was one of the ten largest cities in Europe. But then it was destroyed twice: first by the Mongols in 1240 and then again in 1482 by the Crimean Tatars, after which Kyiv became just a small town at the edge of the steppe. It didn't regain its status as a major city until the late nineteenth century.

This is reminiscent of the fate of Rome, once the largest city in antiquity. After being destroyed by the barbarians, it took until the nineteenth century for it to reach its former size. This analogy shows how the disappearance of the capital, the seat of local power, creates a geopolitical vacuum. And like nature, geopolitics abhors a vacuum. Which can help us to understand why powers from outside were constantly 'pouring' into the empty space of these former capitals. As the interwar Ukrainian sociologist Olgerd Bochkovsky noted, all possible types of *Drangs* or drives of expansion can be classically studied in the history of Ukraine: *Drang nach Westen* during the time of the migration of peoples, *Drang nach Norden* – from ancient Greece, Byzantium and then Turkey; the Polish *Drang nach Osten* and the Muscovite *Drang nach Süden*. This list doesn't even include the incursions from the north by the Vikings and Swedes.

After the Russian Empire annexed Crimea in 1783, intensive agricultural colonisation of the steppes around the Black Sea began. Although the situation had changed, the significance of these territories as a large contact zone did not. The colonisation of the former Wild Field meant, in fact, a new great migration of peoples: Ukrainians, Russians and Jews from neighbouring lands; Bulgarians, Greeks, Germans and others from lands far and near. This led to another striking difference between Western and Eastern Europe. In Western Europe, the Migration Period generally ended in the Viking Age and by the nineteenth century, its ethnic map was largely established. This was not the case in Eastern Europe, where migration took place over a longer period and there were no clear ethnic borders between different groups.

It would be hard to find a region which has been subject to more competing priorities in the building of empires and nations. This is readily visible on the map of various national and imperial projects in Eastern Europe: there was not a single territory on Ukrainian lands that was not simultaneously claimed by at least two nationalisms and two empires.

The complexity of the situation is not exhausted there. In Eastern Europe, traditional ways of life were particularly persistent and ethnic and religious differences coincided with social ones, so that they became mutually reinforcing. Moses Rafes, one of the Kyivan leaders of the Bund (Jewish Socialist Party), wrote: 'In Ukraine, where the landowner was a Russian or a Pole and the banker and merchant were most often Jews and neither understand the common speech, for a Ukrainian, the expression "down with the lords" could mean "down with the Poles, Russians and Jews".'

Taken together, these geographical and historical facts made Ukraine a giant powder keg, similar to the Balkans or the Caucasus. In the early twentieth century, this powder keg was ready to explode. British geographer Halford John Mackinder, one of the fathers of geopolitics, summarised the situation in 1919: 'Who rules Eastern Europe commands the Heartland; who rules the Heartland rules the World Island; who rules the World Island commands the world.' By 'Heartland' Mackinder meant the lands of the Eurasian steppe and by 'World Island' he meant the entire Eurasian continent. According to his calculations, 75 per cent of the world's population and the same percentage of the world's energy resources were concentrated on this continent and 60 per cent of the world's gross domestic product was produced here. The dominance of the Eurasian continent was a direct result of the global expansion of the West. It began with Columbus and was essentially complete by the end of the nineteenth century. Mackinder predicted that due to the fact that Europe had become the centre of the world, future European conflicts would inevitably broaden into world wars. The states that established control over the Heartland would have the greatest chance of military victory. At the beginning of the twentieth century, two states showed the greatest interest in establishing such control. The first was Russia. Over the course of several centuries, starting with the emergence of Muscovy, Russia had conquered most of the Heartland, with the exception of its westernmost edge. The second state with an interest in controlling the Heartland was the newly emerging German Empire, which considered Eastern Europe essential to its vital interests (*Lebensraum*). Accordingly, Eastern Europe became the central arena where Russia and Germany would clash in the struggle for world domination. This confrontation was fundamental and did not depend on who was in power.

Like Turner's theory about the frontier, Mackinder's theory has been subject to criticism. Nonetheless, it has not lost its relevance. In particular, it is rumoured to reflect Putin's way of thinking, except that Putin has replaced Germany in the schema with the entire West. Even in his own time, Mackinder's theory proved to be prophetic (he died in 1947). Both world wars played out according to the scenario he predicted, although you could consider it a self-fulfilling prophecy. Mackinder's thesis influenced American President Woodrow Wilson and his plan for the postwar world order (1918) and, via Nazi geopolitician Karl Haushofer, it 'migrated' to Hitler's *Mein Kampf* (1925).

The Nazi version, however, was a crude caricature of Mackinder. Mackinder believed that geography has a strong influence on politics, but that politicians should not become prisoners of geography. On the contrary, he believed that by recognising the risks inherent in geography, we might overcome them. Mackinder believed that the creation of a wide belt of independent states between the Baltic and Black Seas separating Russia and Germany would serve as a safeguard against future global conflict. Ukraine would be one of those states. Instead, the Nazis believed that all states in Eastern Europe should be either destroyed or turned into vassals of Germany.

Although Lenin, Stalin and the other Bolshevik leaders did not read Mackinder, they acted as though they had. They viewed the Ukrainian lands as a bridge through which the world revolution would spread from Russia to the West and South of Europe. In the end, it wasn't necessary to read Mackinder to understand the new role of Eastern Europe and especially Ukraine.

As a result of these intertwined external and internal

circumstances, not one or two, but numerous conflicts broke out in Ukraine between 1914 and 1945:

- Ukrainian lands were one of the main military theatres in two world wars
- From the start of the Russian Revolution in 1917 until the end of the Second World War, Ukrainian lands were one of the territories where the fate of the Soviet regime was decided
- The First World War gave impetus to the Ukrainian national movement, which aimed to create a Ukrainian nation state
- Each of these lines of conflict was accompanied by local civil wars. The bloodiest was the war between the Russian Whites and Reds from 1918–20, but smaller wars were fought in parallel between the Ukrainian left (the UNR government) and the Ukrainian right (the government of Hetman Skoropadsky) in 1918. During the Second World War different factions of the Ukrainian nationalist movement (Bandera and Melnyk) battled each other
- In conjunction with these wars or following them, local interethnic conflicts arose, particularly between Poles and Ukrainians, and both against the Jews
- Finally, a mass peasant movement emerged that combined elements of the social and national revolutions but could not be reduced to either of them. In 1917–20, this movement resulted in anti-landlord pogroms and the struggle of Makhno's peasant army in the South and peasant insurgent groups in Central Ukraine. In 1930, it was seen in the mass peasant uprisings against collectivisation. During the Second World War, elements of the peasant movement could be seen in the activities of the nationalist Ukrainian Insurgent Army of the 1940s.

None of these conflicts existed in isolation, they were all intertwined. The combinations increased the violence to almost astronomical proportions. The severity of the conflicts was dictated by the high stakes. The struggle for Ukraine would decide not just the fate of Ukraine, or even just of Eastern Europe. Given the region's significance for global geopolitics, the fate of Ukraine had global significance.

Perhaps in other circumstances, Ukraine's significance could be a source of pride. But not in the period 1914–45, when the inhabitants of Ukrainian lands found themselves on a geopolitically vulnerable border in times of war and revolution. In the first half of the twentieth century, Ukraine became one of the most dangerous places in the world. And it all started with the First World War.

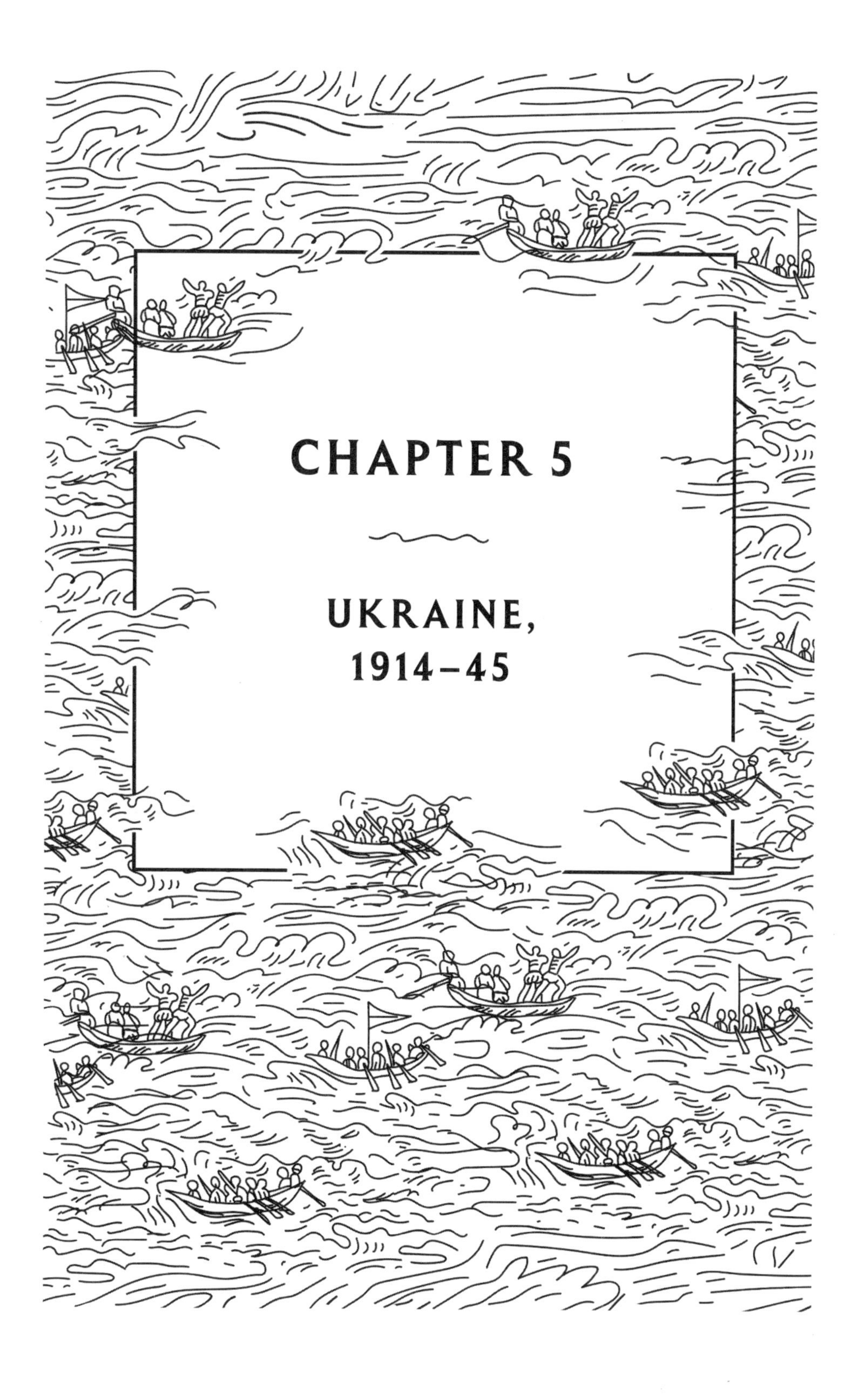

CHAPTER 5

UKRAINE, 1914–45

UKRAINIAN NATIONAL REPUBLIC, AFTER ITS UNION WITH THE ZUNR

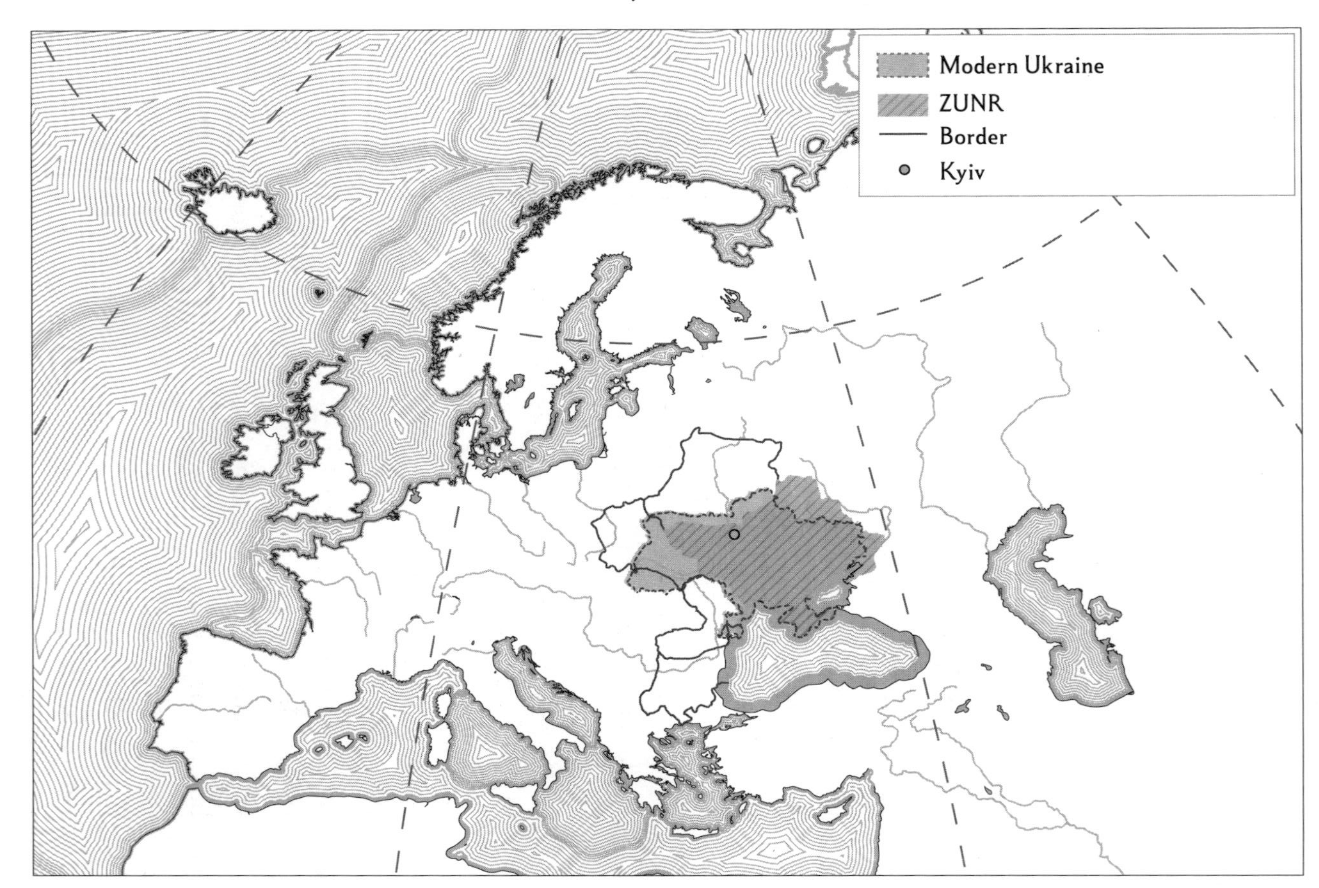

The Great War

If nations had passports, Ukraine's year of birth would be recorded as 1914. This isn't to suggest that the Ukrainian nation did not exist before that. It did, but mostly in the imagination of those people living in Ukrainian lands who considered themselves Ukrainians. Approximately 90 per cent of the nearly 30 million potential Ukrainians were peasants who generally had only a very vague sense that they belonged to a single national community and that this community was called Ukraine.

The First World War turned this 'soft' reality into a 'hard' one. This happened due to a variety of factors and in various ways. The strategic importance of Ukraine was the most significant factor. As British historian Dominic Lieven has noted, 'As much as anything, the First World War turned on the fate of Ukraine.' The significance of Ukraine was largely determined by the nature of the war. It was not only the first world war, but also the first total war, meaning that it required the total mobilisation of resources both at the front and in the rear. In such a war, the side that controls the most resources and can hold out for the longest has the best chance of winning. The Ukrainian lands represented an almost inexhaustible reservoir of resources – most importantly of bread. Keep in mind that both the 1917 Russian Revolution in Petrograd and the 1918 German Revolution in Berlin started with bread riots. Before the war, in 1913, a record 16,000 metric tons of grain had been harvested in the Ukrainian provinces of the Russian Empire. This figure acted like a magnet on the imagination of all parties. It is no surprise that the 1918 Brest Peace between the Central Powers and Ukraine was referred to as the 'peace for bread' agreement: it promised access to Ukrainian bread for the Austro-Hungarian and German armies.

Coal and iron ore were other strategic resources. In the Russian Empire, the lion's share of these resources was extracted and processed in the industrial centres of southeastern Ukraine, in the Donbas region and neighbouring Ekaterinoslav. And in Austrian Ukraine, there was Galician oil. The German navy fought on Galician oil in the First World War and the oil issue was one of the main factors that determined the fate of Galicia at the Paris Peace Conference.

People are another essential resource. The first widespread use of heavy artillery and poison gas led to enormous casualty rates among the troops; the armies required constant replenishment of 'cannon fodder'. Ukrainians were the second-largest ethnic group in the Russian Empire and the sixth largest in the Austro-Hungarian Empire and so represented an essential resource of manpower for both.

The First World War also revitalised the national question in another way. Before the war, there was an unwritten gentlemen's agreement between the European empires that none would use the national question as a weapon against the other. The First World War was not a gentleman's war. The Russian Empire claimed to be waging a war to liberate the Slavic peoples from the 'German yoke'. The conflict between Austria-Hungary and the Russian Empire over Galicia was one of the casus belli for the war, second in importance only to the Balkans. The Russian imperial government believed that Vienna was supporting Ukrainian independence/unification in Galicia and were determined to eliminate this nest of 'Mazepism'. It is unsurprising that Russia moved against Galicia in the first days of the war. During the Russian occupation, Ukrainian activists were among the main targets of military repressions.

Initially, people imagined that the war would be short and that everyone would be 'home by Christmas'. However, it quickly became entrenched. With a fairly equal balance of power, even large battles with massive losses did not lead to radical movement of the frontline in either direction. In the spring of 1917, British officers ironically commented that if the Western Front continued to move at its current pace, they would reach the Rhine in 180 years!

It was different on the Eastern Front. Lines were stretched thin, which allowed for large and significant breakthroughs which took place primarily in the Ukrainian lands. Russian troops occupied Galicia at the start of the war. In the spring and summer of 1915, Austro-Hungarian units pushed them all the way back to Volhynia. In the summer of 1916, the Russian army's Brusilov Offensive broke through again to the west. Then the biggest changes at the front took place in the last months of the war. From the winter of 1917 to early spring of 1918, German and Austrian troops took advantage of the collapse of the Russian imperial army following the revolution and went on the offensive, occupying almost all of the western edges of the Russian Empire, including Ukraine.

The Ukrainian question played an important role in German and Austrian plans. As German publicist Paul Rohrbach wrote before the war, whoever takes Kyiv can control Russia. At the beginning of the war, the Austrian government authorised the creation of the Sich Riflemen, which was made up of Galician Ukrainians. Near the end of the war, two additional divisions were formed from Ukrainian prisoners of war in German camps. These units, known as the 'Blue Coat' and 'Grey Coat' divisions, were to fight against Russian troops. They were formed with the active support of the Union for the Liberation of Ukraine, an organisation of Ukrainian emigrants from the Russian Empire that operated with the support of Berlin and Vienna.

The Habsburgs recognised that their empire might not hold and could eventually disintegrate into nation-states. They prudently prepared male representatives of the family to take over as monarchs in any newly created states that might emerge after the war. Wilhelm Habsburg, known by his Ukrainianised name Vasyl Vyshyvany, was slated to become the king of Ukraine.

The Entente powers became interested in the Ukrainian movement in autumn 1917, when Ukraine appeared to be the only region of order and stability as the centre of the Russian Empire plunged into anarchy after the revolution. That interest evaporated when the Ukrainian government entered negotiations with Germany in early 1918 to avoid the threat of Bolshevik occupation. Under the terms of the Treaty of Brest, Germany recognised Ukraine's independence – but only in order to occupy it. This decision resulted in a cruel twist of fate after the war when the victorious Entente powers viewed the Ukrainian government as pro-German and offered only ultimatums.

When we say that the First World War activated the Ukrainian question, we must take into account not only individual factors, but also the broader backdrop. The First World War was a major turning point in world history. It finished what the French Revolution of 1789 had begun: the destruction of the old regime. The war began as a battle between empires and monarchies and ended as a war of nations and republics. Near the end of the war, both American President Woodrow Wilson and Russian Bolshevik leader Vladimir Lenin, the leaders of two great powers whose voices played an outsize role in the fate of Europe, proclaimed the right of nations to self-determination as one of the core principles of the postwar world.

The First World War created situations and phenomena that

would have been unimaginable in peacetime. For example, there were 6 million refugees in the Russian Empire in early 1917. Of course, they didn't exist as a group before the war, but they became one of the largest groups in the empire. For comparison, the entire industrial proletariat of the empire numbered only 3.5 million. One group consisted of Galician Ukrainians who ended up in Kyiv, after being deported by the Russian occupation authorities when they retreated in spring 1915. After the Poles arranged a separate building for their fellow Galicians, Kyiv's Ukrainians did the same to house Ukrainians deported from Galicia. And so the first 'officially Ukrainian' institution appeared in Kyiv. Around the same time, the first Ukrainian-language educational institutions in the lands of the Russian Empire appeared when the Sich Riflemen began to establish Ukrainian schools in occupied Volhynia.

The peasantry, who were the most numerous group in these lands, experienced the greatest changes. The First World War brought a massive invasion of modernity into the traditional peasant world. Peasants made up the majority of soldiers on both sides of the front. Before the war, Ukrainian peasants could choose whether they wanted to go to work at a neighbouring factory or mine. In the First World War, there was no choice. All peasants of military age were mobilised. In terms of its influence, the army was actually similar to a factory or plant. Peasants had to master the use of military equipment which included the most modern technologies. The army taught them such principles of the modern world as discipline and organisation. In the trenches, the peasants became the targets of propagandists and, towards the end of the war, revolutionary agitators. They learned about modern ideologies – socialism and nationalism in particular. The war also opened social elevators, allowing a measure of upward mobility. The group that proportionally suffered the greatest losses at the front were field officers, so the officer corps required constant replenishment. Thus, the most skilled peasants could reach the rank of junior officer.

There were also significant changes in mental geography. The peasants drafted to both armies travelled over large areas and, like Columbus, discovered a new world. The peasant soldiers who occupied Galicia as part of the Russian Army were surprised to discover that most of the local population spoke almost the same language as they did. Alcohol and Shevchenko's *Kobzar* were the goods in highest demand.

The war modernised the peasants and activated their national self-awareness. When they came back from the front, they were entirely different people. In 1924, a rural communist from the Zhytomyr region wrote a letter to *Pravda* complaining that 'every village in our district now has a politically opinionated and active group of "worldly" peasants who travelled during the war and revolution, saw the world, developed the habit of reading the papers and now they have all kinds of things to say and make us look like idiots.'

Wars and revolutions are powerful accelerators: processes that would normally require decades take place within a matter of years or even months. This is certainly true of Ukrainian nation-building, which progressed much faster after 1914 than before – particularly the transformation of 'peasants into a nation'. Their old, small, personal homeland was being replaced by a new, large and nationally aware homeland. Later in the war, after the initial patriotic fervour had passed, the contours of their new homeland coincided less and less with those of the empire for which they had fought.

This isn't to suggest that the homeland envisioned by the peasants and the homeland of the national elites were necessarily one and the same. No one had abolished class and class differences remained significant. Even among the Ukrainian Sich Riflemen, the most battle ready and nationally conscious military unit, officers looked down on the rank-and-file soldiers and the sentiment was mutual.

Our description would be incomplete without referencing one additional element: several years of experience in bloody and senseless slaughter combined with harsh living conditions in the trenches, where they were often cold and hungry, had undermined the usual moral foundations and norms of behaviour among soldiers. Moreover, the weapons in their hands gave them a sense of power and impunity for even the most disgraceful crimes. The 'man with a gun' or 'front-line soldier', usually a former peasant in a soldier's overcoat, brought their experience of wartime violence back to civilian life.

The bitter irony of the Ukrainian situation is that the end of the First World War did not mean the end of war at all. It was immediately followed by the even more brutal revolutionary and civil wars.

The Ukrainian Revolution

The Russian Revolution began in March (February, OS) 1917 with massive street protests in Petrograd that led to the abdication of the Russian Tsar. For nine months the Provisional Government attempted to build a liberal democracy in Russia, but never achieved stability. In November (October, OS), the Bolsheviks, led by Vladimir Lenin, seized power in a coup that later Soviet propaganda would call the 'Great October Revolution'. This event opened a new chapter in world history: the birth, growth and death of a superpower, the Union of Soviet Socialist Republics. The 'short twentieth century' (1914–91) was largely the 'Soviet century'.

The Russian Revolution was a turning point in the history of revolutions. Like many other phenomena of modernity, Western Europe was the historic fatherland of revolution. Until 1917, revolutions were largely confined to the European continent. The exceptions were revolutions in states that had emerged following the global expansion of the West: the United States (1776–87), South America (1810–20s) and Meiji Japan (1868–69). The Russian Revolution of 1917 was the first global revolution. From Russia, communism spread to the whole world, including to Asia and Africa.

Karl Marx was the first to foresee the global nature of the coming revolution in *The Communist Manifesto* (1848). He argued that capitalists, in pursuit of new markets and profits, were spreading capitalism around the world – and simultaneously producing their own gravediggers, the world proletariat. Thus, the future proletarian revolution would inevitably be global in nature. Marx and his followers placed their main hopes in Germany with its strong industrial base, large working class and massive social democratic party. The world revolution would begin with the uprising of the German proletariat.

However, toward the end of his life, Marx came to believe that world revolution was also possible in backward agrarian Russia, where social and political conflicts had become particularly acute. Lenin expanded on this theory before the First World War. He argued that Russia was the weakest link in the imperialist system, which he viewed as the highest and last stage of capitalism.

But according to Marx and Lenin, Russia could only ignite the revolutionary spark. The real flame of the revolution would burn in Germany and the rest of Western Europe and from there would spread around the world. The 1917 revolution seemed to confirm Marx and Lenin's prophecies. It began in Russia. Then, in November 1918, revolution broke out in Germany and over the next five years (1918–22), in Hungary, Finland, Italy, Slovakia, Bulgaria, Estonia and other countries. In this model, the Ukrainian lands would serve as a bridge for the Russian Revolution to reach Western Europe and then conquer the world.

In 1918, Stalin wrote that the essential knot of the modern international order was being tied in Ukraine. But Ukraine was experiencing its own revolution and its revolutionary flames, although they burned the local lands to the ground, prevented the revolutions in Russia and the West from connecting.

The Ukrainian Revolution is like Verdi's opera *Il trovatore*: it's impossible to describe the incredibly complicated plot without going off track or leaving out important episodes. Therefore, descriptions of the Ukrainian Revolution are inevitably selective. Historians choose the aspects that best fit their outline. For example, Soviet historians described events in Ukraine as part of the October Revolution; many Russian and Western historians continue to hold that view. From that perspective, there is no Ukrainian Revolution. And the fate of the real revolution, the Russian Revolution, was decided in the centre, in the deadly struggle between the Reds (Bolsheviks) and the Whites (their enemies). Ukraine was just one of the peripheral territories in which the conflict played out and so the revolutionary events on Ukrainian soil have no meaning of their own. We might say that the revolution was *on* Ukraine, but not *in* Ukraine.

Most Ukrainian historians see things differently. They say that there was a Ukrainian Revolution, but they generally mean only the *national* revolution, the national liberation struggle. Accordingly, they present the history of the Ukrainian Revolution almost as a history of the emergence, short existence and defeat of four Ukrainian states: the Ukrainian National Republic of the Central Rada (March 1917–March 1918), Hetman Skoropadsky's Ukrainian State (March–December 1918), the Ukrainian National Republic of the Directory period (December 1918–December 1919) and the Western Ukrainian National Republic (November 1918–July 1919). All of which were followed by the joint Polish-Ukrainian campaign against Soviet Ukraine (April–July 1920).

The Ukrainian Revolution was actually a much broader

phenomenon than just the Bolshevik or national revolutions. It included a third, peasant revolution. This corresponded to its character as a revolution on the frontier, where several conflicts were intertwined. This dense intertwining of conflicts was the main feature of the Ukrainian Revolution, forming its identity, logic and dynamics. And since Ukraine was not simply a border region, but a strategically important borderland, the course of the Ukrainian Revolution influenced the centres of power in Central and Eastern Europe: in Berlin, Warsaw and Vienna and above all in Moscow, the new Russian capital (transferred from Petrograd in 1918).

However, it was the national revolution that gave the Ukrainian Revolution its unique flavour. In any revolution, the primary issue is a change in power. But this issue differed between the Russian and Ukrainian contexts. For the Russian Revolution, the main issue was the transfer of power in the existing state. For the Ukrainian national revolution, the challenge was to build a state that did not yet exist. The Ukrainian Revolution also had a specific geographical dimension. Unlike the Russian Revolution, the Ukrainian Revolution involved lands in two different empires. The chronology of the Ukrainian Revolution also differed from the Russian one. Like the Czechs, Slovaks, Lithuanians and Poles, the Ukrainians began their national liberation struggle not in 1917, but in 1914, with the creation of national committees and military formations in the first months of the war, as activists aimed to take advantage of the military situation to build a nation state.

Initially, the Ukrainian leaders weren't especially revolutionary – in fact, they weren't revolutionary at all. At the start of the war, they declared their loyalty to their respective states: those in the east to the Russian Empire and the Galicians to the Austro-Hungarian Empire. Each side believed that the defeat of the *other* empire would lead to the unification of Ukrainian territories within their empire and thus increase the importance of the Ukrainian question. For the most part, they did not raise the question of creating an independent national state on Ukrainian lands. On the one hand, this was simply pragmatic. The Ukrainian movement in the Russian Empire was poorly organised and therefore its leaders didn't aim for what they couldn't hope to achieve. On the other hand, they continued the central line of nineteenth-century Ukrainian political thought, whose origins went back to the Cyril and Methodius Brotherhood: the transformation of the empire into a federation of nations in which Ukrainians would enjoy political and cultural autonomy. This distinguished them from the Polish and Finnish national movements, whose leaders sought full national independence. The Ukrainian movement was more similar to movements in Belarus, Armenia and Georgia, which also supported plans of federation. The Ukrainian movement was an important indicator in this group. Their successes and failures would show the extent to which the national question could be resolved within the former Russian Empire.

It came to a test of strength in the first weeks of the Russian Revolution of 1917. When the Tsar abdicated, the Provisional Government took over, acting with the support of various councils or soviets of workers' and soldiers' deputies, nationalities, trade groups, etc. In St Petersburg and in central Russia, control was quickly established in the form of 'dual power': the Soviet of Workers' and Soldiers' Deputies began to act as a counterweight to the Provisional Government. In the Ukrainian lands, a third power centre appeared: the Central Rada, created in March 1917 in Kyiv and headed by Mykhailo Hrushevsky.

The Central Rada proclaimed their control over all ethnic Ukrainian territory. This was not a bluff. Of the three centres of power in Ukraine, the Central Rada was the strongest. The Kyiv Rada of Workers' and Soldiers' Deputies was weak and had no connection with the corresponding councils in Russia, so the Central Rada could afford to ignore them. The Provisional

Government in Petrograd, composed of Russian liberals and moderate socialists, was stronger. They were prepared to recognise Ukrainians as a separate nation in the sense of ethnic group but were opposed to the transformation of Russia into a federation. The Provisional Government was forced to make concessions. It recognised the authority of the Central Rada, but only over 'old' Ukraine. From their perspective, 'new' Ukraine (the steppe) was still 'Novorossiya' (New Russia), even though Ukrainian peasants made up most of the population. Therefore, up until the Bolshevik coup, relations between the revolutionary centres of Kyiv and Petrograd revolved around the question of what degree of autonomy Ukraine would enjoy and within what borders.

During the spring and summer of 1917, the Provisional Government was losing power and the Central Rada was gaining power. Ukrainian leaders spoke of 1917 as a year of great miracles. They felt like gods creating a new world out of nothing. The concept of a federal Ukraine spoke to the peasants. The Ukrainian peasantry was suffering from a land hunger and believed that a local, Ukrainian government would be able to solve the land issue better than the government in distant Petrograd. The war-weary Ukrainian soldiers of the Russian army also supported the Central Rada. A Ukrainian state would need a Ukrainian army and this opened the way for them to return home to Ukraine.

The moment of truth came with elections to the Constituent Assembly in November-December 1917. The assembly was envisioned as a parliament that would decide the fate of the entire former Russian Empire. In Ukraine, the Central Rada was the clear winner. The two major parties of the Rada – the Social Democrats and the Socialist Revolutionaries – together won about 70 per cent of the vote.

As the Russian centre grew weaker, Ukrainian demands became more radical. When the Bolsheviks took power in Petrograd that autumn, the Central Rada proclaimed the Ukrainian National

Republic (UNR). But again: not as an independent state, but as an autonomous state in a federal union with democratic Russia and other peoples of the former empire.

The Bolsheviks simultaneously recognised the UNR and declared war on it. They had no significant support in Ukraine. In the elections to the Constituent Assembly, the Bolshevik Party had garnered only 10 per cent of the vote in the Ukrainian provinces of the former empire. Their main support in the region was among soldiers at the front and the industrial cities of the East. In December 1917, local Bolsheviks attempted to seize power in Kyiv but failed. After their defeat in Kyiv, they moved to the Russian-Ukrainian border, to Kharkiv and proclaimed the Soviet Ukrainian Republic. By creating an allegedly separate Ukrainian government in Kharkiv, the Bolsheviks tried to create the impression that their war with the Central Rada was not an external aggression, but a civil war along class lines between Ukrainian workers and the 'bourgeois' Central Rada. (This is the same tactic the Kremlin used after the invasion of Ukraine in 2014, when it tried to present the struggle for the Donbas region as an internal civil war.)

In 1917, the local Bolsheviks were too weak to establish themselves on the Ukrainian lands and Bolshevism could only be introduced to Ukraine from outside, from Russia, 'at the tip of a bayonet'. In late 1917, Russian Bolshevik units attacked Ukraine. The war between the Russian Bolsheviks and the Ukrainian Central Rada in 1917–18 was the first war ever between two socialist states. The Central Rada proved to be the weaker of the two. The miracle of 1917 was short-lived: like straw, it caught fire quickly but was easily extinguished. The support of Ukrainian peasants and soldiers evaporated as soon as the peasants received land and the soldiers returned home from the front. The Bolsheviks had slogans to satisfy both groups: 'Land to the peasants' and 'Down with war!'

Deprived of support from below, the Central Rada began negotiations with Germany. On 22 January 1918, the Ukrainian government in Kyiv proclaimed an independent Ukraine and in early February 1919 signed a separate peace in Brest with Germany and the other Central Powers. (The Bolshevik government signed their own Brest Peace a month later.)

After the defeat of the Ukrainian Revolution, Ukrainian nationalists blamed Ukrainian socialists, saying that their delay in proclaiming national independence had led to their failure. These accusations are unfair. In 1918, several states declared independence: Lithuanians (16 February), Estonians (24 February), Belarusians (25 March), Georgians (26 May), Armenians and Azerbaijanis (28 May) and, at the very end of the German occupation, Latvians (18 November). All of them hoped that by declaring independence, they would gain a protective German umbrella against Russian Bolshevism. If we look at the chronology, the Ukrainian government was actually the first to take the radical step of a complete break from Russia.

The German government made peace with the Ukrainian socialist government hoping to gain access to Ukrainian bread. In early March 1918, German and Austrian occupation forces entered Ukraine. The Germans occupied the central and northern part, while the Austrians occupied the south and east. However, the Central Rada was already only a pale reflection of its former glory. It could not fulfil its commitments to supply bread to the occupying forces. Disappointed with the Central Rada, the German occupation authorities dispersed it and organised a coup d'état on 29 April 2018. Hetman Pavlo Skoropadsky (1873–1945) came to power. He immediately proclaimed that his fatherland would no longer be a testing ground for socialist experiments. The new head of the new Ukrainian state had been a general in the Russian imperial army. He has been compared to the 'father of the Finnish state' Carl Mannerheim, who was also a general in the Russian army. The difference is that Mannerheim was a Swede without Finnish blood, while Skoropadsky was a direct descendant of Ukrainian hetmans and deliberately imposed the traditions of the eighteenth-century Cossack state. His rule can be described as a conservative Ukrainian government with a Little Russian orientation under German occupation.

Skoropadsky's alliance with Germany was a marriage of convenience. He put up with the German occupation as a temporary evil because he believed that in the broader war the Entente would win and Ukraine's fate would continue to be linked to that of Russia. Only now it would be a new Russia, not autocratic, but liberal and in this new Russia Ukraine's rights would be respected.

Due to the presence of the German army, Skoropadsky's rule was the most stable period of the Ukrainian Revolution. Trains ran on time and Kyiv's restaurants, cafés and theatres were packed with people – many of whom had fled Bolshevik Russia. Never had Kyiv been such a Russian city as it was under Skoropadsky. Contemporaries wrote that 'all of Petrograd' and 'all of Moscow' had taken refuge there. The emigres lived with the consent of the German command and the Skoropadsky regime, but didn't like either one of them. As far as the Russians were concerned, they were living under a hostile government working with a collaborator. For his part, Skoropadsky sought an alliance with the Russian Volunteer Army (associated with the Whites), which was being formed in Southern Russia, adjacent to Ukraine. He aimed to form a joint anti-Bolshevik front composed of Ukraine, the Volunteer Army, the Don, the Kuban and Crimea.

The white movement is often portrayed as a reactionary monarchist movement. This is not true. The foundation of the white movement wasn't monarchists, but the Russian liberals who were at the core of the Provisional Government. They sought to return Russia not to the monarchy but to the liberal republic of the spring and summer of 1917 and they saw themselves as a Russian version of Western liberalism. Their liberalism, however, had a clear line that they would not cross: the concept of a centralised

Russia – 'one and indivisible'. And so they couldn't quite decide who their main enemy was: the Russian Bolsheviks or the Ukrainian nationalists. To the Russian liberals, the Bolsheviks looked like a temporary and artificial government that would be blown away by the winds of history. The Ukrainian movement, on the other hand, had deeper, popular roots. In any case, the White Guards rejected the idea of any alliance with Skoropadsky.

Skoropadsky's relationship with the Russian White Guards was like a mirror image of the relationship between the Central Rada and the Bolsheviks: for both the Russian left and the Russian right, the idea of Ukraine as a separate, autonomous state was anathema. National priorities held more weight than shared ideologies. It was said of Russian liberals that their liberalism ended where the Ukrainian question began.

There is no doubt that if the Central Powers rather than the Entente had won the war in 1918, Ukraine would have achieved statehood. It would certainly have shared the weaknesses of similar young states from the interwar period, such as Poland, Lithuania, Romania and others. It would have been plagued by political and economic crises, its elite would have tended toward authoritarianism and attempted to assimilate national minorities. But it most likely would not have evolved toward totalitarianism, like Bolshevik Russia did and certainly would not have used mass terror against its own population. Another big question is how long the Bolsheviks wouldhave lasted had Ukraine gained independence.

A War of All Against All

When the First World War ended in November 1918, the Ukrainian lands were in a state of total chaos. Ten days earlier, the Polish-Ukrainian war had broken out in Western Ukraine. Ukrainian troops seized power in Lviv on 1 November 1918 and a few days later proclaimed the West Ukrainian National

Republic (WUNR). In response, Polish units, with the support of the local Polish population, began military operations. In the third week of the war, they took complete control of Lviv. The West Ukrainian government first moved to Ternopil and then in January 1919 to Stanyslaviv. They also began negotiations with Kyiv to unite Western and Eastern Ukraine into a single state – although it wasn't entirely clear who they should negotiate with. On 14 November 1918, three days after Germany's surrender and the end of the First World War, Skoropadsky had abolished Ukrainian independence and proclaimed a federal union between Ukraine and Russia. On that very day, the new army of the Ukrainian National Republic marched on Kyiv under the leadership of the new revolutionary authority, the Directory. By that time, Hrushevsky had already retired from politics and emigrated. The Ukrainian government was now headed by Volodymyr Vynnychenko, a good writer but a naive politician, and Symon Petliura, a journalist who became commander-in-chief of the army by force of circumstance. On 14 December, the Directory occupied Kyiv and on 22 January 1919, representatives of the two Ukrainian republics solemnly proclaimed the Act of Unification of the Ukrainian National Republic and the WUNR. Two weeks later, the Bolsheviks retook Kyiv.

The Ukrainian National Republic government and troops retreated to Central Ukraine. There, in July 1919, they were joined by the government and army of the WUNR, which had lost the war in Galicia and moved to the former Russian lands. The unification of the two armies gave a second wind to the Ukrainian Revolution. On 30 August 1919, the united Ukrainian forces entered Kyiv. However, their stay in the Ukrainian capital lasted exactly one day. The Ukrainian government was pushed back by the Russian Volunteer Army, which entered Kyiv from the other side of the Dnipro River. The Ukrainians retreated to Kamianets-Podilskyi. In the autumn of 1919, the cold weather arrived early and the Ukrainian army found itself in a 'triangle of death', squeezed on three sides by the Polish, Red and White armies, where they suffered huge losses due to a lack of ammunition or medicines and a typhus outbreak.

In early December 1919, Petliura recognised that the situation was hopeless and moved to Poland with most of his troops. The leaders of the WUNR went to Vienna. The Ukrainian Galician Army first sided with Denikin's army and later with the Red Army. Meanwhile, the Volunteer Army's offensive against the Bolsheviks also ended in ignominious defeat. By October 1919, Denikin had made it two-thirds of the way from the south to Moscow, but then was forced to retreat after Nestor Makhno's anarchist peasant army attacked from the rear. In the winter of 1919–20, Denikin's troops abandoned Kharkiv, Kyiv and Donbas and dug in on the Crimean Peninsula.

The period from the end of 1918 to the end of 1919 is known as the 'Period of the Directory' in Ukrainian history. However, this name should be taken with a grain of salt as the Directory had no decisive influence on events. At times, its power extended no more than a few kilometres from the headquarters of the Ukrainian National Republic Army. Although the same could be said of any of the forces fighting for control of the Ukrainian lands of the former Russian Empire in 1919. In Ukraine, organised authority could be found only in large cities and along railroads. Beyond that, a sea of anarchy raged where the authorities were powerless. The fate of the French occupation can serve as an example. The Entente had determined that France would take control of Ukraine after the war. In December 1918, French troops landed in Odesa, Mykolaiv and Kherson. They were to prepare for the arrival of French occupation forces. The French authorities tried to govern, supporting the Volunteer Army and issuing ultimatums to the Directory. But in March 1919, Ataman Nykyfor Hryhoriev's insurgent army successfully drove the French out.

It was a real Hobbesian war of 'all against all'. In the course of a single year, from the end of 1918 to the end of 1919, eight armies operated on the Ukrainian lands of the former Russian Empire: the German and Austrian armies, French troops, the armies of the Ukrainian National Republic and West Ukrainian National Republic, the Red, White and Makhno armies as well as at least sixty groupings of self-styled atamans. Ukraine effectively splintered into into separate territories – cities, districts and often even villages. Researchers count 120 such 'republics', each with its own 'government', 'army' and 'front'.

No government in the Ukrainian lands of the former Russian Empire could last longer than six months. Constant regime change led to the complete collapse of the state monopoly on violence. All sides resorted to violence and each side was both perpetrator and victim. But the Jews were the main victims. Between 1918 and 1921, approximately two thousand pogroms took place on the territory of the former Russian Empire, most of which occurred on Ukrainian lands (75 per cent). All of the local armies, without exception, participated in these pogroms. As contemporaries wrote, anti-Semitism among soldiers and officers reached the point of madness. The Red Army, the army of the WUNR and Makhno's peasant army accounted for the smallest share of violence, while the Ukrainian National Republic Army and units affiliated with it were responsible for the largest share (40 per cent).

Ukrainian-Jewish relations during the revolution present a paradox. On the one hand, the worst wave of anti-Jewish violence took place on the territory of the Ukrainian National Republic. And yet, the Ukrainian National Republic was distinguished by exceptionally liberal legislation regarding national minorities, especially Jews, who were granted more rights than in neighbouring Lithuania, Latvia, Estonia and Belarus.

There are a number of possible causes for this contrast. One is geographical. The Ukrainian National Republic was strongest in Central Ukraine, where the majority of the Jewish population lived. The intensity of contacts and stereotypes among Jews and non-Jews was highest here which explains in part the high involvement of the Ukrainian National Republic Army in overall anti-Jewish violence. In the South, where the number of Jews was lower, Makhno's peasant army did not resort to pogroms. On the contrary, many Jews fought in its units. Makhno's biggest enemies were the German colonists and they suffered the most from his violence. Even many years later colonist mothers would frighten their children with the name Makhno.

Another reason was that the pogroms of 1919 represented a late wave of the violence that had begun during the First World War and had rolled across Ukrainian lands as one of the main military theatres. When they occupied Ukraine in the spring of 1918, the Germans naively thought that the social anarchy was simply a consequence of the Bolshevik occupation and that the anarchy would end with the end of the Bolshevik presence. Over time, it became clear that the anarchy had deeper causes and that the disintegration of social ties had become irreversible. It's important to note that the anti-Jewish pogroms of 1919 were not the only waves of violence. In southern Ukraine they went hand in hand with the pogroms against the German colonies and everywhere they were accompanied by pogroms against the landowners: by the end of 1919, not a single landowner's household remained on Ukrainian lands.

We must recognise the pogroms as part of not only a national but also a peasant revolution. Usually, the revolutionary armies are referred to in terms of ethnicity or class: the Red Army was allegedly composed of Russian workers, the Ukrainian National Republic Army seemed to be composed of Ukrainian peasants and the White Army of Russian old regime officers. In reality, they were all peasant armies. Peasants constituted the majority in all of them and they did not join the armies of their own free will, but were drafted as cannon fodder. There are instances when the same peasant served at various times in the White, Red and Ukrainian National Republic armies.

The career of Ataman Hryhoriev, one of the worst pogromists, is illustrative. During the first half of 1919, he managed to serve as a commander in the Ukrainian National Republic Army, as a soldier in the Red Army and as the leader of an anti-Bolshevik revolt, right up until has was shot and killed by Nestor Makhno in summer 1919, apparently for his anti-Semitic pogroms. These and other similar examples undermine the myth of the pogromists as 'nationally conscious Ukrainians'. In fact, one of the armies with the fewest pogroms was the nationally conscious WUNR Army.

The army of the Ukrainian National Republic was first and foremost a peasant army – perhaps the most 'peasant' of all. This leads to another plausible cause of the above paradox. When we talk about Ukrainian nationalism, we must keep in mind its heterogeneity: there was the educated nationalism of the intelligentsia, on the one hand and the spontaneous nationalism of the peasantry, on the other. As already mentioned, during the years of war and revolution, peasants came to realise that they had a new homeland. But their understanding of that homeland differed from that of the educated classes. In one respect particularly, the peasant vision of Ukraine differed radically from that of the intelligentsia: while the intelligentsia's nationalism was primarily inclusive, the nationalism of the peasantry was more exclusive. This can help us to understand how the liberal legislation of the intelligentsia coexisted with peasant xenophobia and pogroms. Of course, the people who suffered in the pogroms weren't concerned with these distinctions: they just saw Ukrainian nationalism. In fact, Petliura and other Ukrainian National Republic leaders did not initiate pogroms. On the contrary, they created special commissions to identify and punish the pogromists. The problem was that the Ukrainian National Republic command had no real influence on the peasant rebels. Its power often ended a few kilometres from its headquarters.

None of this is to say that Petliura and other Ukrainian leaders were completely innocent. In their statements and texts, they 'hinted' that the Bolshevik government was Jewish and none of the initiators of the pogroms seem to have actually been punished, despite the harsh sentences that were meted out. It's impossible to say whether this lack of consequences was solely due to the wartime situation. And there can be no doubt of a broader guilt beyond these smaller 'failures'. It is not so much about anti-Semitism as populism: the belief that the people and especially the 'working people' are always right. The reality was different. What Ukrainian socialists called 'the people' quickly became an unruly mob during periods of crisis. And you can't expect anything other than lynch law from a mob.

For a state to properly function, it requires lawyers, police, prison guards and so on – the people who can guarantee a minimum of security and stability. Ukrainian peasants were not suited for this role. The only people who could have fulfilled those roles were former Russian officials and officers and Polish landowners, but from the very beginning of the revolution, the leaders of the Ukrainian National Republic saw these groups as a threat to their power. The Ukrainian National Republic was like a wizard who has released an evil spirit he can't control.

Against this background of radicalisation and mass violence, the Western Ukrainian National Republic was a strange exception. The history of the WUNR is so unique that historians struggle to fit it into the general history of the Ukrainian Revolution. First, unlike the Ukrainian National Republic government, the majority of those involved in the WUNR were liberal democrats, not socialists. Secondly, in Western Ukraine, unlike during the revolution in Greater Ukraine, there was no mass seizure of landowners' lands by the peasants. Galician peasants agreed to take land only if they could pay for it and it was legal. And third, unlike in the Ukrainian National Republic, there were very few anti-Jewish pogroms on the territory of the WUNR. When there were pogroms, they generally involved looting, not mass murder. The WUNR authorities also made an effort to put an immediate end to violence and paid compensation to the victims wherever possible. The real pogroms in Galicia began with the arrival of Polish troops: Polish soldiers took revenge on local Jews for allegedly supporting Ukrainians.

In the Ukrainian Revolution, the regimes of Skoropadsky and the WUNR were the only more or less successful examples of rule of law. But Skoropadsky's government maintained law and order thanks only to the German occupation forces. The WUNR government managed on its own, without external support. This suggests that behind the wave of violence, in addition to the brutalisation and general instability caused by the war, stood the long shadow of Russian autocracy. Unlike the subjects of the Austro-Hungarian Empire, Russian subjects had much less experience in legally resolving social conflicts.

The overall course of the Ukrainian Revolution was a drive toward socialism and national independence with an emphasis on democracy. Their socialist orientation was a source of both the strength of the Ukrainian liberation movement and its weakness. A strength because its leaders successfully mobilised a significant part of the population under their banner during critical moments. A weakness because they failed to establish the rule of law, which resulted in an escalation of violence.

As the conflicts escalated, the balance between nationalism, democracy and socialism could no longer be maintained. One wing abandoned socialism. In April 1920, Symon Petliura formed an alliance with Józef Piłsudski, the leader of the newly reconstituted Poland. Petliura and Piłsudski had similar views on the world. They had both been socialists in the past but, as Piłsudski said, he got off the socialist tram at Independence Station. Petliura did the same. But not only did he 'betray' socialism; he also 'betrayed' the unity of the Ukrainian lands. The price of his alliance with Piłsudski was the Ukrainian National Republic's renunciation of its claims to Galicia and Volhynia. Petliura followed the tactics of a lizard that sheds its tail to escape danger, hoping the tail will grow back. As soon as the treaty was signed, the Polish-Ukrainian army marched on Kyiv and even briefly captured it. This adventure almost resulted in the death of the young Polish state. The Red Army quickly went on the offensive and in the summer of 1920 almost took Warsaw, only to be defeated by the Polish army in a battle that was later called the Miracle on the Vistula.

The other wing of the Ukrainian National Republic leadership moved in the direction of Bolshevism. On the one hand, this reflected the general radicalisation of public sentiment in Ukraine, especially among local peasants. On the other hand, they were impressed by the communist revolutions that seemed to be winning throughout Europe in 1919. Volodymyr Vynnychenko was the most famous leader of this faction, but he left Ukraine, unwilling to take responsibility for further developments. Lesser-known leaders remained. In 1920, they merged with the Bolshevik Party, forming a national wing called the Borotbysts.

In the war of 'all against all' in Ukraine, no one had a decisive advantage. In May 1919, the ratio between Bolsheviks, Poles, the Ukrainian National Republic Army, the White Guards, Grigoriev's units and the WUNR Army (Ukrainian Galician Army) was 30:21:14:10:8:17. This count doesn't include Makhno's Army, which some estimates suggest was equal to or even larger than the size of the Red Army in Ukraine in 1919. In these conditions, any advantage was only temporary. For example, the unification of the Ukrainian National Republic and WUNR armies (31 per cent) would have made them equal in number to the Bolsheviks (30 per cent). However, unlike the Bolsheviks, the Ukrainian armies had no access to medications or ammunition as the main military factories of the Russian Empire, including the Kyiv Arsenal, were under Bolshevik control. Help with ammunition and medicines could only come from outside. But the Entente was in no hurry to assist the Ukrainian movement, considering it both pro-German and pro-Bolshevik.

If someone were placing bets in the summer of 1919, the Volunteer Army would have been a clear favourite: it was well organised and, thanks to the Entente, well supplied. But it was primarily fighting far from the Russian border since ethnic Russian territory was under Bolshevik control. This was one of the chief weaknesses of the Volunteer Army, which the Bolsheviks actively exploited. The Bolsheviks depicted the Volunteer Army as a tool under foreign control and themselves as defending national interests. The White Movement could have won had it formed an alliance with the local movements. British intelligence tried to convince Denikin of the necessity of an alliance with Petliura. Admiral Alexander Kolchak, who was recognised by the leaders of the White Movement and the Entente as the Supreme Ruler of Russia, advised the same from Siberia. Denikin flatly refused. He rejected any possibility of compromise with Ukrainian separatists.

The Bolsheviks were less dogmatic. Lenin has been called a genius of pragmatism. This pragmatism can be clearly seen in his attitude toward Ukraine and the Ukrainian question. Before the war, Lenin was opposed to any form of federation. Then his experience in the revolution forced him to change his position. In order to retain power, he was ready to compromise and establish some sort of federation with groups on the peripheries of the empire. German communist Rosa Luxemburg accused Lenin of flirting with rabid Ukrainian nationalism. In response, he pointed to the results of the elections to the Constituent Assembly in the autumn of 1917: the 5 million votes that Ukrainian parties received then were, in his view, proof that the Ukrainian movement had to be reckoned with.

The Bolsheviks' willingness to compromise with national movements on the periphery is one of the main reasons for their victory. The compromise between two forces, neither of which could fully establish control on the peripheries of the former Russian Empire, took the form of the Union of Soviet Socialist Republics. Ironically, although Hrushevsky and Vynnychenko were not present when the USSR was created, the Union was created according to their formula. The strategic goal of the Ukrainian movement was to transform Russia into a federal union in which Ukraine would have broad national rights as a separate republic. In its own, very modified way, the 'Ukrainian Soviet Socialist Republic' (Ukrainian SSR) created by the Bolsheviks was the embodiment of the dreams that the Ukrainian movement had been cherishing since the days of the Cyril and Methodius Brotherhood. In other words, there would have been no Ukrainian SSR if there had been no Ukrainian National Republic.

Therefore, it is a mistake to talk about the *complete* defeat of the Ukrainian Revolution. In the words of historian Ivan Lysiak-Rudnytsky, '[i]t did not achieve its ultimate goal, but it led to a rebirth within Ukrainian society; it created Ukraine as a modern political nation. Ukrainian life has been developing on this foundation ever since.'

The Peasant Revolution

By the end of 1920, the Bolshevik government had successfully defeated all the other armies in Ukraine and driven out all other would-be governments. There remained, however, a force that the Bolsheviks could neither defeat nor expel. That force was the peasantry.

The Bolsheviks experienced firsthand the rebellious nature of the Ukrainian peasantry. Between 1917 and 1920, the Bolsheviks entered Ukraine three times and three times they retreated, each time with the flames of anti-Bolshevik uprisings burning in their rear. There were actually peasant revolts in all the major grain-growing areas of the former Empire: in Siberia, the Volga region and the Caucasus. But some of the largest peasant uprisings took place in Ukraine and they continued there long after 1920.

It was difficult to wage war against peasants. Their tactics were based more on peasant wit than on military knowledge, which made their actions unpredictable. They had a firmer knowledge of the local area and could appear and disappear without warning. In addition, they had a firm local base. Solidarity is one of the main features of traditional peasant culture. Peasants might not like their relatives or neighbours, but in times of trouble, they would support each other in the hope that the favour would one day be returned. So the Bolsheviks found themselves fighting the entire peasantry rather than individual detachments.

One of the Bolshevik commanders recalled that from the outside, a Ukrainian village 'was like a peaceful cherry orchard. A picture of peasant prosperity, where a sense of peace and quiet reigned among the little white-washed houses. Girls behind wattle fences, oxen and screeching cranes. But it was all just a masquerade. The reality that lay hidden behind the scenery bore no resemblance to a peasant idyll. The slippery body of a bandit was slinking behind the scenes of this Little Russian opera and a sawn-off shotgun and a grenade were hiding under the skirt of the Ukrainian beauty.'

From 1917–20, the peasants rebelled not only against the Bolsheviks but also against the Austrian and German occupation authorities, Skoropadsky's troops, the Volunteer Army and even (in the case of Makhno's army) the Ukrainian National Republic. However, revolts were neither the only nor even the main course of action. The behaviour of Ukrainian peasants during the revolution followed a certain pattern. Initially, they would welcome each new government, expecting them to resolve the land issue.

Then, when the government resorted to extortion and requisitioning, they would grow frustrated and angry. Finally, they would reject it or rebel, then welcome the next government and the cycle repeated.

Given these fluctuations in sentiment, it could seem as though the Ukrainian peasants' reactions lacked any logic. In fact, they were entirely logical. We just have to recognise that the land issue was the driving force for the peasants. They believed that God had created the land so that people could work on it and live off the products of their labour. Therefore, the land should belong to those who worked it – the peasants, not the lords. The revolution and the abdication of the tsar removed the last barrier protecting the lords from the peasants. The time had come to settle scores. Between 1917 and 1919, the peasants seized and divided almost all the landowners' land among themselves. However, they were aware that they possessed it illegally. Therefore, they needed a government that would legalise their 'justified' robbery. The indecisiveness of the Provisional Government in St Petersburg in resolving the agrarian issue forced Ukrainian peasants to turn to the government in Kyiv. They had hopes that the Ukrainian government, composed of 'their' people, would know and understand them and meet their needs. Therefore, they supported the demand to transform Russia into a federal republic in which Ukraine would have autonomy. For them, the slogan of federation was equivalent to the right to own the land. When Russian speakers at the All-Ukrainian Peasant Congress in Kyiv (June 1917) ended their speeches with the words: 'Long live the Russian democratic republic,' the peasant delegates added, shouting and stomping: 'A federal one!'

The Jews who lived side-by-side with the peasantry watched in shock as some sort of 'demon' possessed their neighbours. Previously peaceful and almost somnolent, they suddenly awoke and started talking about some 'Ukraine'. When the peasants drafted their petitions themselves, without the help of educated people, their language on paper sounded like the words of children who had just learned to speak: 'Mother Ukraine has territorial cultural national autonomy, a national parliament with minority rights.' But that doesn't mean they acted like children. It's just that the revolutionary village and the revolutionary city spoke two different languages – and in the case of the Bolsheviks and the Ukrainian peasants, they were also two different *national* languages.

After the Bolshevik coup in late 1917, the sympathies of the peasants shifted to the Bolshevik government. The Bolsheviks campaigned with the slogan 'Down with the war, factories to the workers, land to the peasants' or in a simpler form, 'Take back what was stolen!' Therefore, when war broke out between the Central Rada and the Russian Bolsheviks in late 1917–18, the peasants observed the course of the war with indifference. They were more interested in their own 'small wars', in which villages were fighting over disputed borders.

However, you could only like the Bolsheviks from a distance. As soon as they established power, they set about confiscating grain and forcing the peasants into 'communes' – collective farms, that were actually state enterprises. The peasants responded with riots and revolts.

It's clear that the fluid loyalties of the peasants did not mean the peasantry lacked a political programme. They did have a programme and it consisted of the following points: a) legal recognition of the redistribution of landowners' lands; b) an end to the requisitioning of grain and food products and a return to the free market; c) peasant self-government; d) no communal farms; e) respect for religion, local customs and traditions.

While these demands constituted a political programme of action for peasants throughout the Russian Empire, there were some features unique to Ukraine. If before the revolution, the enemies of the peasants were Russian and Polish landlords along with Jewish merchants, during the revolution, communists were added to the list. The communists most often were not Ukrainian, but more likely to be Russian, Jewish and sometimes Latvian. Of course, the Bolsheviks weren't especially interested in ethnicity: they were internationalists and considered themselves communists first and foremost. The peasants did not share this perspective. For them, the ethnic and religious division into 'us' and 'them' was of fundamental importance. The slogan, 'We are for Soviet government, but without communists!' was both a national and social statement. It was accompanied by purely nationalist slogans: 'Long live independent Ukraine!', 'No bread to Muscovy!', 'Beat the Yids and Moskals!' Historian Andrea Graziosi writes that '[w]ith the possible exception of the contemporary Mexican Revolution, what developed was the first peasant-based national-socialist liberation movement in a century that was to see so many of them. Of course, precisely because it was the first one and because of Ukrainian peculiarities, its traits were sometimes ambiguous, although unmistakable.'

Peasant movements are doomed to failure. The centres of power are in the city, not the village, and that is where the fate of a country is decided. The story of Makhno's army, one of the largest peasant armies in world history, clearly demonstrates this fact. At its peak, it included 100,000 peasants. Makhno was a self-taught anarchist and the capital of the army was his native village of Huliaipole in the Ekaterinoslav region, former Cossack territory. Makhno rejected the Ukrainian National Republic and sided with the Bolsheviks against the Skoropadsky regime. In the autumn of 1919, his army saved the Bolsheviks from defeat by attacking Denikin's White Army from the rear when they marched on Moscow. Nevertheless, the Bolsheviks declared war on him a year later and by the end of the summer of 1921, he and what was left of his army had been driven out of Ukraine.

The story of Makhno's movement allows us to see the spontaneous nationalisation of the peasant revolution. One reason for the Ukrainisation of Makhno's army may have been the influence of his wife, Ukrainian language teacher Halyna Kuzmenko, whom Makhno married in autumn 1919. Makhno's last proclamations clearly showed a national element. For example, one of the appeals written by Halyna Kuzmenko and signed by Makhno began with the words: 'Hard times have come to our dear Ukraine.' This appeal referred to the 'historical enemy' of Ukrainians, the Polish lords. In the summer of 1921, when his army was deciding how to retreat from Ukraine, Makhno seriously considered the possibility of sending his troops to Eastern Galicia to help Galician Ukrainians fight the Poles and then later launch a new offensive against the Bolsheviks from there. Both Makhno's enemies and allies wrote that his army resembled the Cossacks of the Zaporozhian Sich. When he later wrote his memoirs from exile, one of his main themes was how the 'Russian Revolution in Ukraine' became the 'Ukrainian Revolution'. Makhno considered it his duty to 'Ukrainianise' the anarchist movement and regretted that he did not speak better Ukrainian.

This spontaneous focus on national identity went hand in hand with the Bolshevisation of the peasantry. However, for the Ukrainian peasants, Bolshevism didn't mean Russian Bolshevism. On the contrary, they wanted Soviet rule without communists, especially when those communists were Russian or Jewish. The Bolsheviks could not ignore this sentiment. Before the war, they had believed that the future of Europe was socialism and that nationalism was just a relic. The Bolsheviks' position on the Ukrainian movement boiled down to two mutually exclusive points: when they were winning in Ukraine, they called the movement 'nonsense'; when they were forced to retreat under the pressure of the uprisings, they insisted that it had to be taken into account.

Christian Rakovsky, a Romanian Bulgarian, provides an

interesting example of these fluctuations. Rakovsky was one of the most educated Bolsheviks and an internationalist to the core. Before arriving in Ukraine, he mocked the Ukrainian movement, calling it a delusion of a few dozen urban intellectuals. In 1920–23, he was appointed to lead the Bolshevik government in Ukraine and his stay in Ukraine changed his perspective. Rakovsky became convinced that the Ukrainian national movement was primarily a movement of the peasantry and that the Bolsheviks would not retain power in Ukraine if they couldn't find a common ground with the Ukrainian peasantry.

In the spring of 1921, Lenin recognised that the Bolshevik government was on the verge of collapse. If they hoped to save it, compromises would have to be made. On the national question, that compromise was the creation of the USSR with its nominally federal structure. In the economic sphere, the compromise was the New Economic Policy. The main point of this policy was to replace the forced requisitioning of bread with a system of taxation. These compromises were linked by their response to demands of the peasantry, who had been awakened by the war and revolution.

Bolshevik rule began as Russian rule and in 1917–18 in Ukraine it had an obviously imported flavour. In 1919, it started to take on local characteristics due both to the radicalisation of public sentiment, on the one hand, and the Bolsheviks' willingness to compromise, on the other. However, the domestication of the Bolshevik regime in Ukraine did not lead to the emergence of an identical copy of the Russian regime. Ukrainian communism had a distinctly nationalist tone. Ukrainian communists differed from their Russian counterparts in the belief that the only basis for socialism in Ukraine would be a Ukrainian Soviet Republic. They asked Lenin an uncomfortable question: 'Is it possible to remain a member of the Russian Communist Party and defend Ukraine's independence?'

The nationalist communists felt that the only path forwards

for genuine Ukrainian independence would be to transform the Bolshevik Party of Ukraine from a regional branch of the All-Russian Party into an independent Ukrainian communist party as a necessary condition for genuine Ukrainian independence. It would rule in a coalition with other socialist Ukrainian parties representing the interests of the petty bourgeoisie and peasantry.

When people talk about the genesis of the Soviet regime, they generally focus on the political struggle in the big cities. In reality, the fate of the Bolsheviks was largely decided in their relations with the peasants. In the early 1920s, these relations were essentially a forced compromise between two forces, neither of which had been able to establish total control over the territory separately. The compromise could not last long when both sides preferred to see each other through a rifle sight. Sooner or later, it would come to a decisive battle.

Ukrainisation

The Soviet era was a golden age for political anecdotes. One of the earliest was recorded in 1928 in the diary of Ukrainian activist Serhiy Yefremov: 'It doesn't burn in the north or in the south, not in the east, or even the west. What is it?' – 'The fire of world revolution.'

After the communist revolts of 1919 were defeated in Germany and Hungary, the Bolsheviks were left to fend for themselves in their backward agrarian country. The Soviet regime hung by a thread. There were entire remote districts in Soviet Ukraine without a single communist cell. This resulted in a paralysis of power. In the early 1920s, Kharkiv was the capital of the Ukrainian SSR. Officials from the communist government there could not collect data on the rural harvest because Soviet officials were afraid to even go to the villages, especially if they weren't Ukrainian. Which they usually weren't. The Communist Party in Ukraine was not Ukrainian. The majority of its members were Russian (54 per cent). Only 19 per cent of party members identified as Ukrainian, of those only 11 per cent considered Ukrainian to be their native language and only 2 per cent spoke it regularly. The disproportion was even greater in the Bolshevik secret services and in the army, which was 85 per cent Russians.

In 1923, the Kremlin proclaimed a policy of indigenisation of the party and state apparatus in non-Russian republics. The scope of this Ukrainisation was impressive. In just five years, from 1923 to 1928, the Soviet government published two and a half times more books in Ukrainian than had been published in the previous 120 years (1789–1917) of Ukrainian book printing. In the early 1930s, the Ukrainian-language press accounted for 89 per cent of the total circulation of newspapers. This is the highest figure in the history of Ukraine (for comparison: in 2010–15, it ranged from 10–20 per cent). Mastery of Ukrainian became mandatory for government and party work. In the mid-20s, the share of Ukrainians reached a majority in the main strategic sectors for the first time: the state and party apparatus, the population of large cities and workers.

These figures were largely for show. In 1925, Vasily Shulgin, a leader of the Russian White movement and former editor of the pre-revolutionary Russian ultra nationalist newspaper *Kievlyanin*, made a clandestine visit to Kyiv. There, he did not hear a single Ukrainian word from the lips of Kyivites or their children. He proclaimed his gratitude, writing: 'Glory to you, Little Russian bourgeoisie! Not in words, but in deeds, you defend the mother of Russian cities!' Russian also continued to dominate in the capital city of Kharkiv. In Stalino (formerly Hughesovka, now Donetsk), the signs were in Ukrainian but they all had errors. A sign in Ukrainian without errors would have been the exception. Most government employees who took Ukrainian courses and passed the required exam never used it and quickly forgot it.

More importantly, state sponsored Ukrainisation had clear limitations. It did not apply to the most important positions. For instance, no ethnic Ukrainian was ever appointed First Secretary of the Communist Party of Ukraine. Emanuel Kviring (in post from 1923–25) was a Volga German from Russia and an opponent of Ukrainisation. He was replaced by Lazar Kaganovich (1925–28), a Kyivan Jew who spoke fluent Ukrainian and was therefore put in charge of Ukrainisation. The next First Secretary, in 1928, was Stanisław Kosior, a Pole. His successor in 1938 was Nikita Khrushchev, a Russian. The same was true for the heads of the Soviet secret services (Cheka): Stanislav Redens (1931–32) was Polish; Israil Leplevsky (1937–38) was Jewish, Alexander Uspensky (1938) and Ivan Serov (1938–39) were Russian and Amayak Kobulov (1938–39) was of Armenian descent and born in Georgia. Maybe Vsevolod Balytsky (1923–31 and 1933–37) could have claimed to be a Ukrainian. But he was only registered as Ukrainian during Ukrainisation. Before and after, he recorded his nationality as 'Russian'.

Despite the official policy of indigenisation, the percentage of Russians as a share of the population in Ukraine actually increased during the interwar period. This paradox is relatively easy to explain if we keep in mind that for the Kremlin, indigenisation was simply a tool, not an end in itself. The actual goal was the triumph of communism. This revolutionary song written by young, communist railroad workers in Kyiv expressed the sentiment 'Fly on, our locomotive/ There's a station in the commune/We have no other path/With rifles in our hands.' On this route, the 'nation' station was just an intermediate stop, not the end of the journey.

The communists believed that a largely illiterate population would grasp the message of communism better in a familiar language, i.e., a national language. This was not a novel concept. The leaders of the Haskalah (Jewish Enlightenment) used a similar tactic: they initially created secular literature in 'jargon'

(Yiddish) as a medium to convey modern ideas to uneducated Jews. Likewise, Lenin's father, Ilya Ulyanov, a prominent Russian educator, organised efforts to create national elementary schools to teach the Chuvash and other peoples of the Volga region in their own languages. In other words, in order to become modern, it was first necessary to become national.

Marxism offered a theory for the radical modernisation of the world, but for a long time it lacked a theory of nationalism. It wasn't seen as necessary. As Marx and Engels wrote in *The Communist Manifesto*, 'the proletariat have no fatherland'. Lenin and Stalin didn't start to formulate a position on the national question until 1912, on the eve of the First World War, when it became obvious that the question could not simply be ignored. But Lenin's and Stalin's position was marked by the so-called Marxist dialectic, the 'unity of opposites': the Russian Bolsheviks advocated the *right* of nations to self-determination but did not support self-determination *itself*. Many of them believed that with the approach of communism, nations would be replaced by a new historical community: the Soviet people. While feudalism spoke French and capitalism spoke English, communism would speak Russian. Therefore, although indigenisation encompassed all ethnic groups, it did not apply to the largest nationality, the Russians themselves. Communism was already Russian by default.

Indigenisation went furthest in the Ukrainian Soviet Republic. There were several reasons for this. First and foremost was the geopolitical importance of the Ukrainian question. The First World War had raised the question, but not solved it and the Bolsheviks intended to capitalise on this fact. The Fifth Congress of the Communist International in 1924 called the Ukrainian question the most important unresolved national issue in Europe. The Bolsheviks saw the Ukrainian question as a battering ram they could use to break down the gates of the capitalist fortress of the West. Secondly, Bolshevik national policy wasn't only oriented toward the republics of the Soviet Union: it was also oriented toward the peoples of Asia and Africa. The Kremlin wanted to see the anti-colonial struggle there become an ally of the communist revolution. They wanted to show that only communism could offer a fair resolution of the national question and the Ukrainian question offered the perfect opportunity. Ukrainians were the largest non-Russian nationality in the USSR. Therefore, Ukrainisation was to serve as a communist showcase for the outside world.

In addition to the roles of 'battering ram' and 'showcase', there was another reason that indigenisation in Soviet Ukraine went the furthest – the long shadow of the Ukrainian Revolution. In fact, we should talk about not one but two Ukrainisations: Ukrainisation from above carried out by the Bolsheviks and Ukrainisation from below as a continuation of the national revolutionary ferment. The logic of the former was conveyed by Mikhail Frunze, the commander of the Red Army in Ukraine. He believed that as the number of Ukrainian villagers swelled in the army, the threat of Petliurism would increase. He argued that to overcome this threat, the Soviet government would have to wrest its main weapon, the Ukrainian language, from Petliura's hands and learn to wield it. The logic of the other Ukrainisation, 'Ukrainisation from below' was described by Mykhailo Hrushevsky. In 1924, he returned from exile to Ukraine and quickly became convinced that it was precisely here, at the moment when Ukrainian peasants were moving to cities en masse and would soon constitute a majority among workers and bourgeoisie, that the future of the Ukrainian nation would be decided. He argued that the Ukrainian national intelligentsia needed to participate in that process.

Ukrainisation went furthest in two institutions that had their roots in the revolutionary era, the Ukrainian Autocephalous Orthodox Church and the Ukrainian Academy of Sciences. Many of the leading figures in Ukrainisation had anti-Communist backgrounds. Within the Communist Party, the strongest supporters of Ukrainisation were representatives of the most radical wings of the main socialist parties of the former Central Rada, the Ukrainian Social-Democratic Party and the Social-Revolutionary Party. They didn't leave the country and, following the radicalisation of Ukraine during the revolution, they became national communists who attempted to reconcile the communist movement with national interests and self-determination.

Even non-communist Ukrainian patriots were surprised to observe that the Ukrainian communists had gained national spirit and begun to agitate for 'independence'. In 1926, the People's Commissar of Education and former Borotbyst, Oleksandr Shumsky, sent a letter to Stalin. In the context of the Ukrainian revival, he wrote, the important positions in Soviet Ukraine should be held by Ukrainians. Shumsky demanded that Kaganovich be replaced by the Ukrainian Vlas Chubar. In 1928, the journal *Bolshevik Ukrainy* published an article by a young economist, Mykhailo Volobuiev, which argued that the status of Ukraine within the USSR had all the characteristics of a colony.

The charismatic young communist writer Mykola Khvylovy garnered the most attention. While Spengler was writing about the decline of Europe, Khvylovy believed in its revolutionary revitalisation. He believed that the impetus for revival would come from the communist East, including Ukraine. All of which meant that young revolutionary Ukrainian culture had to stop being a provincial copy of Russian culture and meet high European standards. Khvylovy's position in the literary debate of the 1920s is best expressed by the slogan: 'Away from Moscow! To Europe!'

The Kremlin condemned 'Shumskyism', 'Volobuievism' and 'Khvylovism', but this did not reverse the trend. Mykola Skrypnyk was one of the few Ukrainians in the Bolshevik Party before 1917 and his trajectory is fairly characteristic. Skrypnyk had played a significant role in the defeat of the national communist opposition. But when he replaced Shumsky as Commissar of Education, he took the course of Ukrainisation even deeper and further, including plans to Ukrainianise the Kuban, which was part of the Russian Republic.

These conflicts between the Kremlin and Ukrainian communists revealed how shaky the compromise of the early 1920s actually was. Then, in 1926, the spectre of war with England added fuel to the fire. In May 1926, Józef Piłsudski returned to power in neighbouring Poland via coup d'état. This aroused Stalin's fears of a possible renewal of the alliance between Piłsudski and Petliura. Exactly two weeks after the coup, Petliura was shot dead in Paris by Jewish anarchist Samuel Schwarzbard in retaliation for the 1919 Jewish pogroms in Ukraine. It was suspected that Bolshevik secret services were behind the murder. Although no conclusive evidence was ever found, the murder proved to be extremely beneficial to the Kremlin.

Soviet Ukraine was slipping out of the Kremlin's grip. The revolutionary train built by the Bolsheviks had stopped responding to the driver's commands and started running on its own track. Ukrainians were becoming a nation with their own political elite and a fully fledged, sophisticated, not 'peasant' culture. The younger generation of Ukrainian artists experimented with modernist movements such as cubism, constructivism and futurism. Ukrainisation was especially important in the two most popular art forms: theatre (Les Kurbas's experimental theatre) and cinema (most significantly the films of Oleksandr Dovzhenko). The Ukrainian language, the central symbol of Ukrainian identity, also underwent a transformation. In 1926, Ukrainian spelling was codified in Kharkiv with the participation of Ukrainian linguists from both Soviet and Polish Ukraine. At the Kharkiv Public Library, one could listen to a lecture on Einstein's theory of relativity in Ukrainian, which had been considered only a 'peasant language' just five to ten years earlier. Any run-of-the-mill journalist could readily use words in his articles that the Ukrainian patriots of the nineteenth century wouldn't have recognised.

Young Ukrainians were creating an entirely new, modern vision of Ukraine. The traditional embroidered shirts as symbols of Ukraine were entirely alien to them: they were considered symbols only fit for a museum. Their Ukraine was an industrial Ukraine, represented by Ukrainian-speaking doctors, mathematicians, physicists and metallurgists who would gradually conquer the big cities and give the whole country, in the words of one of them, Hryhorii Kostiuk, 'a modern Ukrainian style and character'.

There was a sense that Ukrainians no longer needed Russian culture to mediate their entry into the modern world. Of course, it wouldn't have ended there. Cultural emancipation would sooner or later have led to political separatism. The Bolsheviks weren't the only ones who feared that outcome. Russian émigrés abroad may have hated the Bolsheviks, but they considered the restoration of the Russian Empire to be the main merit of the Bolshevik government. Communism would pass, they thought, but the empire would remain.

Inside the country, things looked somewhat different. In 1929, the Soviet scholar Vladimir Vernadsky, Ukrainian by birth and Little Russian by conviction, wrote a letter to his son, who became a historian of Russia in exile: 'My greatest fear is the collapse of the Russian state. It is generally impossible to restore that which has been torn asunder. Ukraine and Georgia are the greatest risks.'

The situation in Ukraine could develop unchecked while the Kremlin was weakened by the power struggle after Lenin's death in 1924. In 1929, Stalin emerged victorious from that struggle. Once he had consolidated power, he announced a sharp change of course. The period of retreat, Stalin declared, was over and it was time to go on the offensive. The new course meant the end of the NEP and indigenisation. And here the Ukrainian issue again played the role of a litmus test: the signal for the abolition of the policy of indigenisation throughout the USSR was the abolition of Ukrainisation in Kuban in 1932.

The decisive battle was approaching.

The Holodomor

The Bolsheviks were winning on many fronts, but they couldn't seem to manage everyday life. In the summer of 1930, the virtuoso Austrian pianist Paul Wittgenstein, brother of Ludwig Wittgenstein, came on tour to Kharkiv, the capital of Soviet Ukraine. For breakfast at the hotel, he could not get milk and coffee (because there was no milk), tea with lemon (there were no lemons), or even a fried egg (there were no eggs or butter). The only thing available was crusty old cheese. Wittgenstein's tablemate, a Soviet official on a business trip, admitted that he had forgotten the taste of butter. Wittgenstein was stunned that this was possible in Ukraine, the largest agricultural country in Europe!

A few months earlier, a wave of peasant uprisings had swept across Ukraine rejecting the Bolshevik efforts to force the peasants into collective farms. One of the reasons for collectivisation (though not the main one) was the peasants' refusal to supply bread and other products to the market. And it wasn't because the peasants themselves lacked these goods. In fact, the Ukrainian village had never lived so well as it did in the 1920s.

These were the best years in the history of the Ukrainian village. The old peasant utopia of living off the labour of their own hands with minimal government interference had become a reality. After the revolution, the peasants had finally satisfied their 'land hunger'. The elimination of landowners' farms in 1917–19 resulted in a 67 per cent increase in the area of land controlled by the peasants. It was also a peasant-style utopia in the fact that it was oriented towards the past. The revolution and postwar devastation threw the Ukrainian village back several decades to the traditional peasant world. Farms once again relied on the labour of large families with the involvement of children and were oriented not towards the market, but towards meeting the needs of the family.

There was no point in selling the products of one's labour on the open market due to the 'price scissors': industrial goods were too expensive and prices for food too low. The peasants mocked, 'Just because you bought a collar, doesn't mean the nag will carry you' and 'Here's your worker-peasant union: wheat sells for a ruble, but a wagon costs two hundred'. To modernise agriculture, loans would be needed to purchase machinery and fertilisers. One solution was to create cooperatives, an association of several farms that bought machinery together, cultivated the land and sold products on the market. But this was only a partial solution. A large-scale solution would require government support.

There were two ways out of this situation: the market or violence. The former dominated in the 1920s and was called the New Economic Policy. As long as the Bolshevik government in Ukraine was weak, it did not dare to openly fight the peasantry. But in 1929, Stalin 'sent the NEP to hell'. When it became clear that the world communist revolution had failed, he set out to 'build socialism in one country'. He set about forced modernisation from above to rapidly transform the USSR from an agrarian to an industrial country.

Stalin's plan included three elements: industrialisation, collectivisation and cultural revolution. Although industrialisation was the most important, it would rely on collectivisation to achieve its goals. Stalin was convinced that modernisation in the West had been achieved through the exploitation of colonies. The USSR had no external colonies, but it did have one, very large internal one: the peasantry. In the mid-20s, NEP opponent Yevgeny Preobrazhensky proposed going through a phase of 'primitive socialist accumulation'. Anyone who had read Marx understood what he was talking about: in *Capital*, Marx described the process of initial capital accumulation in England as a violent robbery of the peasants. At the time, Stalin condemned Preobrazhensky's theory. It was too cynical even for him. But in the late 1920s, Stalin's policy of 'building socialism in one single country' was actually a version of Preobrazhensky's theory: the peasantry was to pay the main price for Soviet modernisation. By taking away peasants' land and selling grain and other products of their labour to the West, the Soviet government would gain the funds it needed for industrialisation.

The peasants did not like the Soviet government. Literary critic Serhii Yefremov recorded in his diary that the peasants called their own fighters 'Cossacks', whereas they called the Bolsheviks 'comrades' using the Russian word and 'you should hear how much contempt they put into that word'. When the threat of war between the USSR and Great Britain arose in 1926, the Soviet secret services reported that Ukrainian peasants were looking forward to the war as a salvation. They pinned their hopes on Petliura's return. After he was killed, they looked to Piłsudski, the exile Trotsky (because they thought he was against the Bolsheviks) and even the Pope – anyone to destroy the godless communist government.

Since the start of the First World War, the village had lived in constant expectation of the Apocalypse. In the 1920s, they viewed the Bolsheviks as the Antichrist. Their opposition to Soviet rule had material, political *and* religious bases. The goals of the cultural revolution included putting an end to illiteracy and 'religious superstition'. Closing and tearing down churches, dissolving monasteries and arresting priests went hand in hand with collectivisation. All of which only strengthened peasant resistance.

Peasant uprisings against collectivisation took place throughout the USSR, particularly in the grain-growing regions. But Ukraine was the most rebellious: almost half the uprisings took place there. Moreover, the uprisings in Ukraine were gaining a national dimension. The peasant slogans included calls to fight for a free Ukraine. In some villages, the rebels sang what would become the anthem, 'Ukraine has not perished.' And the closer you got to the western border with Poland, the stronger this national dimension was.

Stalin knew the statistics. He was certain that Piłsudski and the Petliurists were responsible for the scale of the Ukrainian uprisings. There was a grain of truth in this, though very distorted. Just as the Soviets wanted to use the Ukrainian issue as a battering ram against Poland, Poland tried to use it against the USSR. In 1922, Piłsudski, the creator of the Polish state, had decided to retire from political affairs. However, the catastrophic state of these affairs in the first years of Polish independence forced him to reconsider his plans. In 1926, he organised a coup d'état and returned to power. Piłsudski appointed his friend, the Kyiv-born Polish artist and former Petliura minister Henryk Józewski, as governor of Volhynia. Józewski pursued a policy of Ukrainisation in Volhynia that mirrored Soviet Ukrainisation. For example, when Kharkiv invited Ukrainians from Lviv to move to the Ukrainian SSR to participate in Soviet Ukrainisation, Józewski brought former Petliura officers from Warsaw to Lutsk, his capital, and appointed them to key positions in the Volhynia Voivodeship. He also supported and developed Ukrainian schools, credit unions, etc. The goal of this 'Volhynia experiment' was to convince Ukrainians in the USSR that Warsaw cared about Ukrainians more than Moscow. Józewski also had another, secret task: to build a Polish spy network in Soviet Ukraine. The forests and swamps of Volhynia were ideal for smuggling Polish spies across the border. Most of these spies were Polish in name only. They were actually Petliura's soldiers and officers, whom Piłsudski had granted asylum. They would prepare the ground in case of war between Poland and the USSR.

In 1929–30, Polish intelligence reported that Ukraine was burning in the flames of peasant uprisings. Józef Piłsudski took this news as a signal to action. He ordered his general staff to prepare a plan to repeat the 1920 offensive against Kyiv. Stalin knew about this plan. Soviet counterintelligence had exposed and neutralised the Polish spy network in Soviet Ukraine and recruited double agents. As a result, their reports were simultaneously placed on the desks of both Piłsudski and Stalin. All of this 'convinced' Stalin that the strong resistance of Ukrainian peasants and their nationalist slogans were no more than the result of a conspiracy between Polish agents and Ukrainian nationalists.

Piłsudski did not repeat the Kyiv campaign. Maybe he felt too old to take on such an adventure. In any case, the moment was lost and without an ally, the peasant revolts were doomed. Moreover, the villages did not have their own leaders. In 1930–31, wealthy and enterprising peasants and their families were exiled to Siberia as 'kulaks'. The Bolsheviks used the term 'kulaks' very broadly: it was applied not only to those with large farms, but also to anyone who had publicly expressed anti-Soviet feelings.

Collectivisation was a disaster for agriculture. Peasants didn't want to work on collective farms instead of their own land. The situation was exacerbated by the fact that the Kremlin had drawn up inflated grain supply plans and failure to meet those plans was seen as a new form of peasant resistance. To break the peasants, the Soviets didn't take only the grain: they took all the food. In the summer of 1930, the first signs of famine could be seen. By the spring of 1932, famine had become widespread in Ukraine.

Ukraine's communist leadership was fully aware that Moscow's grain procurement plans were impossible. They were afraid that implementation would lead to a catastrophe for which they would ultimately be held responsible. Ukrainian communists tried to convince Stalin to change his plans. Stalin viewed their resistance as proof that Ukrainian nationalists and Polish agents had infiltrated even the highest Soviet bodies. Instead of becoming a stronghold of Bolshevism, Ukraine was turning into a Trojan horse.

Therefore, in addition to the widespread 'spontaneous' famine of 1932, an additional, intentional famine was organised for Ukraine in 1933. Stalin most likely made this decision in the summer of 1932. The decision may have been prompted by a report from the secret services about the mood in Ukraine that suggested that the Soviet government had effectively ceased to function there.

We cannot know what was going on in Stalin's mind. However, it is certainly reasonable to suppose that in the Ukrainian situation of 1930–32, he saw a repeat of the revolutionary events of 1917–20, when the Bolsheviks had been forced to retreat from Ukrainian lands several times. For Stalin, this was a personally traumatic experience. During the revolution, he had acted as a party leader and military commander in the south of the former Russian Empire, including Ukraine, and during the Polish-Soviet war he was viewed as partially responsible for their defeat in the summer of 1920. In addition, it should be remembered that Stalin himself was a 'man from the borderlands'. He was from Georgia and knew very well that the borderlands are a territory that constantly generates disorder and revolt. And finally, as the main Bolshevik theorist on the national question, Stalin was convinced that the peasantry was the main base of the national movement and the behaviour of Ukrainian peasants confirmed it.

Stalin had no shortage of reasons to single out Ukraine and deal it a punishing blow. But any conjecture about Stalin's motives in handling the Ukrainian crisis is based on the assumption that he acted rationally. In reality, the more power he concentrated in his hands, the more paranoid his behaviour became – a common reaction for a person who fears that the situation is slipping out of control. And in the early 1930s, Stalin had the feeling that he was losing Ukraine.

Regardless, the famine of 1932–33 was the largest national catastrophe in Ukraine in the twentieth century. The total number of victims was about 4 million. The vast majority of them were ethnic Ukrainians, but other groups living off the land, such as rural Jews and German colonists, also experienced the famine.

There is ongoing debate among historians about whether the famine of 1932–33 was genocide. Those who deny the genocidal nature of the famine point to the fact that it occurred not only in Ukraine but in all grain-growing areas of the USSR and that proportionally, it was not Ukrainians but Kazakhs who suffered the most. Those who consider the famine to be genocide (the Holodomor) point to the fact that not only grain but also all food was taken from Ukrainian peasants and the borders were sealed by military detachments deployed along the Ukrainian-Russian border to prevent peasants from leaving Ukrainian territories.

The resolution to this debate lies in recognising the fact that *in 1932–33 there were not one but two famines in Ukraine.* The first, in 1932, was truly throughout the Soviet Union; the second, in 1933, was deliberately directed against Ukraine. Without this second famine, Ukraine's human losses would have been several orders of magnitude lower.

The famine of 1932–33 finally broke the back of the Ukrainian peasantry. It ended the transformation of the peasantry into a nation, a process that had begun so dynamically in 1914 as part of a pan-European process and continued in fits and starts until the '30s. While in 'old' Europe the mass transition 'from peasants to nation' lasted from the end of the nineteenth century through the interwar period, in Ukraine it began later, during the Great War and the revolution. In the early 1930s, the process was forcibly stopped and then reversed. Peasants who survived the famine recall that from that time on, saying just the words 'Ukraine' or 'mother Ukraine' would get you arrested. It had to be 'Soviet Ukraine'.

Stalin's plans to build socialism in one country accelerated the transformation of the USSR from a formal federation into an actual empire. In the early 1930s, at the height of collectivisation, Stalin started publicly appealing to Russian nationalism. He claimed that Russia had previously been defeated by the Turks, Poles, Swedes, French and Japanese due to its backwardness, but now, thanks to the revolution, that would never happen again.

Collective farm peasants and workers were the two main groups of the 'Soviet people'. In addition, the Bolsheviks intended for the revolution to create a separate stratum, the Soviet intelligentsia, the bearers of a culture that was 'national in form, socialist in content'. Under Ukrainisation, the young Ukrainian culture became national in both form and content. Thus, the Ukrainian intelligentsia then became primary targets of the Stalinist repressions. Out of 260 Ukrainian writers publishing in 1930, 230 died during the purges. The communist leadership of the Ukrainian Republic was also targeted. By the end of the purges in 1938, only two former leaders of the Communist Party of Ukraine were still alive. When Nikita Khrushchev arrived in Ukraine in 1938 as the new First Secretary for Ukraine, he had the impression that another Mongol invasion had taken place.

Stalin's repressions affected all of the Soviet republics, including Russia. One difference between the Russian and non-Russian republics was that Russia was already a part of world culture. Even the loss of an entire generation of the governing and cultural elite could not eliminate Russian national culture entirely. In contrast, for Ukraine, with its young culture, the new elite was almost all it had. The destruction of this elite threatened the very existence of Ukraine as a nation.

The reaction of the West, or rather the lack of it, marks a separate page in the history of the famine. It was not a secret that large numbers of people were dying in Ukraine. Foreign consulates reported the famine to their governments; some journalists reported it. However, the general stance was to avoid discussion of the famine. There were various reasons. For some, like Walter Duranty of *The New York Times*, silence was the key to success. He had access to the highest echelons of the Soviet government and had no intention of losing that access. His calculations paid off: in 1932, he was awarded the Pulitzer Prize for the 'profundity, impartiality, sound judgement and exceptional clarity' of his reporting from the USSR. Others fell victim to deception, such as former French Prime Minister Edouard Herriot. During his visit to the USSR, he was taken to a specially organised 'Potemkin village' in Ukraine, where he was shown well-fed peasants.

Many were deceived because they wanted to be deceived. The famine of 1932–33 coincided with two other major events: the Great Depression of 1929–33 and Hitler's rise to power in 1933. Both the Depression and Hitler's victory provided further evidence of the deep crisis of the liberal West. The Soviet Union, with its promise to build a new world of social equality and an economy that seemed immune to the crisis, appeared to offer a genuine alternative to both liberalism and fascism. Many intellectuals in the West viewed Stalin as a saviour of humanity and therefore were ready to forgive him everything.

The Ukrainian famine showed the dark side of modernity, which many people preferred to ignore. In this 'brave new world', it was possible to rob and kill millions of people in the name of progress and to do so with complete impunity if the killings were based on 'historical necessity'.

Western Ukraine

From 1914–39, the parts of Ukraine which fell under Soviet rule experienced a journey 'back and forth': from ethnos (people) to nation and then back to ethnos. For Ukrainians in the West, beyond the borders of the Soviet Union, the interwar journey went in only one direction: from a people to a nation. In other words, from Rus (or Rusyn) to Ukrainians. In his memoirs, the abstract artist Karlo Zvirynsky, who came from a remote mountain village in Western Ukraine, wrote that in the 1920s few people in his village identified themselves as Ukrainians; by the 1930s, few identified themselves as Rus anymore.

The Ukrainian lands that were outside the USSR in the 1920s and '30s had a collective name: Western Ukraine. It existed as an *official* name for just a few months, as the Western Ukrainian National Republic (WUNR). The WUNR had tried to establish authority over all the Ukrainian lands of the Austro-Hungarian Empire: Galicia, Bukovyna and Transcarpathia. However, their aspirations remained just that: aspirations. By the middle of 1919, they didn't control any of those territories. Although the WUNR itself disappeared, the name 'Western Ukraine' did not. The local Ukrainian politicians used the term and so did the Bolsheviks (this became the basis for the myth that 'Western Ukraine' was invented by the Kremlin). After its annexation by Poland in 1919, Volhynia, formerly part of the Russian empire, also became part of 'Western Ukraine'.

The area was diverse, with parts of it falling under three different governments. Galicia and Volhynia were part of Poland, Transcarpathia was in Czechoslovakia and Bukovyna was part of Romania. Western Ukraine was also divided into three major zones geographically: a southern, mountainous zone around the Carpathians; a central zone characterised by hills with plains that merged into Podolia in the east; and a northern zone of forests and swamps. This area roughly coincided with the territory of the medieval principality of Galicia-Volhynia. However, following its decline in the fourteenth century, those lands had been under a variety of states for almost six hundred years and each had left its mark. This was most clearly seen in the character of the ruling elite. In Galicia, the ruling elite were primarily Polish. In Transcarpathia, they were Hungarian. Bukovyna had many Romanians among the elite and in Volhynia there were many Russians.

Over the years, these states had introduced groups of various ethnicities and religions to economically and politically colonise the local lands – German and Czech farmers, Austrian officials in Bukovina and Galicia, Russian officials in Volhynia and a broad range of Jewish communities. The large Jewish population was as mixed as Western Ukraine itself. Religiously, it was divided into three main groups: Orthodox, Hasidim and Progressive Jews. Progressive Jews lived primarily in large cities where the breath of progress was felt, such as Lviv, Chernivtsi, Brody and Drohobych. Some Orthodox and Hasidic Jews lived in these cities, but more lived in the towns and villages. Rural Jews became emblematic of the region, embodying its agricultural character.

From the perspective of London, Paris or Berlin, the western Ukrainian lands looked like classic Ruritania – a backward and uncivilised corner of the world with Carpathian castles, behind whose walls the owners indulged in forbidden pleasures, dirty Jewish shtetls and squalid villages of primitive, superstitious peasants. There was no scope in this stereotype for the population of Ruritania to have a national identity; national identity is the prerogative of educated and civilised 'Megalomaniacs', the major, industrialised states.

There was some basis for this stereotype. We can see it quite clearly on the basis of the ethnic Ukrainians. Western Ukraine was Ukrainian because Ukrainians constituted the majority.

In total, 7–7.5 million Ukrainians lived in the region, with the largest number (5–6 million) in Poland and smaller numbers in Romania and Czechoslovakia (somewhere between half a million and a million in each). This is a significant number of people, larger than the combined populations of the Baltic states and equal to the population of Belgium at the time. However, if we take a closer look, the initial impression of a homogeneous Ukrainian majority gets rather clouded. In the mountainous Carpathians and in marshy Polesia, there were nominally Ukrainian ethnic groups with very distinct local cultures and identities, including the Boykos, Hutsuls, Lemkos and Polesians. Ukrainians were also split into two large groups by religion: Ukrainians in Galicia and Transcarpathia were predominantly Greek Catholic, while those in Bukovyna and Volhynia were more often Orthodox.

The level of Ukrainian national consciousness also varied, from the highest in Galicia and Bukovyna to the lowest in Polesia, where a significant number of residents simply called themselves 'tuteishchy' or locals. Transcarpathia occupied a middle position. In terms of national awareness, they were close to Galicia, but to the Galicia of 1848 rather than 1918. In 1848, during the 'Spring of Nations', the Galician Rusyns couldn't decide whether they were Ukrainians, Russians or Poles. Similarly, Rusyns in interwar Transcarpathia continued to argue about which nation – Ukrainian, Russian or Hungarian – they belonged to or whether they constituted a separate, Rusyn nation. The latter was a local creation. Its theorists believed that Transcarpathian Rusyns differed in language and customs not only from Russians and Ukrainians, but even from Galician Rusyns on the other side of the Carpathian Mountains.

All of this shows us that at the beginning of the interwar period, it would be a stretch to speak of Western Ukraine as a single, coherent region. However, by the end of that timeframe, Western Ukraine actually appeared quite united. The number of people who identified themselves as Ukrainians had significantly increased.

In part, this nationalisation, or growth in self-awareness as a nation, can be attributed to the Versailles System that was established at the 1919 Paris Peace Conference. The Versailles System enshrined the principle of one state per nation, with 'nation' meaning an ethnic group. Although the victorious powers created this system, it was never consistently implemented. Stateless nations existed after the war just as they had before it. What the Versailles System did accomplish, however, was to reduce their numbers on the European continent from 50 per cent of all recognised nations to 25 per cent. Those nations that found themselves either without a state or living outside the borders of their state were granted the status of national minorities. The League of Nations, which only included nations with states, took responsibility for protecting the rights of the national minorities.

In postwar Central and Eastern Europe, the states that benefited most from the postwar order were those that had been allies of the Entente in the war – Romania and the newly formed Poland and Czechoslovakia. Their territorial claims were achieved to the greatest extent: Romania almost doubled its land after the war; the Czech national elite, in addition to Bohemia, Moravia and Silesia, also gained Slovak and Rusyn territories; and Poland swallowed so much land that it could not digest it. The Entente powers did not consider these states to be civilised enough to protect national minorities. Therefore, the Entente required Poland and Czechoslovakia to sign separate treaties that further protected the rights of national minorities and demanded that Galicia and Transcarpathia be granted autonomy in order to protect them.

Both Jews and Ukrainians constituted national minorities in each of these states and in Poland Ukrainians were the largest minority group, making up 14 per cent of the population in the

1931 census. The fate of these scattered Ukrainians could be seen as a litmus test for the viability of the Versailles System.

In the interwar era, the Ukrainian question became what the Polish question had been in the nineteenth century: the largest unresolved national issue in Central and Eastern Europe. Its resolution impacted the fate of four different countries: the Soviet Union, Poland, Romania and Czechoslovakia. By the end of the interwar period, that list came to include Germany and Hungary, who also hoped to establish control over all or part of the Ukrainian lands. None could afford the luxury of ignoring the Ukrainian question.

In the 1920s, the main game on the Ukrainian question was played between the USSR and Poland. Each side claimed to hold the trump card, the central core of a future united Ukraine. In the early 1920s, Bolsheviks in Moscow and Kharkiv were drawing up plans for a Ukrainian uprising in Volhynia and Galicia. The Kremlin financed and encouraged local communist organisations, the émigré government of the WUNR and even, believe it or not, Ukrainian nationalists – their future enemies.

Soviet hopes for a Western Ukrainian uprising were abandoned in the mid-20s, when it became clear that plans for a world proletarian revolution would have to be shelved. At that point, the active role in playing the Ukrainian card passed to Poland, where Józef Piłsudski had staged a coup d'état and returned to power in 1926. His return coincided with a diplomatic conflict between the USSR and Great Britain. The smell of war was in the air. The Kremlin considered Piłsudski to be a 'dog on the leash of British imperialism' and believed that Britain would wage war with Polish hands.

Piłsudski developed a plan for a Polish-Lithuanian-Ukrainian federation. These plans were a mixture of pragmatism and the romantic slogan of nineteenth-century Polish democratic nationalism, 'For our freedom and yours.' The pragmatic calculations were dictated by issues of national security. Piłsudski considered Russia the main threat to Polish independence – regardless of whether it was a Red Russia or a White. This led him to support 'Prometheanism', a movement of his former associates, Polish socialists and his former military allies, Ukrainians, Georgians and other emigrants in Warsaw. The goal of Prometheanism was to support the national awakening of non-Russian peoples, leading to the dissolution of the USSR. Ukraine and the Ukrainian question were central to the Prometheans. Henryk Józewski's 'Volhynia experiment' was another card Piłsudski held in this game.

The Piłsudski group's Ukrainian policy was characterised by a peculiar lack of consistency. While trying to Ukrainianise Volhynia, they were simultaneously trying to de-Ukrainianise Galicia. An internal border was established between the two regions to protect Volhynia from 'harmful' Galician influences. In Galicia itself, the majority of Ukrainian schools were made bilingual. In addition to the Polish language, Polish history and Polish literature also became compulsory. At the University of Lviv, the Ukrainian departments were shut down and, initially, Ukrainian youth could attend only if they could provide proof of having served in the Polish army. This denationalisation even affected naming. The name 'Galicia' in official documents was replaced by 'Little Poland' and 'Ukrainians' were to be called 'Rusyns'. In this way, an opposing pair was created: 'obedient Rusyns' vs 'rebellious Ukrainians'. Ukrainian public organisations whose activities were considered a threat to the state, such as Plast, the Peasant-Worker Alliance, Prosvita and the Union of Ukrainian Women, were intermittently banned. To strengthen the Polish presence, Polish veterans were granted land on Ukrainian territory, even though the local Ukrainian peasantry was suffering extreme land hunger.

When any 'ism' becomes state ideology, it is immediately at

risk of degradation. We can see this at play in the case of Marxism in the case of the Soviet Union. The degradation of nationalism began earlier, in the 1870s, with the emergence of a united Italy and a united Germany. These states were entirely different from what liberal nationalist revolutionaries had envisioned during the 1848 'Spring of Nations'. As German Chancellor Otto von Bismarck declared, 'The great questions of our time will not be resolved by speeches and majority resolutions – that was the great mistake of 1848–49 – but by iron and blood.' We can also see this general trend towards degradation in late-nineteenth-century Poland where, as one researcher has noted, Polish nationalism 'began learning to hate'. The figure of Roman Dmowski embodies this evolution. Dmowski was a chief ideologist of Poland's ultra nationalist and anti-Semitic National Democratic Party. He called on Poles to forget the romantic slogans of old Polish nationalism, arguing that they should be guided by a healthy national egoism instead. Dmowski saw Germany as the main threat to Polish independence. He was willing to ally with Russia to counter the threat. The peoples between Poland and Russia were to face a tough choice: fight for independence or be divided between Poland and Russia to then disappear through assimilation.

In interwar Poland, Dmowski was Piłsudski's main opponent. Ironically, Piłsudski actually followed Dmowski's line after his return to power in 1926. It was under Piłsudski that the most outrageous violation of the rights of national minorities took place: the so-called 'pacification' of Ukrainians. In 1930, Polish estates throughout Galicia were destroyed in a wave of arson attacks. Ukrainian nationalists claimed responsibility, but the entire Ukrainian population of neighbouring villages was punished in the 'pacification' of Galicia.

It has been said of the policy of interwar Poland that it was worse than criminal – it was idiotic. Instead of drawing Ukrainians closer and winning their loyalty, particularly in light of what was being done to their countrymen in Soviet Ukraine in the 1930s, it alienated them.

Romania was pursuing similar policies. They also closed Ukrainian university departments, Ukrainian schools and organisations and settled loyal military veterans in the Ukrainian lands. All of this was part of a broader trend: the collapse of the idea of a liberal state and the rise of authoritarianism. In Poland, this trend was manifested in the creation of the Bereza Kartuska internment camp in 1934, where political opponents were imprisoned, often without trial. This included not only communists and Ukrainian nationalists, but also members of Polish opposition parties. In Romania, the restriction of political parties took the form of martial law, introduced in 1919–28 and then again in the late 1930s, when the activities of political parties, including Ukrainian ones, were banned.

It was very naive to imagine that young states born on the corpses of three empires would instantly become models of liberal democracy. Both Poland and Romania had the typical problems of young states; their state apparatuses were plagued by corruption and their finances by inflation. They were two of the poorest countries in Europe and their political life was marked by extreme instability. The first Polish president, Gabriel Narutowicz, was assassinated, as were two Romanian prime ministers, Ion Duca and Armand Călinescu. They were killed not by outsiders, but by their own people, that is to say, by Polish and Romanian nationalists. These assassinations once again demonstrated that the slide into authoritarianism was linked to the national question.

Formally, interwar Poland and Romania were nation-states. In fact, they became a classic example of 'nationalising states' – states whose ruling elite believes that there are numerous alien groups among its subjects that threaten its existence. These 'alien' groups were the national minorities. For the sake of national security, they would have to be nationalised – assimilated if possible, or neutralised if necessary. Germans and Jews would have to be neutralised. All other minorities, including Ukrainians, were subject to assimilation.

The policy of nationalisation, however, had the opposite effect: instead of assimilating, Ukrainians were strengthened in their Ukrainianness. No one did more to Ukrainianise the children in Galician schools than teachers of Polish history and literature. They presented the Polish past in the best possible light, enthusiastically recounting tales of Polish uprisings, Polish heroes and national prophets. Ukrainian children naturally transferred these stories to the Ukrainian situation. After these lessons, they would ask their Ukrainian teachers and parents: 'Where are our heroes?'

Ukrainians were especially disturbed by the fact that the Polish authorities added humiliation to national discrimination. Young Poles were raised on the historical novels of Henryk Sienkiewicz, which depicted Ukrainian Cossacks as wild barbarians from the east. There was a belief that Ukrainians were actually an inferior race and had 'black palates', like dogs. It was commonplace to address a Ukrainian as 'Hey, pig'. In Lviv, people said the Polish government was worse than the Soviet: the Soviets 'only' took away the body, while the Polish authorities took aim at their souls as well.

It must be plainly stated that Ukrainians were not the only victims of discriminatory policies. Jews were also subject to persecution; interwar Poland and Romania were 'renowned' for their anti-Semitism. However, unlike the Ukrainians, the Jews of Poland and Romania did not live compactly in a single territory and there was no neighbouring state with designs on annexing them, so they weren't seen as presenting the same existential threat. The Jewish 'homeland' could only exist in some distant future and in distant Palestine. Therefore, the anti-Semitism of interwar Poland and Romania was, so to speak, optional, while discrimination against Ukrainians, given the threat of Ukrainian irredentism, seemed to be a necessity.

But was it inevitable? Interwar Czechoslovakia showed that it was not. Unlike the governments of Poland and Romania, the Czechoslovak authorities did not deliberately settle veterans on Ukrainian lands, or close schools for the children of minority groups, or persecute their civil institutions. On the contrary, during the interwar period in Transcarpathia, schooling was improved, new roads were built and agrarian reforms benefited the peasantry. Prague itself had three universities: the old German university, the new Czech one and the newly established Ukrainian Free University (1921). There were two other Ukrainian higher education institutions as well: the Ukrainian Higher Pedagogical Institute and the Ukrainian Academy of Economics. Students from Galicia and Volhynia could study in Prague if they wanted to leave Poland.

The liberal policies of the interwar Czechoslovak state made it seem like a smaller copy of the old Habsburg monarchy. It could afford liberalism because it had inherited a strong, well-established industrial core from Austria-Hungary and was thus one of the richest countries in Europe: stable democracy requires a certain level of prosperity.

Of course, the Czechoslovak governing elite did consciously choose liberal democracy. Tomáš Masaryk, Czechoslovakia's philosopher president, recognised that the status of national minorities was central to the viability of the nation-state. However, his conclusions in that regard were categorically opposed to Dmowski's. He felt that the national minorities must be supported, not repressed. Masaryk's model was not an ethnic monoculture, but a political, multicultural nation. This was even reflected in the name of the state: it was not Czechia, but Czechoslovakia.

Czechoslovakia was an exception not only in the context of Central and Eastern Europe, but also in continental Europe as a whole. The Versailles System, with its emphasis on the protection of national minorities, was deteriorating in most places. One proof was the failure of the League of Nations to respond to the 'pacification' of Ukrainians. The League showed itself to be toothless and hypocritical. Against the backdrop of this deterioration, Italian fascism and German Nazism seemed to offer an increasingly attractive alternative. Hitler destroyed the Versailles System step by step after coming to power in 1933.

The rise of Hitler put the Ukrainian question back on the agenda, but now in a new context: the National Socialist Revolution in Germany. This revolution envisioned the destruction of both the Versailles System and the Soviet Union, which aligned with the interests of Ukrainian nationalists. Most Ukrainian parties in exile and in Western Ukraine hoped that Hitler would support the Ukrainian cause. These hopes were unfounded. The Ukrainian question was not among Hitler's political priorities. Suffice it to say, Nazi propagandists of the 1930s did not exploit the story of the Ukrainian famine, which could have been a very useful topic for them, as they preferred to increase their cooperation with the Soviet Union, which shared their interest in the collapse of the Versailles System.

In reality, the Nazi authorities were already seeking common ground with the Soviets, who also wanted to see the Versailles System dismantled. For Hitler, the Ukrainian issue was just a bargaining chip in his preparations for a new war. In 1935–38, when Hitler was trying to form an alliance with Poland against the USSR, he promised to give Poland a part of Soviet Ukraine.

But in the autumn of 1938, despite his intentions, the Ukrainian issue became more relevant in connection with the Czechoslovakian crisis. Hitler successfully dismembered Czechoslovakia under the pretext of protecting the German minority in the Czech Sudetenland. As a result, Transcarpathia finally received its long-promised autonomy. The Transcarpathian autonomy revived hopes among Ukrainians for Hitler's support in establishing a Ukrainian state. Transcarpathia could become the kernel around which the rest of the Ukrainian lands would unite. The smell of war was in the air again: this time between Stalin and Hitler over Ukraine. Western politicians, diplomats and journalists were all discussing the possibility. Stalin ridiculed these conversations in March of 1939 as akin to annexing an elephant to a gnat (i.e., Soviet Ukraine to Transcarpathia). Meanwhile, Hitler allowed his ally, Hungary, to occupy Transcarpathia. These events paved the way for the signing of the Molotov-Ribbentrop Pact on 23 August 1939, clearing Hitler's path to start the Second World War.

The Czechoslovak crisis had another specifically Ukrainian dimension: it revealed the victory of Ukrainian identity in Transcarpathia. Newly autonomous Transcarpathia selected the name 'Carpathian Ukraine,' and Ukrainian activists formed the backbone of the local government. When Hitler approved the Hungarian occupation of Transcarpathia, the autonomous government declared national independence.

Carpathian Ukraine lasted exactly a day as an independent state. It was crushed by Hungarian troops. But unlike Czechoslovakia, which surrendered without a fight, the armed forces of Carpathian Ukraine resisted the Hungarian invasion. Their resistance was as fearless as it was hopeless. However, the deaths of the defenders of Carpathian Ukraine created a heroic national myth that the local population of Transcarpathia had lacked up until that point.

The fate of Carpathian Ukraine showed the actual significance of the Ukrainian question: it had deteriorated from being one of the most important issues in postwar Europe to the status of spare change. This degradation coincided with the degradation of liberal democracy. By the outbreak of the Second World War, the number of remaining liberal democracies could be counted on one hand. Most of the countries and peoples of Europe faced a very narrow choice: communism or fascism. The Ukrainian national movement in Western Ukraine went through similar shifts, as the influence of centrist parties weakened and the influence of the extreme left and right wings grew significantly stronger.

Radicalisation of the Ukrainian National Movement

These changes had a generational dimension. The rise of extremist sentiment was closely related to the rebellion of young Ukrainians against the older politicians. In most of Western Ukraine (with the exception of Volhynia), the older generation had been brought up under the influence of Austrian rule of law. Their politics were based on democratic governance and legal parliamentary struggle. Liberal democracy was the only norm they knew and they tried to implement it in the WUNR. They were unable to pursue this goal in interwar Bukovyna due to the excesses of the Romanian regime but continued in Galicia, where the Polish authorities, despite restrictions, left room for political activity. Just as in the 'good old Austrian times', the entirety of Polish Galicia was covered by a network of Ukrainian party organisations, village 'Prosvita' and agricultural cooperatives, and for some time there was even an underground Ukrainian University in Lviv.

In essence, they created a 'state within a state'. The 'power' in this state was held by the same parties as before the war. The dominant centrist party was the Ukrainian National Democrats – not to be confused with the Polish National Democrats – the Ukrainian version was actually democratic. The opposition was represented by two moderate left-wing parties – the Radical Party and the Social Democrats. Between the wars, the officially allowed Ukrainian movement even surpassed the prewar movement in some respects. Agricultural cooperatives were quite successful and even exported products to Western markets, and Ukrainian organisations managed to reach two groups that are often the last to join national movements: women and the peasantry.

Young Ukrainians had never experienced liberal democracy. The only political reality they knew was authoritarian regimes with cults of personality and without the rule of law, and from the 1930s onwards, the totalitarian regimes of Stalinist communism, Italian fascism and German Nazism.

The emergence of a new, nationalistic generation was not an exclusively Ukrainian phenomenon. The same phenomenon existed among Poles, Jews, Romanians and others. All of them were part of the interwar European generation which is associated with the transition to 'reactionary modernism'. This modernism hated nineteenth-century modernity with its ideals of universal progress, liberal democracy and the free market. In the field of ideology, its main characteristic was the idealisation of revolutionary violence; in the field of politics – the tendency to authoritarianism; and in the field of economics – state regulation of the economy. In the Ukrainian case, two additional features were the bitterness of national defeat and the lack of economic and social opportunity.

Researchers of nationalism often suffer from social myopia: they overlook the social roots of national movements. For Ukrainian nationalism in the western Ukrainian lands, the fact that these were some of the poorest territories in Europe was of key importance. After the war, the machine of demographic transformation slowed but did not stop. The population grew and so did the land hunger. The type of rich farmer who was called a 'kulak' in eastern Ukraine scarcely existed in the west. Just as before the war, the lack of large-scale industry meant the likelihood of finding work outside agriculture was low. In fact, conditions had actually deteriorated. Before the First World War, emigration to North America had offered one solution. Then in the 1920s, the United States and Canada imposed severe restrictions on the entry of emigrants from Eastern Europe. And, of course, the global economic crisis of 1929–33 had local effects as well.

Education was one ticket out of poverty. Theoretically, the interwar years offered such an opportunity. The Krzemieniec Lyceum opened in Volhynia and high schools were also founded in Berehove and Mukachevo in Transcarpathia. Although the network of Ukrainian schools in Galicia shrank, Galician Ukrainians and Transcarpathian Rusyns could take advantage of the newly opened higher education institutions in Czechoslovakia. However, one thing dramatically changed the situation: the connection between the matura (high school graduation exam) and a government position was severed. In Volhynia and Galicia, the local administration was dominated by Poles, in Bukovyna – Romanians, and in Transcarpathia – Czechs. Ukrainians had limited or no access to public office. Those who had been bureaucrats before the war lost their jobs after the war, along with the prospect of a state pension. The fate of Yaroslav Okunevsky, an admiral in the Austro-Hungarian navy is illustrative. Okunevsky was left with no means of support after the war and ended up committing suicide. There was some possibility of work in Ukrainian public organisations, primarily in cooperatives. Veterans of the liberation struggle found material support there. But the employment opportunities in Ukrainian cooperatives compared to the needs of the Ukrainian population were a drop in the bucket.

The general history of modernisation in Europe fits into a simple pattern: as you move east, the state has played a greater and greater role in its implementation. The state became the main provider of employment. This meant that the defeat of the Ukrainian state was not only a national defeat but also a socioeconomic catastrophe for Ukrainians.

Educated young Ukrainians felt this particularly powerfully. They were essentially an intellectual proletariat. Their anger was directed not only against the foreign government, but also against the older generation: it was they who had lost the national revolution along with the possibility of a better life.

The defeat of their national aspirations led to the radicalisation of the Ukrainian movement in two directions simultaneously: a 'turn to the left' and a 'turn to the right'. The 'turn to the left' in the 1920s took the form of 'Sovietophilia', or sympathy for Soviet Ukraine. Many Galician Ukrainians saw Soviet Ukraine as the genuine embodiment of the Ukrainian state and they believed that Galicia should resign from its aspirations as the centre of a Ukrainian state. Many of them moved to the Soviet Ukrainian Republic – some for patriotic reasons to help build the Ukrainian state and others simply to find work.

Within Western Ukraine, Sovietophilia could be seen in the activities of the Communist Party of Western Ukraine. Its social makeup varied greatly from region to region. In Galicia, the communist movement was popular primarily among young intellectuals. Their communism had a strong national dimension. When in 1926 it came to a conflict between the Ukrainian national communists, on the one hand, and Stalin, on the other, they sided with the Ukrainians. In the history of the international communist movement, this was one of the first revolts against the Kremlin. In Volhynia, however, the Communist Party was composed of peasants rather than intellectuals.

Any Sovietophile sympathies evaporated against the backdrop of the Holodomor and Stalinist repressions against Ukraine in the 1930s. Almost all the Western Ukrainians who had left for Soviet Ukraine in the 1930s fell victim to these repressions. Stalin dealt the final blow to Western Ukrainian communism in 1938, when he ordered the dissolution of both the Communist Party of Poland and the Communist Party of Western Ukraine under the pretext that Trotskyists and agents of the Polish secret service had allegedly infiltrated their leadership.

In the 1930s, the alternative to the centrist parties was no longer Sovietophilia, but rather radical integral Ukrainian nationalism. It was represented most clearly by the Organisation of Ukrainian Nationalists, which was founded in 1929. Support for OUN came from two main groups. The first was primarily military veterans of the liberation struggle who had already formed an underground military organisation in 1920. The most authoritative among the veterans, Colonel Yevhen Konovalets, became the first head of the OUN. Senior nationalists saw the OUN as a kind of underground army that was supposed to defend legal Ukrainian civil society.

The second source of support for the OUN were high school and college students. They viewed legal activity as a form of collaboration. The younger nationalists weren't interested in political chess – they just flipped the table and the chessboard along with it. Their attitude was captured in the words of poet Oleh Olzhych, 'the age is cruel as a wolf'. They were poor, so they scorned comfort. Instead of nineteenth-century nationalism which taught love, they chose a new nationalism which taught hate. Their texts show contempt for death. The first paragraph of the 'Ten Commandments of the Ukrainian Nationalist' read, 'You will gain the Ukrainian state or die fighting for it.' Since they did not value their own lives, they had no respect for the lives of others.

Although the OUN was by definition extremely nationalist, its activities were transnational: the organisation was founded in Vienna, some of its core members were students in Prague, its leaders included veterans of the war for independence from tsarist Russia, its main theatre of operations was interwar Poland and its main enemy was the USSR. Broadly, it was similar to many other revolutionary groups, including the Russian narodniks of the 1870s and 1880s or the Polish liberation groups. In Poland, Piłsudski's memoirs describing how he robbed a train for the party treasury in his revolutionary youth were part of the required literature for the education of Ukrainian nationalist youth. Unlike the Russian narodniks, Polish revolutionaries and the older Ukrainian figures, many young Ukrainian nationalists did not receive an education due to lack of funds or arrests: prison camps were their only universities. This negatively impacted their intellectual maturity. They needed simple formulations and slogans rather than complex theories. Dmytro Dontsov supplied them. Dontsov was a Ukrainian nationalist from the Russian Empire who Konovalets and his colleagues brought to Lviv. Dontsov became the editor of one of the most popular journals of the time, the *Literary and Scientific Bulletin*. Dontsov was the Ukrainian version of Dmowski, insisting on the necessity of national egoism for Ukrainians. Dontsov despised Drahomanov and his followers, who saw the Ukrainian cause as part of the universal progress towards democracy. He thought they undermined the cause of Ukrainian independence with their humanism. He preferred the examples of Mussolini and Hitler. Dontsov reinforced the trend that had already developed in Galicia before the war to view Russia, rather than Poland, as enemy number one to the Ukrainian cause. The fact that the government in Russia had changed did not matter much: the Bolshevik government was just as hostile to Ukraine as the tsars had been. According to Dontsov, it didn't matter who was in charge: Russia was a fundamentally Asiatic power that was a threat not just to Ukraine, but to the whole of Europe. He made anti-Russianism into an indicator of Ukraine's true European character. Dontsov claimed that abandoning liberal democracy in favour of aggressive nationalism actually embodied the spirit of a new Europe.

Armed with these ideas, young nationalists turned against their elders. The Greek Catholic Church under the leadership of Metropolitan Andrei Sheptytsky was one of the first targets of their attack. There was no room for Christian morality in their vision of nationalism. In 1933, they boycotted the Greek Catholic

'Ukrainian Youth for Christ' rally and attempted to mobilise young people under their banner. The older generation of nationalists were also targeted. The young activists viewed them as 'armchair nationalists', unprepared for real action. Moreover, most of the veterans were living in exile, they had less knowledge of what was happening on the ground and their social circles were infiltrated by foreign security services. For a while, Yevhen Konovalets' authority restrained the 'revolt of the young'. When he was murdered by a Soviet agent in 1938, power passed into the hands of another veteran Andrii Melnyk. The young then rejected Melnyk and chose Stepan Bandera instead. In 1940, the OUN split into two irreconcilable factions, the Melnykites and the Banderites.

The new page in Ukrainian nationalism is directly associated with Bandera. In the early 1930s, he became active in the leadership of the Galician OUN and announced the transition to active terrorism. Their most high-profile action was the 1934 assassination of Polish Interior Minister Bronisław Pieracki, who was responsible for the pacification policies. Bandera's fearless attitude in his trial for Pieracki's murder won him many supporters. He refused to respond to questioning in Polish, responded to every question with the slogans of Ukrainian nationalism and accepted his death sentence calmly (it was commuted to life imprisonment). Bandera's conduct satisfied Ukrainian youth's burning psychological need for a national hero.

The young nationalists proclaimed a 'permanent revolution', of which terror was to be a part. They didn't specify how exactly to foment a revolution in a region where Ukrainians held no more than a hundred hunting rifles. Most likely, they intended to deliberately destabilise political life, bringing it to a boil when the 'right time' came. The list of their victims shows the OUN regional leadership's terror campaign was focused not so much against the Polish authorities as against Ukrainians who supported legal activism and Poles who advocated for Polish-Ukrainian reconciliation. The young nationalists aimed to drive all Ukrainian life underground, where they would automatically become the main Ukrainian political force.

At first, the OUN was an entirely marginal group. The coverage of their criminal trials brought them increased attention and popularity. These trials demonstrated the hypocrisy of the Polish authorities – even to Poles: young Ukrainian nationalists were sentenced to death for the same crimes that Piłsudski and other Polish nationalists had committed before 1914. The OUN was in crisis from 1935–38 due to arrests and trials. They actively supported Carpathian Ukraine, forming the core of the Carpathian Sich. Their acceptance of 'baptism by fire' set an example of heroic self-sacrifice for the national cause.

There were aspects of the OUN that appear similar to the German and Italian fascists: the cult of a strong leader, forms of greeting, open xenophobia, and so on. One of the main debates surrounding the history of the OUN concerns the question of whether the Ukrainian nationalists can be considered fascists. There is no definitive answer to that question. Not only because historians rarely agree on anything, but also because of certain peculiarities of the object of discussion, i.e. the OUN. First, OUN members actually held a wide range of political views. One wing held views that could be considered fascist. But others held views that were not fascist and were even anti-fascist. Here, the OUN is entirely different from the Nazi or Bolshevik parties, who did not tolerate ideological heterogeneity. Second, the OUN's attitude towards Nazism and fascism depended on the attitude of the Nazis and fascists towards Ukrainian independence. Here, the spectrum of attitudes was also wide, ranging from hope for Hitler as an ally of the Ukrainian cause to disappointment in him and even hostility, especially after he 'betrayed' Carpathian Ukraine.

Therefore, the question of whether or not the OUN was a fascist organisation needs to be reformulated to ask to what *extent* was it fascist or not? From the mid-30s, a current within the OUN that can be considered pro-fascist grew in strength. It's impossible to say whether it would have become fascist. When the Germans invaded the Soviet Union on 30 June 1941, the Banderites immediately proclaimed an independent Ukrainian state in Lviv. Shortly afterward, a huge pogrom against the Jews in Lviv took place. The degree of connection between those two events is still debated. The state itself lasted only a few days before it was dissolved by the Nazi authorities. Many of Bandera's supporters were arrested along with Bandera himself and Yaroslav Stetsko, the prime minister of the self-proclaimed Ukrainian state. Some were immediately executed. Ironically, it may have been the Nazis who prevented the OUN from becoming a fully fledged fascist organisation.

During the Nazi occupation, the OUN shifted from Dontsov-style nationalism towards social democracy. There were new splits in the ranks of Ukrainian nationalists after the war. This time the split turned against Bandera himself, whose fate was much like that of the 'older nationalists' before him. From the moment of his arrest in 1934 until he was killed by a Soviet agent in 1959, he never again lived in Ukraine and never altered his beliefs.

István Deák, an American historian of Central and Eastern Europe addressed the xenophobia of this period. He was commenting on an OUN rallying cry: 'Long live a greater independent Ukraine without Jews, Poles and Germans; Poles beyond the river San, Germans to Berlin and Jews to the gallows.' Deák writes: 'I don't know how many Ukrainians subscribed to this slogan. I have no doubt, however, that its underlying philosophy was the philosophy of millions of Europeans.'

It was the spirit of the times. This can't justify the Ukrainians who committed terrible crimes, it simply demonstrates once more the ways in which the Ukrainian idea was firmly tied to the European idea and evolved with it.

If we want to speak of the 'Westernness' of Western Ukraine, we need to remember what the West was at that time and what sort of example it set.

The Ukrainian Question in the Second World War

Yevgeny Khaldei was born to a Jewish family in Hughesovka (now Donetsk) in 1916. In 1918, his mother was killed in a pogrom. The bullet that killed her passed through her and lodged in the body of two-year-old Yevgeny. He was saved by a local medic. Khaldei grew up poor, and at the age of thirteen, he left school to work in a factory. Unlike so many of his peers, he didn't remain a factory worker: he became a photographer. He constructed his first camera out of a pair of glasses and other materials at hand. In the 1930s, he photographed the construction of the Dnipro Hydroelectric Plant and the renowned miner, Aleksei Stakhanov, Hero of Socialist Labour. In 1941, Khaldei was drafted and sent to the front as a war photographer. His best works date to this period.

Khaldei's most famous photograph is the raising of the Soviet flag over the Reichstag. It was taken on 2 May 1945, when the fighting in Berlin was already over. The idea for the photo had come to him a year earlier. After the liberation of Sevastopol, he picked up a postcard in the street that one of the Germans had lost during the retreat. It depicted the victory parade of Berliners welcoming the Prussian army at the Brandenburg Gate after their victory over France in 1871. Khaldei decided that he wanted to make a similar photograph when the Red Army entered Berlin. He stole a red tablecloth from the Moscow office of his newspaper and asked his uncle, a tailor, to make a flag out of it. He practised this future photograph in every city the Red Army entered on its journey west.

In Berlin, he invited a few Red Army soldiers to pose on the roof of the Reichstag. He chose the photo in which a soldier with the flag is supported from below by a Soviet officer. When the photo was printed, it became clear that the officer had watches on both wrists. Khaldei used a needle to scratch the extra watch off the negative. He also added smoke to the finished photo to make it look as though the battle was ongoing.

When the retouched picture was shown to Stalin, he asked who the brave warriors were. He was told that it was a Russian and a Ukrainian. Stalin replied that there could not be a Ukrainian there. Ever since that time, the photo has been known by the caption '[Russian] Yegorov and [Georgian] Kantaria raising the flag on the Reichstag'. Generations of Soviets were raised with that image in their textbooks. And it's a perfect illustration of the Soviet version of history: a retouched story built on theft – from the tablecloth and wristwatches to the stolen identities of the participants.

Plenty of examples demonstrate Stalin's distrust of Ukrainians. In the victory over Hitler, Stalin emphasised the decisive role of the great Russian people, 'the greatest of all nations'. The tradition of glossing over the Ukrainian experience of the Second World War dates back to Stalin's time. This disregard of Ukraine is blatantly unjust. After visiting Ukraine in 1945, American journalist Edgar Snow wrote,

> What some are so apt to dismiss as 'the Russian glory' has, in all truth and in many costly ways, been first of all a Ukrainian war ... No single European country has suffered deeper wounds to its cities, its industry, its farmlands and its humanity.

This habit of describing the 'Russian victory' is firmly entrenched in books about the Second World War in both the West and the East. I will try here to bring Ukraine back into the history of the Second World War, focusing only on the key points.

The first point concerns the Soviet annexation of Western Ukraine. The Second World War immediately resolved the Ukrainian question. On 17 September 1939, just over two weeks after the German attack on Poland, the Red Army crossed the Polish-Soviet border and entered the territory of Galicia and Volhynia. A few weeks later, they were officially annexed to Soviet Ukraine. In the summer of 1940, Bukovina and Bessarabia, Romanian territories that the Kremlin seized via threats and blackmail, suffered the same fate. By the end of the first year of the war, almost all Ukrainian ethnic territory except Transcarpathia had been annexed to Soviet Ukraine.

The annexation of western Ukrainian lands was a partial realisation of the prewar plan to establish an entirely Soviet Ukraine. The war provided the opportunity to expand the zone of communism closer to the 'old West'. At the same time, this annexation represented partial realisation of the old Russian imperial vision of 'gathering the Rus lands'. Western Belarus and the Baltic republics were also annexed. The Soviet army also attempted to annexe another former Russian province, Finland, but the Finns successfully defended their independence in the Russo-Finnish War. From 1939–41, the Kremlin's communist and imperialist plans merged. The annexation of Western Ukraine and other western regions further demonstrated that the USSR had been transformed from a communist federation into a communist empire.

The Bolshevik 'revolution from abroad' of 1939–41 was a repetition of the 'revolution at the tip of the bayonet' of 1917–20. The difference was that in twenty years, the Bolsheviks had transformed their backward country into a modern industrialised state. In 1936, Stalin declared that the Soviets had essentially already achieved socialism and that a new social type, the Soviet Man, had been formed in the process. The Soviet Union would serve as an example to show the world the advantages of communism over capitalism. The story of Western Ukraine in 1939–41 showed these advantages to be few or nonexistent. When Red Army soldiers crossed the Soviet-Polish border in September 1939, they were convinced that they were going to save local Belarusians and Ukrainians from starvation. However, when they arrived, they saw that people lived better, with greater prosperity, in capitalist countries than under communism. Soviet officials made a sport of vying for the opportunity to travel to Western Ukraine where they could buy up goods whose existence had been long since forgotten or never even imagined in the Soviet Union. And this was Western Ukraine, the poorest part of Poland, which, in turn, was one of the poorest countries in Europe between the wars!

The Sovietisation of Western Ukraine in 1939–41 looked like Ukrainisation. Universities and schools switched to Ukrainian. Ukrainian became the language of governance and business. Streets were renamed after significant Ukrainian cultural figures, etc. But this was 'Ukrainisation without indigenisation'. Soviets were placed at the head of state and party bodies. Local Ukrainians were not promoted to higher state and party positions and local communists from the former Communist Party of Western Ukraine were some of the first victims of repression.

The initial Sovietisation of Western Ukraine was implemented rather cautiously: there were no attacks on the Greek Catholic Church, no mass collectivisation and no mass executions – at least not until the last days of Soviet rule when they had to rapidly evacuate to the east following Germany's attack on the USSR on 22 June 1941. Before that, the repressions had taken the form of shutting down local parties and civic organisations, confiscations of personal property and mass deportations to Siberia. These efforts, along with communist indoctrination and the dullness and poverty of Soviet life, made the Soviet government hateful not only to the local Poles who had just lost their state, but also to the Ukrainians and Jews who were supposedly liberated from the oppression of aristocratic Poland. Many local residents were extremely happy to see the Soviet regime go, or rather flee, in the summer of 1941.

In the decades after the Second World War, Western Ukraine remembered the 'first Soviets' as the good ones: they left just as quickly as they came. This is in contrast to the 'second Soviets' who arrived in 1944 and stayed. There are anecdotes that summarise the experience of Sovietisation in 1939–41. Ukrainian composer Stanislav Liudkevych is reported to have said, 'Well, we've been liberated and there's nothing we can do about it.' An unnamed Volhynian Jew supposedly said, 'Thank you very much for the liberation – just make sure it never happens again!'

However, there are no jokes to describe the summer of 1941. The retreating Soviets shot prisoners they were holding, including people who had just been picked up off the street on the basis of a denunciation or simply suspicion. The first thing the Germans would do when they entered a city was to open the prisons to allow people to see what had happened there. The sight of mutilated bodies decomposing in the summer heat cried out for revenge. Pogroms rocked the entire region between the Baltic and Black Seas after the Soviet retreat. The Jews were blamed for Soviet crimes. Several factors played a role in the outbreak of pogroms. There was a widespread belief in the power of 'Judeo-Communism'. (This belief was based in part on the fact that Jews were overrepresented among the ranks of the NKVD, but that didn't mean that the local Jews, most of whom were deeply religious, supported the communists.) Some local Lithuanian and Ukrainian nationalists promoted anti-Semitism. The German authorities directly encouraged the pogroms. However, there is also a Soviet factor here. We should consider why simultaneous pogroms took place throughout the territory that had so recently been subjected to forced Sovietisation. Sovietisation destroyed the local elite and social structures that could have contained the violence. It had led to the atomisation of society, with a complete loss of public trust and solidarity. As a result, there was almost no capacity to oppose violence. It is easy to impose your power and will on an atomised society: any well-organised minority can do it.

The annexation of Western Ukraine and the Baltic states is considered to have been one of Stalin's biggest mistakes. Until the very end of Soviet rule, Western Ukrainians and the people of the Baltics were the least Sovietised population and significantly contributed to the collapse of the USSR. The experience of 1939–41 showed that the Soviets had problems with Western Ukraine from the very beginning of the Second World War. The Soviet government didn't only impact Western Ukraine; Western Ukraine impacted Soviet Ukraine.

Another aspect of the Ukrainian experience of the Second World War was the catastrophe of the Soviet military following the German attack on 22 June 1941. Ukraine immediately fell to the German blitzkrieg. Ukraine was almost entirely occupied by the end of September. The Germans were welcomed as liberators throughout Ukraine, not just in the west. People welcomed them with flowers and the traditional hospitality gifts of bread and salt. This warm welcome led one German officer to write in his journal that 'there are still people who love us Germans'. The Wehrmacht sometimes reciprocated: some Ukrainian prisoners of war were released, often so that they could harvest the crops needed by the German army.

The local population was impressed by the discipline and appearance of the German army, which contrasted sharply with the deplorable state of the Red Army. There were rumours that the Ukrainian state would be restored, led by Vynnychenko and other leaders of the Ukrainian National Republic. Ukrainian nationalists from Galicia worked with the Germans in the occupied territories. Officially, they served as translators and in other support roles tasked with managing local government and establishing cultural life in Central and Eastern Ukraine. Indeed, in the first weeks of the German occupation, one could observe a certain national revival: Prosvita reopened; the Autocephalous Church and its parishes were restored; books on the history of Ukraine, which had been banned in the 1930s, were published; Ukrainian-language newspapers were founded in major cities; and concerts were held, at which various previously banned songs were sung including 'Ukraine Has Not Perished'.

All these stories convinced Stalin and the Soviet leadership that the Ukrainians had gone over to Hitler's side in the summer of 1941. Soviet pilots feared being shot down over occupied Ukraine because they thought that Ukrainians would immediately hand them over to the Germans. When the Soviet government retreated, they left behind party members who were expected to develop an underground resistance to fight the occupiers. However, in the first year there were few credible reports of partisan groups in Ukraine. Most communists preferred to surrender. Ukraine seemed so well pacified that Hitler's favourite, the architect Albert Speer, travelled around the Ukrainian forests without an escort in the first months of the war.

The behaviour of Ukrainians in the summer of 1941 was the result of the recent experiences of collectivisation, famine, deportations and purges. Research shows that there was a broadly felt sense of relief, of 'Thank God, the Germans have finally come' in other occupied territories as well, including in Russia. However, one thing that distinguished Ukrainians from the rest of the Soviet population, was that middle-aged and older residents could still remember the German occupation of 1918.

Those memories of the last great war sometimes guided decision-making during the current one. But memory is a poor guide. In the summer of 1941, some Kyiv Jews refused to evacuate to the east because they remembered the Germans from 1918 as a cultural nation. They thought the stories about Nazi atrocities and Hitler's anti-Semitism were just Soviet propaganda.

Memory also led the Western Ukrainian nationalists astray. They worried about a repeat of the situation after the First World War when the Polish-Ukrainian war broke out immediately following the end of the war. Then, Polish military superiority had determined the outcome of events. These concerns led them to create the Galician Division, a Ukrainian division within the German army. It also motivated preventive ethnic cleansing of the Poles of Western Ukraine.

Memories of the first German occupation also influenced Hitler's attitude towards Ukrainians. He believed that they lacked any sense of gratitude or responsibility. As proof, he cited the 'fact' that they had killed 'the greatest friend of the Ukrainian people', Marshal Hermann von Eichhorn, commander of the German occupation forces in Ukraine in 1918. Eichhorn was actually killed by a Russian Socialist Revolutionary, but that was an insignificant 'detail'. As far as Hitler was concerned, Ukraine's catastrophic losses in the 1930s only confirmed the fact that they didn't merit a state.

The Nazis did not have firm plans for Ukraine. They adapted their plans according to circumstances. A year before attacking the USSR, in July 1940, Hitler entertained the possibility of establishing a Ukrainian state as a German protectorate, similar to those which existed in Slovakia and Croatia. The prominent Nazi ideologue Alfred Rosenberg pushed for this scenario, advocating the creation of an expanded Ukrainian state (stretching 'from Lviv to Saratov') with a German ruling elite.

Hitler abandoned these plans in the summer of 1941. No one knows what made him change his mind. He was likely 'dizzy with success'. The final plans for Ukraine were announced in late summer 1941. The Ukrainian lands would be divided into several different zones. Most of the Ukrainian lands would be ruled as the Reichskommissariat Ukraine. The administrative capital was established in the provincial town of Rivne in Volhynia rather than the Ukrainian capital of Kyiv, to demonstrate that the Nazis did not consider the Reichskommissariat Ukraine a nation state, nor the Ukrainians as a nation. Galicia was transferred to the General Government for occupied Poland with the capital based in Krakow, marking another blow to the vision of Ukrainian independence. Bukovyna and Bessarabia were returned to Romania. A narrow strip of southern Ukrainian lands centred in Odesa became a separate Romanian governorate of Transnistria. Transcarpathia had already been given to another German ally, Hungary, in 1939. And eastern Ukraine with its industrial regions remained under front-line military rule.

Erich Koch, one of Rosenberg's rivals, was appointed Reichskommissar of Ukraine. Rosenberg had hoped to have Koch appointed to govern Russia, where the occupation regime was supposed to be exceptionally brutal, but instead he was assigned to Ukraine. Koch called himself a 'vicious dog', and the German command considered him 'another Stalin, the best man to carry out the assignment in Ukraine'. When choosing methods of punishment, he recommended the most cruel: executions and hangings. Under Koch's rule, Ukraine was like an open-air concentration camp. The local population was treated as prisoners whose lives had no value. Executions and physical punishment were performed in public, in broad daylight, sometimes to musical accompaniment.

What the Germans saw in Ukraine seemed to convince them of the racial inferiority of Ukrainians. First of all, the level of poverty despite such obvious natural wealth, suggested a people who were incapable of managing things. Despite the Soviet industrialisation and urbanisation, most Ukrainians continued to live in small villages, in thatched-roofed houses without electricity or running water.

Hitler often 'visited' Ukraine. He had a bunker on the outskirts of Vinnytsia, where he would come to inspect affairs on the Eastern Front. Here, amidst the riches of nature, he would indulge his fantasies about Ukraine. He imagined that within twenty years, there would be 20 million Germans living there and that in three hundred years Ukraine would have become a paradise on earth for German farmers. Large cities and industrial centres were to be completely destroyed and the native population would be reduced to the minimum adequate number to serve the Aryan race. The rest would be liquidated or deported to Siberia. The intelligentsia and the populations of large cities would be deliberately starved to death. Starting in the summer of 1942, officials sent young, healthy Ukrainians to Germany for forced labour. Public organisations were dissolved and universities closed. According to Hitler's plan, Ukrainians only needed to be able to read and understand road signs so they wouldn't fall under the wheels of German vehicles and obstruct their movements.

In the race hierarchy of local peoples, Ukrainians were below Estonians, Latvians and Lithuanians, but above Poles, Belarusians and Russians. The Roma and Jews were at the very bottom of the racial pyramid: they were subject to complete extermination. The Holocaust was a catastrophe on a global scale. It is conceivable that the decision to begin the Holocaust was connected with the challenge of occupying Ukraine. In the summer of 1941, there were 2.7 million Jews in Ukraine, one of the largest Jewish populations in Europe. The fact that so many 'extra mouths' were living on fertile Ukrainian lands led the Nazi authorities to an extreme decision. The systematic murder of Jews began almost immediately after the wave of pogroms in the first weeks of the war, in August 1941 and continued almost until the last day of the German occupation. The Roma were subject to the same fate.

Red Army prisoners of war were also killed in massive numbers. The fact that the USSR had not signed the Geneva Convention on the treatment of prisoners of war gave the Nazis an excuse to treat captured Soviet soldiers as 'subhuman'. Unlike the Jews, most of the prisoners of war were not shot; instead, they were condemned to a slow and painful death from hunger, disease and physical exhaustion in open-air camps before the eyes of the local population.

The fact that the territory of Soviet Ukraine was almost completely occupied by the Nazis permits a comparison of the Nazi and Soviet regimes. It is immediately striking how much the Nazi occupation powers resembled the Soviet regime. In particular, they retained the Soviet collective farm system. Ukrainians experienced the German requisitions of grain and agricultural products as similar to Soviet requisitions. The Germans deported Ukrainians to work in Germany much as the Soviets had deported them to Siberia. And the starvation of prisoners-of-war and people in the major cities reminded Ukrainians of the Holodomor. This was not simply coincidence. German officials openly discussed the need to preserve those elements of the Soviet regime that would allow for the effective exploitation of Ukraine's resources.

However, there were some fundamental differences. The Soviet system demanded that its citizens constantly demonstrate loyalty and love. The German regime was not concerned with such 'details'. They demanded obedience and that obedience was obtained almost exclusively through terror. Another difference concerned the terror itself. The Soviet authorities hid the terror: arrests were carried out at night and executions took place in basements and camps. The Nazi authorities carried out punishments and executions in public places in broad daylight. The mass murders of Jews and Roma were an exception: they were shot in secluded places away from public view.

In some ways, the German terror did have a certain 'advantage'. Soviet terror affected everyone, even Stalin's inner circle, so there was no way to hide from it. Under German terror, if you understood its logic and followed its laws, you could be saved, as long as you were not a Jew or Roma.

Nazi ideology was the primary determinant in the behaviour of German occupation authorities. However, recent research has drawn attention to another source: colonial power as practised by European powers in Africa at the turn of the twentieth century. This is another point that connects Ukrainian history with global history. The Germans ruled Ukraine as a colony and treated the Ukrainians like slaves. The Soviet government left its citizens at least some vestige of human dignity; the German government saw no place for it.

Ultimately, the Nazi occupation of Ukraine ended in complete disaster for the Germans themselves. Contrary to the stereotype of German discipline and organisation, the actions of the German authorities in Ukraine were marked by chaos, corruption and inefficiency. Just as in 1918, the Germans were not able to extract sufficient food from Ukraine to provision their army and occupation forces. Instead of exporting coal from Donbas to Germany, the German authorities had to import German coal to Ukraine. However, the local German officials did provide well for themselves and their families. The Nazi occupation left almost nothing behind in Ukraine other than mass graves and ruined land. The only exception was the highways built for military purposes: those still serve Ukraine, where the lack of good roads remains a problem of national significance.

In summary, two years under German occupation produced dramatic shifts in public attitudes. If at the beginning many Ukrainians viewed the Germans with a mix of hope and optimism, by the end the dominant feeling was hatred. While in 1941, there were almost no partisans in Ukraine, by 1943 some districts were under partisan control and awaited the Red Army for salvation.

The exception was Galicia, where the occupation regime was

far less harsh. The Germans placed local Ukrainians higher than Poles and Jews in their racial hierarchy, though still far inferior to themselves. For Galician Ukrainians, the Soviet government was still the main enemy and people feared its return.

The Nazi occupation ended in the autumn of 1943. After the Soviet army's victory at Stalingrad in the winter of 1942–43 and the Battle of Kursk in the summer of 1943, the front line shifted in the other direction. In the early autumn of 1943, the Red Army liberated the Donbas region from the Germans, in late autumn they took back Kyiv and by the end of the summer of 1944, they had freed Galicia and Volhynia and reached the 1941 border. By the end of autumn 1944, Transcarpathia, the last Ukrainian territory, had been conquered and was annexed to Soviet Ukraine.

It is said that Hitler could have won if he had hung the Ukrainian trident in Kyiv instead of the swastika. But then he would not have been Hitler. Stalin played the Ukrainian card much more skilfully. The events of the summer of 1941 once again 'convinced' him that Ukraine was completely unreliable. Nikita Khrushchev, in his secret speech about the cult of Stalin at the Twentieth Congress of the Communist Party (1956), claimed that Stalin intended to deport all Ukrainians to Siberia; they escaped this fate only because there were too many of them. This statement is repeated in the memoirs of other Soviet figures, but there is no documentary evidence to confirm it. There is no doubt, however, that Stalin was distrustful of Ukrainians, especially those who had lived under German occupation from 1941–44.

Many Red Army officers and soldiers shared his suspicions. In his memoirs, the Yugoslav communist Milovan Djilas described his impressions of life in central Ukraine just after its liberation from the Germans. He arrived there with the Soviet military and Communist Party leadership and immediately felt the tension between local Ukrainians and the Soviet victors:

> It was impossible to hide the passive attitude of Ukrainians towards the war and the Soviet victors. The population left an impression of sullen restraint and they paid very little attention to us. Although the officers who accompanied us tried to hide or explain away the behaviour of the Ukrainians, our Russian driver cursed them up and down, saying that the Ukrainians didn't fight and that was why the Russians had to liberate them.

Djilas wrote that another problem for the Soviet government was the underground Ukrainian Insurgent Army, known as the UPA (Ukrainska Povstanska Armiia). The UPA assassinated General Nikolai Vatutin, the commander of the Red Army forces that liberated Kyiv. The UPA was rarely known by its official name. Instead, its fighters were called 'Banderites', after the leader of the revolutionary wing of the OUN. Bandera himself had been arrested by the Germans and sent to the Sachsenhausen concentration camp after his attempt to proclaim a Ukrainian state. Two of his brothers died in Auschwitz. Banderites were banned and German authorities pursued them. When caught, they were arrested and executed as criminals.

The Melnykites shared the same fate later. They chose Kyiv as the centre of their activities and worked with the local authorities there, but they showed too much independence and grew careless. In the winter of 1941–42, the Germans arrested and shot part of the Melnykite leadership and Melnyk himself was sent to the same camp as Bandera. Those Banderites and Melnykites who managed to escape started forming partisan groups in Volhynia. Starting in the summer of 1941, Taras Bulba-Borovets units also operated in Polesia, where Borovets tried to build his own mini-state, the Polesian Sich. Towards the end of 1942, members of the Bandera, Melnyk and Bulba groups began negotiations to create a Ukrainian partisan army.

The Banderites eventually won control of this army. They subjugated the units of other factions and killed anyone who disagreed. One of the first decisions made by the UPA was to undertake ethnic cleansing of the local Polish population of Volhynia. It is still unclear whether it was a coincidence that the Lviv pogrom of 1–2 July immediately followed the proclamation of the Ukrainian state in Lviv on 30 June 1941. However, there were no coincidences in the attack on the Poles in 1943. Although it is still unknown who gave the order to start, the UPA's anti-Polish action was thoroughly planned and organised. In a single night, from 11–12 July 1943, between fifty and one hundred Polish villages were attacked.

The struggle of the UPA as a 'third force' against both Hitler and Stalin is another significant aspect of the Ukrainian dimension of the Second World War. The UPA fought everyone: they fought the Poles and the Germans. They almost certainly exterminated Jews hiding in the Volhynia forests. But the Soviet government was their main enemy. The fight against Soviet rule was the UPA's finest hour. They battled the Soviet state into the early 1950s (and some units operated even longer), which would have been impossible without the support of the local Ukrainian population. Almost 400,000 people passed through the ranks of the UPA – twice as many as the Red partisan units, who were organised and equipped by the Soviet authorities. The UPA did not receive any help because it fought against everyone under a slogan of self reliance. They hoped that Stalin and Hitler would exhaust their resources in their battle with each other. They believed that after the Second World War, a new war would begin, this time between the USSR and UPA allies, Great Britain and the United States. It must be said that Washington and London cynically supported this illusion among the Banderites and Lithuanian 'forest brothers' immediately following the war. Moreover, British intelligence was infiltrated by Soviet agents, as were parts of the insurgent leadership. The lack of external support doomed the UPA to failure. This was a chronic disease of Ukrainian nationalism: it repeatedly found itself facing multiple enemies at critical moments. Which makes the very existence of the UPA even more surprising. They are far from perfect and some of their actions were undeniably criminal. Still, their struggle was one of the most significant examples of mass resistance to communism, on a par with the Hungarian Revolution of 1956, the Prague Spring of 1968 and Poland's Solidarity movement in the 1980s.

The situation in Ukraine during the last years of the war was reminiscent of the situation in 1919. It was the same war of 'all against all'. The German and Soviet armies fought massive battles in open areas and around large cities. Three large partisan armies were operating in the forests of Volhynia: the Red Army, the Ukrainian Insurgent Army and the Polish Home Army. Ukraine, Belarus, Greece, Italy, France and Yugoslavia were some of the few territories in German-occupied Europe where mass partisan struggle unfolded. The majority of the European population either preferred to collaborate with the Germans or silently endured the occupation.

When you consider the scale of resistance to German occupation, statements about large-scale Ukrainian collaborationism sound strange, especially in the case of Ukrainian nationalists whose leaders spent the war in German concentration camps. The scale of collaboration is determined by the occupying power, not the occupied population. The Nazi regime was far more brutal in Eastern Europe than in the West. Here, unlike in Western Europe, the Germans did not practise 'indirect rule' over the occupied territories – the Ukrainians weren't permitted to create local administrations. Ukrainians could only participate in the government at the lowest levels. For many of them, it was the only way they could survive and feed their families. There was also no clear dividing line between collaboration and resistance: one person might cooperate with the occupation regime during the day and post leaflets or listen to enemy radio broadcasts at night.

This is not to suggest that there were no active collaborators among Ukrainians. The actions of many of them, most of all the participation of the Ukrainian police in the Holocaust, are among the most shameful pages of Ukrainian history. Without going into details, it is still interesting to carry out a thought experiment. Try to imagine how historians would assess Ukrainians if Hitler had won the war. They would almost certainly be depicted as Soviet collaborators, given their high proportion among Red Army troops (even in Galicia, more young people fought in the Soviet army than in the UPA) and their participation in the lower rungs of the Soviet government. Banderites would almost certainly be included among the Soviet collaborators, as German propaganda generally presented them as 'agents of the Kremlin'.

The same phenomenon could be seen later in postwar Soviet Ukraine: Ukrainians filled the ranks of both collaborators and dissidents. Both groups were in the minority, however. The majority occupied a position somewhere in between and shifted depending on the situation. It's difficult to pin down the identity of this majority. When they said 'us', that included Belarusians, Russians and sometimes, less often, Galician Ukrainians and Georgians. It did not include Poles, Jews, or Germans. It wasn't based on national identity. It was more like a 'Rus' identity (East Slavic) that preceded the concept of nations. This shouldn't be surprising. The Soviets and the Nazis had twice destroyed the most active portion of society, that part that articulated a national identity and built the civil institutions through which an identity could take root. After that experience, it should come as no surprise that most Ukrainians returned to traditional, pre-modern ways of thinking.

In any case, the entire population of the Ukrainian lands was never of one mind – either before or after the German occupation. There were a whole range of perspectives.

Stalin continued to view Ukraine as a problem. But now they were seen as having fallen under enemy influence during the German occupation. The next taming of Ukraine took place with the arrival of the Red Army in 1943–44 and mass repressions. When they retook a town or village, the Soviet authorities would start by shooting or hanging everyone they considered a collaborator. Another form of reprisal was the mobilisation of local men between the ages of seventeen and fifty. The revenge was not the fact of mobilisation, but what actually happened to them. They were thrown into battle without training or weapons (one rifle for ten to fifteen people), to face certain death, so that they could wash away their guilt towards the government with blood. Until the very end of the USSR, any time spent living under German occupation created an obstacle to a career in the party or government.

But the Soviet government would never have won if it had relied exclusively on repression. After the victory over Hitler, its soft power lay in the fact that it could now pose as Ukraine's salvation from the fascist threat. It's not a complete fiction. It is difficult to imagine the fate of Ukrainians if the German occupation had lasted any longer. Although Hitler did not aim for the complete physical extermination of Ukrainians, unlike Jews or Roma, he did intend to eliminate as many as possible. He represented a mortal threat to the existence of Ukrainians as a people and as a nation. Stalin also saw to it that Ukrainians did not become a fully fledged nation. However, he did take measures to create the appearance of a nation state in Ukraine. In February 1944, the Ministry of Foreign Affairs of the Ukrainian SSR and the Ministry of Defence of the Ukrainian SSR were established. In the autumn of 1945, the Ukrainian and Belarusian Soviet Republics became founding members of the United Nations.

One emigrant author described the paradoxical situation that arose at the end of the war by saying that the Ukrainians were an unfree nation with their own state. Ukraine was a nation state insofar as its ethnic lands were united within a single state, which, in addition to the word 'Ukrainian' in its name, had other structural elements: a capital, an elite, and high culture in the Ukrainian language (not only folklore). But these elements were actually only a simulacrum: the important decisions about Ukraine were made in Moscow, not Kyiv. Nevertheless, officially it was a Ukrainian nation state.

The future of Ukraine under Stalin can be imagined from the answer of a party official to the question of the Polish poet Czesław Milosz immediately after the war about what would happen to Lithuania: 'There will be a Lithuania, but no Lithuanians.' Lithuanians, like Ukrainians, Georgians and others, were to be dissolved into a single Soviet nation. One step towards this goal was to erase Ukrainians from the history of the Second World War. Another was to erase everything that showed that Ukrainians were different from Russians.

Stalin solved the Ukrainian question by uniting all Ukrainians within a single Ukrainian state, then depriving it of any international existence. Ukrainians were now to be sealed up tight within the Soviet borders like a tin of sardines. From that point until the fall of the communist regime, the Ukrainian question was just an internal issue for the USSR.

A final aspect to consider of the Ukrainian experience in the Second World War is the number of victims, which could give the clearest idea of the impact of the war in Ukraine. Unfortunately, it's impossible to get accurate numbers because the Soviet government deliberately underestimated its losses. They wanted to create the impression that the USSR won due to the advantages of the socialist system rather than sheer numbers. Therefore, it understated the figures to make them close to the Wehrmacht's losses (4.3 million). Immediately after the war, Stalin spoke of 7 million casualties. Under Khrushchev and Brezhnev, the number rose to 20 million. Gorbachev referred to 27.5 million. In 2017, the Russian State Duma published the largest number of casualties with an estimated 42 million people, 19 million military losses and 23 million civilians. However, this is only a rough estimate; there is no breakdown by republic or ethnic group. A very rough estimate of Ukrainian losses can be calculated if we consider that Ukrainians accounted for about 20–25 per cent of the Red Army's soldiers and Ukraine accounted for 40 per cent of all occupied territories. Taking these factors into account, it can be assumed that Ukraine lost 13–14 million people, including 3.8 to 4.7 million military deaths and 9.2 million civilians. A conservative estimate would be 8–9 million people.

Depending on whether we accept a figure of 8 or 14 million, the proportion of deaths relative to the pre-war population for Ukraine ranges from 1:3 to 1:5. This is much higher than for other countries: for Yugoslavia, the proportion is 1:8, for the USSR as a whole – 1:11, Greece – 1:14, Germany – 1:15, France – 1:77 and Britain – 1:125. Only Poland's losses can be compared to Ukraine's (1:5) and only Belarus has higher figures. However, in terms of the absolute number of losses, Ukraine has the highest death toll among all of the European nations and is second only to China globally. During the Second World War, China lost about 20 million people, Germany about 7.4 million, Poland up to 5.8 million, Japan 3.1 million, Yugoslavia 1.7 million, Romania 1.2 million, France 0.6 million, Italy 0.5 million, Great Britain 0.45 million and the United States 0.42 million.

Of course, these figures are all approximate. They often reflect the desire of particular countries or groups to win the oppression Olympics. For this purpose, the victims of other nationalities may be appropriated, especially the Jews, whose fate is the central tragedy of the Second World War. Regardless of how approximate these figures may be, they clearly show where the 'heart of darkness' was located. And they serve as a sad illustration of the metaphor of Ukraine as a seagull that has built her nest by the side of the road.

1914–45: Summing Up

Ukraine's birth as a modern nation took place in the fires of war and revolution, the period 1914–45, and constitutes a distinct chapter in Ukrainian history. We can focus on distinct processes and phenomena, such as the national liberation struggle, the genesis and establishment of Bolshevism, the Nazi occupation, the Holodomor, the Holocaust, the Volhynia massacre, deportations, collaboration and resistance.

I propose to consider all of these events and phenomena as interconnected, as parts of an entangled history united by one theme: modernisation. Both world wars and the revolution were massive and brutal invasions of modernity into the world of Ukrainian villages, Jewish shtetls and Crimean Tatar settlements and led to the almost complete destruction of traditional society. At the same time, large ethnic groups that had been important actors in Ukrainian history for centuries were eliminated. Hitler murdered most of the local Jews and Stalin deported Poles, Germans and Crimean Tatars from Ukraine. These groups did not disappear completely, but they fell from 20 to 30 per cent of the population before the war to only 1 or 2 per cent after it. They became insignificant minorities. The only group that not only maintained but increased its presence was the Russians. Overall, Ukraine became much a more ethnically homogeneous and predominantly urban society – in short, a modern nation.

In this sense, 1914 is as powerful a symbol as 1492. These are two points at which global history became closely linked to

Ukraine's national history and set in action large-scale transformations that put Ukraine on the world map.

Both processes began in 'old' Europe. This is even true of Bolshevism: Marxism, with its idea of world revolution, originated in the West, not in the East. Of course Russia showed the deadly mutations that concept could take on when it spread beyond its 'historical homeland'.

Violence lay at the heart of both processes. This has to be emphasised because we often hold a very sanitised understanding of modernisation. When we talk about modernity, we often mean phenomena and processes that made human life easier and more comfortable: railroads, modern communications, medical progress and the development of education. But all of these innovations were products of the second wave of global modernisation, which occurred during the 'long' nineteenth century, the most peaceful in European history. In contrast, the first wave of globalisation, which began in 1492, and the third wave, which began in 1914, were exceedingly violent.

In the *Divine Comedy*, Dante writes that we cannot understand the greatness of human nature if we do not see the depths of its greatest downfall. The same is true of modernisation: we can't understand its brightness without the dark side. In the Ukrainian 'short' twentieth century, this dark side dominated. Ukrainian identity was most clearly manifested during the revolutionary and military crises.

This is not to say that the Ukrainian nation would not have emerged without war and revolution. The nineteenth century had set in motion nation-building processes that seemed unstoppable. Even before 1914, Russian Minister Sergei Witte was already convinced that over the next fifty years the nobility would become utterly impoverished and disappear from the socio-political scene. Anton Chekhov offered the same image, but in different words, in his play *The Cherry Orchard*, which, by the way, is set in the vicinity of Kharkiv. In the early 1920s, Stalin spoke of the historical inevitability ('one cannot go against history') of the Ukrainisation of cities in Ukraine. To illustrate the point, he cited the fate of Riga in Latvia or cities in Hungary that had once been German but became Hungarian. Economic historian Franciszek Bujak made a similar argument regarding Austrian Galicia. He compared the prospects of the local Poles to the fate of the English nation in Ireland and the German nation in the Czech lands and Silesia. In the 1890s, Ukrainian Marxists were convinced that it was the Rus-Ukrainian peasantry of Galicia who were doomed to disappear from those lands. They viewed the mass peasant emigration to North America as the initial stages of this process.

We can look for the answer as to whether modernisation is possible without violence by exploring statistics from the time. Following the Bolshevik cultural revolution, the literacy rate in Soviet Ukraine doubled from 44 per cent to 88 per cent between 1926 and 1939. In Czechoslovak-ruled Transcarpathia, the rate almost tripled – from 22 per cent in 1910 to 60 per cent in 1930. (We do not have data for 1939 but can safely assume that it was even higher.) In other words, Transcarpathia experienced a small-scale cultural revolution without collectivisation of the peasantry, closure and destruction of churches, repression of the clergy, etc. Even in 'backward' Volhynia, the interwar years of Polish rule brought new schools and roads, increased electrification and so on – all those things we call civilisational changes. If we step back to broaden our view, we will see that in the period between the world wars, countries from across the European periphery – Bulgaria, Greece, Spain, Portugal, Turkey, Sweden and Yugoslavia – were slowly modernising and catching up.

In other words, traditional society throughout Europe was crumbling and dying, without war or revolution. Barbara Kirshenblatt-Gimblett, a scholar of Eastern European Jewry, has provided an excellent summary of the balance between tradition and modernity in the first half of the twentieth century. She writes that although many Jews were already leaving behind the traditional world of the shtetl in the early twentieth century, it took the Russian Revolution and the Holocaust to put the final nails in the coffin. Analogies to the Ukrainian village and the Holodomor are obvious.

Of course, the Ukrainian nation might have had different borders without the war and the revolution. Frankly, it is unlikely that the Ukraine nation would have stretched from Transcarpathia in the southwest all the way to Donbas in the east. The unification of all these lands into a single state was undoubtedly due to the Bolsheviks. But the Bolsheviks did not gather the lands out of goodwill. They wanted to control the geopolitically important and resource-rich borderlands. They would have struggled to retain power in the centre without them.

It bears repeating: Ukraine was born in the fires of war and revolution. This means that it has the birth trauma of war and revolutionary violence.

The first trauma is related to material damages. When Ukrainian independence was proclaimed in 1991, it would have been hard to find a family in Ukraine where property had passed from hand to hand for three generations-from grandparents to parents, from parents to children. Only a few isolated things survived: an old, yellowed photograph, an embroidered shirt from a trunk, a musical instrument. There are almost no instances where the main family capital – houses, jewellery, stocks or cash savings – were passed down through the family line for three generations. Each generation had to start from scratch.

Certainly there were material losses as the result of two world wars. But the main blow to property came during the collectivisation of peasant farms. As a result, the attitude to property changed radically. For instance, in a traditional village, theft was treated very harshly. Thieves were punished, sometimes severely, and if the theft involved horses or cattle, they might be beaten to death. There is an obvious explanation for this norm: in a subsistence-level society, the loss of a horse or cow could mean starvation for a family. In contrast, when private property was eliminated after collectivisation, theft became the norm. New proverbs even appeared during the Soviet era: 'If you don't steal, you won't live.' The logic is simple: since the state has robbed us and continues to rob us, we have the right and even a sacred duty to respond in kind. This new 'tradition' survived the Soviet era. Owners of modern large agricultural firms in Ukraine complain that they lose up to 30 per cent of their profits to theft. Reducing it to 7–8 per cent is considered a great achievement.

Another change concerns cities. In contrast to the First World War, when the main battles were fought outside of cities, in the Second World War the biggest battles involved urban combat. The population groups targeted for elimination first were also predominantly urban: the Jews and the political and cultural elites. The urban population suffered enormous losses during the war. In some cases, such as in Kyiv and Lviv, up to 80 per cent of the population. All of which meant that a significant number of people who moved to the cities after the war moved into houses and apartments that had belonged to someone else before the war.

Disrespect for property has become normalised: we can see it in the businessmen who organise raider attacks on other people's property and in the government officials who tolerate these attacks and sometimes even organise them. In any case, Ukraine's history means that it will take a lot of time and effort to make a culture of honest business the norm.

The next consequence is corruption. Of course, corruption is a complex phenomenon with a variety of causes. But often the most corrupt countries are also those that have suffered extreme violence. This is understandable: in such circumstances, corruption is a survival strategy. Independent Ukraine is 'famed' for corruption. How long the traces of extreme violence continue is anyone's guess.

But Ukraine's greatest birth trauma is socio-demographic in nature. The wars caused huge losses among all population groups. There were, however, some groups who proportionally suffered the most losses: Jews, men of military age and the middle class. There appeared to be a reverse Darwinian selection: those who died in in the first turn at the front were often the most active, honest, intelligent and hardworking people. Those who survived included, more often than not, opportunists, the people who did not take a stance and were socially apathetic. Overall, the war and revolution of 1914–45 deprived Ukrainian society of many of its most dedicated members. Such a society can be more easily controlled and manipulated.

This doesn't mean that there were no Ukrainians who supported the Soviet government. There weren't many in 1941, but far more from 1943–44. Experience on the front and under Nazi occupation represents a turning point. A new generation of elites emerged from the war: men with frontline experience. Living under constant threat of death on the frontlines had freed them from the fear of Stalin's terror and made them proactive and self-confident. The victory over Nazi Germany granted new legitimacy to the Soviet regime. The Ukrainians felt that they owed their survival to the Kremlin and their alliance with the Russian people.

In postwar Ukraine, there were two forms of Ukrainian identity: national and Soviet. Geographically, the differences between these two forms more or less coincided with the pre-war border of 1939. The national form of identity dominated in Western Ukraine, while the Soviet form dominated everywhere else. Even before the war there had been significant differences within the Ukrainian population. The war exacerbated them many times over due to the very different experiences of the German occupation and the anti-communist nationalist underground.

But the image of 'two Ukraines', a Soviet one and a national one, does not describe the actual situation well. Neither the Soviet nor the national formula of Ukrainian identity has successfully formed the identity of the majority. The majority has existed in a condition of profound ambivalence in which people incorporated fragments of both identities.

This condition is the result of the cumulative effects of Soviet and Nazi violence which led Ukrainians to be apathetic and passive. At the point when communism fell, Ukrainians were not inclined to trust each other: the circle of trust rarely extended beyond family and a circle of close friends. Research shows that Ukrainian behaviour during the German occupation was characterised by a profound lack of trust. But Ukrainian society had been in this state long before the Germans arrived in 1941. The disintegration of social ties began during the First World War and the revolution; the Soviet terror of the 1930s dealt the fatal blow.

Ambivalence doesn't just describe the state of Ukrainian Soviet society. It also describes the general effect of 'modernisation through violence'. Over time, some victories turn into defeats. From the 1960s–80s, even the 'defeated' European countries had significantly better social and economic indicators than the 'victorious' USSR. Eventually, what became important wasn't who had won or lost the war, but who successfully modernised without war and revolution. The secret to successful modernisation is not rapid development, but sustainable development. The USSR may have modernised rapidly in the 1920s and '30s and even achieved dizzying results. However, Soviet modernisation proved to be uncompetitive as soon as mass violence began to decline on the European continent. Violence doesn't create anything that can be sustained.

INTERLUDE
A Brief History of Violence

Anyone with cardiac issues should likely skip over this section and go straight to the next. Everyone else should read it only to get some idea of the levels of violence in Ukraine from 1914–45.

Statistics show the scale of this violence. But statistics have little effect on the imagination and depersonalise the victims. Timothy Snyder makes an important point in his book *Bloodlands*: when we talk about the millions of dead, we must remember that we are not talking about abstract millions, but about millions of individual deaths.

The most direct way to overcome the indifference of statistics is to imagine, every time you read these numbers, that your sister or your brother, husband, wife, child or parents – any of your loved ones – were killed.

This is how the imagination of children who witnessed violence worked. In the mid-1920s, teachers asked a group of students at a school in Przemyśl about their most vivid childhood memories. They would describe how a friend was shot and killed by the enemy, how their brother was led to the firing squad and how their older sister was raped: their most vivid memories were of death and of corpses on the battlefield.

The year 1914 became the trigger for mass violence. In the very first weeks of the war, entire groups of civilians were victimised.

People who were considered unreliable or suspected of treason were hanged or sent to concentration camps. On the Austro-Hungarian side, suspicion fell on Galician and Transcarpathian Rusyns, especially Russophile Rusyns. On the Russian side, it was the Germans, Jews and nationally conscious Ukrainians. One small, but telling detail, which would happen again later, speaks to the degeneration of society: those who carried out the sentences, formerly ordinary civilians, liked to have themselves photographed in front of the people they had hanged, even when they were children or women, like successful hunters being photographed in front of their trophies, the prey they had killed.

On 15 September 1914, Hungarian soldiers committed a massacre in Przemyśl, during the retreat of the Austro-Hungarian army. A group of prisoners from a nearby village, who had been arrested under suspicion of treason, were being marched through the city. One of the Hungarian soldiers recognised people who had attacked a cavalry patrol and killed his comrades. (As it turned out later, their village was not even in the combat zone.) He stopped the convoy, approached a seventeen-year-old girl, put a revolver to her head and fired. The shot set off a massacre. The villagers were cut down with sabres and beaten to death with sticks. The convoy guards stood by without interfering. The attack lasted for half an hour. When the police finally arrived at the scene of the massacre, they found human bodies turned to pulp. Only two of the forty-six victims survived.

The Bolshevik seizure of power in November 1917 set off a new wave of mass terror. There was a direct connection between the waves of violence of war and revolution. Research into the 1918–19 pogroms shows that many of those who carried them out had also participated in anti-Jewish riots at the start of the war when they were soldiers in the regular army. The same is true of the anti-landowner riots of 1917, which were often instigated by soldiers who had returned home from the front. However, this wave of violence was relatively bloodless. For the most part, the landlords were not killed – they and their families were 'simply' expelled from their properties. This 'gentle' wave ended in early 1918.

That's when the Red Terror began. On 23 January 1918, the Red Army Commander Mikhail Muravyov entered the Ukrainian capital. He issued an order that very day calling for the 'ruthless elimination of all officers and cadets, Haidamaks, monarchists and enemies of the revolution'. Anything might become a pretext for execution: a 'bourgeois appearance' (such as a lack of calluses on the hands) or a 'nationalist' Cossack moustache. In three days of terror (26–28 January), the Bolsheviks killed between 1,300 and 5,000 people according to estimates.

The Bolsheviks later condemned the excesses in Kyiv, but they didn't abandon revolutionary violence. 'Do you really think,' Lenin asked, 'that we took power in order to coddle our enemies?' The Bolshevik terror was an order of magnitude beyond the terror of other regimes. Other instigators of terror were scary, but almost amateurish with their spontaneous pogroms and massacres. The Bolshevik terror was professional, proactive and systematic, directed at the achievement of strategic goals. At one point Moscow received complaints from the Odesa region about the outrages of Bolshevik units that not only requisitioned grain from local peasants, but also robbed and shot them. The head of the Odesa Revolutionary Committee, Pavel Blyakhin, was sent to investigate. And although his investigation showed that the complaints were justified, his conclusion was the opposite of what one might expect. Blyakhin advised more revolutionary terror, not less. The terror should serve strategic goals and it was necessary to 'screw Ukraine tighter and tighter so that its lifeblood would flow not just as far as Kharkiv, but all the way to Moscow'.

The first wave of Bolshevik terror ended in the spring of 1918, when the Bolsheviks were forced to retreat from Ukrainian lands after the conclusion of the Treaty of Brest-Litovsk. German and Austro-Hungarian occupation forces took over. The cities where the troops were stationed became oases of peace and stability, particularly in comparison to what was happening in Russia under Bolshevik rule. The situation was rather different in the villages. The occupation authorities tried to restore the landowners and seize grain from the peasants to satisfy the needs of the army and the home front. When they encountered resistance, they meted out severe punishments. The peasants were beaten with whips and shot; their houses and property were burned.

After the war ended, the wheel of violence spun faster and faster. When the Central Powers surrendered, the Austro-German occupation forces left Ukraine. Any semblance of stable governance disappeared along with them. A new wave of violence against landowners commenced. This time the landowners were killed so that it would be impossible for them to return. A doctor in Poltava recorded the mood of the rebels in a diary entry on 29 November 1918 when Ukrainian National Republic troops entered the city. They discussed dividing Poltava into districts and to kill 'all bourgeoisie over the age of ten, because otherwise they'll just grow into more bourgeoisie'.

While attacks against landowners continued in the parts of Ukraine which had been part of the Russian empire, the Polish-Ukrainian War broke out in Galicia. People would later call it the last 'romantic' war of the nineteenth century, in which both sides showed mutual respect in battle and avoided repressions against the civilian population. While there were individual cases of such gallantry, they didn't actually characterise the war overall. Like every war, it involved arrests, detention camps and executions. The unromantic nature of the war can be seen in the anti-Jewish pogrom committed by Polish troops as soon as they occupied Lviv on 22 November 1918. Officers and soldiers were seething with the desire to retaliate against Jews who had allegedly sided with the Ukrainian authorities. According to various estimates, between fifty and 150 Jews were killed, over fifty Jewish homes were burned and over five hundred shops were looted. The official reports afterward made claims that would become familiar in other reports: so-called 'troublemakers', workers and criminals that the Ukrainians had supposedly released from prison as they retreated were responsible for the killing and looting. In reality, later research showed that the pogrom was carried out by the regular army and that the Polish intelligentsia watched with pleasure as Jews were shot at as they fled from burning houses and Polish ladies came to loot with their maids so that they would have someone to carry their looted items home.

In one episode, an elegant-looking Polish soldier and two companions entered the home of the Neuer family and shot the apartment's owner, a Jewish soldier in the Austrian army who had returned from Russian captivity just a few weeks earlier. The pogromist took his wedding ring and pocket watch and the jewellery his wife had hidden under her shirt. Then he knocked out her gold tooth with a revolver and started beating her elderly mother and children as they screamed. Tired, he sat down at the piano in the next room and played skilfully for an hour and a half, after which he returned and robbed the women again. As he left the apartment with two bags of loot, he tossed the dead body at the women and children: 'Now deal with your corpse.'

The Lviv pogrom, however, paled in comparison to what was happening on the other side of the former Austrian-Russian border. There, the largest wave of pogroms against Jews in world history began, to be exceeded only by the Holocaust. Among them was the infamous pogrom in Proskuriv (now Khmelnytskyi) on 14–15 February 1919. The pretext was an attempt by young Jewish Bolsheviks to revolt against the Ukrainian National Republic. The uprising failed. And then, Ataman Ivan Semosenko addressed the Ukrainian soldiers with a speech: 'The Jews are the most dangerous enemy of the Ukrainian people. They must be slaughtered to save Ukraine.' The soldiers lined up in marching order and marched into town while a band played. The local Jews didn't know anything about the Bolshevik uprising. They were religious Jews, far removed from Bolshevism and politics. The pogrom began on Shabbat, just after the Jews had returned from synagogue and were sitting down to the meal. Investigation results and survivor testimonies allow us to understand what took place. In one house, an old woman was so mutilated by bayonets that her own son could barely identify her. The bodies of her other son and two daughters lay next to her. A girl from a neighbouring home survived, but had twenty-eight stab wounds. In another house, a mother begged them to leave her children alive and offered the perpetrators money, but they replied that they 'only came for her soul'. Elsewhere, the looters saw a girl so beautiful that no one dared to stab her; the one who finally did boasted of the feat afterwards. One local Orthodox priest, a Fr Klymentiy Kachurovsky, ran out into the street, grabbed a child who was running away from the rioters and shouted at them: 'Christian people, what are you doing?' He and the child were killed on the spot. Nearly 1,500 people were killed in the Proskuriov pogrom, almost 10 per cent of the Jewish population, without regard to gender or age.

As we've noted, Makhno's army did not commit anti-Jewish pogroms. They attacked and murdered German colonists instead. And not only. Here is an episode recounted by Makhno's chief of staff, Viktor Bilash:

> Makhno's train was standing on the platform and people were crowded around the locomotive. Makhno was shouting: 'Toss the shaggy devil into the furnace! Look how fat the parasite's gotten off us!'
>
> As we got closer, we saw Shchus, Liuty and Lenetchenko on

> the locomotive struggling with an extremely fat, bearded old man in black robes who was on his knees next to the firebox ... Everyone was just standing there. The priest tried to defend himself, but they grabbed him firmly. His head disappeared into the door with his hands still waving around a bit. A moment later, his legs disappeared as well. The fire flared up and black smoke poured out of the chimney. People in the crowd spit on the ground without saying anything and moved away.
>
> It turned out that the priest had been at the station urging the rebels to stop fighting the Germans in the name of God and humanity ...

All the local armies, without exception, carried out pogroms. In the Red Army, Semyon Budyonny's cavalry was especially 'renowned' and is described in Isaac Babel's *Red Cavalry*. However, the percentage of pogroms led by Bolsheviks was relatively low: they preferred systematic mass terror. In any case, the Bolshevik command decisively stopped the pogroms and punished the perpetrators. It is unsurprising that many Jews saw the Red Army as their protector and young people signed up as volunteers. Often, the main motive was a desire for revenge (German colonists did the same by joining the White Army to settle scores with the Makhnovists). Here is a description of a scene after a battle in which a Red Army unit defeated a unit of the Ukrainian National Republic Army and the wounded Ukrainian soldiers lay on the battlefield:

> One Jewish soldier from Berdychiv went crazy. He would wipe the blood off his saber onto the grass and with each severed head, he shouted: 'This is for my murdered sister, this is payback for my murdered mother!' The Jewish crowd stood silent, holding their breath.

The Soviet government enabled social mobility for young Jews that they could never have imagined under the old regime. This was most noticeable in the government enforcement organs. Before the revolution, there was not a single Jew in the police force or imperial guard; after the revolution, they constituted a sizeable portion of the security organs, especially in the former Pale of Settlement. Here is an event from Stalin's terror of the late 1930s. Ukraine was one of his main targets. In 1938, Nikolai Yezhov, head of the NKVD, took the 'Ukrainian' operation under his direct control. Before leaving for Kyiv, he gathered the Moscow NKVD staff who were to travel with him to Ukraine. Yezhov asked: 'Who here speaks Ukrainian?' One of them just laughed: 'There's no Ukrainians there [in the Ukrainian NKVD], just Jews.' Yezhov instructed someone to check the personnel of the Ukrainian NKVD and report on the results. Looking through the inspection materials, he said: 'I looked at the staff lists; that's not Ukraine, it's pure Birobidzhan' (the Jewish Autonomous Oblast in the Soviet Far East).

Materials from the case of the Uman group who operated out of the prison in the town of Uman illustrate some of the forms of Stalinist terror. Prisoners were kept standing continuously for ten to fifteen days to force confessions. The commanders of the prison organised what they called concerts, demanding that the prisoners beat one another, sing and dance. Those who confessed were shot right in the prison yard, then their gold teeth would be knocked out with a revolver and the guards would divide up their belongings among themselves. Attractive girls among the arrestees were raped and then penetrated with various implements.

The most numerous group among the victims of Stalinist terror were the peasants. According to one NKVD officer in Kharkiv, Ukrainians were not 'suited to' communism, so they should be replaced as 'ethnographic material.' Subjugation of the Ukrainian peasants took place in several waves. The essential and final one was the Holodomor of 1932–33.

Starvation is one of the worst ways to die. Death by bullet or sabre is quick, whereas death by starvation takes a long time. In addition to the physical suffering, there is moral anguish: the victims did not suffer alone, they saw the torment and slow death of their loved ones. The famine destroyed the internal solidarity that was key to the culture of the traditional village. The survivors recalled that a person will stop at nothing in the face of hunger and pain. Few people have a faith that is stronger than the body. People were prepared to commit any crime for a crust of bread: theft, murder, looting. They sometimes resorted to cannibalism. In his memoirs, Nikita Khrushchev cited an episode from the later, postwar famine of 1946–49, that the first secretary of the Odesa Communist Party committee had described to him. Kyrychenko described entering the house of a collective farmer, where he saw a woman cutting into her child's dead body on the table saying: 'We've already eaten Manechka and now we'll salt Vanechka. That will last us for a while.' 'She went mad from hunger and stabbed her own children to death. Can you imagine?' asked Kyrychenko.

While the peasantry were being destroyed in Soviet Ukraine, Ukrainian villages in Polish Galicia were being subjected to 'pacification'. Pacifications lasted from July to December 1930 and impacted about 450 villages with 1,700 people arrested. The actions all followed the same scenario: a police unit would enter the village, villagers were prevented from leaving and then the houses were searched for weapons and nationalist literature. During the searches, the property of villagers and Ukrainian civic organisations was deliberately destroyed and then the physical violence would begin. The villagers, regardless of gender and age (the youngest victim was three and the oldest was eighty-three), were beaten with rifle butts and police batons, sometimes until they lost consciousness, after which they were revived by pouring water on them and then beaten again. This was accompanied by the words: 'Here's your Ukraine!' Villagers were forced to shout: 'Long live Piłsudski', sing the Polish anthem and eat dirt until they said whose soil it was – Polish or Ukrainian.

In the summer of 1938, state-sponsored terror in Poland reached the population of the Chelm and Podlasie regions, territories where there had been no particular interethnic tensions. This time the Orthodox Church was targeted. The action was carried out under the slogan of 'Revindication of everything that had been Polish and Catholic before the partitions (of Poland)'. The claim was that the local population had been forcibly converted to Orthodoxy under the Russian Empire and the time had come to correct historical injustices. One hundred and twenty-seven Orthodox churches were destroyed over the course of two months. People who attempted to maintain access to the churches were dispersed with rifle butts and beaten with rubber batons. Although there were no fatalities, there was plenty of blood. The event formed a significant barrier blocking any route towards Polish-Ukrainian reconciliation. The Polish art historian and poet Tadeusz Chrzanowski, whose childhood was spent in the interwar Chelm region, recalled how his father, upon hearing about the brutal destruction of the Orthodox churches, 'cursed the Polish government ... saying that we (the Poles) would be slaughtered here by the Rusyns, slaughtered without the slightest mercy, that we would be held accountable'.

Regardless of how disturbing these attacks on the Ukrainian population of interwar Poland were, they don't compare to Bolshevik terror. For instance, 90 per cent of those arrested during the pacification were acquitted and released – this was unimaginable under the Soviets! Terror was more than just a tool for the Soviet government; it was the essence of Soviet power. We can look at figures of repressions on the territory of Poland from 1939–41, when it was under dual German-Soviet occupation. The rates of physical repression, including imprisonment, deportations and murders, were three to four times higher in the Soviet-occupied zone than in the German zone.

The final act of Soviet violence in Western Ukraine in 1939–41 took place in the days immediately following the German invasion, when they murdered 10–40,000 prisoners. Many of these people had simply been picked up in the streets and held based on suspicion or denunciation. There were members of multiple ethnic and social groups, including members of Polish and Jewish organisations and particularly Ukrainians. When the Germans entered Lviv and other western Ukrainian cities at the end of June 1941, they opened the doors of prisons to reveal the atrocities of the NKVD. The sight of mutilated bodies revealed that many prisoners had been tortured before their deaths. And then Germans, Ukrainians from the newly created police force, relatives of the murdered prisoners and ordinary citizens carried out a large-scale massacre of local Jews in retaliation for their alleged support of the Soviet regime.

The son of a rabbi in Lviv described the pogrom in his memoirs:

> I can clearly remember one of those Ukrainian policemen. He was dressed in an embroidered shirt and an elegant traditional jacket. He beat us with an iron rod. His blows gradually became more methodical and began to fall even on our heads. Each blow tore a piece of flesh from our bodies. The politsai officer gouged people's eyes out and ripped off their ears. When his stick broke, he just grabbed a piece of wood from the fireplace and hit my neighbour on the head with it. His brain splashed out of his crushed skull and pieces landed on my face and clothes. The unfortunate man died immediately. Breathing heavily, the killer turned to the wall to rest for a moment. His rapacious face, red eyes and swollen veins looked terrifying and repulsive.

The only group in occupied Ukraine who were not targeted by the German terror were ethnic Germans: the Volksdeutsch and German colonists. Unlike Western European Jews, who died in death camps, Eastern European Jews were shot in the 'Holocaust by bullets'. In Babyn Yar in Kyiv, the Nazis, assisted by the local police, shot approximately 34,000 Jews in a single day on 29 September 1941. There are approximately five thousand Nazi execution sites throughout Ukraine.

Ukraine became an experimental site for the extermination of Jews. Here the Germans first tested the method of 'sardine packing'. Victims were undressed and ordered to lie down at the bottom of a dug pit. They were shot right in the hold and their bodies were covered with dirt. (This resulted in some people, primarily children, being buried alive.) Then, in order to save space, the next layer of bodies was placed on top of them and so on, until the hole was filled. In almost every village, there are reports of the ground continuing to move for days after the shootings.

The extermination of Jewish children created a separate 'problem'. During the German offensive in the summer of 1941, in one Ukrainian village, military chaplains came upon a house full of children whose parents had been shot a day or two before. The children had been left in the heat without food or water. The chaplains were shocked by the conditions in which the children were kept. Their recommendations, however, had nothing to do with Christian charity. They wrote in their report that the children's incessant crying could be heard by German soldiers and local Ukrainians. They advised that in the future, such circumstances should be better concealed from the public.

Between 1941 and 1944, about 1.5 million Jews died in Ukraine, one quarter of the 6 million victims of the Holocaust. The Holocaust represents the top of a pyramid of violence on Ukrainian lands, as the 'purest' and 'most complete' genocide. Below it were others, not as complete, but with many victims. The mass murder of Red Army prisoners of war by the Nazis is one of them. The number of victims (4 million, including 1.6 million in Ukraine) approaches the number of victims of the Holocaust.

It is impossible to accurately estimate the frontline losses in the Soviet-German War. In the summer of 1941, the Germans passed through Soviet territory like a knife through butter. In the words of one veteran, the only way to stop them was to 'pour blood on the blade of the knife. Gradually, it began to rust and grow dull and move more and more slowly'. Orders to end military operations by certain favoured dates resulted in particularly heavy losses. For instance, Soviet forces were ordered to take Kyiv by the anniversary of the October Revolution on 7 November 1943. The highest casualty rates of the entire war were tallied in the concomitant Battle of the Dnieper, averaging 27,300 people per day.

Soviet soldiers were pointlessly sent to their deaths. The officers drove them to their deaths regiment after regiment. Some of the officers who had a conscience, went into battle and died with their soldiers. Anyone who retreated would be gunned down by the NKVD, who lay just behind the trenches. The soldiers were as scared of the NKVD as they were of the Germans. Frontline veterans who tried to tell the truth about what had happened called it the 'Stalin-Hitler genocide'.

Behind the front lines, the partisan war was also characterised by extreme violence, particularly in Volhynia. There were three partisan armies operating in the forests and swamps of Volhynia: Soviet partisans, the Polish Home Army, the Ukrainian Insurgent Army. Other groups were also hiding in the forests including Jews who had escaped the Germans, groups of Borovets' men (called Bulbashi) and just plain bandits. In those circumstances, anything could trigger a long chain of violence. Soviet partisans would stage a provocation near Ukrainian villages and the local police, which consisted mainly of Ukrainians, would be sent to carry out a punitive action. Instead, they would refuse to kill

Ukrainian villagers and end up joining the UPA. Many of these policemen had participated in the extermination of Jews and were prepared to kill again. When the Ukrainian policemen had disappeared into the forest, the German authorities replaced them with local Poles. The Polish police were much more prepared to deal with the Ukrainian peasants: the long shadow of the Polish-Ukrainian hostilities of 1918–39 hung over Volhynia. Late in the war, an additional factor came into play: with the Red Army approaching from the east and American troops landing in southern Italy, the question arose as to who would own the western Ukrainian lands after the war – a restored Poland or Ukraine?

In the summer of 1943, the UPA decided to resolve the issue by fait accompli. On the night of Sunday, 11 July 1943, UPA units simultaneously attacked several dozen Polish villages. The insurgent commander Klym Savur (Dmytro Kliachkivsky) was one of the leaders of the punitive action. Standing on a high grave on the night of the action, he surveyed the fires burning the surrounding Polish villages with pleasure, according to the memoirs of one of the nationalists. For Savur, this was a 'protest against all of the interlopers and foreigners encroaching on Ukrainian freedom and land'.

One of the most infamous of the anti-Polish actions took place in the village of Poryck (Pavlivka). A group of Banderites entered the Catholic church during the service. Within half an hour, they had killed three hundred Poles, regardless of age or gender, and then set the church on fire. Once they had eliminated the population of Poryck, they moved on to a neighbouring village and two hamlets. There, they killed another 180 people, again, regardless of age or gender, looted and burned homes and took livestock.

The Poles' Ukrainian neighbours also took part in these actions. This is shown by the fact that the victims were killed not only with bullets, but also with sickles, scythes and axes. Sometimes it can be difficult to draw a clear line between peasants and insurgents. The UPA was largely a peasant army and Ukrainian insurgents used axes as weapons. For instance, when they discovered a Gestapo agent in their ranks, a UPA court sentenced him to death by beheading with an axe. The sentence was carried out publicly by a field commander, one of those who, together with Klym Savur, had participated in the destruction of Polish villages.

The Polish Home Army turned to preventive and retaliatory actions. The Pawłokoma massacre took place from 1–3 March 1945, after the front line had already moved to the west. It was set off by the appearance of an unidentified military unit that arrested seven Poles and took them into the forest. The identity of the unit is still unknown: there were no UPA units operating in the area. There has been speculation that it may have been an NKVD unit in disguise. In any case, the arrested men disappeared without a trace. At a meeting in a neighbouring Polish village, the Home Army led by Lt Józef Biss and local men decided to take revenge by killing all Ukrainian males over the age of fifteen. During the retaliatory action, the age limit was significantly lowered and gender didn't matter. The village was surrounded while its residents were attending church. According to survivors, the Poles separated girls under ten and boys under seven and shot everyone else at the Greek Catholic Cemetery near the church. Some of the men were beaten to death with chains. The attackers cut a cross into the chest of the Orthodox priest, wrapped him in barbed wire, dragged him by horses around the church and then beat him with chains. Before they died, the victims were stripped of their clothing and shoes, which the killers shared among themselves. The surviving women and children were taken to the forest and told: 'Cross the Zbruch River and never come back!'

Soviet partisans were responsible for similar actions. In 1943, they attacked the village of Stara Rafalivka. A Banderite detachment had briefly entered the town and left behind a small outpost. The next morning, Soviet partisans attacked. The villagers hid wherever they could. One girl ran into a barn to save her kittens. The Soviet partisans set fire to the barn and threw her into the fire alive. Her burned body was found afterwards. In one root cellar, the body of a young boy was found with his stomach split open by a bayonet. His mother had been hiding somewhere else and when her son was found, she walked around clutching his dead body oblivious to her surroundings – grief had driven her mad. The partisans took some of the men to a memorial mound the Banderites had erected to commemorate their dead. The partisans forced the villagers to dig out the entire mound with their hands. When the ground was level, they were shot. All that remained of the village were a few cottages.

One might suppose that the eyewitness accounts of the atrocities are exaggerated, but the stories of the perpetrators themselves convince us that this is not the case. Oleksandr Dovzhenko recorded the words of an acquaintance who worked with the NKVD, who said, 'I hung the nationalist upside down and burned him over a slow fire, cutting pieces of flesh off of him (. . .) and the snake died screaming: "Glory to Ukraine!" I slaughtered so many of them . . . '

These examples help us understand the nature of extreme violence. It is often described as the terror of a brutal regime against a single large group: Nazi Germany against the Jews or the Soviet government against Ukrainian peasants. While the general image is correct, it is too narrow. There were many more acts of mass terror, often interconnected, that came wave after wave, with short or long breaks between them. The violence built until it reached extreme levels and no group was excluded. Every ethnic, social and professional group had both perpetrators and victims. The lines between military and civilians were blurred. Murder often took on an almost intimate character: the killers and victims knew each other by sight and had normal, even friendly, relations during peacetime.

The high number of victims in Ukraine was the result of extreme geopolitical instability, the large number of forces fighting for control and frequent changes of control. The state lost its monopoly on violence; it spilled out into the streets and became the standard solution to any conflict. In many periods of terror, such as in 1919, Ukraine perfectly demonstrated the old maxim that even the worst state is better than no state at all.

But the maxim is only partially true. It was not just the collapse of the state that caused rampant violence. Extreme violence was due to the fact that a new type of state, the 'spoiler state', was operating on the lands of Ukraine. A spoiler state goes beyond holding a monopoly on violence: violence becomes the very essence of the state, which cannot exist without it.

The USSR and Nazi Germany were two such states. The emergence of this type of state coincided with the emergence of modern technology, particularly technologies of violence. The nineteenth-century Russian exile Alexander Herzen predicted that the symbol of future Russia could be 'Genghis Khan with a telegraph', while Bukharin is said to have called Stalin 'Genghis Khan with a telephone'. Along that line, Hitler could be called 'Genghis Khan with gas chambers'. The Holocaust would not have been possible without technological progress: Hitler's concentration camps became modern death factories, their chimneys resembling those of factories and plants.

Of course, modern technology alone is not responsible for the extreme nature of the terror. The key role was played by the fact that both the Bolshevik and Nazi regimes were revolutionary regimes with global ambitions.

The Bolshevik regime professed world proletarian revolution, while Hitler's regime proselytised a national socialist revolution. The former was supposed to lead to the world domination of the proletariat, the latter to the world domination of the Aryan race. Revolutions are periods of 'beautiful madness' – the illusion that a 'brave new world' is just around the corner. All that remains is to destroy the last obstacles to victory: landowners, kulaks, Jews, etc. The initiators of mass terror believed that truth and the logic of history were on their side, so they justified the hecatomb of victims as a historical necessity.

These millennial visions were not unique to the Soviet or Nazi regimes. The peasants saw signs of the Apocalypse in both the First World War and the 1917 revolution. This explains why they were ready to carry out the 'last judgement' on their oppressors and take revenge for the injustices they had experienced in 1917–19. Similarly, the Banderites had a millennial vision with their theory of 'permanent revolution': an independent Ukrainian state would rise from Ukrainian victims and the corpses of their enemies.

In modern accounts, Russian and Polish narratives portray Ukrainian nationalism in general and the Bandera movement in particular, as the largest and most violent force in this period. This is false. The Banderites didn't unleash the terror. As Ukrainian poet Marianna Kiyanovska has succinctly put it, without Piłsudski, Bandera would have remained an ordinary insignificant agronomist. Moreover, the number of Bandera's victims pales in comparison to the scale of Bolshevik and Nazi terror.

The long nineteenth century in Ukraine has been called a 'laboratory of modernity'. The experience of 1914–45 allows us to use this metaphor in a different sense: the history of Ukraine provides an opportunity to study violence as an aspect of modernity with forensic precision. The history of modernity is largely the history of mass murder in the service of modernist visions. This idea of the connection between modernity and violence is nothing new. Social scientist Zygmunt Bauman studied this connection in relation to the Holocaust, the greatest tragedy of modern history. The history of Ukraine provides the opportunity to view this connection in the context of an entire region and across three decades.

It is surprising that so few people have examined Ukraine's

history from this perspective and drawn the appropriate conclusions. There are several possible reasons. First, every society seeks to normalise its experience. According to social psychologists, even during periods of massive change, most people continue to try to live a normal life: they get a job, fall in love, raise children ... In addition, people who have experienced significant trauma often didn't want to talk about it to avoid retraumatising themselves and to protect their children and grandchildren.

Second, the Soviet government's policy of collective amnesia after the war played an important and even decisive role. This policy seems to have reached a peak specifically in Ukraine (more on this later). The situation changed with the fall of communism. But here, the selectivity of national memory and the desire to create a 'convenient past' come into play. All of the countries that emerged from the fragments of the communist empire prefer to talk about *their* victims and not so much about *their* criminals. In today's Russia, any negative depiction of Russian history is a crime. Ukraine puts the memory of the Holodomor as one of the greatest acts of genocide in world history at the heart of its historical policy but does not have the courage to speak openly about the participation of Ukrainians in the Holocaust and in the Volhynia massacres. The current Polish government interprets the Volhynia massacre as genocide against Poles but chooses not to discuss the participation of Poles in the extermination of Jews and Ukrainians. Jews do not acknowledge Jewish NKVD officers, preferring to consider them communists rather than Jews.

An alternative to this egoistic morality is the solution proposed by Albert Camus: that we aim 'not to be on the side of the executioners'. We must stand in solidarity not with the executioners, but with the victims. Not only is this position morally honest, it corresponds accurately with history: the Ukrainian nation is not composed solely of heroes. In fact, executioners and heroes have always been in the minority. Ukrainians were more often victims.

Although Ukrainians compose the greatest number of victims by sheer numbers, all nations on these lands have suffered extreme violence, whether Ukrainian, Jewish, Crimean Tatar or any other of the multitude of nationalities who have lived on these lands.

Of course, a nation can't be built solely on victimhood. No nation can do without a heroic myth, especially during periods of major transformations or when fighting against external aggression. This is exactly the situation in Ukraine today. It is dramatic, but not hopeless. To build a new Ukrainian nation, we don't only need heroes ready to sacrifice their lives for the sake of ideals. We also need heroes who will show simple human decency and sacrifice their lives for the sake of others. There are plenty of examples of this type of heroism. When we read about prisoners in Hitler's and Stalin's camps, we find that the survivors almost always point to someone who helped them.

The Greek Catholic priest, Father Omelian Kovch, embodies this type of heroism. Kovch was born in Austrian Galicia in 1884 and lived under five different regimes in his sixty years of life. During the revolution, he was a chaplain in the Ukrainian Galician Army. When he and other prisoners were being transported to execution, he was saved by a Russian Red Army soldier who let him off the train with the words: 'Father, don't forget to pray for Luka.' In interwar Poland, Kovch defended the rights of Ukrainians and may have been a member of the OUN. In 1939–41, under the first Soviet regime, he helped the families of Polish officers deported to Siberia. During the German occupation, he saved Jews, for which he was sent to the Majdanek concentration camp, where he died. When his family tried to get him released, he wrote them a letter:

> I understand that you are trying to free me, but I ask you not to do anything ... Other than heaven, this is the only place I want to be. Here we are all equal. Poles, Jews, Ukrainians,

> Russians, Lithuanians, or Estonians. I am the only priest here. I can't imagine what they would do without me ... When I celebrate the Liturgy, they all pray. They pray in different languages, but doesn't the Lord understand all languages? They die in different ways and I help them cross the bridge.

The current Russian-Ukrainian war has brought great sacrifices to Ukraine, but there will also be many heroes, including, or above all, those who sacrifice themselves for others. Most of them have probably never heard of Omelian Kovch. But I hope that after the war, people like this Greek Catholic priest will occupy the highest place in the pantheon of Ukrainian heroes.

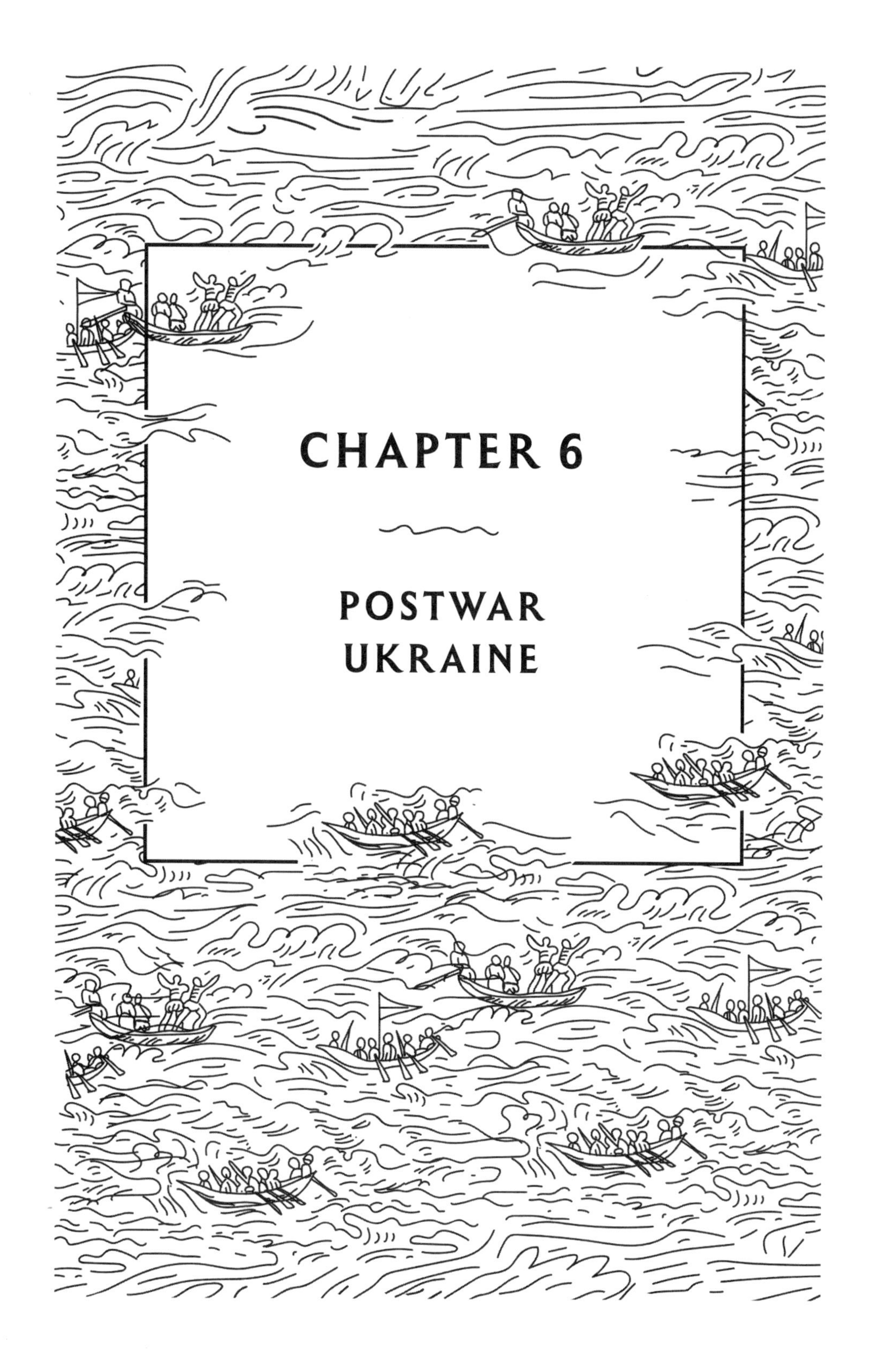

CHAPTER 6

POSTWAR UKRAINE

SOVIET UKRAINE, 1945–1991

A Country Without a Past

The story of the fate of the criminals who became 'famous' for the violence of 1914–45, what happened to them personally or to the memory of them after the war, tells something important about Soviet Ukraine after 1945. Let's start with those who were involved in the three largest pogroms of the revolutionary period, the Kyiv and Lviv pogroms of 1918 and the Proskuriv pogrom of 1919.

Mikhail Muravyov, the organiser of the mass terror in Kyiv in February 1918, was shot by the Bolsheviks themselves a few months later, not for the pogrom, but for his participation in an anti-Bolshevik coup in July 1918.

Ivan Semesenko, the military leader in the Proskuriv pogrom, was treated for syphilis in Proskuriv. According to Jewish legend, the ghost of a local rabbi would appear to him at night ordering him to leave the city immediately. The Ukrainian National Republic government investigated Semesenko's case and sentenced him to death. This sentence wasn't carried out because Kamianets-Podilskyi, where the Ukrainian government was located, was attacked by the Denikin Army, the court fled and Semesenko went free. As it turned out, he was executed, but only a year later during the Polish-Ukrainian march on Kyiv in the spring of 1920. One version says he was executed for the

Proskuriv pogrom, another for rebelling against Petliura. These two versions actually coincide, given that Semesenko criticised Petliura for 'trying to please both the socialists and the right-wing, the peasants and the landowners, the Jews and Europe'. He did have his admirers though among Petliura's followers. A veteran of the Ukrainian national liberation struggle wrote in his memoirs about Semesenko with regret, '. . . in other revolutionary circumstances, Ukraine would have had its own Mussolini in the figure of this iron dictator'.

Czesław Monczynski, who was responsible for the pogrom of Lviv Jews in November 1918, was more fortunate. He held high military positions in interwar Poland and even became a member of parliament. After he retired, he lived out the rest of his life on an estate in the Ternopil region. He was buried with honours in 1935 at the Cemetery of the Defenders of Lviv, which he had helped to create and which was intended to demonstrate the greatness and indomitability of the Polish martial spirit.

These three major pogroms and their main 'heroes' were never mentioned in postwar Soviet Ukraine. The only revolutionary events that mattered were those that affirmed the heroic version of the Bolshevik victory. One of the creators of that Bolshevik myth was Pavel Blyakhin, the man who had demanded in the early 1920s that Odesa-area peasants be shot. He became a writer after the revolution and wrote an adventure story called 'Red Devils'. One of the first Soviet adventure films was based on this story in 1923. Fate was kind to Blyakhin. He was one of the Old Bolsheviks and few of his cohort died a natural death – most of them were shot, imprisoned or exiled in the 1930s. He was again lucky when he was sent to the front in the summer of 1941 and his division was almost completely destroyed during the defence of Moscow in the autumn of that year: he survived. After the war, he became a member of the Soviet Writers' Union and died of natural causes in 1961. After his death, three films in the style of a

Soviet comedy western were made based on his novel: *The Elusive Avengers* (1966), *The New Adventures of the Elusive Avengers* (1968) and *The Crown of the Russian Empire, or The Elusive Again* (1971). The main storyline depicts young communists heroically fighting against Petliura bandits and brutal White Guards. All three films were very popular in the USSR and were later shown on television in independent Ukraine.

Nikolai Yezhov was shot in the next wave of Stalin's terror. His investigation materials included a denunciation from an NKVD agent that reported Yezhov's comment about the Ukrainian NKVD being a 'Birobidzhan'. That agent was also shot later.

In April 1941, Samuil Abramovych, the head of the Uman prison, was sentenced to six years in prison. In 1943, he was released early and sent to the front. However, he was not sent to the front line, but to a safer place as a driver. He was awarded the Order of the Red Star and the Medal for Battle Merit after the war. Two members of the Uman group who were sentenced to shorter terms, were also released early due to the war. Both 'fought' in their area of speciality, in the NKVD and one even rose to the position of deputy director of the SMERSH counter-intelligence department of the First Belorussian Front.

Lazar Kaganovich, one of the main organisers of the Holodomor, lived to the age of ninety-eight and died in Moscow in the summer of 1991, missing the collapse of the USSR by only a few months. In 1997, his memoirs, which he wrote in retirement, were published. Not only does he fail to express a single word of remorse, but he also doesn't even mention the Ukrainian famine. While Stalin was alive, Kaganovich was awarded four Orders of Lenin and received various other honours. Numerous places and institutions were named after him, including cities in Soviet Russia and Ukraine, the Moscow subway system and several institutions of higher education. When he lost the struggle for power after Stalin's death, Khrushchev had his name removed from public entities and he was expelled from government in 1957. Kaganovich's memory was unexpectedly rehabilitated after the fall of the USSR. A village in Russia was named in his honour, and in 2018, a monument was erected in Yekaterinburg depicting Kaganovich and Felix Dzerzhinsky together. There is also a village in Crimea named Lazarivka. In 2016, the Ukrainian parliament voted to return it to its old, Crimean Tatar name. This decision will take effect when Crimea returns to Ukraine.

Like Kaganovich, Erich Koch, the chief Nazi executioner of Ukraine, lived a long life. After the war, he hid in the British occupation zone and even received unemployment benefits, until he accidentally, through his own stupidity, revealed himself. He was arrested and turned over to the Soviet authorities, who then handed him over to communist Poland. There he was tried not for crimes in Ukraine, but for the deaths of 400,000 Poles killed when he was Gauleiter of West Prussia (1939–41). The investigation lasted almost ten years. During interrogations, Koch claimed credit for opposing Rosenberg's plans to create a Ukrainian state. In 1959, he was finally sentenced to death. However, the sentence was not carried out. One explanation suggests that he was not executed because he was terminally ill, another claims that he was a secret agent of Stalin. According to the Polish anti-communist opposition, Koch lived in comfortable conditions in prison, with access to television and daily newspapers. He died in 1986 at the age of ninety. In an interview with a West German journalist not long before his death, Koch said that he had no regrets and did not feel the need to repent of anything.

One of the initiators of the Volhynia massacres, Klym Savur (Dmytro Kliachkivsky), died in a battle with the Soviet NKVD on 12 February 1945, at the age of thirty-four. The UPA leadership posthumously awarded him the Order of the Iron Cross of Merit and the Iron Cross of Military Merit, first class. In independent Ukraine, streets in Lutsk, Ternopil and Rivne are named after him and two monuments have been erected – one in his hometown of Zbarazh and one in Rivne. A recent study shows that people in Rivne who pass this monument every day have only a very vague idea of who Klym Savur was.

Józef Biss, the commander of the Polish Home Army unit that committed the massacre in Pawłokoma, was arrested immediately after the war by the Polish communist authorities. The murder of Ukrainians was initially part of the case, but those charges were dropped. He was only convicted for participating in the anti-communist armed underground and was sentenced to eight years in prison. He served only half of this sentence. Biss was arrested several more times after his release from prison. He was offered the opportunity to join the Polish Communist Party at one point, but refused because he considered himself a 'man of honour'. Biss died of natural causes in 1977, and in 1992, a Polish court posthumously dropped all charges against him and ordered compensation to his family.

We don't know with certainty the identity of the NKVD officer described in screenwriter and director Oleksandr Dovzhenko's diary, the one who burned a Banderite over a slow fire and skinned him. In Lviv, I heard that Dovzhenko was referring to Anton Odukha, who before the war had worked at various times as an NKVD agent, an electrical engineer and a schoolteacher. During the war, he commanded a partisan unit and was awarded the title of Hero of the Soviet Union (1944). After the war, Odukha was appointed director of the Vasyl Stefanyk Scientific Library in Lviv, the second largest academic library in Ukraine. He held this position for ten years and then was granted special status as a 'political pensioner'. Even if Odukha was not the NKVD officer in Dovzhenko's diary, he was still credited with other 'exploits'. Villagers from the outskirts of the Khmelnytsky region, where his guerrilla unit operated, recall that he was responsible for robberies, rapes and the murders of old people and children. Immediately after his death in 1967, a monument to him was erected in Slavuta. According to Wikipedia, it was demolished in February 2022.

The one thing these 'heroes' have in common is the fact that none faced any consequences for the crimes they committed in Ukraine. The only ones who faced trial at all were typically tried for their connections with the German occupation regime or the Ukrainian nationalist underground. The two groups were often lumped together to create the impression that Ukrainian nationalists were Nazi collaborators. UPA soldiers were treated mercilessly, sentenced to maximum terms of up to twenty-five years or to the highest form of punishment, execution. The last execution of a UPA member was in the summer of 1989.

The KGB also organised the assassinations of nationalist movement leaders Lev Rebet in 1957 and Stepan Bandera in 1959. They were murdered secretly in exile, as was Yevhen Konovalets in Rotterdam in 1938 and, most likely, Petliura in 1926. The systematic way in which the Soviet secret services killed the leaders of Ukrainian nationalism shows that the Kremlin took the movement very seriously, although it was publicly portrayed as an insignificant force, lacking mass support and surviving only thanks to the West: the German General Staff during the revolution and the First World War, the Nazis during the Second World War and the American and West German governments in the postwar years.

All of the blame for Soviet mass repressions was later assigned to Stalin personally, as in Khrushchev's famous 1956 speech 'On the Cult of Stalin and Its Consequences' at the Twentieth Party Congress. Khrushchev had blood on his hands himself, just like everyone in Stalin's inner circle did, but he never admitted it. The 'Secret Speech' as it was called was not published in the USSR until 1989. From 1956 until 1989, the main Soviet line was reduced to the formula: 'Lenin – good, Stalin – bad.' Stalinist-era repressions were presented as a deviation in Soviet governance. In reality, the terror began not under Stalin, but under Lenin. And it was not a distortion, but the very essence of communist power. People only began openly addressing this fact towards the end of Gorbachev's *perestroika*. Even then it wasn't the government, but the anti-communist opposition who initiated the discussion. The government itself preferred not to mention Stalin at all, except for the occasional attempt to rehabilitate him in view of his supposed contributions, such as building socialism, winning the war and turning the USSR into a superpower.

The Soviet Union was like Hogwarts: there were names that must never be said. The Jews who died in the Holocaust could not be called Jews, only 'Soviet citizens'. It was the same with 'bourgeois Ukrainian nationalism': it existed, but without the names of Hrushevsky, Petliura and Bandera. The mere mention of these names was considered veiled propaganda for Ukrainian nationalism. After Stalin's death, Khrushchev eliminated his rivals in the resulting power struggle and became the first secretary of the CPSU Central Committee. He lasted there until he was ousted by Brezhnev in 1964, after which Khrushchev was not to be mentioned either. There was an unwritten rule: as soon as one of the top party figures faded into the shadows, his name should never be spoken aloud again (a Soviet leader was always a man, never a woman!). There was no official order as to who or what was to be forgotten. Conscious Soviet citizens had to sense it for themselves.

Historical memory is not only about what a society remembers but also about what is better forgotten. The policy of collective forgetting is especially important for a society undergoing radical change: amnesia helps facilitate a smooth transformation. This was the case in postwar West Germany after the fall of Hitler, in Spain after the death of the dictator Franco and even in Israel after its emergence as a young postwar state. However, in each of these cases, the policy of forgetting was only partial and it lasted only one or two decades. Then, when the transformation was over, discussions about the past were rekindled. The Kremlin's policies under Khrushchev and in the early years of Brezhnev can also be seen as efforts to reset the Soviet system. But those efforts ended after the late 1960s. Instead of reform, the top priority was stability. Therefore, the policy of collective amnesia in the Soviet Union continued almost up until the very end.

This was true in every single Soviet republic, but it seems to have taken an extreme form in Ukraine. Not only did Soviet repression need to be forgotten – anything that suggested any differences between Ukrainian history and Russian history were also subject to relegation. This ban extended to almost every Cossack hetman, with the sole exception of Khmelnytsky. Shevchenko's works were not officially banned, but his anti-Russian poems were not read in public, the unauthorised laying of flowers at his monument was equated with anti-Soviet activity and research into the Cyril and Methodius Brotherhood that was prepared for publication in the 1960s, ended up being shelved for several decades until it was finally published in 1990. You could compile an entire volume from Ivan Franko's works that were censored by the Soviets. Millions of copies of the works of the Russian prerevolutionary imperial historians Solovyov and Klyuchevsky were published in postwar USSR, while the works of the Ukrainian historian Hrushevsky were banned – despite the fact that he was a Soviet academic by the end of his life.

The Second World War was the central organising event of official memory policy. In the Soviet Union, it was called the 'Great Patriotic War' and shortened by two years: the war began with the 'treacherous attack of Nazi Germany' on 22 June 1941, as if the Molotov-Ribbentrop Pact had not given the green light to this war and the Red Army had not been at war since September 1939. The memory of the war pushed the memory of the revolution into the background. This is hardly surprising: while the revolution and the civil war divided the population into several hostile camps, the Great Patriotic War was a symbol of the unity of Soviet citizens in the fight against a common enemy. In other words, it was ideally suited to create an image of a cohesive and homogeneous society.

This model of memory began to dominate in the early years of Brezhnev's rule. In 1965, 9 May, the day the Germans surrendered, was declared a public holiday (under Stalin and Khrushchev, it was a regular workday). Although the cult of personality was officially condemned in 1956, in reality, the cults of Khrushchev and Brezhnev were created. One example is the story of the defence of Malaya Zemlya, a small outpost in the Second World War, which was blown into a major event in Brezhnev's public biography. There was a joke in Brezhnev's time: 'What is the Great Patriotic War? A local episode in the battle of Malaya Zemlya.'

The reality of the frontline was sacrificed to this model of memory: Brezhnev 'fought' as a party bureaucrat nowhere near the front line. Nikolai Nikulin, a front-line officer, wrote:

> Memoirs are written by those who were only somewhere near the war – in the second echelon, sitting at headquarters . . . They will survive, return home and eventually form the core of the veterans' organisations. They'll get fat, go bald, cover their chests in distinguished medals and orders and tell how heroically they fought, how they defeated Hitler. And they will believe it themselves! And they will bury the bright memory of those who died . . . They'll depict the war, that they actually know so little about, with a romantic halo. How good everything was, how beautiful! What heroes we are! And the fact that war is horror, death, hunger and absolute, utter hell, will fade into the background. And the ones who were actually on the frontlines, of whom there are just one and a half people left and even they are mindless and destroyed, they'll keep silent.

Another victim of this memory is the price Ukraine paid for the victory. Oleksandr Dovzhenko wrote in his diary:

> Ukraine lost 13 million people in the war. Even that is likely an undercount . . . Thus, the Great Widow lost 40 per cent of her people killed, burned, tortured, exiled and expelled to foreign lands to eternally wander . . . Not a single person has ever told me about this historical horror with tears or even sadness. No. Either they are silent, or avoid speaking, are indifferent, or smile in a way so no one will guess they're troubled, because it would be dangerous politically.

Certain acts of mass violence against civilians had to be passed over in silence. In the Soviet Union, not only was it impossible to speak of the Holodomor, the Holocaust and the Volhynia massacre were also off-limits. The silence around the Holocaust in postwar Ukraine reached extremes. In contrast, in the Estonian Soviet Socialist Republic, the Holocaust was even discussed in official school textbooks. In Lithuania, the history was presented, although touched up. Meanwhile, in the official history of the Ukrainian SSR, published in 1977–79, there was absolutely no mention of the Holocaust, or even the existence of Jews. Thus, the victims of mass violence were killed twice: once physically and again by eliminating the memory of them.

The existence of a nation is dependent on its memory. Take away its memory and it loses the ability to act independently. First, the nation forgets about itself and then the world begins to forget about it. This is exactly what happened to postwar Soviet Ukraine. It still had the formal features of a nation-state, but it was deprived of any memory of itself as a nation.

The USSR consisted of fifteen Soviet republics, but there could be only one nation: 'a new historical community – the Soviet people'. Its main features were the shared socialist homeland, shared socialist economy, shared socialist culture and shared goal of building communism. The Kremlin had been talking about the formation of this community since before the war. At the Twenty-Second Congress of the Communist Party (1961), Khrushchev announced that socialist society had been achieved. The difference between the prewar and postwar 'Soviet people' was especially clear in the status of Ukrainians. Before Stalin's death, Ukrainians were not trusted even to govern their own republic – not a single first secretary of the Ukrainian Communist Party had been Ukrainian. That changed immediately after Stalin's death. In 1953, Oleksii Kyrychenko, the same man who told Khrushchev about the horrors of the Ukrainian famine, was appointed First Secretary. From then on, Ukrainians not only appeared in leadership positions in the Ukrainian SSR, but also began to play a key role in the governance of the USSR. Both Khrushchev and Brezhnev had spent time in leadership positions in Soviet Ukraine before becoming leaders of the USSR. They relied on their Ukrainian ties in their struggle for power in the Kremlin and when they came to power, they brought their Ukrainian allies to Moscow.

In 1954, the USSR celebrated the great tricentenary of the 'reunification of Ukraine with Russia'. Behind the scenes of the official celebrations, a 'new Pereiaslav agreement' was being formed: Ukrainians were offered partnership in managing the empire. In return, they would accept the new rules of the game. One of the requirements was that they reject their own national memory. It is impossible to say how many Ukrainians accepted these rules. Suffice to say, there were many. Like the 'Little Russian colony' in St Petersburg at the turn of the nineteenth century, the 'Ukrainian group' occupied a dominant position in Moscow in the last decades of the Soviet Union. Some Russians in the party nomenklatura complained that khokhols had taken up every spot 'like cockroaches' and that Russia, having freed itself from the Tatar-Mongol yoke, was now suffering under the 'khokhol yoke at the top'.

The new rules of the game paid dividends not only in the form of high positions. The Soviet version of the past was useful because it covered over the traumas of the past. Someone who didn't know the past could see the world from a fairy tale perspective – a fairy tale about the struggle between communist good and capitalist evil, which would eventually end in victory over this evil on a global scale. By building communism, Soviet people could feel personally involved in this victory. The discrepancy between perception and reality was dismissed as a temporary issue. These discrepancies could be endured for the sake of the future victory – just as the previous generation had done when they bore the burden of the war against Nazism. This was the Soviet version of progress. It took root especially strongly among young people who had seen no reality other than the Soviet one. It was indeed possible to have a happy childhood in the Soviet Union. Almost everyone who was born in the USSR remembers the feeling of happiness that teachers instilled in elementary school – happiness that we were born here and not in the West, where children lived in poverty and were brutally exploited by capitalists. The price of that 'happiness' was ignorance of everything that had happened to the older generations.

It was unclear, however, how long it would be possible to keep society in this state. Almost everyone had family stories that contradicted the Soviet version of the past. Although children were shielded from these stories for the sake of their safety and mental health, they did learn about the past in one way or another as they grew up. It is logical to suppose that people are less likely to recall the terrible past if their personal lives don't give them cause to do so. However, the example of postwar Western Europe showed that the opposite can also be true. It was the generation who didn't personally experience mass violence, the generation that came of age in the Sixties, who began to ask uncomfortable questions about the past.

The Sixties Generation

On 4 September 1965, the movie *Shadows of Forgotten Ancestors* premiered at the Ukraina Cinema in Kyiv. The film was based on a short story of the same name by Mykhailo Kotsiubynskyi, which is a Ukrainian *Romeo and Juliet* story. The film combines folklore and avant-garde imagery and was made in a specific genre of poetic cinema, that was founded by Oleksandr Dovzhenko in the 1930s. *Shadows of Forgotten Ancestors* was hailed in Ukraine and beyond and received multiple awards and honours at international film festivals.

Before the screening, the young literary critic Ivan Dziuba took the floor. Instead of discussing the film, he announced that dozens of young people had just been arrested in Ukraine. The theatre manager tried to take the microphone away from him, but Dziuba began reading out the names of those who had been arrested. Someone set off the fire alarm to drown him out. Then Viacheslav Chornovil, a young journalist, shouted over the noise of the siren: 'If you're against tyranny – stand up!' A third of the audience stood up. The movie finally started. During the intermission, Vasyl Stus, a graduate student at the Kyiv Institute of Literature, addressed the audience again: 'Everyone needs to protest: today they take Ukrainians, tomorrow it will be Jews and Russians will be next!' The film's director, Sergei Parajanov, an Armenian who lived in Kyiv, joined the protestors.

Nineteen sixty-five was exactly halfway between the end of the war (1945) and Gorbachev's rise to power (1985), when the Soviet system entered its death throes. Chronologically, this protest of the young Kyiv intelligentsia emerged at the centre of the postwar era. It was central in another, broader sense as well. It embodied the emergence of a new, global generation that went on to largely define the outlines of the modern world. In Ukraine, this generation was personified by Ivan Dziuba, Viacheslav Chornovil and Vasyl Stus. In the Soviet Union, they were called the Sixties Group. Despite the fact that young people in the communist East and the capitalist West were separated by the Iron Curtain, they had certain features in common.

Every generation forms its values during adolescence. People from the Sixties Group were born in the 1930s and '40s, which means they were teenagers during the first postwar decades. Politically, these were decades of liberalisation. In the West, it was seen in the return of liberal democracy, a political model that had been weakened in interwar Europe. In the communist East, liberalisation meant an end to mass terror. After Stalin's death in 1953, mass arrests, imprisonments and executions stopped, prisoners were released from the camps (especially after a wave of camp uprisings in which, incidentally, Ukrainian nationalists played first violin) and the camp system itself ceased to exist in 1960. The generation of the 1960s was the first generation not to be decimated by war and repression. They had a sense of security denied to previous generations.

There were economic changes as well. The 1960s were the best decade the world economy had ever experienced, the decade of 'economic miracles': German, French, Italian, Japanese, etc. The Western economy in the 1950s reached pre-1914 levels and then continued to grow. These quantitative changes were associated with qualitative ones. In the 1960s, Western economies began the transition from industrial to post-industrial. Post-industrial society was based on knowledge-intensive technologies – when, in the language of metaphors, the gross national product came not from factory pipes, but from a cup of coffee. Radios, refrigerators, televisions and even cars became commonplace in almost every family. Unemployment was very low. Young people were not looking for work; work was looking for them. Another innovation in Western Europe was the introduction of the welfare state model, a state that provided support in case of unemployment, paid vacation time, or paid leave to care for a newborn child. Therefore, young people felt protected not only politically but also socially.

In the Soviet Union, living standards were lower than in the West. For example, cars were still a luxury item. But even here, the 1960s were the best decade economically. Soviet gross domestic product grew by 6 per cent annually. In 1961, Nobel Prize-winning economist Paul Samuelson predicted that at its current rate of development, the USSR would catch up with the United States in 1984 at the earliest and in 1997 at the latest. This prediction coincided with Khrushchev's 1957 call to 'Catch up and overtake America!' At the Twenty-Second Congress of the Communist Party, Khrushchev proclaimed that socialism had been built in the Soviet Union and the next generation would live under communism.

It's hard to have much faith in Soviet statistics: careful studies have shown that economic indicators were inflated. There was, however, another, more reliable indicator: life expectancy. The 1960s was the only decade when life expectancy in Soviet Ukraine equalled that of Europe.

Finally, the postwar decades were decades of social elevators. To a large extent, this was due to the need to replenish the demographic losses of the war. But there was another factor. The industries of the new economy required engineers, researchers and managers. Accordingly, the number of students increased significantly. In Western countries, their numbers doubled or tripled. The same processes took place in the USSR: in Soviet Ukraine, the number of students doubled from 400,000 to 800,000 during the 1960s. Young people were much more educated than their parents or grandparents and, accordingly, now had jobs that did not require hard physical labour.

The values of a society change primarily through the change of generations. We can find indirect evidence for this in sociological surveys conducted at the beginning and end of the postwar period, i.e. before the emergence of a new generation and after it reached adulthood. A survey of Ukrainian refugees in the United States in the early 1950s showed that, despite their general hostility to the Soviet system, they accepted certain basic elements of it, such as the state's guarantee of jobs and its control over heavy industry. The first authorised polls in Soviet Ukraine in the late 1980s revealed unexpectedly high support for individual rights and free democratic expression – what might be loosely termed 'Western values'.

Higher education was the ticket to the middle class, which was growing in both the West and the East. If in the West it was made up of independent professionals and intellectuals, in the communist East it took the form of the Soviet technical and humanitarian intelligentsia. Since the processes were similar, this gave rise to optimistic hopes that over time, the capitalist and communist systems would converge, becoming ever more similar.

Optimism was another feature of the 1960s. In the USSR, this was particularly vivid in music, literature and films, which developed the 'golden age' of Soviet mass culture. There was a feeling that nothing was impossible. In the words of a popular song of the time, 'You're twenty, I'm twenty and the seventh heaven is just ahead'. By the way, when one encounters nostalgia for the Soviet era among some older Ukrainians today, it is often a nostalgia for the happy 1960s. Optimism characterises a generation that benefits from social elevators. In this sense, the Ukrainian youth of the 1960s resembled the generation at the end of the nineteenth century or the Ukrainian national communists of the 1920s.

A belief in socialism strengthened the similarity between East and West. In the West, socialism experienced a renaissance. Since the early 1950s, almost every Western European state has had a socialist or social democratic government. The fact that the Soviet Union had taken the brunt of the war and defeated Nazi Germany convinced people of the advantages of communism. Many Western intellectuals were sure that it was only a matter of time before Soviet troops would enter Paris. The revelation of Stalin's crimes and the anti-communist uprising in Budapest in 1956 undermined faith in communism but did not destroy it entirely. New Soviet achievements, such as the launch of a space satellite (1957) and the first man in space (1961), gave socialism a second wind. There was a feeling that a new socialism, not Stalinist socialism, but socialism 'with a human face', was the future.

Most of the participants of the Sixties Group in Ukraine shared that belief. Except for the ones from Western Ukraine, most believed in the ideals of communism. They were largely unaware of the ideas of Ukrainian nationalism and uninterested. First of all, most of the people who might have shared those ideas had either died in the postwar struggle or emigrated to the West. Those who survived and were released from the Soviet camps were most often not allowed to settle in the large cities that had become incubators of educated youth. Secondly, in the eyes of many young people, Ukrainian nationalism was compromised by the image promulgated by Soviet propaganda, which equated Ukrainian nationalism with Nazism. In any case, there were no ties between the fighters of the UPA and the Sixties Group.

It is worth emphasising that initially the Sixties Group were not remotely anti-Soviet. They were all products of the Soviet system. This can be clearly seen in one trait that sharply distinguished them from the Sixties in the West: there was no youth culture of 'sex, drugs and rock and roll'. In the USSR, poets played the role of rock stars, particularly the Russian poets Bella

Akhmadulina, Andrei Voznesensky, Yevgeny Yevtushenko and Robert Rozhdestvensky. Ukraine had its own poetic quartet: Mykola Vinhranovsky, Ivan Drach, Lina Kostenko and Vasyl Symonenko.

What made the Sixties in Ukraine most similar to the Sixties in the West was the desire for self-expression. This trait was a consequence of their formative experience: once the basic needs of security and survival are met, the desire to express oneself follows. Valentyn Moroz was one of the Sixties Group who later became a dissident. He wrote that they were artists who wanted to paint, but not just portraits of Lenin; poets who wanted to write poetry, but not just about Stalin and peace; scientists who wanted to conduct research, not just follow directives from above. They were 'bodies in search of souls'.

The 1960s had its dark sides: the construction of the Berlin Wall; the Cuban Missile Crisis; political assassinations including John F Kennedy and Martin Luther King Jr; and the American war in Vietnam. And the shadow of nuclear war loomed over all of it. In the Soviet Union, an economic crisis in the early 1960s almost caused another famine. From the early 1960s until the very end of the USSR's existence, the Soviet government had to buy large quantities of grain from America and Canada, despite the fact that they controlled some of the most fertile land in the world! Khrushchev's Thaw was cut short by Leonid Brezhnev's ascent to power in 1964. In Ukraine, this return to the past was immediately felt in a string of arrests in 1965, the first such event since the death of Stalin. Moreover, the improvements in standard of living scarcely affected the lives of collective farm workers, who made up about 40 per cent of the population. Their labour was hard, their earnings were meagre and their legal status resembled serfdom: until 1974, they were not issued passports, which prevented them from leaving the village, and their children were automatically enrolled in the collective farm upon reaching the age of sixteen.

The situation in Ukraine had its own distinctive features and they also affected the fate of the Sixties Group. Ukraine was one of the republics most impacted by the war. The destruction was particularly severe in large cities. Almost all of them had lost more than half their population and industrial enterprises were in ruins. Reconstruction required a massive labour force and so the Ukrainian Soviet government had to allow rural youth to move to the cities. From 1959–70, Ukrainian-speaking rural immigrants were the fastest growing group in metropolitan Kyiv and Lviv. In the 1960s, more people lived in urban centres than in the countryside for the first time in Ukrainian history. This is considered one of the main indicators of the modernisation of society, so Ukraine officially became a modern urbanised nation.

The collective biography of the Sixties Group mirrors these changes. Most of them were born in the countryside and moved to the city to study after graduating from the village school. They combined two cultures: the folk rural culture remained close and dear to them, but Russian culture was not alien and its moral heroes were examples to follow. However, the balance was upset when they encountered condescending or even hostile attitudes towards Ukrainian culture when they arrived in the cities. For people raised in the spirit of communist internationalism, this was a blatant manifestation of injustice and a violation of Leninist norms: Lenin had described the Ukrainisation of the cities as a positive process!

Reading Lenin opened their eyes to other inconsistencies between communist theory and Soviet practice. For instance, Lenin demanded that the salaries of the Communist Party nomenklatura should not exceed the salaries of workers – but that requirement was never met. All of these inconsistencies could be perceived as a legacy of Stalinism, but the cult of Stalin had been officially condemned in the Soviet Union! In 1958, five years after Stalin's death, school reform was initiated throughout the

USSR. With the reforms, the study of the Ukrainian language in Ukrainian schools became optional, while Russian remained compulsory.

With time, national differences started to take on the character of social differences. These and other inconsistencies inspired Ivan Dziuba to write his 1965 essay titled 'Internationalism or Russification?', which became the political manifesto of the Sixties Group. Dziuba wrote about the construction of the Kyiv hydroelectric power plant, where Ukrainians were engaged primarily in physical labour, while all the managerial positions (construction manager, chief engineer, heads of most departments and offices) were occupied by Russians who were brought in from Russia. What kind of Leninist nationality policy can we speak of, he asked, when in the fiftieth year of Soviet rule, a republic with a population of 45 million, with numerous universities, colleges and research institutes, is unable to meet its own national staffing needs?

In addition to the 'violation of Leninist norms', there was the risk of a return to Stalinist repressions. The Sixties Group viewed the 1965 arrests of young Ukrainian intellectuals as proof of this threat. Tensions were increasing. In a certain sense, things developed into a conflict between two generations of the Ukrainian Soviet elite – the older generation, who were willing to accept the terms of the 'new Pereiaslav agreement' and the younger generation, who viewed it as a violation of communist principles.

A 'generation' is obviously an amorphous concept. On the one hand, there were a few among the older generation who sided with the young, such as the writers and war veterans Oles Honchar and Viktor Nekrasov. On the other hand, it is hard to expect that a milkmaid from Poltava, a villager from Transcarpathia, a miner from Donbas and a student from Kyiv, Lviv, or Kharkiv would have much in common just because they were born in the same time period and lived within the borders of the same republic.

Generations are like unleavened dough: they have no flavour on their own. In the 1960s, there was a chance that the Sixties Group thinkers and artists would become the salt of their generation and that people from across the different regions of Ukraine would be united by the music of the young songwriter Volodymyr Ivasyuk, the poetry of Lina Kostenko and the films of Sergei Parajanov.

Ultimately, the question was the same as it had been before the start of Stalinist repressions in the 1930s: is it possible to have a modernisation that is both Ukrainian and Soviet? It is significant that this question was being posed by a generation who had no ties to pre-war or wartime Ukrainian nationalism, who were almost entirely a product of the post-Stalinist Soviet system. This showed that the Soviet system in Ukraine had built-in structural problems that made almost every major issue become national in nature.

The Revolution that Wasn't

The emergence of the 1960s generation has been called a 'silent revolution'. In 1968, the revolution got loud. In May of that year, students in Paris took to the streets, and for the first time since the Paris Commune, barricades appeared on the streets of the French capital. In a short time, student strikes and riots spread to major universities all over the world, from San Francisco to Tokyo. It was a youthful rebellion against the older generation, the political establishment and it often took place under leftist slogans.

Something similar was taking place in communist Poland, Czechoslovakia and Yugoslavia, but while students in the West were revolting against capitalism, the youth in Warsaw and revolutionaries in Prague demanded that socialism be given 'a human face'. In the USSR in general and in Soviet Ukraine in particular, there were not mass protests, but there were many individual acts of revolt. It is worth remembering that after the war, in addition to the great Iron Curtain that divided Europe into the capitalist West and the communist East, there was another, unacknowledged iron wall that ran along the western border of the USSR separated Ukraine and other western Soviet republics from neighbouring communist Poland, Czechoslovakia, Hungary and Romania.

In the postwar years, the Ukrainian question remained almost exclusively an internal issue of the USSR. However, within the Soviet Union, its explosive potential never disappeared. The events of 1968 offer proof of this observation. Although the 1968 revolution bypassed Ukraine, there was actually a Ukrainian factor. The 'Prague Spring' was crushed by the invasion of the Soviet army. The person who pushed hardest to bring Soviet tanks into Prague was Petro Shelest, First Secretary of the Ukrainian Communist Party. His logic was impeccable and straightforward. In 1968, Czechoslovak leaders legalised the Greek Catholic Church, which was still popular in the Slovak region of Prešov, which had a significant Ukrainian minority. The church had been banned in Western Ukraine since 1946. Shelest was concerned that legalisation of the Church in Prešov might have a dangerous impact on neighbouring Transcarpathia and on Galicia, two regions where the majority of the Ukrainian population had been Greek Catholics before the war. Moreover, the memory of the anti-communist underground was still fresh in Galicia and neighbouring Volhynia. The last UPA units had only been liquidated in the early 1960s and even the elimination of the nationalist underground had not solved the problem of Western Ukraine. It was still one of the least Sovietised and least Russified territories of the USSR, along with the Baltic republics. In the Soviet collective consciousness, Western Ukrainians were still 'Westerners' and 'Banderites'. Suffice it to say that in the 1960s and 1970s, Galicia was home to only 10 per cent of the population of Soviet Ukrainians, but it produced one-third of all Ukrainian dissidents and was home to a quarter of all Orthodox parishes in the USSR. (With Greek Catholicism banned, the faithful attended Orthodox parishes in Ukraine.)

The emergence of Lviv as Ukraine's hidden cultural capital had particular significance. It started with the postwar Soviet industrialisation drive. Before the Second World War, Lviv was not an industrial centre; Soviet rule brought factories and plants to the city. As in all Ukrainian cities, young people from the surrounding villages came to the city to meet the need for workers. But while in other cities these young workers quickly adopted the Russian-speaking urban culture, in Lviv, on the contrary, the rural youth Ukrainianised the city. For the first time in its history, Lviv became a Ukrainian-speaking city – in fact, the largest Ukrainian-speaking city in the country.

While Lviv may have been the hidden capital of Ukraine, Kyiv was the real capital. By the end of Soviet rule, its population of 2.6 million almost equalled the combined population of the next two largest cities (Kharkiv with a population of 1.6 million and Odesa with its population of 1.1 million). Kyiv had finally established itself as the 'first city' of Ukraine. It was home to the largest institutions of higher education, research institutes, publishing houses, film studios, theatres and the editorial offices of the most popular newspapers and magazines. Due to this status, Kyiv attracted people from all regions of Soviet Ukraine. This was the place where the Ukrainian East and Ukrainian West mingled most intensively.

This mingling resulted in the emergence of the Lviv-Kyiv axis. This axis was especially noticeable in the activities of the Sixties Group. At the start of the Sixties, the young creative intelligentsia of the two cities established contacts. After one visit, the Kyiv poet Vasyl Symonenko wrote a poem that ended with the following lines:

Grey Lviv! Capital of my dreams,
Epicentre of my joys and hopes! . . .
I came to you with the elation of a son
From the steppes where the Dnipro weaves her legends,
So that your valiant lion heart
Could splash a drop of strength into my own heart.

Another key territory of Soviet Ukraine was the Donbas region. Extractive industries tend to create a relationship based on a cult of violence, whether it is diamond mining in Africa or gold mining in California. Donbas added its own unique traits to this formula. The harsh working conditions and the constant need for labour meant that criminals and other 'anti-Soviet elements' were sent here to work after they had served their terms. According to one historian of the city of Donetsk, in the postwar years, 'everything associated with the prisons and camps literally hung in the air. This is no surprise considering that one-fifth of the population here had passed through the penal system.' Rebellion was at the heart of the culture and postwar Donbas produced many dissidents, including Ivan Dziuba; Vasyl Stus; Ivan Svitlychnyi, the spiritual father of the; his sister, the dissident Nadiya Svitlychna; and Soviet dissident Natan Sharansky, who is now one of the most prominent political figures in Israel.

The Soviet Union was an industrial civilisation. Donetsk, due to its status as the capital of a large industrial centre, should have been a model Soviet city. Although a genuine cult was created around the working class, the Soviet propaganda was contradicted by the high injury rates and low life expectancy of the miners. They were also accustomed to danger every day working in the mines, so they had nothing to lose. During the food crisis of the early 1960s, workers in Donbas went on strike and anti-government leaflets were distributed. In 1968, a local engineer, Vladimir Klebanov, tried to organise an independent trade union to monitor the implementation of labour laws and safety regulations. In the summer of 1968, speaking at a closed plenary session of the CPSU Central Committee in Moscow, a session that decided the fate of the Prague Spring, the first secretary of the Donetsk regional committee of the party, Degtyaryov, assured the plenum that Donbas remained loyal. However, he also said that nationalist and revisionist elements were sowing seeds of dissent among the local working class.

There are numerous examples of solidarity with the Czechoslovak revolution in other Soviet republics. However, the situation of the Ukrainian Republic was unique in that it shared a border with Czechoslovakia. The leadership of Soviet Ukraine demanded that Soviet troops be sent to Prague because they were afraid of losing control in Ukraine. These fears dissipated after the Prague Spring was crushed in the summer of 1968.

The revolutions of 1968 didn't fail just in Prague; they failed all over the world. The political establishment retained power everywhere. In that sense, the 1968 revolutions resembled the 1848 revolutions, which have been called 'the turning point that failed to turn'. However, as was the case in 1848, the changes the revolutionaries initially failed to achieve became a new reality just a few decades later – for the Sixties generation in 1989–91.

Lost Decades

Just two years after the crushing of the Prague Spring, Shelest himself, initiator of the invasion of Czechoslovakia, found himself on shaky ground. In 1970, he published a book, *O Ukraine, Our Soviet Land*. The Kremlin condemned the book as a work of 'low ideological quality' and the entire hundred-thousand-copy edition was confiscated. Shelest's sin was 'idealisation of the Ukrainian past', especially the Ukrainian Cossacks and his attention to Ukraine's exceptionally important role in the Soviet economy.

Shelest was no Ukrainian nationalist. On the contrary, he called nationalism 'frightening'. He fell victim to power games and his own ambitions in the struggle for power. However, regardless of his personal attitude, Soviet Ukraine during his rule underwent processes that can be called Ukrainisation. By the 1970s, three-quarters of all leadership positions in the Ukrainian Republic were held by Ukrainians. As the proportion of Ukrainians among the local nomenklatura grew, autonomous sentiments emerged. For example, in 1963, even before Shelest took office as First Secretary in Ukraine, representatives from a conference held at Kyiv University demanded that Ukrainian be recognised as an official state language. In 1965, the Minister of Education put forward a proposal to Ukrainianise higher education. Shelest himself sent letters to central Moscow institutions demanding recognition of Ukraine's constitutional rights as a sovereign republic and arguing for Ukraine's key role in preserving the USSR.

Shelest overestimated his strength. The Kremlin grew increasingly irritated and in 1972 he was dismissed from his post. The First Secretary of the Georgian Communist Party, Vasily Mzhavanadze, was also purged, probably based on false accusations like Shelest. Their dismissals revealed a certain trend: the symptoms of 'national deviationism' were most pronounced in those 'border' republics such as Armenia, Estonia, Georgia, Latvia, Lithuania and Ukraine, where a developed sense of national consciousness among the population was combined with high representation in the party leadership. Nationalism turned out to be stronger than Marxism.

The purge of 'national deviationism' was part of a broader campaign to combat dissent throughout the Soviet Union in the 1960s. From 1971–74, about sixty thousand people were arrested and/or subjected to 'preventive measures'. In pure percentages, this was less than 1 per cent of the population. But it was a very high-quality percentage. It included two Nobel Prize winners – physicist Andrei Sakharov and writer Alexander Solzhenitsyn, poets, movie directors, philosophers, historians. In other words, the people who would normally serve as the jewel of any nation, but not of the 'Soviet people'! After the crackdown on dissent, everything 'Soviet' became synonymous with dullness, utter lack of taste and boredom. Ukraine experienced a new wave of mass arrests. All the figures from the *Shadows of Forgotten Ancestors* premiere were arrested, including Parajanov.

Volodymyr Shcherbytsky replaced Shelest in Kyiv. His policy was the opposite of Shelest's. Those who knew Shcherbytsky well remembered him as a man who radiated hostility to everything Ukrainian. It is noteworthy that he used only Russian in public and at the end of his career, he recorded his nationality as 'Russian' rather than 'Ukrainian', just as he had done before his time leading the republic. Shcherbytsky tried to turn Ukraine into the most loyal Soviet republic. There could be no hint of an autonomous policy. One issue discussed in the Ukrainian Central Committee after he came to power was: 'Does the Central Committee of the Communist Party of Ukraine make policy or implement it?' To make policy is to direct and only the Central Committee of the Communist Party (in Moscow) can direct policy! They decided on 'implementing'.

Shcherbytsky came from industrial Dnipropetrovsk (now renamed Dnipro), the city where Leonid Brezhnev had worked for many years. During Brezhnev's time, there was a popular joke about Russian history. According to the joke, Russian history can be divided into three major stages: pre-Petrine (before Peter the Great), Petrine (during Peter's reign) and Dnipro-Petrine (the Dnipropetrovsk period). Indeed, under Brezhnev and Shcherbytsky Ukraine was similar to the 'good old days', when Little Russians could make great careers in the imperial administration.

Unlike during the Russian Empire, the Ukrainian language and literature were not banned under the Soviets. Ukrainians could read Shevchenko (censored, of course), listen to and watch programmes in Ukrainian (though in language so artificial that no one but television announcers spoke it) and sing some of their songs (as long as they sang Russian and Soviet songs too), etc. They needed to look like lucky, primitive collective farmers or newly arrived workers and intellectuals who accepted the gifts of Soviet civilisation with gratitude and joy.

The reality looked rather different. The Russian language dominated almost every sphere of life. The proportion of Ukrainian speakers in Ukraine was declining throughout the 1960s to the 1980s. Book publishing, one of the key indicators of nation-building, offers a significant perspective. In terms of number of books per capita in the native language, Ukraine in the 1970s ranked last among all the republics of the USSR and the countries of the so-called People's Democracies (i.e., communist Poland, Czechoslovakia and Hungary).

Officially, this was viewed as a manifestation of inevitable natural processes. As socialism was built and the Soviet people were formed, national differences would die out. As Khrushchev said, the sooner we start speaking Russian, the sooner communism will come.

In fact, Russification was not a natural occurrence – it was constantly being pushed from the centre. Although the Kremlin's true motives were never openly discussed, we can glean a sense of them from what Soviet leaders said in private. Fedir Ovcharenko, former Secretary for Ideology of the Ukrainian Communist Party recalled his first meeting with Brezhnev in 1968, in which Brezhnev told him that he should intensify the fight against bourgeois Ukrainian nationalism and accelerate the assimilation of the Ukrainian nation in every way possible.

Soviet policy towards Ukraine relied on a combination of

carrots and sticks. Given the size and status of the republic, the figures were high. There were large numbers of Ukrainians both among those who built the Soviet empire and among those who brought it down. There were so many Ukrainians involved in building the Soviet state during the Brezhnevian stagnation that party apparatchiks called it the period of 'Ukrainian domination'. As for those undermining the empire, Ukrainians made up 50–70 per cent of all prisoners in the camps during Brezhnev's rule.

The same was true of the Sixties Group: they fell into both groups. Some repented and were nurtured by the authorities, while others went on to become dissidents. However it went, the outcome was the same: the Sixties Group never became the voice of their generation.

In the late Soviet Union, the voice of the 'Brezhnev generation', those born before the Second World War or at the dawn of Soviet power, dominated. In the late 1970s and early '80s, the situation was completely under their control and public dissent was put to rest. However, there were still powerful factors working against them. First was their age. The average age in Brezhnev's inner circle was seventy-five. A joke at the time said that the Politburo members' working day began with artificial resuscitation; whoever arrived late for work had died. The Kremlin was failing at one of the key elements of political stability: the integration of the younger generation into power structures.

The second challenge for Brezhnev and his team was a loss of political legitimacy. The crushing of the Prague Spring in 1968 destroyed any belief that socialism could be resuscitated and given a human face. As Leszek Kołakowski, a former Marxist himself, wrote, 'this skull will never smile again'. The aging Soviet elite had nothing in common with the communist enthusiasm of the early Soviet era. Without faith in communist ideals, the Soviet nomenklatura resembled nothing so much as bored, old bureaucrats fighting amongst themselves for influence and power.

The third and chief challenge to Soviet power was daily life itself. The Soviet system could launch rockets into space, but it could not harvest potatoes from the collective farm fields or get them onto store shelves. The constant shortage of basic consumer goods was a persistent feature of Soviet life in both the prewar and postwar decades. The difference was that after the war and the Thaw, the USSR was less closed off than it had been before the war. Foreign films and imported goods were like holes in the Iron Curtain through which people could glimpse the higher standards of living in the West. This gave rise to mass consumerism, which, in turn, undermined the legitimacy of the communist system, which had rested on the promise of a better life.

One of the biggest holes in the Soviet system was created by transistor radios: radio waves broke through the ideological blockade. In large cities and in western areas of the Soviet Union, it became commonplace for people to listen to anti-Soviet stations like Radio Liberty, Voice of America, or the BBC. Although the Soviet authorities successfully silenced their own artists and activists of the Sixties, with the advent of transistor radios they couldn't hold back the avalanche of Sixties music from the West. Young people liked listening to rock rather than Soviet music. Rock brought a sense of drive and inner freedom; unlike Soviet songs, rock music didn't work for marching. For the younger generation, Lenin couldn't compete with Lennon. And since rock could not exist legally in the USSR, anyone who listened became a potential anti-Soviet activist, just like the generation of the Sixties before them.

Non-Civil Revolution

These individual stories added up to a broader picture: the failure of the Soviet formula for modernisation. Khrushchev called for catching up with and overtaking America in the production of agricultural products, steel, coal and ore. He did not realise that he was running in the wrong direction. America and the West were already moving towards a post-industrial economy in the 1960s. Centralised management of the economy had produced impressive results during the industrial stage, from the 1920s to the 1950s. The construction of Soviet factories, plants and industrial districts resembled the construction of the Egyptian pyramids, both of which required a strong vertical of power to mobilise a servile population that was promised collective immortality for its hard work. But centralised management was worthless when it came to the creative economy.

The crisis of Soviet modernisation was most dramatically demonstrated in the accident at the Chernobyl nuclear power plant on 26 April 1986. The plant had been constructed with gross safety violations, in an environmentally sensitive area, near the capital, where there was a large concentration of people. Scientists and journalists had repeatedly warned of the danger. When the accident occurred, the Soviet authorities tried to keep it quiet. There were May Day celebrations scheduled which would include many children. When Shcherbytsky called the Kremlin to cancel the demonstration, he was threatened with dismissal.

Chernobyl has become one of the most recognised global symbols of the threat posed by modern technology. In the context of Soviet history, the Chernobyl disaster showed that despite post-Stalinist changes and attempts at liberalisation, the Soviet system still lacked respect for human life. It also highlighted Ukraine's position as a colony: local leadership could not make independent decisions on life-threatening issues and the centre was not interested in protecting the local population.

The Chernobyl disaster occurred almost a year before the young Gorbachev ('only' fifty-four years old!) came to power in the Kremlin. He tried to do what the Soviet government had failed to accomplish in the 1960s: to reboot the system.

Gorbachev himself was a Sixties man himself to some degree: his worldview had been formed in the optimistic atmosphere of the 1960s and he still retained illusions about the reality of socialism 'with a human face'. As for Ukraine, he believed that it was the most loyal Soviet republic. There were people around Gorbachev who warned him that 'the Ukrainians will show their true character yet', but he chose to ignore those voices.

It's impossible to know how sincere Gorbachev was. But in the case of Ukraine, his policies didn't match his words. Ukraine remained an oasis of stagnation long after Gorbachev came to power. In the party leadership, Shcherbytsky was the last of Brezhnev's Mohicans. He remained in power until September 1989 and didn't retire until three months after the anti-communist opposition had won at the polls in neighbouring Poland and just two months before the fall of the Berlin Wall. It does appear that the Kremlin realised the explosive nature of the Ukrainian issue and so they tried to control the development of events in Ukraine. Indirect proof of this can be seen in the fact that the magazine *Ogonyok*, which covered many of the crimes of communism and was very popular, did not touch Ukrainian issues until 1989 – despite the fact that its editor was the Kyiv poet Vadym Korotych, who had been part of the Sixties Group!

The big public discussions and mass rallies took place in Moscow, Leningrad and the Baltic republics, but not in Ukraine, with the exception of the western regions of Lviv and Galicia. There events followed the Polish and Baltic scenario: first, the emergence of unofficial organisations and an independent press, then mass rallies under the banned national flags (blue and yellow). The first democratic elections were held in the spring of 1990 and the communists were completely defeated in all three regions of Galicia. When the democratic opposition came to power, one of their first acts was the demolition of monuments to Lenin.

However, decommunisation started even earlier in the Donbas region. In a series of labour strikes in the summer of 1989, the miners expelled Communist Party organisations from the mines. Despite what Degtyaryov had claimed in 1968, Donbas was not under control. This became apparent as soon as Moscow's centralised power began to weaken.

Kyiv, with its large creative and technical class, was a third centre of the opposition. The idea of Rukh, a mass opposition organisation modelled on Polish Solidarity and the Lithuanian Rukh, was formed in Kyiv. It was impossible to realise the idea as long as Shcherbytsky was still in power. The opposite was also true: when Rukh finally successfully held its founding congress, Shcherbytsky resigned. The Ukrainian Communist Party itself was divided between people who wanted to maintain the status quo and those who were developing a more national character under the pressure of the changes that were happening. Leonid Kravchuk, who had initially opposed Rukh, became the leader of the party faction that supported changes.

Participants in the peaceful revolutions of 1989 in Berlin, Warsaw and Prague are said to have held posters with the inscription '68' which, if turned upside down, read '89'. They were drawing a connection between the revolutions of 1968 and 1989. The connection was not only symbolic, but also literal – some of the leaders in 1989 had participated as young people in the rebellions of 1968.

There was a connection between 1968 and 1989 in Ukraine, as well. Just as in 1968, the main centres of opposition to the central government were Galicia, Kyiv and Donbas. In 1989, the Ukrainian opposition was not as numerous as the opposition in neighbouring Poland. What they did have in common, however, was that many leaders of both Polish Solidarity and the Ukrainian Rukh had been active in the movements of the 1960s.

The Ukrainian opposition was not strong enough to bring about large-scale political change. Most of the population took a wait-and-see attitude. By the spring of 1990, the overall balance of public opinion was as follows: the majority (70 per cent) of Ukrainians voted to preserve the USSR, but with recognition of Ukrainian sovereignty, while only Galicia was in favour of complete independence.

However, as the centre weakened, the opposition grew bolder. The summer of 1991 was a turning point. In June, the leaders of Rukh and the miners of Donbas agreed to work together against the centre. By the end of the summer, the centre itself had collapsed. On 19–21 August, a coup attempt by the nomenklatura in Moscow to oust Gorbachev failed. When it became clear that the coup had failed, the Supreme Council of the Ukrainian SSR proclaimed Ukraine's full independence and secession from the Union on 24 August 1991.

Empires don't die due to separatism on the borders, but from crises in the centre. In the case of the USSR, the decisive crisis was the struggle for power in Moscow: between opponents and supporters of perestroika, on the one hand, and within the perestroika camp, between Soviet President Mikhail Gorbachev and newly elected Russian President Boris Yeltsin, on the other.

The main role of national movements on the borderlands was to determine the seams along which the empire would fall apart. For Ukraine, the strategic alliance of three very unlikely allies was crucial: Western Ukraine, Kyiv and Donbas. Without this alliance, it is difficult to understand further developments, including the results of the 1 December 1991 referendum. The referendum had one question: 'Do you support the Act of Declaration of Independence of Ukraine?' Ninety-one per cent of the Ukrainian population answered 'Yes' and there was majority support throughout the country, including in Donbas and Crimea.

There are arguments today about the circumstances under which Ukraine became independent. There are some people who argue that Ukraine's proclamation of independence was manipulation by local communist elite, since there was no mass anti-communist national movement in Ukraine, such as those which existed in the Baltic republics or in neighbouring Poland, Czechoslovakia, or Hungary. This theory is based on a misunderstanding of how communism actually fell in Central and Eastern Europe. In reality, a completely new type of revolution emerged in 1989. Its central symbol was not the guillotine, as it had been two hundred years earlier in revolutionary France, but the round table. Under the pressure of massive civil protests, the old communist government sat down to negotiate with the anti-communist opposition and agreed to transfer power.

At first it may look like this scenario is only true for Poland. There, the opposition was truly a mass movement. At its peak, Solidarity included almost 80 per cent of the working population. After a long history of confrontation, it forced the communist government to negotiate and hand over power. Countries that followed a similar path in the years 1989–91 include Lithuania, Latvia and Estonia. This was similar to the situation in Western Ukraine. In contrast, the opposition movements in Czechoslovakia, Hungary, East Germany, Romania and most Soviet republics were not mass movements. In those areas, communism collapsed under its own weight, rather than under pressure from below, from organised civil society. Anti-communist demonstrations became massive only in the last months or even weeks of the revolutions. In other words, these revolutions were 'non-civil' revolutions and the Ukrainian events of 1991 fall into this category.

Ukraine's independence in 1991 was the result of a compromise between several forces, none of which had enough strength to establish its own authority over the country. In that sense, the end of the Ukrainian Socialist Republic resembled its beginning. The main difference was that it had undergone a long and complex evolution during its existence. Without rethinking this evolution, it is impossible to understand how and where independent Ukraine came from.

Rethinking Ukraine

As leading Polish dissident Adam Michnik joked, the worst thing about communism is what comes after. Communism did not solve problems, it just drove them underground, making them explosive. This was particularly true of the national question. In December 1969, Jerzy Giedroyc, the editor of the Polish émigré magazine *Kultura*, wrote to Czesław Milosz:

> For several years now and especially recently, I have been obsessed with the thought of a coming catastrophe. I mean, of course, first of all, Eastern Europe with Russia at the head ... I don't think that I am exaggerating: in '70 or in '71 at the latest, we will witness an explosion not only in Poland, but also in the Soviet Union. Not because people there are so terribly busy thinking about freedom, democracy, improving socialism, etc., but because they cannot continue to live like this when it comes to 'everyday' conditions ... Politically, we are facing the rise of Nazi-style nationalisms. This is the case in Russia itself, this is the case in Ukraine and the other republics, this is the case in Poland itself ... If this explosion occurs, it will be completely blind, people will slaughter each other, the problem of Lviv, the Peace of Riga, etc. will be revived and this time we will be ready to perish forever under the rubble of the cataclysm.

The Russian Soviet writer Konstantin Paustovsky expressed similar fears. After Stalin's death, Paustovsky was allowed to travel through Europe on a speaking tour. Speaking in Paris, the very city where Giedroyc published *Kultura*, Paustovsky said that if communism ended and the time of reckoning came, he would think of Ukraine with fear, because Ukrainians would massacre all the Jews and Russians.

American President George H. W. Bush also addressed the threat posed by the revival of Ukrainian nationalism. On 1 August 1991, he visited Kyiv and addressed the Supreme Council of the Ukrainian Republic. In his speech, he stated that the United States would not support those seeking independence and promoting suicidal nationalism based on ethnic hatred. Bush's Kyiv speech (which was dubbed the 'Chicken Kiev' speech in the American press) was a classic example of shortsightedness. He delivered it just twenty days before Ukraine declared independence.

There was some logic in the warning against 'suicidal nationalism'. Bush's advisors who wrote the speech were thinking of the Yugoslav War that had begun in June 1991. Josip Broz Tito, Yugoslavia's communist leader, had been credited with burying local nationalisms in the Balkans and thus solving the national question. It took just over a decade after his death for these nationalisms to surface and lead to the bloody disintegration of Yugoslavia, complete with genocide.

The 'Yugoslav scenario' loomed over Ukraine as the USSR collapsed. The Ukrainian scenario was particularly ominous due to the two hundred ballistic missiles and two thousand nuclear warheads on its territory at the moment the Soviet Union collapsed. After declaring independence, Ukraine instantly became the third largest nuclear power in the world. A conflict in Ukraine or around Ukraine could have turned into the Third World War.

Ukraine managed to avoid pogroms and nuclear apocalypse. It is commonly believed that one of the reasons is the fact that representatives of the communist elite took power in independent Ukraine. This ensured a smooth transition and political stability. In post-Soviet countries where the opposition came to power, there were intense ethnic conflicts as in the Baltic states and even civil war as happened in Georgia.

But the behaviour of the old communist elite is not the only reason Ukraine did not follow the Yugoslav scenario. The anti-communist opposition also wanted to preserve interethnic peace in Ukraine. Even if they had come to power, the Ukrainian situation would hardly have been different. Before the collapse of the Soviet Union, Ivan Drach, the leader of Rukh and a poet of the Sixties Group, declared that 'a Jew in Ukraine should live better than in Israel, a Russian in Ukraine should live better than in Russia'.

To understand the radical nature of this statement, we should look at social attitudes. A survey of Jewish immigrants who left the USSR for the United States in the late 1990s showed that among the countries and peoples that evoked the most negative reactions, Ukraine and Ukrainians were in first place. And this was despite the fact that many of the respondents had friends or even family members who were Ukrainian: stereotypes are stronger than reality. Polls taken in neighbouring Poland after the fall of communism showed similar results: Ukrainians evoked mostly negative feelings among Poles.

Ukrainian national leaders had work to do. The first noteworthy step was Ivan Dziuba's speech in 1966 at an unofficial gathering in Babyn Yar to commemorate the twenty-fifth anniversary of the mass shooting of Kyiv's Jews. His speech was spontaneous – people who had gathered wanted one of the writers present to speak. Dziuba's fundamental rejection of anti-Semitism or any other form of xenophobia was characteristic of the writers of the Sixties. Dziuba said that as a Ukrainian, he felt shame that there was anti-Semitism among the Ukrainian nation. He said that Ukrainians must fight all manifestations of anti-Semitism or disrespect towards Jews. He also urged that Jews in Ukraine fight disrespect for Ukrainian culture and language and try not to see every Ukrainian as a secret anti-Semite. Dziuba concluded by saying that this fight for mutual respect was what they owed to the victims of despotism, to the Ukrainian land and to humanity.

The opposition did most of their 'homework' on Ukrainian-Jewish relations in Brezhnev's camps. The Soviet regime was just as hostile to Zionism as it was to Ukrainian nationalism, so Ukrainians and Jews were two of the most numerous groups among political prisoners. Nothing unites people like a common enemy, and imprisonment provides time and opportunity for thoughtful conversations, some of which concerned mutual national grievances. Accusations of anti-Semitism were contradicted by the behaviour of Ukrainian prisoners, including UPA soldiers, who supported the Jewish prisoners. One Jewish prisoner responded to Ukrainian 'reminders' that Jews were responsible for Bolshevism by saying: 'Even if we did help build this state, we will also destroy it.'

Ukrainian dissidents and Crimean Tatar leaders also found a common language. During the deportation of 1944, most Crimean Tatars had been deported to Soviet Uzbekistan, while the rest were deported to Kazakhstan and selected regions of Russia. After Stalin's death, they sought to return to their homeland. One of the most vocal defenders of the rights of Crimean Tatars was a former Soviet general, Petro Grigorenko, who became a Ukrainian dissident. The collaboration between the dissidents and Crimean Tatars built a sense of shared Ukrainian space.

Geopolitical changes also played a separate role in the transformation of the Ukrainian national movement. In the early 1970s, the Kremlin proclaimed a policy of international détente. This essentially marked an abandonment of the concept of a world communist revolution and the search for a modus vivendi with the capitalist West. In 1975, the Helsinki Accords were signed, which recognised the postwar status quo in Europe and included a commitment against the use of force to resolve international conflicts. In signing these agreements, the Soviet government and other countries also committed themselves to respect human rights, including freedom of thought, conscience and religion. The anti-Soviet opposition immediately saw an opportunity. Henceforth, it would fight the Soviet state on legal grounds, based on international agreements ratified by the USSR.

In 1976, the first Helsinki Group appeared in Moscow. The second emerged in Ukraine and then groups organised in Lithuania, Georgia and Armenia. In the non-Russian republics, the struggle for these rights took on the character of a struggle for national rights, but linking national rights to human rights worked both ways. The Ukrainian opposition declared that in a free Ukraine, not only would the rights of Ukrainians be respected, but also the rights of Russians, Jews, Tatars and other national minorities. It was a true transformation. Ukrainian dissidents rejected the logic of both integral nationalism and communism and prepared the Ukrainian movement to fight for democracy. It was essentially a return to the democratic traditions of the Ukrainian movement at the turn of the twentieth century, but this time the national democratic slogans reflected not only local, but also global circumstances.

There were no Poles in this dialogue of interethnic reconciliation. It was impossible in Soviet Ukraine. After the mass deportations following the war, Poles had virtually ceased to exist as a national minority in Ukraine. There was no freedom of travel between Soviet Ukraine and communist Poland. Therefore, the Polish-Ukrainian dialogue took place in exile. A central question regarded what would happen after the fall of communism to the western Ukrainian lands that had been part of interwar Poland until 1939. The magazine *Kultura* became the main discussion platform. One of the first proposals was a joint Polish-Ukrainian protectorate. Then a Polish priest from South Africa, Józef Majewski, made a radical proposal: for the good of Poland, Poles should agree that Vilnius was a Lithuanian city and Lviv was a Ukrainian city. This proposal was so radical that even Giedroyc did not immediately dare to accept it. And when he did, he drew sharp criticism from the Polish government-in-exile in London and the Polish diaspora. For them, giving up Lviv was tantamount to treason.

However, the Paris-based *Kultura* was popular among the anti-communist opposition within Poland. They adopted the 'Giedroyc Doctrine' as part of their platform. Jacek Kuroń was particularly influential among Polish oppositionists. His father was a Polish socialist from Lviv and had raised his son in the spirit of socialist internationalism. Their family was deported to Poland after the war. There, Kuroń founded a communist youth movement called the Walterites. The name of the movement came from communist Polish general Karol Świerczewski (call sign Walter), who was killed by UPA soldiers in 1947. Świerczewski's assassination had triggered the forced resettlement of Ukrainians from Ukrainian ethnic lands in communist Poland during Operation Vistula. Kuroń organised camps for the Walterites in that area and when he saw the empty villages, he began to understand the scale of the wrongs that the Polish communist authorities had inflicted on Ukrainians. Kuroń was extremely sensitive to human injustice and became an uncompromising advocate for the Ukrainian cause.

Adam Michnik was one of Kuroń's students and Michnik's father, Ozjasz Szechter, was born in a Galician village a couple of dozen kilometres from Lviv. Szechter had been a member of the Communist Party of Western Ukraine in his youth. When the Ukrainian members went against the Kremlin in 1926, Szechter joined many other Polish and Jewish communists in supporting Stalin. He later considered it the biggest mistake of his life and told his son that if he ever opposed the Ukrainians, he would rise from the grave to curse him. In June 1989,

Solidarity won the Polish elections and came to power. Three months later, Michnik spoke at the first Rukh congress in Kyiv. His appearance on the stage was greeted with a standing ovation by the deputies. There he repeated the old slogan: 'Without a free Ukraine, there is no free Poland.' The press reported that he had come to Kyiv as a delegate from Solidarity. Michnik countered that he had come as a delegate from his father. When he got back to Warsaw, he went straight to his father's grave to say, 'Father, I did as you said.'

There were many such stories from Polish and Ukrainian emigrants in the West. Three emigrant historians deserve special mention here: Ihor Ševčenko, Omeljan Pritsak and Ivan Lysiak Rudnytsky. All three were born and raised in interwar Poland. Ševčenko's father was a Petliura officer who took refuge in Warsaw after the defeat of the Ukrainian Revolution. His son went to school with the children of the Polish intelligentsia. Lysiak Rudnytsky was born into a Galician Jewish-Ukrainian family, and Pritsak's stepfather was Polish. The multicultural, intellectual environment these three men grew up in helped them avoid falling under the influence of communism or nationalism. Both Pritsak and Lysiak Rudnytsky cited their reading of Vyacheslav Lypynsky as an antidote to radical ideologies. Lypynsky rejected all forms of totalitarianism and was already advocating the concept of a civic, inclusive Ukrainian identity in the early twentieth century.

All three men survived the war as students in Nazi Germany and emigrated to the United States after the war. There they took up the main project of their lives – rethinking Ukrainian history. The scholarly aspect of the project consisted of bringing Ukrainian history out of the shadow of Russian history and placing it in the broader context, each according to his own speciality: Byzantine (Ihor Ševčenko), Turkic (Omeljan Pritsak) and European (Ivan Lysiak Rudnytsky). The political element of the project consisted of building bridges between Ukrainians, Jews, Poles and Russians.

Institutions would be required to bring this process to fruition. The Ukrainian Research Institute at Harvard University was founded in 1973. This institute was the brainchild of Omeljan Pritsak, who had joined the Harvard faculty in the early 1960s. At the time, it seemed completely unrealistic. Ukrainian history didn't even exist as an object of study for most of the American academic world. Anyone who did study Ukrainian history was branded a Ukrainian nationalist and by extension, an anti-Semite and Nazi collaborator. Pritsak's idea became a reality thanks to support from his colleagues at Harvard, Ihor Ševčenko, Wiktor Weintraub, Richard Pipes and Adam Ulam. They were members of the Committee on Ukrainian Studies, which would form the core of the Institute. All five of them were from interwar Poland, so the committee was a kind of 'Harvard Commonwealth'. Moreover, Weintraub, Pipes and Ulam were all Polish Jews. Their participation certainly guaranteed that the Ukrainian Institute at Harvard would not be a 'nationalist institution'. During the 1967 Six-Day Arab-Israeli War, Omeljan Pritsak encouraged Ukrainian students to create a Ukrainian legion to support the Israelis and thus show the world and all Jews that Ukrainians were ready to atone for their sins with their own blood.

Ivan Lysiak Rudnytsky was instrumental in the creation of a similar institute in Canada in 1976, the Canadian Institute of Ukrainian Studies at the University of Alberta. His most significant contribution to Ukrainian studies was to redefine Ukraine itself, to determine how to deal with the postwar political realities in Eastern Europe, particularly Soviet Ukraine. Most Ukrainian emigrants did not consider Soviet Ukraine a state, viewing Ukraine as living under an occupation regime. To a large extent, this was true. However, there were two major problems with denying the national character of the Ukrainian Soviet Socialist

Republic. First, it undermined the significance of the Ukrainian question, which was actually a key issue for the survival of the USSR. Secondly, it called into question the accession of Western Ukraine to the Ukrainian state.

The way out of this conundrum was to recognise the Ukrainian SSR as a Ukrainian state with all the required elements: postwar borders, a capital and an elite, but of course only as a quasi-nation. This was the position taken by liberal and left-leaning Ukrainian emigrants who called themselves 'realists'. Ivan Lysiak Rudnytsky became one of the leading theorists of this group. His position was that Soviet Ukraine did not emerge at the whim of Lenin, Stalin and their Ukrainian collaborators. In fact, it was a successor state of the revolutionary Ukrainian National Republic: without the Ukrainian National Republic, there would have been no Ukrainian SSR. Therefore, an independent Ukraine would be reborn from Soviet Ukraine after the collapse of communism. Lysiak Rudnytsky and other realists tried to maintain contacts with any circles 'in country' that worked towards this rebirth, deliberately or not, including the Sixties Group, dissidents and the Soviet nomenklatura.

The realists were a marginal group in the Ukrainian diaspora. Ukrainian nationalists dominated the emigration, primarily Banderites. They viewed the recognition of Soviet Ukraine as an act of national betrayal and contacts with Soviet Ukrainians as collaboration. Bandera's concept was 'national revolution, not anti-regime resistance'. Ukrainian nationalists believed that an independent Ukraine would emerge from a national revolution against the occupying regime and saw the national liberation struggle of 1914–40 as its prototype.

The main question in the discussion between realists and nationalists was 'evolution or revolution?' There was a similar conflict within the Polish emigration. The Polish government-in-exile in London refused to acknowledge communist Poland as a legitimate Polish state, whereas the stance of the *Kultura* group in Paris was closer to that of the Ukrainian realists. The similarities between the Polish and Ukrainian groups were reinforced by the fact that they were in regular contact and sometimes worked together.

The 'evolution or revolution?' debate ended in favour of the realists. Communism fell due to its own internal exhaustion, not a revolutionary explosion. And in Poland and Ukraine's part of the communist world, it fell quietly and without blood.

On the night of 1 December 1991, when the votes were being counted for the referendum on Ukrainian independence, Lech Wałęsa, former leader of Solidarity and newly elected president of the new Poland, Jacek Kuroń and Adam Michnik, did not sleep. They were waiting for the results to be announced. They wanted independent Poland to be the first country in the world to recognise independent Ukraine. They were 'worried' that Canada, with its large and influential Ukrainian community, would be the first to do so.

Poland and Canada were the first countries to recognise Ukraine's independence – but Poland did beat Canada. Russia recognised it later, together with other countries. It would seem as though Russia should have the least issue with Ukrainian independence. After all, Russia, not Ukraine, was the first to secede from the USSR, declaring sovereignty in June 1990. Moreover, the first free polls showed no hostility between Russians and Ukrainians. However, the expectations of problem-free Russian-Ukrainian relations did not materialise. There was no 'Russian Giedroyc'.

The closest candidate for the role was the Nobel Prize-winning anti-communist writer Alexander Solzhenitsyn. His mother was Ukrainian and he wrote that Ukrainian and Russian were combined in his 'blood, heart and mind'. In the autumn of 1990, he published a long article titled 'Rebuilding Russia'. In it, he called for preserving the union of the three Slavic peoples and Kazakhstan, which had large populations of Russians and Ukrainians. He also called on Ukrainians separately not to declare independence – and he could not resist calling the Ukrainian language 'artificial'.

If Solzhenitsyn could have become Russia's Giedroyc, then Boris Yeltsin seemed to be Wałęsa's Russian equivalent. He won the Russian presidential election in the summer of 1990 as an opposition candidate and acknowledged Ukraine's independence. But unofficially, he and his inner circle believed that Ukrainian independence would not last long and that after a while Ukraine would 'come crawling back on its knees', asking to be taken back. When Ukraine did secede, Yeltsin's press secretary issued a statement that Russia reserved the right to put the issue of the Russian-Ukrainian border on the agenda.

Looking back on these events, it becomes easier to understand why, despite Giedroyc's fears, there was no Polish-Ukrainian war for Lviv after the fall of communism and why there was a Russian-Ukrainian war for Donbas, Crimea and the other Russian-speaking parts of Ukraine. Few people anticipated this war; before it happened people said it was impossible. But nothing is impossible in history. We cannot take historical reality as something that is already provided, we have to work against it to create a new reality. Or, as Ivan Franko wrote, to 'fight against the prod, swim against the tide'.

This is exactly what Ukrainian, Polish, Jewish and Crimean Tatar intellectuals did in the camps and in exile. The story of their work convinces us that the past can be overcome. This is part of the overall pattern of overcoming the past in postwar Europe. The two world wars began on the European continent. And so 'Never Again' became the rallying call for rebuilding after the war. The creation of the European Coal and Steel Community in 1951 served as the starting point for the unification of Europe.

The treaty establishing the Community was signed by Italy, Germany, France and the three Benelux countries of Belgium, Netherlands and Luxembourg, the territories which were the sites of the largest battles in Western Europe during both world wars. French Foreign Minister Robert Schuman had proposed the union in 1950. He believed that such an alliance would make war impossible both ideologically and materially. Alsace and Lorraine, two large industrial regions where coal was mined and steel was produced, stood at the very centre of this agreement. France and Germany had been fighting over these regions since 1870.

What French-German reconciliation was for Western Europe, Polish-Ukrainian reconciliation was for Eastern Europe. It avoided a new Polish-Ukrainian war over Volhynia and Galicia after the fall of communism and moved the formula for European reconciliation farther east. How far east is one of the key questions of contemporary geopolitics. The Donbas region and the Russian-Ukrainian border play the same role in today's Eastern Europe as Alsace and Lorraine did for France and Germany. Giedroyc believed that Polish-Ukrainian reconciliation could never be truly complete until reconciliation was reached with Russia. The current Kremlin does not understand the language of reconciliation – for it, compromises are an expression of weakness. The only language it understands is the language of force.

This is not to say that Ukrainian-Russian or Polish-Russian reconciliation is impossible in principle. It will be possible when Putin is gone and a new Russia emerges. After all, Schuman did not propose French-German reconciliation when Hitler was in power and Germany was occupying France. The key prerequisite was the defeat of Nazi Germany.

But before Ukrainian-Russian reconciliation occurs (if it ever does), Ukrainians need to focus on Ukrainian-Ukrainian reconciliation, to achieve a shared vision of the past and the future. Ukrainian leaders managed to rethink Ukraine in the 1960s and

1980s under much worse conditions. The fact that they succeeded once should give us hope that it can be done again.

This raises another question: the role of intellectuals in articulating the concept of the nation. In his classic work *Nations and Nationalism*, Ernest Gellner argued that nationalist thinkers 'did not make much of a difference. If one of them had fallen, others would have stepped into his place ... No one was indispensable. The quality of nationalist thought would hardly have been affected much by such substitutions. Their precise doctrines are hardly worth analysing'. It's hard to agree with this statement. The example of postwar Ukraine, in particular, refutes it. Try to imagine a world without Dziuba, Stus, Lysiak Rudnytsky, Giedroyc, Kuroń, Michnik and other opposition thinkers. Without them, it would not only be a completely different world; without them, given the risk of nuclear apocalypse which they worked hard to avert, this world might not exist at all.

INTERLUDE A Brief History of the Ukrainian Language

One of Russia's main arguments as proof that Ukrainians and Russians are one people and therefore need to live in a single nation, is the language argument. They claim that Russian and Ukrainian came from a common source and are so similar that their speakers can communicate without a translator. They even claim that Russians and Ukrainians spoke the same language at some point in the past and that the only differences are due to the Polonisation of those lands that were included in the Polish-Lithuanian Commonwealth. Therefore, the Ukrainian language is an artificial construct, just like the Ukrainian people and the Ukrainian state.

In reality, languages don't grow on trees. Like all fruits of civilisation, they are indeed artificial. Polish, Russian, Ukrainian and Belarusian were different from each other before the Polish-Lithuanian Commonwealth even existed. The current similarities between Ukrainian and Russian are the result of two hundred years during which Russian had superior status on Ukrainian lands and most Ukrainians learned to speak Russian. Ukrainians who grew up without Russian influence, in Western Europe or North America, don't actually understand much Russian.

Ukrainians from Ukraine don't actually understand much Polish either. People in the western part of the country are more likely to understand Polish as they were under direct Polish influence for longer than the rest of the country. Also, their proximity allowed them to tune in to Polish radio and television during the Soviet period, which was many times better than what was being broadcast out of Moscow.

These examples of Russian and Polish influence demonstrate a reality that may sound trite but is all too often forgotten: language is a tool of communication. The similarity and mutual comprehensibility of any two languages depends primarily on the intensity of communicative ties between them.

A comparative analysis of vocabulary and grammar shows that modern Ukrainian is equidistant from Polish and Russian. Belarusian is actually closer than either to Ukrainian, which is hardly surprising given the close historical ties between Belarus and Ukraine.

While the Russians claim that Ukrainians and Russians are one people, you can occasionally hear a different argument from the Ukrainian side: Russians are not actually Slavs at all, but Slavicised Ugro-Finns, while the Ukrainian language is older than Russian and at least as old as Sanskrit, to which it is similar.

The arguments of both sides provide an excellent demonstration of the ways elites use language as a tool in building either empires or nation-states. Those who want to absorb another nation or ethnic group attempt to minimise the differences between their language and the language of those they want to assimilate, they deprive the other language of dignity. Those who want to preserve their distinctness and avoid being absorbed emphasise the differences and attribute an almost sacred significance to language.

Despite their mutual hostility, both camps are united by a common set of beliefs: a) language is the basis of national identity; b) the language is as old as the nation; c) the borders of the nation stretch as far as the language can be heard. This set of beliefs is known as 'ethnolinguistic nationalism', and it is especially common in Central and Eastern Europe. This helps explains why the language issue is so thorny between Russia and Ukraine. It stems from the beliefs of nineteenth-century German nationalism. The German poet Ernst Moritz Arndt (1769–1860) expressed the linguistic credo of that nationalism, claiming that Germany stretches 'as far as the German tongue is heard'.

When it comes to the age of a language, even the most brilliant linguist can't pinpoint the exact moment a language is born. The choice of a birth date for a language is arbitrary and often determined by political or other subjective preferences. We can only very roughly say that Ukrainian, like other Slavic languages, emerged from Proto-Slavic, which itself split off from the Baltic-Slavic language group sometime in the sixth century. Ukrainian began to emerge as a separate language around the eleventh century, so we can estimate that the development of the Ukrainian language took almost a thousand years.

The first written traces of Ukrainian can be found in inscriptions on the walls of St Sophia Cathedral in Kyiv and in other churches of Kyivan Rus. These inscriptions exhibit features that are characteristic of modern Ukrainian and do not exist in Russian: the vocative case (which no longer exists in Russian), the Ukrainian form of the dative case and the Ukrainian form of the prince's name ('Volodymyr' rather than 'Vladimir'). Ukrainianisms can also be seen in the eleventh century Reims Gospel, one of the oldest texts created in the Ukrainian lands. However, these are only isolated traces. Like much of the graffiti in the church, the Reims Gospel is written in Old Church Slavonic. Or to be more precise, in the Ukrainian recension of Church Slavonic.

Church Slavonic is based on the language spoken by Cyril and Methodius, who translated the Gospels and other Christian texts into this old Slavic language. Due to their translations, Church Slavonic became the sacred language of the Eastern Christian church and it spread along with the church, sometimes extending beyond the territories of the Eastern Slavs (at certain points, it was the liturgical language among the Czechs, Croats and Romanians). In addition to the Ukrainian recension of Church Slavonic, there were also Russian, Serbian, Slovak, Croatian and Moravian recensions. These variations aren't due to deliberate language policies of local rulers or scribes. They emerged spontaneously because as Church Slavonic spread from its origins in the old Bulgarian kingdom, it inevitably absorbed elements of local dialects – in our case, Ukrainianisms. Other historical sacred languages, including Latin and Arabic, have similar characteristics. Very few people could write or speak them; those who could introduced errors into the texts that betrayed their origins.

The great majority of people were illiterate and spoke local vernaculars. It is impossible to determine the exact number of these local dialects. The author of *The Tale of Bygone Years* lists twenty-five Slavic tribes, eight of whom lived on the territory of modern Ukraine. According to the chronicler, each of these tribes had its own 'customs, laws of their ancestors and covenants'. It's not difficult to imagine that they also had their own dialects. We can't confirm this with any certainty as local tribes left few written texts behind. However, we do have the birch bark documents, short texts written on the bark that was used instead of paper in the north of ancient Rus and which was preserved in the saturated mud of Novgorod. Analysis of these texts clearly shows that the dialects of the northern Slavic tribes in the vicinity of Novgorod were very different from those in the vicinity of Kyiv.

However, we also know that these dialects were mutually intelligible. Travellers who journeyed from Constantinople to Lviv or from Vienna to Moscow from the fourteenth to seventeenth centuries reported that a person who knew one Slavic dialect could communicate with other Slavs without needing an interpreter. The differences between Slavic dialects were less significant than between, say, different dialects of English, German, or French.

These similarities between Slavic dialects do not indicate that the population of ancient Rus all spoke the same 'Old Rus language'. It is unlikely that any such language existed. It is a figment of the imagination of politicians and unscrupulous scholars. At the same time, separate and distinct Ukrainian, Belarusian and Russian languages did not exist either. What did exist was the raw material for their creation. Linguists identify five major regions which served as the basis on which modern East Slavic languages were formed: Kyiv-Polesia; Galicia-Podolia; Polotsk-Smolensk; Novgorod-Tver; and Murom-Ryazan. The Ukrainian language emerged in the first two regions, Belarusian in the third and Russian in the latter two.

The Belarusian language offers the most straightforward case: the ratio of language to region is 1:1. It is a bit more difficult, but still possible to understand why Russian emerged on the territory of two different regions. After Moscow conquered and subjugated Novgorod, there was very little likelihood that a separate 'Novgorodian language' would emerge. It is harder to explain why Ukrainian emerged on the territory of two different regions. After all, Kyiv never conquered Lviv and Lviv didn't conquer Kyiv. The explanation can be found in geography. Most of the Ukrainian lands lie on the vast East European Plain. On the plain, there are no natural barriers to limit communication between different regions and this helped to create a certain linguistic continuum. Exceptions include the relative geographical isolation of Polesia with its swamps and the lands on the far side of the Carpathians. The dialects in those two regions differ significantly from elsewhere. The other decisive factor was the decision of western and eastern Ukrainian elites in the nineteenth century to create a common literary language. This wasn't a simple or obvious choice. There were linguistic disputes over which dialect should form the basis of the Ukrainian literary language. But that does not change the broad conclusion: it is not the language that creates the nation, but the nation that creates the language.

In any case, the formation of the modern Ukrainian language was not a journey from point A to point B down a one-way highway. It was more like a trip with multiple side routes. For instance, it is not hard to imagine that a common Belarusian-Ukrainian language could have emerged rather than the two separate languages. There are no criteria that can tell you in advance which dialects or groups of dialects will eventually be recognised as separate languages. There are no linguistic laws, for instance, that can tell you why the Rusyn dialect is recognised as a distinct language in Slovakia, but in Ukraine it is considered a dialect. Dialects become standardised languages when they are codified – when they gain a unified grammar, spelling, dictionaries and a sufficiently large number of written texts, including textbooks.

Politics also plays a role in the elevation of a spoken dialect into a written language. The simplest definition says that a language is a dialect with an army. The military forces of the first Kyivan princes most likely spoke a Scandinavian dialect. As their Varangian military trading company grew into a state, they needed a language for record keeping and this is how the Rus written language called 'prosta mova' (simple language) emerged. And they didn't use a Scandinavian language: it was Slavic. The language of the first (non-Slavic) conquerors of Bulgaria underwent a similar evolution as they gradually Slavicised under the influence of their predominantly Slavic environment. The prosta mova was most likely based on the dialects of Kyiv, as Kyiv was the capital of Kyivan Rus.

The Rus prosta mova outlived Kyivan Rus as a chancery language and became one of the official languages in Moldova and the Grand Duchy of Lithuania. There is little scholarly consensus about the language. It can be viewed as a transitional hybrid from a language for record-keeping to a literary language. It was not used solely for official documents; polemical works, poetry (verses) and dramas were also written in prosta mova. Although it certainly had Ukrainian elements, for a long time the Rus language used in Lithuania was more similar to modern Belarusian, due to the fact that the main centres of Rus cultural life in the Polish-Lithuanian Commonwealth were Vilnius, Navahrudak, Polotsk and Smolensk. Later, at the turn of the sixteenth century, they gradually lost ground to Lviv, Ostroh, Lutsk and Kyiv. Over time, in the Ukrainian lands, the prosta mova gains more and more local features to the point that it becomes recognisable as Old Ukrainian. We can track these shifts through documents written by scribes who attempted to reproduce what they heard as accurately as possible. For instance, a modern-day Ukrainian can easily read a speech by Khmelnytsky recorded by a scribe five hundred years ago.

Due to the adoption of terms from Polish, German, Czech and Latin, the vocabulary of prosta mova was more similar to the West Slavic languages than to Russian. When the Cossack lands came under the rule of the Moscow Tsar, Great Russian officials had to hire translators to communicate with the Ukrainian Cossacks.

The Cossack period of Ukrainian history took place during a key period for the formation of modern standardised languages on the European continent. Grammars and textbooks were being written on a large scale for the first time. The Reformation played a key role in this. Protestantism introduced the idea that the word of Christ should be available and understandable for everyone, not just for priests and monks. The translations of the Bible into local vernaculars can be marked as a birthdate for European literary languages. The Peresopnytsia Gospel and other translations into the vernacular first appeared in the Ukrainian lands in the 1550s–60s.

In addition, Catholic pressure on the Orthodox Church unexpectedly led to the revival of Church Slavonic. Efforts to resist Catholic influence motivated the publication of the Ostroh Bible, which translated the gospel into a new, modernised version of Church Slavonic. At the same time, the first local Church Slavonic grammars and dictionaries by Meletii Smotrytsky, Pamvo Berynda and Lavrentii Zyzan appeared.

The linguistic situation of the pre-modern and early modern periods is best described as diglossia or triglossia: the coexistence of two or even three languages, each with its own sphere of use. For example, Cossack officers prayed in Church Slavonic, kept records in Old Ukrainian and spoke to peasants and servants in the local dialect.

There were no impenetrable barriers between these languages, rather the levels overflowed freely from one into the other. In his correspondence with his beloved, Ivan Mazepa would switch to conversational language when he wanted to be easily understood. The poetry attributed to Mazepa ('Duma' and 'Chaika') is written in the same colloquial language. The interaction of different levels of diglossia or triglossia can give rise to a shared national language. An important pre-condition is the widest possible penetration into all levels of society. By the early eighteenth century, Old Ukrainian was rapidly approaching this state.

This linguistic growth stopped at the end of the eighteenth century. In the part of the Ukrainian lands that remained under the rule of the Polish-Lithuanian Commonwealth, Old Polish developed more intensively than Old Ukrainian and achieved what Old Ukrainian had not: Old Polish almost completely displaced the sacred language (for them, Latin) as the language of education and literature. It also displaced Old Ukrainian. Polish spread not only among secular elites, but also among the church elites, and not only among Greek Catholics or Protestants, but even among Orthodox believers.

Old Ukrainian survived longer in the Cossack state. However, after the defeat of Mazepa in 1709 and the transformation of the

Tsardom of Muscovy into the Russian Empire in 1721, it was subject to increasing Russification and when the Hetmanate was dissolved, Old Ukrainian was replaced by Russian. A similar fate befell the local recension of Church Slavonic: government bans on Ukrainian led it to be replaced by the Russian recension. The Ukrainian version of Church Slavonic survived only in Galicia, which fell under the rule of Austria rather than Russia after the collapse of the Polish-Lithuanian Commonwealth. Here it took the form of *Yazychia*, a mixture of the Church Slavonic, Polish, Rus and Russian languages that remained the language of high culture of Galician Rusyns until the late nineteenth century. In the Habsburg monarchy, the Rus language was recognised as one of the fourteen official languages. In this status, it coexisted in Galicia with German and Polish, in Bukovyna with German and Romanian and in Transcarpathia with German and Hungarian.

With the exception of Galicia, the efforts of the Rus elite to develop two languages of their own, a sacred and a secular, had ended with them being left without either. They had to start over. The first contribution to this fresh start was Kotliarevsky's parody of the *Aeneid*, written in 1798 in a new, vernacular language.

The formation of this modern language faced greater obstacles in its development than Old Ukrainian had. On the one hand, Rus-Ukrainian society had lost its layer of state and secular elite. It had gone from being a nation of Cossacks to being a nation of 'priests and peasants'. In addition, it now faced the challenge of the Russian language, which had greater political and cultural resources, including a long, uninterrupted period of development, unlike Ukrainian. In the eighteenth century, Russian moved ahead in the competition between the two languages. The modern Russian language also incorporated many features of Church Slavonic which conveyed a special, almost sacred status onto Russian. Nonetheless, in the Ukrainian lands of the former Polish-Lithuanian Commonwealth, Polish remained the dominant language of the elites, even after it lost its official status in the early nineteenth century.

The Ukrainian ethnic territories were also part of 'Yiddishland', the lands where Eastern European Jews lived. Comparison with the Jewish case helps to better highlight the uniqueness of the Ukrainian case. While Hebrew was the sacred language of the Jews, Yiddish was the language of daily life. Yiddish is a Germanic language with many words and concepts adopted from local cultures. There are significant differences between the northern ('Lithuanian'), central ('Polish' or 'Galician') and southern ('Ukrainian') dialects of Yiddish.

As the Jewish elite secularised, they followed two linguistic paths. One portion of the elite chose to adopt the local dominant language: German, Polish or Russian, depending on their time and place of residence. Others followed the same path as the Ukrainian elite: they attempted to turn the language of everyday life into a modern literary language. The writer Sholem Aleichem (1859–16), who was born and spent most of his life in the Ukrainian lands, took this path and wrote primarily in Yiddish. In 1917, Ukrainian and Yiddish became the two official languages of the Ukrainian People's Republic. However, it is rare for a primarily oral language to become the official language of a state and the State of Israel chose Hebrew rather than Yiddish.

The linguistic diversity of Central and Eastern Europe made it resemble the Tower of Babel. In addition to large communities of Belarusians, Jews, Poles, Russians, Slovaks, Ukrainians and Czechs, there were also Armenians, Greeks, Karaites, Crimean Tatars, Roma and Russian Old Believers. Each group had their own language or dialect. A look at the situation in Austrian Galicia offers a sense of the linguistic diversity of the region. The four dominant languages were German, Russian, Polish and Yiddish, but the list of words in daily use included borrowings from Romanian, Hungarian, Latin, Armenian, French, Czech, Church Slavonic, Russian, Italian, English, Turkish and Arabic.

This diversity did not prevent the inhabitants of these territories from communicating. Knowledge of a few hundred basic words was enough. People from the area joked that they 'could *not* speak three languages' – that is, they spoke them all badly. The level of language skills a person needed depended on their status and profession. A peasant working the land needed one or two languages, while a merchant who traded with the broader population needed to master several.

There is often a lingua franca, a language of interethnic communication used by the educated public. In medieval times, the lingua franca was one of the sacred languages, such as Latin or Arabic. In early modern Europe, it was French, the language of the largest and most powerful state in Europe. In the nineteenth century, following the revolutions of 1789–1870, French lost its stature and was gradually squeezed out by German in Central Europe and by Russian in the Russian Empire. In the twentieth century, English became a global lingua franca. In the circumstances of di- or tri-glossia, the choice of language depended on the circumstances. For instance, French shielded Polish aristocrats from Russification and Germanisation. But when they wanted to emphasise their superiority over the petty gentry, they would switch to English.

These are all nuances. They should not prevent us from seeing two fundamental features of the pre-modern linguistic situation. First, there were few large areas that were purely monolingual. Even in isolated mountain villages in the Carpathians or swamp settlements of Polesia, the language of the church existed side by side with a local Rus dialect. Second, for a long time, language was not viewed in relation to either nationality or imperial loyalty. The Ukrainian separatist Vasyl Kapnist wrote his 1783 'Ode on Slavery' in Russian. The Russian aristocracy (and the Polish) spoke French on the eve of the war with Napoleon. The greatest Ukrainian poet, Taras Shevchenko, kept his diary in Russian. Another great Ukrainian poet, Ivan Franko, wrote to his beloved, the daughter of a Greek Catholic priest, in German.

Pre-modern authorities generally had very little interest in what language their subjects spoke – they were more interested in taxes for the treasury and recruits for the army.

Modern society is more demanding. If yesterday's peasants are going to be able to work in a factory or fight in the army, they need some baseline knowledge and education should be provided in a single language that is readily understood by the students. These demands give dialects their chance to develop into standardised languages. In addition to these pragmatic requirements, ideological considerations also play a role. The nineteenth century was a time of social emancipation, the birth of mass politics and new ideologies. Each of these projects demanded the loyalty of the masses and loyalty requires emotional attachment: it is hard to love under duress. Here again, dialects come to the fore. 'High' languages are important for cognitive transformations, giving yesterday's peasants and their children the ability to think in abstract terms so that they can master modern technologies or vote in elections. But the emotional attachment is still to the traditional, oral language – the language they heard at home as children.

The nineteenth century was an era of linguistic and political revolution. Romanticism imbued this revolution with a sacred dimension. The Romantics believed that peasant culture, unspoiled by civilisation, contained deep ancient wisdom and truth. The largely peasant nature of Ukrainian lent it an elevated status in the eyes of European romantics. This explains why, despite a poverty of resources and problems of linguistic competition, the creators of the new literary Ukrainian language quite readily overcame the obstacles in their path: the wind of change was filling their sails. During the Romantic era, grammars, dictionaries and textbooks in the vernacular appeared. And, most importantly, national poets emerged. These national poets all shared one specific trait: they knew the peasant language well, either because they came from families of peasants or village priests, or because they were raised by peasant nannies who rocked them to sleep with traditional lullabies and told them folktales. In any case, they were able to use this language fluently.

The language these poets used wasn't purely the peasant language. The oral culture of traditional peasant society lacked certain concepts to express complex feelings and thoughts. For example, peasants knew that a beggar at a church should be given alms and a guest should be fed and provided with a place to stay, but they didn't know the words 'sacrifice' or 'hospitality'. The abstract terms had to be borrowed or forged from the languages of high culture. Therefore, modern languages are inherently syncretic; they are created from multiple sources. Shevchenko created his language on the basis of three Ukrainian dialects (southeastern, northern and northwestern), elements of Church Slavonic and the linguistic material of early Ukrainian literary works. The quality of the synthesis was important; it should sound melodious to an untrained ear. Listening to Shevchenko's poems, the peasants might not fully understand them. But they never ceased to marvel: how could something like this exist in *their* language?

National activists claim that language is the core of national identity, believing that it encrypts the cultural code and historical memory of the nation. Switching to another language is treated as the gravest sin. In 1869, Ukrainian poet Sydir Vorobkevych wrote:

Native language, native word!
Whoever forgets you,
Has a stone in his chest
Instead of a heart.

The fact that there were far more languages available in Central and Eastern Europe than nations meant that nation-building inevitably revolved around the question: which language is worthy of becoming a national language? There were many contenders, few prizes and the choice was a zero-sum game: I win, you lose. This made the language issue particularly acute and emotionally charged. Hetman Pavlo Skoropadsky, himself a man of Russian culture and a critic of 'Galician (i.e. Ukrainian-speaking) Ukraine', wrote that the tsarist Russian émigrés in Kyiv in 1918 hated nothing as much as the Ukrainian language.

If a language was to become a national language, it had to function at all levels, from low to high, including in scholarly works. The German-speaking elite ridiculed the Poles' attempts to establish a Polish university in Lviv: although there was good Polish literature, only amateurs would use Polish in scholarly writing. Nonetheless, the Poles did successfully establish their own universities and technical schools. Then when the Ukrainians tried to open their own university in Lviv, the Poles used the same argument as the Germans had: although Ukrainian might have a rich folk literature, it couldn't possibly convey scientific terminology!

All of these language disputes and insults centred on a key question: could Ukrainian become a language of modernity? This question was not a linguistic one, but a purely political one. In principle, any language can meet the needs of a modern society with appropriate effort and support. The state took on the role of arbiter in this matter. Until the end of its existence, the official policy of the Russian Empire was that 'the Ukrainian language never existed, does not exist and shall never exist'.

Historians argue whether the decision to ban the public use of the Ukrainian language was a strategic decision or simply a response to changed circumstances after the Polish uprising of 1863. The answer to this question can be found if we take a broader view. In the Russian Empire, not only the modern ('peasant') Ukrainian language was subject to repression, but also the two earlier ones: the Ukrainian version of Church Slavonic and the Rus language. The Russian authorities were determined that none of the three historical languages of Ukrainians would become a language of administration, education or the Church. So it was a strategic decision: allowing Ukrainians to have their own language could have led to Ukrainian separatism. And, given Ukraine's importance in the imperial system, that could have put an end to the empire itself.

In the Austrian Empire, Ruthenian (as Rus was known in Austria-Hungary) was one of the fourteen official languages. However, compared to the others, it was like a historical relic that was poorly suited to modern needs. Even the Rus Greek Catholic clergy spoke mostly Polish at home! Another issue was its use of 'etymological spelling' in which the way a word was spelled did not correspond to how it was pronounced (similar to the case with English and French). In the eyes of the Austrian and Polish elites, this made the Ruthenian language suspiciously similar to Russian, which also used etymological spelling, thus calling into question the loyalty of Ruthenian subjects in the event of an Austrian-Russian war. As a result, the Ruthenian language became the object of alphabet wars for years. There were attempts to implement use of the Latin alphabet in order to distance it as much as possible from Russian. The more Ukrainian-oriented Rus elite began to use a simplified phonetic spelling based on the principle: 'Write what you hear and read what you see.' The fight between etymological and phonetic spelling was a fight between tradition and modernity. In Galicia, there was a report of a Russophile grandfather who beat his grandson to death with a stick when he caught him reading a newspaper printed in phonetic script. In 1890, Vienna pushed for an agreement between Polish and Ukrainian factions, as they sought to resolve internal disputes in anticipation of potential war with Russia. In the agreement, phonetic spelling was granted official status.

Polish officials continued to use the outdated term 'Rus' and claimed that Ukrainian itself was a Bolshevik invention. No, the Bolsheviks did not invent Ukrainian. However, they did use Shevchenko's poetry for revolutionary propaganda and presented the tsarist ban on Ukrainian as another reason to fight the tsarist regime. The 1917 revolution and the national liberation struggle led to a striking expansion of the sphere of use for Ukrainian. For the first time, Ukrainian became the language of the government apparatus. Even the defeat of the Ukrainian national liberation struggle of 1917–20 did not stop its development, because it was the language of the revolutionary peasant element, which the Bolshevik government could not disregard. Even before the official Ukrainisation policy of the 1920s, Lenin required all Red Army military institutions in Ukraine to have translators from Russian to Ukrainian. And during Ukrainisation, the revolutionary Bolshevik poet Vladimir Mayakovsky wrote:

I say to myself: comrade Muscovite,
Don't mock Ukraine.
Learn this language from its Red banners,
This language both majestic and simple:
'Hear the trumpets blow, the hour of reckoning has come . . . '

(The last line is a quote from a Ukrainian translation of 'The Internationale'.)

The 1920s mark a high point in the development of the Ukrainian language. Official Ukrainisation from above and unofficial Ukrainisation from below jointly led Ukrainian to become a language of modernity. But even at that high point, it hit a glass ceiling. It was never widely adopted in large cities. That would have required several generations and Ukrainisation lasted barely a decade. Moreover, Ukrainian never penetrated to the highest levels of the Soviet regime – the Bolshevik elite, the security organs, or the army leadership.

When Ukrainisation was curtailed in the 1930s, the Ukrainian language again began to lose its relevance. The policies of the Russian Empire and the Soviet Union are clear linguistic genocide. At some points, linguistic genocide went hand in hand with physical genocide. It is interesting to note that a significant fraction of peoples who no longer speak their traditional tongue are also nations who have survived mass famine, including the Irish, Kazakhs and Ukrainians. Most of the creators and supporters of Ukrainisation were killed in the Stalinist terror. The hidden limits of 1920s Ukrainisation became the solid limits of Soviet torture chambers and camps in the 1930s. Not only were Ukrainians subject to Stalinist repression – the Ukrainian language was as well. According to the spelling 'reforms' of 1933, most of the elements and features that distinguished Ukrainian from Russian were removed. This included elimination of the Ukrainian letter to indicate a hard 'g', which did not exist in Russian, and changes in transliteration, such as the requirement that the German diphthong 'ei' would now be transliterated to sound more like Russian than German (Einstein would now be pronounced Ejnstejn).

After Stalin's death, the next major blow to Ukrainian was the educational reform of the late 1950s, which abolished the compulsory study of Ukrainian in schools within Ukraine. Russian remained mandatory. In fact, it was a death sentence for the language. Ukrainian was gradually being pushed out of all spheres of modern life just as Soviet modernisation was reaching its peak: Ukraine was becoming an urbanised society for the first time, compulsory secondary education was introduced and new means of communication like radio and television were emerging. To be urban, educated and successful in Soviet Ukraine almost automatically meant to be Russian speaking.

From the 1960s to the 1980s, Russian achieved unofficial status as the 'normal' language of daily life in Soviet Ukraine. There was one phrase that was repeated again and again, anytime someone spoke Ukrainian in public, in shops, public transportation, or libraries: 'Speak human language.' As if the Ukrainian language was spoken by non-humans!

In Brezhnev's time, people joked that only academics and house cleaners spoke Ukrainian in Kyiv. Academics because they had to and cleaners because no one cared. For everyone else, a normal career in Soviet Ukraine required use of the 'normal' language, i.e. Russian.

The Ukrainian language was dying out, in line with the official principle that nations will disappear under communism. It might have completely died if the Soviet regime had lasted even one more generation.

The collapse of the USSR and the proclamation of Ukrainian independence raised the language issue in a new way: a nation-state requires a national language. Ukraine had declared Ukrainian an official language in October 1989. This happened immediately after the resignation of Brezhnev's last Mohican, Vladimir Shcherbytsky, who had actively pursued a course of Russification in Ukraine. In 1996, the status of Ukrainian as the official language was enshrined in the Constitution of Ukraine.

In independent Ukraine, the status of Ukrainian as an official language is not a matter of dispute. There is strong consensus around the issue. The disputes arise over the status of Russian. Although most residents of the young Ukrainian state identified Ukrainian as their native language, they reported using Russian more often (57 per cent in 1991). Many demanded that Russian be recognised as a second official language.

In theory, that shouldn't be a problem. Ireland and Canada both have two official languages, Belgium and Luxembourg have three, Singapore has four, South Africa has thirteen and Bolivia has more than thirty-seven. Countries with more than one official language usually have a history of colonisation: one language is the language of the metropolis and the others are local languages. Ukraine was a colony, but a strange one. Neither the Irish nor the Canadian, let alone the Singaporean or Bolivian elites were allowed to govern in the imperial centre and their influence on the imperial language was minimal, if any. In contrast, Ukrainians were allowed close to power in the centre during two separate periods: once in the eighteenth century and again after Stalin's death. Therefore, their influence on the formation of the language and culture of the Russian Empire and the USSR was quite significant. On the other hand, in both the Russian Empire and the USSR, the Ukrainian language was subject to systematic repression and pushed out of the public sphere. This aspect makes it more similar to the case of Irish within the British Empire. However, unlike Irish, Ukrainian has remained the language of daily communication for a large portion of the population.

So in the Russian Empire and later the Soviet, Ukrainians started out as the Scots and ended up as the Irish. Russian speakers in Ukraine threatened to follow the same path from loyalty to separatism if their language was not recognised as an official language. Officially, they demanded the consolidation of bilingualism. In reality, they were demanding the preservation of monolingualism in the areas where they dominated – the industrialised east and south of Ukraine. Ironically, if the residents of these regions had actually wanted bilingualism, they would have learned Ukrainian – native Ukrainian speakers already knew Russian!

Ukraine is commonly referred to as a bilingual country and it is argued that it is the division into the Ukrainian-speaking West and the Russian-speaking East that is responsible for the high levels of political conflict. In reality, the linguistic situation in Ukraine is much more complicated than a division into speakers of Ukrainian vs Russian. A significant part of the population regularly uses both Russian and Ukrainian or a blend of the two referred to as *surzhyk*. With the exception of Crimea, linguistic separatism has never been strong in Ukraine. Even in the largely Russian-speaking Donetsk, people more often identified their nationality as Ukrainian than Russian (and even more people claimed a primarily Donetsk identity). In their quest for power, the Donetsk elite went to Kyiv and every Russian-speaking president learned to speak Ukrainian once he came to power in Kyiv.

In independent Ukraine, language and national identity are not necessarily connected. For Ukrainian speakers they are linked, but not for Russian speakers: most Russian speakers consider themselves Ukrainian, not Russian. It is true that sociological research before the full-scale war showed that Russian speakers on the whole were less committed to Ukrainian independence, less prepared to defend it, had less negative attitudes towards Russia as an aggressor and were more likely to consider Ukrainians and Russians as closely related or even one people. These differences between Ukrainian and Russian speakers, however, are quantitative rather than qualitative. There is no pro-Russian majority among Russian speakers. On the contrary, most consider themselves to be part of the Ukrainian tradition and have a negative attitude towards Putin.

Sergei Loiko is a Russian journalist for the *Los Angeles Times* who reported on the war in Donbas. In 2014, he found himself in the hottest spot of this war – the battle for Donetsk airport. In an interview, he described the battle as something out of *The Lord of the Rings* in which 'absolute good' was battling 'absolute evil' and he noted that both sides communicated almost exclusively in Russian. He also commented that the Ukrainian soldiers tended to speak a cleaner, more educated Russian.

The overwhelming majority of Ukrainians do not view language as the main social issue in the country. There are two factors which have 'helped' the tension of the language issue. The first is that the question of language has strong emotional salience and speaks more to the heart than to the mind. This lends itself perfectly to political manipulation, especially during elections. The second factor is Russia: the French language could hardly have developed freely in Quebec if France once invaded Canada!

Until recently, the language situation in Ukraine looked like a stalemate. Those who demanded official status for Russian threatened that Ukraine would disintegrate otherwise. Those who opposed it believed that Ukraine would disintegrate if Russian was granted official status.

Historically, Ukraine has never been monolingual and the big question now is whether it will remain bilingual and for how long. One possibility is a trilingual Ukraine in which English becomes the prerequisite for a successful career. People wouldn't object to that solution. According to sociological surveys in independent Ukraine, Ukrainians might argue about the best language of instruction, but there is broad agreement that the second compulsory language should be English.

One reason Russian has maintained its position in Ukraine has been its status as a world language. Over the past two centuries, thanks to state support and with the development of Russian culture in the nineteenth century and the export of communism in the twentieth century, Russian has made the leap from a provincial language to a language of world culture. For many Ukrainians, Russian has been the language of entry into the wider world and this enhanced its spread and popularity.

After the collapse of the USSR, Russian began to lose its status as a world language. Estimates show that the number of native Russian speakers outside of Russia is constantly decreasing and soon it will no longer be one of the ten most widely spoken languages in the world.

In 2000, most Ukrainians still named Russian as their main

language of communication. By 2002, Ukrainian had drawn equal to Russian and it has been increasing steadily ever since, particularly after the Euromaidan and Russian aggression. There are demographic changes which impact those number including the emergence of a generation fully educated after Ukrainian independence and the impossibility of surveying Russian speakers in Donbas and Crimea. However, the declining prestige of the Russian language is another factor. Modern Russia has nothing to offer the world except gas and war. As Hugh Laurie joked, even Russian vodka is only good for cleaning the oven.

Russia has lost its chance for modernisation and with it, the Russian language has lost its status as a language of modernisation. Moreover, unlike English, Spanish, German and French, Russian has not become a language of democracy – there are no states with Russian as an official language which are classified as democracies.

Independent Ukraine may have been the last country where Russian had a chance to become a language of democracy. Immediately after the victory of Euromaidan in 2014, there were calls for official recognition of a distinctly Ukrainian-Russian, with its many borrowings from Ukrainian that makes it different from the Russian spoken in Russia. The idea never took hold.

Putin declared war under the pretext of protecting the Russian-speaking population of Ukraine, but the reality is entirely different. The war is being waged mainly in the Russian-speaking parts of the country and while claiming to protect the Russian-speaking population of Ukraine, Putin and the Russian army are systematically destroying it. Russian attacks and shelling of Mariupol, Odesa, Kharkiv and Kherson, are killing people and destroying their homes. They are also destroying the special status of the Russian language and culture in Ukraine. One year after the full-scale invasion, 45 per cent of people who identified as Russian speakers or bilingual report that they are now speaking more Ukrainian. Overall, 22 per cent of people report that they are speaking Ukrainian more often.

War is a great accelerator and it makes the impossible possible. This is certainly the case for the language issue in Ukraine, which is simply evaporating as Ukraine's colonial history burns in the fire of the current war.

Most likely, the Russian language in Ukraine will suffer the same fate as the Hungarian language in Slovakia and German in Poland after the Second World War: it will lose its special status and become just one minority language among many. And so, Russian will experience the very fate that Russian and Soviet officials tried to impose on Ukrainian. History loves a paradox.

INSTEAD OF A CONCLUSION

INDEPENDENT UKRAINE

Events

At the start of the 1990s, the disintegration of the USSR became Ukraine's main contribution to world history. Although communism had fallen, the Soviet Union itself could have continued to exist. Ukraine's declaration of independence made that impossible. The Soviet Union could have existed without the Baltics or the republics of the Caucasus but without Ukraine, it lost its raison d'être.

The appearance of independent Ukraine has been placed alongside the two other most important events in the history of the twentieth century, the First and Second World Wars. Ukraine's withdrawal from the Soviet Union put an end to the global superpower that appeared after the First World War, grew stronger after the Second and threatened the world with a Third.

Ukraine's declaration of independence was the last act in the wave of anti-communist revolutions of 1989–91. Revolutions have been called times of beautiful madness. The fall of communism led people to believe that history had reached its happy ending. At least, that's what Francis Fukuyama argued in his well-known article 'The End of History'. Fukuyama relied on a Hegelian philosophy of history, which claims that history has a meaning and that meaning is the gradual liberation of humanity from various forms of oppression. Hegel himself drew this conclusion under the influence of the French Revolution of 1789 and the Haitian Revolution of 1791 – the latter being the first successful slave uprising in modern history. The victory of Western liberal democracy over communism two hundred years later meant that history had reached its highest point: it was over, because there was no one left to liberate. Small conflicts would not disappear, but there would no longer be any major wars. Although life might become dull, it would be comfortable and safe.

As the 1980s turned to the 1990s, Ukrainian history and world history once again became closely intertwined. This time there was a heavy dose of optimism in that intertwining. In 1990, Deutsche Bank assessed the economic potential of all fifteen Soviet republics. It considered such indicators as levels of industrialisation and agricultural development, the education of the population, natural resources, etc. Ukraine was ranked as the republic with the greatest economic potential.

Moreover, Ukraine had the foundations to join the club of the world's most influential players: Ukraine inherited a significant nuclear arsenal after the collapse of the Soviet Union and became the third largest nuclear power in the world, behind the United States and Russia. It was the largest European country in terms of territory and according to population was only slightly smaller than the UK, Italy and France. Optimistic expectations boosted the support for Ukrainian independence in the Russian-speaking south and east of the country.

However, Ukraine's 'fifteen minutes of fame' passed quickly. High expectations gave way to deep disillusionment. The old Soviet economy in Ukraine was falling apart, many factories closed, mass unemployment took hold and millions of Ukrainians fell below the poverty line. While neighbouring Poland was experiencing the shock of rapid but successful reforms, Ukraine was experiencing the shock of no reforms. In 1993, Ukraine's annual inflation rate reached 10,200 per cent. It set a world record at the time.

Ukraine lost yet another advantage – its status as a major nuclear power. Under pressure from Russia and the United States, Kyiv agreed to nuclear disarmament. In December 1994, the Ukrainian government signed the Budapest Memorandum with the United Kingdom, Russia and the United States. Under its terms, these countries pledged to respect Ukraine's independence, sovereignty and borders in exchange for renunciation of its status as a nuclear power.

Ukraine was going through a deep political crisis. The three groups which had formerly been allies, the former national democrats, former national communists and miners in Donbas, had become enemies. The new Ukrainian elite consisted of a mixture of the first two, the national communists and the national democrats. They faced a challenge: how to build a nation, when a large part of the population doesn't feel like part of it?

Many young nation-states have faced this very problem. As Italian politicians said in 1861 after the unification of Italy: 'We have made Italy – now we have to make Italians'. Similarly, Ukraine's elite had 'made' Ukraine and now it had to make Ukrainians. Neighbouring Russia and Poland did not face the same problem as their national identity wasn't under threat. They embarked on radical economic reforms without the step of building a nation.

Nation-building efforts provoked resistance in the Russian-speaking East. Political leaders there demanded the federalisation of the country and the adoption of Russian as a second official language. In the summer of 1993, Donbas miners went on strike and then moved their strike to Kyiv. Under their pressure, the Ukrainian parliament decided to hold early presidential elections in the summer of 1994. The main candidates in the elections were the incumbent president, Leonid Kravchuk and his former prime minister, Leonid Kuchma. Kravchuk was supported by the Ukrainian-speaking West, while Kuchma was supported by the

Russian-speaking East. The fact that political divisions coincided with linguistic and regional ones made the situation particularly dangerous. In late 1993, the CIA predicted that Ukraine was headed for a civil war that would make the Yugoslav wars of the time look like a harmless picnic. A month before the 1994 presidential election, the *Economist* published an article under the alarming headline 'Ukraine: The Birth and Possible Death of a Country'.

Russia was also undergoing a deep crisis at the time. Radical economic reforms had not been as successful as in Poland and Russian democrats did not have the mass support the anti-communist opposition enjoyed in Poland. In December 1992, the Russian parliament rejected the appointment of Yegor Gaidar, 'father of the economic reforms', as acting prime minister. After several months of acrimonious confrontation, Yeltsin dissolved the parliament and the parliament impeached Yeltsin. In response, Yeltsin sent in troops and tanks fired at the parliament building. In early October 1993, several hundred people were killed or wounded in clashes on the streets and squares of Moscow.

Unlike the Russian crisis, the Ukrainian political crisis was resolved without bloodshed. Kravchuk lost the election and peacefully transferred power to Kuchma. This was a key moment in the divergence of political paths between Ukraine and Russia. As Russian historian Dmitry Furman wrote, Ukrainians successfully passed the democracy test that Russians failed. And it's worth noting that Ukrainians passed it on an 'empty stomach', because the economic situation in Ukraine was much worse than in Russia.

The 1994 elections were a crucial moment in the birth of Ukrainian democracy. Ukraine successfully established a mechanism for the change of ruling elites. While Ukraine has had six presidents since the fall of communism, Russia has had only three – in reality, only two, because during the presidency of Dmitry Medvedev, Putin continued to hold all the levers of power.

Of the six Ukrainian presidents, Leonid Kuchma ruled the longest, serving two full terms from 1994–2004. In the first months of his presidency, Kuchma gathered a team of reformers and implemented necessary reforms. Combined with favourable global market conditions, this led to the steady growth of Ukraine's economy from the late 1990s until the global crisis of 2008.

Kuchma unexpectedly made a sharp change in course in Ukraine's relations with Russia. Although he came to power on the promise of bringing Ukraine closer to Russia, he made a U-turn once he was in office. He began speaking Ukrainian and even wrote a book titled 'Ukraine is not Russia'. He tried to maintain good relations with Russia, while simultaneously reorienting Ukraine towards the West. The government declared a policy of integration with Europe.

Kuchma's changes came in response to Russian behaviour. From the first days of Ukrainian independence, Russian politicians would complain from time to time that Ukraine had lands that had historically belonged to Russia. The Kremlin actively prevented the transfer of the Black Sea Fleet to Ukrainian control. A separatist movement developed in Crimea. Thanks to his decisive and peaceful actions, Kuchma was able to resolve it in the first months of his presidency.

Kyiv was successful so long as Moscow was weak. Everything changed when Putin came to power in 1999. Already in 2003, a conflict between Russia and Ukraine over the Black Sea island of Tuzla almost led to armed conflict. We are accustomed to viewing Putin as a product of the KGB. However, we often forget that he began his political career among the Russian democrats. Even before the collapse of the USSR, they were thinking about what to do with Ukraine. The prevailing opinion was that Ukraine should be allowed to leave the Union. However, this permission was based on the calculation that the Ukrainian nation was not viable and that Ukrainian independence would not last long. Sooner or later, Ukraine would come begging back to Russia, this time on its knees, and then it would be possible to dictate tougher conditions for reunification.

Time passed, but Ukraine did not come back. On the contrary: Kuchma's first term in office (1994–99) was a time of political and economic stabilisation of Ukrainian independence. The situation changed at the beginning of his second term. In November 2000, one of the opposition leaders released a recording of secret conversations in Kuchma's office made by Mykola Melnychenko, Kuchma's bodyguard. The recordings appeared to show that the Ukrainian president had violated the US arms embargo on Iraq and secretly sold advanced radar intelligence stations to the Iraqi government. It was never proven that the sale took place, but the incident severely damaged relations between Ukraine and the United States.

Some people see the hand of Russia's special services behind the scandal, but Kuchma had plenty of other problems. It was under his rule that the oligarchic system became firmly entrenched in Ukraine. Most of Ukraine's oligarchs made their fortunes through personal connections with the authorities in Kyiv and Moscow. Corruption reached such proportions that it seemed to have become a central pillar of state power: remove it and the whole state would collapse. Systemic corruption, abuse of the court system and unofficial censorship became deeply entrenched.

In September 2000, the young journalist Georgiy Gongadze, who had been investigating government scandals, went missing in Kyiv. A few weeks later, his decapitated body was found on the outskirts of Kyiv. Melnychenko's tapes implied that Kuchma might be responsible for the killing of Gongadze. In the winter of 2000–01, a wave of protests 'Ukraine without Kuchma' swept through Kyiv. The authorities dispersed the protests by force. The first revolutionary situation emerged in Ukraine.

Kuchma's story is the story of many modern authoritarian rulers. They come to power in response to a demand for improvement. They often succeed initially. But then economic growth leads to the emergence of a large middle class which does not accept authoritarian rule. They demand the expansion of political freedoms. All of which leads us to a paradox: political protests against the government don't begin when the economic situation gets worse, but rather when it improves.

Ukraine was moving towards authoritarianism. Kuchma did not try to Russify Ukraine linguistically or culturally, but he did try to Russify Ukraine politically by copying Russian political patterns. Just as Yeltsin transferred power directly to Putin, Kuchma tried to transfer power to acting Prime Minister Viktor Yanukovych at the end of his second term.

Before becoming Prime Minister, Yanukovych was governor of Donetsk oblast. He was a head of the Donbas clan that had emerged following the merger of the local elite with the criminal underworld. He had two criminal convictions. Locals called his group the 'Donetsk mafia'. The Donetsk clan were planning to replace the Dnipro group headed by Kuchma. The Dnipro group splintered towards the end of Kuchma's rule and Yulia Tymoshenko, who had originally been part of the Dnipro clan, started leading the anti-Kuchma opposition. Splits weren't tolerated in the Donetsk clan. The boss of the Donetsk mafia, Rinat Akhmetov, was the richest oligarch in Ukraine. He gained control of the Donetsk clan after the murder of his business partner, Akhat Bragin, in 1995. This was just one of several murders that accompanied the struggle for power and property in Donbas. The local labour movement was powerless and withdrew from the arena.

It is hard to imagine a worse choice for president than Yanukovych. Kuchma's motivations in selecting Yanukovych as his successor are unknown. He could have chosen the previous prime minister, economist Viktor Yushchenko, who led the 1996 financial reforms and successfully avoided default during the 1998 crisis. Yushchenko remained loyal to Kuchma for a long time and only reluctantly agreed to lead the opposition.

Kuchma most likely chose Yanukovych in exchange for a guarantee of loyalty: when Yanukovych was governor, Donbas was the only region that didn't have mass protests against Kuchma. As a former KGB officer, Putin had only contempt for the convicted criminal Yanukovych. However, the choice of Yanukovych as president suited him, because it would guarantee Ukraine's return to Russia's sphere of influence. Yanukovych's campaign was run by Russian political operatives from the Kremlin. Their intent was to frame the Ukrainian elections as an apocalyptic scenario and bring Ukraine to the brink of collapse. In the words of Gleb Pavlovsky, one of those operatives, it was set up as a contest between two monsters from Hollywood horror films – *Alien* vs *Predator*. Yushchenko was assigned the role of the Alien. Yanukovych's political strategists presented Yushchenko as an extreme nationalist and even a Nazi. On the other hand, Yushchenko's supporters did not even have to create an image of Yanukovych as a 'Predator' – with his mafia background, he already was one.

Russian political advisors used Ukraine as a practice site. They tested out schemes that they could use later in Russian elections. One of their 'experiments' was the poisoning of Yushchenko on the eve of the election – a practice the Kremlin has repeatedly employed against opponents. Exit polls in November of 2004 showed a clear victory for Yushchenko, but the election commission declared Yanukovych the winner. In response to these cynical manipulations, thousands of Kyivans and non-Kyivans took to Independence Square, the central square of the Ukrainian capital. They refused to leave, standing in the cold and snow for weeks until their demands for a re-vote were met.

These events went down in history as the Orange Revolution. The Orange Revolution marks the debut of civil society in Ukraine. In a broader context it was part of a new wave of revolutions, the 'colour revolutions' of the early 2000s that began with a change of government in Serbia (2000) and continued in Georgia (2003), Ukraine (2004), Kyrgyzstan, Lebanon and Uzbekistan (2005). The Orange Revolution looked like a delayed repeat of the revolutions of 1989 in Poland, Hungary, East Germany and Czechoslovakia. Like those revolutions, there was a peaceful mass rally in the central square of the capital, with an immense sense of solidarity and revolutionary creativity. As in the revolutions of 1989, the main symbol of the Orange Revolution was the round table and compromise, not the guillotine and revolutionary terror, as in the early great revolutions of 1789 or 1917. After lengthy negotiations that included Kuchma and Polish President Aleksander Kwaśniewski, both candidates agreed to hold new elections. Yushchenko won and became Ukraine's new president.

Yushchenko's presidency (2005–10) was a period of missed opportunities. Instead of fighting corruption, he focused on cultural policies, such as the status of the Ukrainian language and national memory politics. At the end of 2006, Yushchenko successfully passed a law recognising the Holodomor as genocide. But this was his only achievement. The ruling coalition was split by his personal conflict with Yulia Tymoshenko, who had become second in prominence during the Orange Revolution. They each tried to form coalitions with Yanukovych in order to defeat each other. Moreover, Yushchenko's term coincided with the global economic crisis of 2008, which damaged Ukraine's economy, putting an end to almost a decade of improvement. The Orange government ended in fiasco. In the 2010 elections, Yushchenko lost in the first round and Tymoshenko in the second.

Viktor Yanukovych became Ukraine's new president. Ukraine was once again facing the threat of authoritarianism, but now it took on much more dangerous forms. Yanukovych broke several of the political consensuses that had been established during the first twenty years of Ukraine's independence. Until then, there had been an unspoken understanding that after coming to power, election winners did not pursue the losers, because they might find themselves in their place the next time. When Yanukovych came to power, he immediately imprisoned Yulia Tymoshenko and Yuriy Lutsenko, another Orange leader.

There had also been an unwritten consensus to maintain a balance of power among the different regions. Each new president in turn had come to power from the Ukrainian-speaking West or the Russian-speaking East, but none controlled enough power to rule alone. They had to make informal compromises with regional elites from elsewhere. As they say, compromise is the bread and wine of democracy. Thus, democracy by default was established in independent Ukraine, not so much by established democratic procedures as by accepted norms.

Yanukovych violated those norms. He put people from Donbas in leadership positions throughout Ukraine. Each official governor was assigned an unofficial 'minder' – a role that the Donbas mafia transferred from the criminal underworld into the political sphere. The minder was personally responsible for ensuring that all illegal money flows were transferred 'to the top'. There, they were distributed among Yanukovych, his family and his closest friends. If Kuchma played the role of arbitrator between various oligarchic groups, then Yanukovych aimed to become the biggest oligarch of all.

The Parliament was also under the control of a parliamentary 'minder' who boasted that the parliamentary opposition had been reduced to the level of helpless kittens. This marked a radical departure from all previous rules governing Ukrainian political life: even Kuchma had to take the opposition into account. Once they had consolidated their control of parliament, the Donetsk crowd set about undermining the official status of the Ukrainian language and rewriting Ukrainian history to ensure that it aligned as closely as possible with the Russian version.

Naturally, the Kremlin was pleased with this direction. Putin openly supported Yanukovych. During the fraudulent 2004 elections, he even congratulated him twice on his 'victory'. After Yanukovych's victory in 2010, talks were renewed of an alliance of Belarus, Russia and Ukraine. However, one circumstance had blocked Ukraine's gradual absorption by Russia. That was Yanukovych's personal greed: he didn't intend to share his zone of control with anyone. In 2013, he surprised everyone by announcing that Ukraine would move towards European integration.

The examples of Kuchma and Yanukovych convinced the Kremlin that even presidents from the Russian-speaking East would support closer ties to the West when they came to power in Kyiv. Like most authoritarian leaders, Putin does not believe in the existence of free public opinion or spontaneous public protests. For him, the Ukrainian Orange Revolution, like the Georgian Rose Revolution before it, was a conspiracy by the West against Russia and against his government in particular. In August 2008, Russia invaded Georgia. After a quick and easy victory, the Kremlin adopted a new military strategy towards Ukraine. This was predicated on the plan that if Ukraine continued its movement towards the West, it would suffer the same fate as Georgia. Ukraine's defeat would lead to its dismemberment. The Russian-speaking East, along with Crimea and the entire Black Sea coast, was to be annexed to Russia. Western Ukraine, as a territory with strong anti-Russian sentiments, could go wherever it wanted to go, to hell with it. The rest of Ukraine would be reduced to a small agrarian vassal state with a puppet government in Kyiv.

When these plans were leaked to the newspapers, no one could believe them – they sounded like science fiction. However, during the Euromaidan they gained renewed relevance. The Euromaidan was provoked by Yanukovych's unilateral decision to refuse to sign the Association Agreement between Ukraine and the European Union. He announced the decision only days before the scheduled signing date and immediately after visiting Moscow. Putin may have revealed his plans for Ukraine at that meeting.

Yanukovych's reversal provoked mass protests in Kyiv. Students were at the centre of them. On 30 November 2013, the tenth day of the protests, police severely beat the students. The next day, up to a million people took to the streets of Kyiv. They demanded prosecution of those responsible for the attack on demonstrators, Yanukovych's resignation and new presidential elections. The protests continued throughout the winter. They often resembled the Maidan of 2004. The protests took place in the same city and with the same enemy: Viktor Yanukovych. But this time, the government had no intention of sitting down together for negotiations. They chose violence. In December, the government attempted to disperse the Euromaidan by force. In mid-January the Ukrainian parliament declared the protests illegal and on 22 January, three protestors were killed: Yuri Verbitsky, Serhiy Nigoyan and Mikhail Zhiznevsky. Clashes between government forces and the revolutionaries continued for another month and from 18–20 February over a hundred Euromaidan participants were killed by government forces. They are known now as 'the Heavenly Hundred'.

In the last weeks of the Euromaidan, it became clear that Ukraine's main problem was no longer Yanukovych, but Putin. There were warnings that the protestors had only until the end of the Sochi Olympics in February 2014. Immediately after the Olympics, the Russian army would invade. And that's exactly what happened. On 21 February, Yanukovych fled Ukraine and Russian forces invaded Crimea the following day. But here Putin's gross miscalculation was revealed. He thought the Russians would be greeted with flowers in eastern Ukraine as a 'liberating army' and that a wave of uprisings and seizures of power to be called the 'Russian Spring' would sweep through Russian-speaking cities. That did not happen. In fact, Russian-speaking Dnipro became one of the strongest centres of Ukrainian resistance to Russian aggression. Dnipro was the birthplace of Brezhnev, Kuchma and much of the Ukrainian elite, including one of the richest oligarchs in Ukraine, Ihor Kolomoisky – who led Dnipro's resistance to the Russian invasion.

The 'Russian Spring' of 2014 turned into summer, lasted through the autumn and was completely spent by the end of December. Russia's only conquests were Crimea and part of the Donbas region. Even in Donbas, local separatism was not a spontaneous uprising: it required an invasion by Russian special forces. If not for Russian intervention, relations between Donbas and Kyiv would have remained tense, but it is unlikely they would have come to war.

In any case, the separation of Donbas was a rather minimal achievement compared to Russia's ambitious plans to divide Ukraine and turn it into a vassal state. The failure of Putin's plans showed once again that he does not know or understand Ukraine. It's true that Ukraine struggled with internal conflicts during the first decades of its existence. In 1996, in his *The Clash of Civilisations*, Samuel Huntington cited Ukraine as a classic example of a 'cleft country'. The image of 'two Ukraines', a West and an East, in which 'never the twain shall meet', has become one of the most persistent images in descriptions of the Ukrainian situation.

This image is grossly oversimplified. In reality, neither the Ukrainian East nor the Ukrainian West is monolithic – both are divided into smaller regions with their own political and cultural characteristics. The imagined East and the imagined West were in fact opposite poles on the Ukrainian political map. A much larger and more ambivalent Centre stood between them. And at the centre of that Centre stands the capital, Kyiv, which, according to Harvard historian Roman Szporluk, spoke the same language as the East, but voted like the West. Ukrainians could argue until they were blue in the face about the status of the Ukrainian and Russian languages or who their national heroes were. Sometimes these disputes resembled a cold civil war. But Ukrainians were in agreement when it came to their independence. Surveys have shown that if the referendum of 1 December 1991, were repeated at any time, the result would be the same: the majority would choose independence. Only the level of support varied over time. It declined each time the economic situation worsened and then increased any time there was a threat from Russia, whether real or imagined. Support for independence increased during the two Chechen wars, the Russian-Georgian war and during the conflict over the island of Tuzla and it reached its highest levels ever following the annexation of Crimea in 2014.

In the early 1990s, a British ambassador in Kyiv remarked that independent Ukraine reminded him of the 'bumblebee paradox'. The laws of conventional aerodynamics say that bumblebees should not be able to fly – and yet they do. Numerous expectations and forecasts say that Ukraine should not exist as an independent state – and yet it does. Despite its internal divisions, Ukraine has proven to be a reasonably stable political community. Which is exactly what the Kremlin could not see and doesn't want to see. Putin and his entourage think like the German nationalists of the nineteenth century, who envisioned a Germany that stretched as far as the German language sounded. Since many Ukrainian citizens speak Russian, they must be Russians.

This is not the case. In reality, a new Ukrainian identity has been forged during the years of Ukraine's independence, one that is not based on language or ethnicity. It is based on political loyalty to Ukraine as an independent state. The new political identities have not replaced old ethnic identities: they coexist. However, the political identity has been dominant for some time now. Proof can be seen in the fact that the two Ukrainian presidents who have been elected during the war in Donbas, Petro Poroshenko in 2014 and Volodymyr Zelensky in 2019, won majorities across the country and not just in the East or the West.

Processes

Ukraine's political turmoil reflects much deeper processes – the great social transformation that Ukraine has undergone since independence. The Euromaidan can be viewed as its central symbol. The Euromaidan is now called the Revolution of Dignity or the Revolution of Values in Ukraine. These are not just beautiful phrases; they reflect new Ukrainian realities. The emergence of a large group of people with a new set of values represents a fundamental change in the history of independent Ukraine. We can call them the new urban middle class.

Like most historical phenomena, we can't attribute the emergence of this group to a single factor. There are several. One of the most important is economic. In the mid-2000s, for the first time in Ukraine's history, a significant share of the gross domestic product was generated not in the industrial sector of the economy, but in the service sector – technology, mass media, entertainment, restaurants, tourism, educational and cultural initiatives, etc. The industrial sector has traditionally been closely tied to the state in Eastern Europe. In contrast, the service economy tends to grow from the bottom up, on private initiative. As a result, Ukraine now has a large sector that is less dependent on government influence and less riddled with corruption. To successfully survive and compete, the owners and employees of this sector need to know everyone is playing by the same rules. This makes them potential change agents.

Economic changes have also led to changes in the nature of Ukrainian regionalism. While the industrialised East continues to play an important role in the economy, the Centre and West are developing more dynamically as they move towards a service economy. Since the 2000s, economic capital has been migrating from East to West and the social capital of organised civil society has been migrating from West to East. The 2014 war in Donbas accelerated this bilateral exchange, but it started earlier and constitutes a steady trend.

Regional differences have not disappeared, but another fault line has emerged: generational differences. The shift in values is largely due to the emergence of a generation of Ukrainian independence. They were born after, or just before, the collapse of the USSR and came of age in the late 1990s and early 2000s. It was a time of economic growth and the transition to a service economy. We can look to historical analogies to understand the significance of this timing. In the West, the transition to a service economy began in the 1960s. There, it was accompanied by the emergence of a young generation that valued self-expression. The result was the youth revolution of the 1960s. Something similar happened in the USSR with the emergence of the Sixties generation, but the Soviet authorities neutralised and silenced the leaders of that generation. In independent Ukraine, a generation has emerged that has never known repression, does not remember the Soviet Union and has no affection for Russia. They behave very differently from their parents.

We can see some of the generational differences if we compare the first and second Maidans. The first would have been impossible without a leader and Yushchenko was that leader. The second had three leaders, but they were primarily for show. The actual leader was the Maidan itself. In other words, if the first Maidan was an example of vertical mobilisation, the second one was an example of horizontal self-organisation. The difference between the first and second Maidan can be explained by the fact that people who were children and teenagers in 2004 had grown up and become young adults by 2014. The Euromaidan was largely their revolution. This is particularly evident in the support for Euromaidan on social media. The majority of social media users outside Crimea and Donbas supported the Euromaidan. Since young people were the primary users of social media, support for the Maidan had a generational dimension.

Social media generates different norms of behaviour. They are imbued with an egalitarian ethos. Everyone starts out equal, like the Vikings in their boats or Cossacks on the steppe. The ethos of industrial society, in contrast, is hierarchical. Large industrial enterprises require centralisation and discipline. Political movements in the industrial age were impossible without a party hierarchy and party leaders. In contrast, post-industrial society functions at the level of horizontal connections and can manage without a clear hierarchy.

Social media is also inherently global. Social media broke through the provincialism that the Soviets had forced on Ukraine. The Ukrainian dissidents were like intellectual Robinson Crusoes. They had to independently come up with ideas that were freely available outside the communist camp. The same was true of those who came to power in Ukraine in 1991. None of them really understood the mechanisms of transition to a market economy and they largely believed that as soon as Ukraine broke free of Kremlin control, all its problems would be solved. Donbas miners got their ideas of the outside world mainly from pirated videotapes of Hollywood movies, so they wanted paycheques like the Americans and social benefits like the Swedes.

The independence generation is different. Young Ukrainians are not isolated from the outside world. They have free access to the internet and many of them travel or study abroad. A large percentage of this generation have college degrees. Whereas in previous generations, those who entered higher education were in the minority, today the minority are those who do not. Ukraine is one of the most educated nations in the world and there have been constant reforms in the field of higher education. There is still plenty of room for improvement. Nonetheless, research shows that people who have spent any period of time in college, even at the lowest-ranked school, have a different set of values from those of their peers who went straight to work after school.

Similar shifts in middle-class values have occurred in neighbouring Belarus and Russia. Mass protests took place in Moscow in 2012 to protest Putin's fraudulent re-election and in Minsk in 2020 against Lukashenko's. Those protests were crushed by government forces. In order for the value shift to have political success, a favourable climate must exist – democracy at the minimum. In Ukraine, a generation of young people grew up in freedom. This is precisely what did not happen in Belarus and Russia.

The 2010s are reminiscent of the 1960s, with one essential difference. The younger generation of that time came of age during the postwar recovery, when there was a strong need for workers and educated minds and education was the pass to a relatively comfortable and stable life. Today's youth have been called the precariat. Although they have many of the habits and norms of the middle class, they lack a stable future like the proletariat. The young generation will not live as well as their parents. As the saying goes: tell me the year you were born and I'll tell you how poor you'll be. Although this precarity is relevant everywhere, the lack of a stable future is especially acute in countries with authoritarian and oligarchic regimes. In such circumstances, revolutionary uprisings are a natural response to the problems of the modern world.

Structures

The Euromaidan should be compared not only to the Maidan of 2004, but also to other similar revolutions of the 2010s: the

American 'Occupy Wall Street' movement, the Arab Spring of 2011, the Gezi Park protests in Istanbul in 2013, the Armenian revolution of 2018, the student protest movement in Bulgaria and the Hong Kong protests.

The similarities can be striking. Here is a brief description of events in Chile in 2019. Protests began in Santiago with student demonstrations that were brutally dispersed by the authorities. When the mass media started reporting what was happening, anti-government demonstrations began to snowball. The largest of them attracted over a million people. The central square of the capital became the centre of the protests. Demonstrators renamed it Dignity Square. The President declared a state of emergency. He said the protests were inspired by hostile external forces and that the government was in the right and would restore order. The demonstrators, who had acted peacefully up to that point, began clashing with the police. Street militants armed with homemade shields, paving stones and Molotov cocktails formed the front line. They held the line and successfully blocked the police from advancing into the centre of the protests. Demonstrators of all ages and social backgrounds backed up those on the front line. They formed medical brigades, handed out water and sandwiches, made Molotov cocktails and delivered them to the front line along with more pavers. It may have looked chaotic, but the Chilean uprising functioned like a well-oiled machine. Street violence coexisted with the spirit of carnival and a festive atmosphere.

Even here there was a 'Russian factor'. A majority of Russian-speaking emigrants in Chile supported the government. They created a Facebook group called 'Russians in Chile', where they demanded that the revolutionaries be shot and praised the government's actions. Unsurprisingly, most of them attended the Russian Orthodox Church and glorified Russian Cossacks and Putin.

Replace Chile with Ukraine and Santiago with Kyiv and

you will have a fairly accurate picture of developments during the Euromaidan. The Ukrainian, Chilean and other mass protests shared a similar structure: they had no leaders, their core was made up of young, educated people and they had no clear demands. They demanded things that are difficult to define and even more difficult to measure: justice and respect for human dignity. Their revolutionary language was the language of values, not interests.

The year 2019 could be called the 'year of revolutions'. The geography is global: Paris, La Paz, Beirut, Bogotá, Cairo, Hong Kong, Seoul, Tehran, New Delhi, etc. These are 'leaderless revolutions' in which people go out on the streets in mass protests that are largely peaceful. Their levels of mobilisation are similar to those of the Velvet and Colour Revolutions, but they have been less successful. The success rates of the protests at the end of the twentieth century ranged from 50 to 70 per cent, whereas between 2010 and 2019 they fell to 30 per cent.

Ukraine's Euromaidan was one of the successes. The explanation should be sought in the quest for national identity: revolutions that have a national and anti-colonial dimension are more likely to be successful. Euromaidan participants fought not only against Yanukovych but also against Putin and Russia. Anne Applebaum has written that democracy wins when citizens feel a deep sense of belonging to their own language, literature and history. The opposite is also true: regions without nationalism tend to be corrupt, anarchic, full of rent-a-mobs and mercenaries, like Donbas.

The key challenge for countries like Ukraine is how to translate this surge of national identity into a fair judicial system and effective, functional democratic institutions. Without these changes, Ukraine is doomed to stagnation. Statistics show that before 2013 Ukraine had the worst indicators among the former communist countries of Europe, including the former Soviet republics. The history of Ukrainian independence seems to demonstrate the truth of the biblical parable: who was first shall be last.

Ukraine has been and still is a rich country of poor people. This discrepancy is what drives millions of Ukrainians to take to the streets and squares to protest inefficient and corrupt government. As one of the slogans of Euromaidan read: 'Listen, we're sick of this!'

The Euromaidan succeeded in both the short and long perspective. Its short-term achievement was that Petro Poroshenko, who was connected to the Euromaidan and had previously been part of Yushchenko's team, came to power. And its long-term success can be seen in the fact that after Poroshenko lost in the 2019 elections, there was no counterrevolutionary turn as there was after the first Maidan. Zelensky's election was also a continuation of the youth revolution – after his victory, the number of elected officials under the age of forty in the Supreme Council of Ukraine doubled from 29 per cent in 2012 to 57 per cent in 2019.

Before the war, Zelensky's team was similar to Poroshenko's. After coming to power, both teams started with rapid and radical changes. Then after a few months, they returned to the old rules of the game loaded with corruption scandals, pressure on the opposition, etc., without ever completing the reforms they had started.

One of Ukraine's reformist ministers identified Ukraine's challenge as a 'last mile problem'. In the thirty years since Ukraine gained independence, it has come a long way and has almost reached a radical reset. But 'almost' does not count. We need to go the critical 'last mile' and complete the reforms. History offers too many examples of countries that have gone off track or returned to the starting point.

If we imagine Ukraine's situation as a sports match, we can say that after the victory of Euromaidan, Ukraine entered the finals: between countries that are fighting oppression and authoritarianism and the countries that embody that authoritarianism; countries that are trying to modernise against all odds and countries that have failed at modernisation and now want to compensate for their failure with a 'short victorious war'; countries that want to overcome the past with its primary characteristics of poverty and violence and countries that are sinking deeper and deeper into the past and dragging the entire world with them.

War

Russia is the other team in the finals. On 24 February 2022, Putin launched a full-scale war against Ukraine. He started this war based on the pretext that Russians and Ukrainians are one people, that the existence of a separate Ukraine from Russia is a historical aberration, that the West created Ukraine just to threaten Russia and that therefore Russia has no choice but to eliminate the threat.

Putin was counting on a blitzkrieg. Ukrainians quickly buried those plans. In the first days of the war, Russian troops reached the outskirts of Kyiv and occupied large areas in the south and east. However, they were pushed back within weeks. The war entered a protracted, positional phase. The Ukrainian government is performing effectively and enjoys the trust of its citizens for the first time in the history of Ukrainian independence. The Ukrainian army is fighting better than the Russian army. The army is also backed by a strong citizen movement of volunteer support.

The war clarifies things that were previously unclear and poorly understood. Before the war, Ukraine was broadly characterised by ambivalence. The situation before the war was neither as good nor as bad as it may have seemed. There was a strong civil society, but corrupt political elites; Ukrainians were building democracy, but the primary indicators were declining; Ukraine had pushed away from the 'Russian world' but had not yet reached the western shore. The war ended this ambivalence. The fires of the war have burned away that part of Ukraine's past that was tied to the Russian factor and pulled Ukraine backwards.

Ukrainians buried more of Putin's plans, as well. When he started this war, Putin operated on the belief that the West as such didn't actually exist, only individual western countries existed. He assumed that each of them would pursue their individual interests and that Western values are a fiction. Putin's assumptions were proven false. Helping Ukraine has united the democracies of the world. The war has reaffirmed the relevance of freedom and dignity. Without financial and military assistance from the West, Ukraine could not fight so effectively against Russia. But it is still Ukraine who is doing the fighting. Ukraine is fighting not only for its own future, but for the future of the world.

The Russian-Ukrainian war is a turning point in world history. It has closed the chapter that opened with the fall of communism and raised hopes for the end of history. History is back and events in Ukraine prove it. Ukraine's first thirty years of independence were not a time of comfort and security, they have been a time of wars and revolutions. It is tempting to compare this period with 1914–45. Naturally, any comparison is inexact and Ukraine's current losses don't compare to those times. Still, some comparisons with the thirty-year war of the twentieth century do make sense. Depending on how long this war lasts, Ukraine could lose between a quarter and a third of its population, which is similar to the period from 1914–45. Eight million Ukrainians, mostly women and children, have fled to safety in Europe. Russia has deported another 2 million people to its own territory. The scale of battlefield losses is not equal to those of the First and Second World Wars but is much higher than most recent wars. If we talk only about the civilian population, then during the first year of the war in Ukraine, 8,000 people have died, including five hundred children; 13,000 have been wounded and another 15,000 are missing. The same rule applies to the losses of 1914–45 as it does now: each time you read these figures, imagine that your sister, brother, husband, wife, child, parent, loved one, or closest friend was killed. Many Ukrainians do not even have to imagine: 37.5 per cent of Ukraine's population has loved ones who were killed or injured during the first year of the war.

The return of history includes the return of genocide to these lands. Putin and his entourage make no secret of the fact that they intend to wipe Ukraine off the political map. He cannot kill every Ukrainian. So he will kill the most active part of society, the people without whom Ukrainians cease to be a nation and become silent inhabitants. Another part of this genocidal plan is to make Ukraine uninhabitable. Towns and villages are being wiped off the face of the earth. Businesses, communication lines, energy and water supply facilities are being destroyed. Millions of domestic and wild animals have died. Millions of hectares of fertile land and forests are now wastelands, often contaminated with harmful substances. In just a few months of war, Russia has brought unprecedented levels of destruction to Ukraine.

Russian aggression threatens the entire world with degradation. In 2009, Britain's chief scientific advisor warned that the next twenty years would be decisive for the continued existence of human civilisation. Unprecedented growth in the world's population and economy will lead to acute shortages of food, energy and water by the year 2030. The world is on the verge of a 'perfect storm'. Of course, these predictions were made before the current war. Now the prognosis is even more ominous.

It would be hard to find a corner of the world that is not impacted by the war in Ukraine. Problems with the timber industry and shortfalls in fertiliser production will contribute to deforestation of the Amazon, the natural lungs of the planet.

Ukrainian and world history are once again tied together in a critical knot. This intertwining confirms Hannah Arendt's prediction that the problem of evil will remain the fundamental question of history. The generations who lived through the Second World War in Ukraine and the neighbouring 'bloodlands' understood this very clearly. 'The devil in history' is not just a metaphor, it was their reality. The generations born in the West after the war, who grew up in comfort between the 1960s and the '80s, including the generation of Francis Fukuyama, no longer understand the reality of evil. The irony is that the very year in which Fukuyama published his book declaring the end of history (1992) also had one of the highest numbers of military conflicts at any point in the last two hundred years.

The last two hundred years of human history have seen a quantum leap into the realm of freedom – freedom from the forces of nature and various forms of oppression. For lack of a better word, we call this quantum leap modernisation. During these two hundred years of modernisation, there was not a single peaceful year. There were only a few years during which a new war did not begin and not a single year without war. When we juxtapose these two facts, a question inevitably arises: is historical progress possible without catastrophes?

This question is especially acute for Ukraine. On the one hand, the Ukrainian nation was born out of the process of modernisation. On the other hand, it has paid and continues to pay an exorbitant price for modernisation.

Modernisation is a global process, but it proceeds in different countries at different times and with varying levels of success. Independent Ukraine has experienced the typical problems of a young state trying to build a democracy and a market economy. It makes sense to compare Ukraine not with the much older, established states, but with the United States in 1805, France in 1820. Not all of those states succeeded in becoming what their young revolutionaries had dreamed of. Comparative politics suggests that such transformations require approximately fifty years.

Britain and the United States completed this modernisation from 1800 to 1850, France in about 1880, the Asian Tigers after the Second World War. Obviously, fifty years is an estimate. Some countries in Europe have made this transformation more quickly, for instance Spain after the death of Franco or the countries of Central Europe and the Baltics after the fall of communism. But almost all of those countries went through a long period of revolutions and wars. It seems as though progress is impossible without catastrophe and the time has come for Ukraine to experience this historic tendency.

Given its status as a geopolitically important but vulnerable borderland, the historical legacies of Eastern Christianity, the Russian Empire and communism, the path of Ukrainians to the 'kingdom of freedom' has been particularly difficult and convoluted. Before the war, Ukraine was moving slowly but steadily along that path. War is a great accelerator of time. It shortens that last mile to a few hundred feet. As the 2022 Democracy Index noted, 'Historically, wars have been among the biggest drivers of political and social change; this may also be the case for Ukraine, provided that it wins.'

For Ukraine, there can be no question of 'if' it wins, the only question is when. Even the deepest understanding of history can't answer that question for us. As I noted in the introduction, knowledge of the past won't help us to create a detailed road map. But history can serve as a compass, information on which way to go.

A compass has one remarkable ability: with all its possible variations, its arrow steadily points in one direction. Ukrainian history is similar. Resilience is one of its throughlines. Despite innumerable obstacles and dangers, Ukrainians have managed to survive and become a nation of committed citizens.

Ukrainians have survived primarily due to their own choices. Can you imagine what would have happened to Ukraine if

Zelensky had accepted the offer of Western governments to get him out of the country in the first days of the war? Or if the residents of Kyiv's outskirts and military units had not stopped the advance of Russian troops towards the Ukrainian capital?

At critical moments in history, Ukrainians demonstrate the will to do what their two greatest poets have demanded. Taras Shevchenko told us to 'Fight and you will win!' and Ivan Franko called on Ukrainians to 'Fight against the prod, swim against the tide'. The historian Timothy Garton Ash points out that the Ukrainian word *volya* has two meanings. It means both 'will' and 'freedom'. The word *volya* may just offer the shortest answer to the question of the relationship between progress and catastrophe: of all possible scenarios, the most likely outcome is the one we freely choose and steadfastly defend.

Ukrainian history provides a foundation for a limited but defensible optimism. It's not unique in that sense. Just think of David and Goliath, the Greco-Persian wars, the fall of fascism and communism, the stories of Frodo and Harry Potter. It doesn't matter whether these stories are fictional or real. What matters is that they remind us that the devil – in the Bible or in history – is a pathetic creature. He can destroy, enslave and corrupt, but he cannot win.

Ultimately, we depend on the stories we tell each other. I hope this story of Ukrainian history will strengthen your faith that although progress is impossible without catastrophes, progress is also possible despite catastrophe. Once again, at the next sharp turn in our history, Ukrainians will choose *volya*. And that choice offers hope for a better world.

ACKNOWLEDGEMENTS

This book was first published in Ukrainian three months before the start of the war. In it, I expressed my gratitude to my colleagues – historians who helped me write this text, commented on it, and saved me from oversimplifications, distortions and just plain mistakes – all the things that can destroy an academic reputation.

Since then, the book has gone through a number of reprints, become a bestseller, and been translated into several languages. For the English-language edition, I will not repeat all of the acknowledgements from the original Ukrainian text. I'll limit myself to a few, particularly significant ones.

First of all, I would like to express my gratitude to Professor Frank Sysyn, one of very few historians who can confidently navigate multiple periods of both Ukrainian and non-Ukrainian history. The truth is that he should be writing the global history of Ukraine. His comments were sometimes rather pointed, but always relevant and well intended.

Special thanks are due to my wife, Olenka Dzhedzhora. She has taught world history to her students for many years and taught it to me in the process. While I was writing this global history of Ukraine, she was writing a textbook on world history. From time to time, we would look over one another's shoulders at the computer screen and discuss shared topics. These were the best moments in my work on this book.

I am extremely fortunate that the director of Portal Books, Olena Khirgiy, took an interest in my book. She has set an ambitious task for her publishing house – to publish books on Ukrainian history that will help us to understand and change our country. The war has driven her, like so many others, out of the country. But once she reached London with her children, she continued her work. In particular, she began negotiating for the publication of this book in English. Without her, the book would not exist in either Ukrainian or British editions and for that I owe her double thanks.

The greatest part of the work fell to Nadiyka Gerbish. Nadiyka is a talented Ukrainian writer. Like so many Ukrainian writers, Nadiyka is also an unofficial ambassador for Ukraine in the broader world. Fate brought us together when we collaborated on *A Ukrainian Christmas*. Nadiyka volunteered to manage the publication of my history of Ukraine. She did so with the original version in Ukrainian and she continues to do so for the translations into other languages. No words can describe the scope of her contribution or adequately thank her for it. All I can say is that the contribution is immense, as is my gratitude.

My luck also did not fail me in the case of the English translator of the book, Dominique Hoffman. She managed to translate the book under immense time pressure, but more important than speed is the quality of the translation. I have the impression that thanks to her, my book sounds better in English than in Ukrainian. I am grateful.

Jon Appleton from the British publisher saw to it that the book became more streamlined and more in line with the tastes and expectations of the English reader. Catherine Burke, Deputy Managing Editor at Little, Brown Book Group and Executive Publisher for the Sphere imprint took on the overall coordination of the entire project.

And I'll finish with the traditional reminder that all of these people have significantly contributed to the best aspects of this book. I am entirely responsible for any remaining weaknesses.

SELECTED BIBLIOGRAPHY

This book has relied on many previous works. My main source of inspiration was the project initiated by Ivan Lysiak–Rudnytsky to reconsider Ukraine's past – see: Ivan L. Rudnytsky, John-Paul Himka, (eds.), *Rethinking Ukrainian History* (CIUS Press, 1981). I repeat his main theses in several chapters of the book (see: Ivan L. Rudnytsky, *Essays in Modern Ukrainian History* [CIUS Press, 1987]). The same applies to the work of another influential Ukrainian historian, Roman Szporluk, who taught me and many other colleagues how to think and write about modernisation (see: the collection of his articles: Roman Szporluk, *Russia, Ukraine, and the Breakup of the Soviet Union* (Hoover Institution Press, 2000). Regarding world history, the most significant works for me were Douglass C. North, John Joseph Wallis and Barry R. Weingast, *Violence and Social Orders: A Conceptual Framework for Interpreting Recorded Human History* (Hoover Institution Press, 2009); Daron Acemoglu, James A. Robinson, *Why Nations Fail: The Origins of Power, Prosperity, and Poverty* (Profile, 2012); Ronald Inglehart, Christian Welzel, *Modernization, Cultural Change, and Democracy: The Human Development Sequence* (Cambridge University Press, 2005); Robert Putnam, *Making Democracy Work: Civic Traditions in Modern Italy* (Princeton University Press, 1993); Hernando de Soto, *The Mystery of Capital: Why Capitalism Triumphs in the West and Fails Everywhere Else* (Basic Books, 2003). As in the case of the articles by Ivan Lysiak-Rudnytsky and Roman Szporluk, I repeat the main theses of those books in various chapters of this book.

Introduction

On the defenders of Irpin, see: Petro Shcherbyna, *Bytva za Irpin'* (2022). Maryna Tkachuk's article 'Iakby ne bulo 'Zhirafa' i nas, Kyiv by dobriache potripaly' describes how the fighters of the Irpin Territorial Defence held back the attack on the capital with their bare hands, Novynarnia, 22/06/2022, novynarnia.com/2022/06/22/irpinska-tro-giraffe.

The idea of the decisive role of 1492 in the emergence of a new world is drawn from Felipe Fernández-Armesto, *1492: The Year the World Began* (HarperCollins, 2009). When I was writing the first draft of the book, I was told that Omeljan Pritsak had spoken about the consequences of the opening of America for Ukrainian lands in his lectures at Harvard University in the early 1970s. These lectures remain unpublished, but they have recently become available on the website of the Canadian Institute of Ukrainian Studies: cius-archives.ca/items/show/2503.

In the introduction, I cite Alexander Gerschenkron's *Economic Backwardness in Historical Perspective: A Book of Essays* (Harvard University Press, 1962), p. 6; Marc Bloch, *The Historian's Craft* (Manchester University Press, 1977), p. 26; and Norman Davies, 'The Misunderstood Victory in Europe', *The New York Review of Books*, 25 May 1995.

Chapter 1: What's in a Name?

The most complete description of the evolution of the names 'Rus' and 'Ukraine' is presented by A. L. Khoroshkevich ('V labirinte etno–politiko–geograficheskikh naimenovanii Vostochnoi Evropy serediny XVII veka', *Russkie ob Ukraine i ukraintsakh* (St. Petersburg Press, 2012), pp. 8–68. On the name 'Circassians' see: Hamed Kazemzadeh. *The Circassian Question: The Formation of Linguistic and Cultural Identity in the Caucasus from the Mid-Nineteenth Century to Modern Times*, Ph.D. dissertation (2018). On the name 'khokhol' see: Boris Floria, Kto takoi 'khokhol?', *Rodina*, 1999. number 8, pp. 58–59.

On modernity and theories of modernisation see: Hans–Ulrich Wehler, *Die Gegenwart als Geschichte:* (Cambridge University Press, 1995), pp. 13–60 and Jacques Le Goff, *History and Memory* (Columbia University Press, 1992), pp. 21–50. For the quote regarding the pre-modern world, see: Rodney Stark, *The Victory of Reason: How Christianity Led to Freedom, Capitalism, and Western Success* (Random House, 2005), p. 233.

Chapter 2: Rus

At the beginning of the chapter I quote Vasyl' Stus, *Tvory*. Tom 4 (Kyiv, 1994); A.A. Tsekalova (ed.), *Mir Aleksandra Kazhdana. K 80–letiiu so dnia rozhdeniia* (Aletheia, 2003), p. 486; Ihor Ševčenko, *Ukraine Between East and West: Essays on Cultural History to the Early Eighteenth Century* (CIUS Press, 1996), p.10.

In this chapter, I have drawn most heavily on two books: Christian Raffensperger, *Reimagining Europe: Kievan Rus' in the Medieval World*, (Harvard University Press, 2012), and A. P. Tolochko, *Ocherki iznachal'noy Rusi* (Aletheia, 2015). I am indebted to Tolochko for the thesis that the creation of Ukraine was the end of Rus – see: Oleksii Tolochko, 'Rus' ochyma 'Ukraïny': v poshukakh samoidentyfikatsiï i kontynuitetu.' Suchasnist, 1994, 1, pp. 111–117.

On the Ukrainian steppes as the place where horses were first domesticated, see: David W. Anthony, Dorcas R. Brown, 'The Origins of Horseback Riding,' *Antiquity*, vol. 65, March, 1991, pp 22–38. On the speed of the spread of the Slavs, see: Peter Heather, *Empires and Barbarians: The Fall of Rome and the Birth of Europe* (Oxford University Press, 2010). On the fact that the Slavs originated in the shadow of Byzantine fortifications, see: Florin Curta, *The Making of the Slavs: History and Archeology of the Lower Danube Region c. 500–700* (Cambridge University Press, 2001), p. 350. On the connection between 'sclavus' and 'Slavs' see: Thomas M. Prymak, 'Say "Goodbye," but Pause a Sec Before Saying "Chow,"' slideshare.net/ThomasMPrymak/say-goodbye-but-pause-a-sec-before-saying-chow-56408079. For a discussion of the legend of Volodymyr's choice of religion see: D.E. Furman, 'Vybor kniazia Vladimira,' *Voprosy filosofii*, 1988, 6, pp. 90–103.

On the poverty of the intellectual tradition of early Rus and its slavish dependence on Byzantium, see: George Fedotov, *The Russian Religious Mind, Kievan Christianity: The 10th to the 13th Centuries* (Harvard University Press, 2014), pp. 38, 370, 380. On the fact that Byzantium itself had little to do with the development of science, see: Cyril Mango, 'Byzantium's Role in World History' in E. Jeffreys, J. Haldon, and R. Cormack (eds.), *The Oxford Handbook of Byzantine Studies* (Oxford University Press, 2008), p. 358. The thesis that Western Christianity is more Aristotelian and Eastern Christianity more Platonic is taken from the book: Yves Cognar, *After Nine Hundred Years: The Background of the Schism between the Eastern and Western Churches* (Fordham University Press, 1959), p.44. On the reasons why the scholarly (university) tradition was not adopted in Eastern Christianity: T.V. Chumakova, 'Retseptsiia Aristotelia v drevnerusskoi kul'ture.' Chelovek, no. 2, pp.58–69.

For a complete catalogue of Russian books of the tenth to seventeenth centuries and a comparison of their total number with the library of a Byzantine monastery, see: Francis J. Thomson, *The Reception of Byzantine Culture in Mediaeval Russia* (Routledge, 1999). A comparison of the number of books published in the Catholic and Orthodox worlds can be seen in Markus Osterrieder, 'Von der Sakralgemeinschaft zur modernen Nation. Die Entstehung eines Nationalbewußtseins unter Russen, Ukrainern und Weißruthenen im Lichte der Thesen Benedict Andersons', in Eva Schmidt–Hartmann (ed.), *Formen des nationalen Bewußtseins im Lichte zeitgenössischer Nationalismustheorien* (Bielefield University, 1994), pp. 197–232. The quote regarding nations as book-reading tribes comes from Yuri Slezkine, *The Jewish Century* (Princeton University Press, 2004), p. 11. For the quote regarding the symbolic drama of Canossa, see: George Schöpflin, 'The Political Traditions of Eastern Europe,' *Daedalus,* Vol. 119, 1, Winter 1990, p. 57.

Extracts from from 'Tales of Times Gone By', the Russian Primary Chronicles, can be found here: pages.uoregon.edu/kimball/chronicle.htm.

Interlude: A Brief History of Ukrainian Bread

On the percentages of black soil in Ukraine see: G. Markov, I. Stebelsky, Soil Classification, *Encyclopedia of Ukraine* Vol. IV. Ph-S. (Toronto–Buffalo, 1993). On the spread of the insult kham/Ham in Slavic languages: Adam Leszczyński, *Ludowa historia Polski: Historia wyzysku i oporu. Mitologia panowania* (WAB, 2020), p. 21–22. For the thesis that ethnic and social conflicts on Ukrainian lands in the modern era were largely related to the struggle for land, see: Daniel Beauvois, *La bataille de la terre en Ukraine, 1863–1914: Les Polonais et les conflits socio-ethniques* (Presses Universitaires du Septentrion, 1993); Slawomir Tokarski, *Ethnic Conflict and Economic Development: Jews in Galician Agriculture 1868–1914* (TRIO Press, 2003). I also cite the article: '"Marching towards starvation": UN Warns of Hell on Earth if Ukraine War Goes On', *Guardian*, 17 June 2022. The Pew opinion poll showing Ukraine as the least anti-Semitic of the post–communist countries can be found here: pewresearch.org/fact-tank/2018/03/28/most-poles-accept-jews-as-fellow-citizen s-and-neighbors-but-a-minority-do-not.

Chapter 3: Cossack Ukraine

This chapter relies primarily on the works of three leading specialists on Cossack history: Zenon Kohut, *Russian Centralism and Ukrainian Autonomy: Imperial Absorption of the Hetmanate, 1760s–1830s* (Harvard University Press, 1989); *Korinnia identychnosti: Studiï z rann'omodernoï ta modernoï istoriï Ukraïny* (Krytyka, 2004); Serhiy Plokhy, *The Cossacks and Religion in Early Modern Ukraine* (Oxford University Press, 2001) and Frank Sysyn (his numerous articles, unfortunately, have not yet been published in a separate collection).

On the expectations of the end of the world in 1492 in the Rus lands, see: Michael

Flier, 'Till the End of Time: The Apocalypse in Russian Historical Experience Before 1500' in Valerie A. Kivelson and Robert H. Greene (eds.), *Orthodox Russia: Studies in Belief and Practice* (Pennsylvania State University Press, 2003), p. 149. The quote about the West arriving in Polish garb comes from *Ševčenko*, op. cit., pp.3–4. On the geography of the Cossacks' origin: Susanne Luber, *Die Herkunft von Zaporoger Kosacken des 17. Jahrhunderts nach Personennamen* (Harrassowitz in Komm, 1983), p.108–109. On Bohdan Khmelnytsky's uprising as a revolution, see: Frank E. Sysyn, 'War der Chmel'nyćkyj-Aufstand eine Revolution? Eine Characteristik der 'großen ukrainischen Revolte' und der Bildung des kosakischen Het'manstaates', *Jahrbücher für Geschichte Osteuropas*, Neue Folge, Bd. 43, H. 1 (1995), pp. 1–18. On an alliance between the Old Believers and the Don Cossacks as a possibility for the emergence of a Don nation, see: Geoffrey Hosking, *Russia: People and Empire, 1552–1917* (Fontana, 1997). On Mazepa's uprising in a comparative context: Orest Subtelny, *The Mazepists: Ukrainian Separatism in the Early Eighteenth Century* (Columbia University Press, 1981). On Mazepa as a modernizer: Vasyl' Kononenko, *Modernizatsiia Het'manshchyny: proekty kozats'koï administratsiï* 1687–1764 (Institute of History of Ukraine, NAS of Ukraine, 2017).

Interlude: A Brief History of Ukrainian Song

On the compromise between two views on the emergence of nations: 'We Study Empires as We Do Dinosaurs: Nations, Nationalism, and Empire in a Critical Perspective', interview with Benedict Anderson, *Ab Imperio*, 3/2003, pp. 57–73. On the term 'Ukraine' in Ukrainian folk songs: George Luckyj, *'Rozdumy nad slovom 'Ukraïna' u narodnykh pisniakh', Suchasnist'*, 1993, 8, pp. 117–122. On Cossack *dumas* and their role in the kobzar repertoire: Natalie Kononenko, *Ukrainian Minstrels: ... and the Blind Shall Sing* (M. E. Sharpe, 1998). On the 'energy of self–identification' in the folklore of Ukrainian ostarbeiters, see: K. Chistov, *Preodolenie rabstva. Fol'klor i iazyk ostarbajterov, 1942–1944* (1998), pp. 9–51.

Chapter 4: The Long Nineteenth Century

On the Table of Nations, see: Franz K. Stanzel's *Europäer: ein imagologischer Essay* (Winter, 1997). In this chapter, I have deliberately ignored a recent global history of the nineteenth century, in part because its author has completely ignored the history of Ukraine: Jürgen Osterhammel, *The Transformation of the World: A Global History of the Nineteenth Century* (Princeton University Press, 2014). Instead, I develop and continue the theses of my book *Ivan Franko and His Community* (Academic Studies Press, 2019). This book contains a detailed bibliography. I would like to highlight a few important articles: Orest Pelech, 'The State and the Ukrainian Triumvirate in the Russian Empire, 1831–47'; Bohdan Krawchenko (ed.) *Ukrainian Past, Ukrainian Present* (Palgrave Macmillan, 1992), pp. 1–17; Patricia Herlihy, 'Ukrainian Cities in the Nineteenth Century', *Rethinking Ukrainian History* (CIUS Press, 1981), pp. 135–155; Stephen Velychenko, 'Identities, Loyalties and Service in Imperial Russia: Who Administered the Borderlands?' *The Russian Review*, 1995, 2:188–208 When discussing the Ukrainian national revival and the geopolitical orientations of the Ukrainian elite, I have relied on perspectives from classical works: Miroslav Hroch, *Social Preconditions of National Revival in Europe: A Comparative Analysis of the Social Composition of Patriotic Groups Among the Smaller European Nations* (Columbia University Press, 2000); Albert O. Hirschman, *Exit, Voice, and Loyalty* (Harvard University Press, 1970). On the Russian imperial concept of 'Orthodoxy, Autocracy, Nationality' as a response to the French Revolutionary slogan of 'Liberty, Equality, Fraternity', see: Andrei Zorin's *By Fables*

Alone: Literature and State Ideology in Late-Eighteenth and Early-Nineteenth Century Russia (Academic Studies Press, 2014). The idea that the universal conflict between political and economic modernization reached extreme levels in the Russian Empire can be found in Theodore H. Friedgut, *Iuzovka and Revolution. Vol. 1. Life and Work in Russia's Donbass, 1869–1924* (Princeton University Press, 1989). Lenin's 'Critical Remarks on the National Question' can be found here: marx2mao.com/Lenin/CRNQ13.html.

Interlude: A Brief History of the Ukrainian Borderland

The most complete discussion of the topic of the borderlands in Ukrainian history can be found in a dedicated issue (N 18/2011) of the journal *Ukraina Moderna* titled 'Pohranychchia – okrainy – peryferii.' I also made use of the following works: Alfred J. Rieber, *The Struggle for the Eurasian Borderlands: From the Rise of Early Modern Empires to the End of the First World War* (Cambridge University Press, 2014); Olherd Ipolit Bochkovskii, *Vybrani pratsi ta dokumenty, Tom II* (Moderna, 2018); Holger H. Herwig, op, cit. On the 'Pripet problem' see: A. Filippi, *Pripiatskaia problema: Ocherk operatyvnogo znacheniia Pripiatskoj oblasti dlia voennoi kampanii 1941* (1959).

On mortality in Ukraine and the Western Europe, 1900–2006: E. M. Libanova (ed.), *Smertrnist' naselennia Ukrainy u trudoaktyvnomu vitsi* (Instytut demohraphii ta sotsial'nykh doslidzhen' NAN Ukrainy, 2007), pp. 50-51.

Chapter 5: Ukraine, 1914–45

This chapter is significantly influenced by the work of two historians, Mark von Hagen and Andrea Graziosi. Mark von Hagen was a historian of the revolution. Andrea Graziosi drew attention to the role of the peasant question in the rise and evolution of the Soviet regime – see primarily his book, *The Great Soviet Peasant War: Bolsheviks and Peasants, 1917–1933* (Harvard University Press, 1996). He also presented the most convincing, in my opinion, interpretation of the Holodomor: 'The Soviet 1931–33 Famines and the Ukrainian Holodomor: Is A New Interpretation Possible, What Would Its Consequences Be?', Harvard Ukrainian Studies, 2004–2005, 1/4; 97–115. For his comparison of the Ukrainian and Mexican revolutions, see: Graziosi, *Stalinism, Collectivization and the Great Famine* (Ukrainian Studies Fund, 2009), p. 181.

On the First World War as the most massive invasion of modernity into the traditional world of Eastern Europe, see: Leonid Heretz, *Russia on the Eve of Modernity: Popular Religion and Traditional Culture Under the Last Tsars* (Cambridge University Press, 2008). On the central importance of Ukraine in the First and Second World Wars, see: Dominic Lieven, *Towards the Flame: Empire, War and the End of Tsarist Russia* (Allen Lane, 2015); Timothy Snyder, 'Germany's Historical Responsibility to Ukraine', transcript available here: marieluisebeck.de/artikel/20-06-2017/timothy-snyder-germanys-historical-responsibility-ukraine. Timothy Snyder's book *Bloodlands: Europe Between Hitler and Stalin* (Basic Books, 2010) is an absolute must-read for anyone who wants to understand what was done to and around Ukraine in the 1930s and 1940s. On the Russian Whites as a liberal movement and their attitude towards Ukraine, see: Anna Procyk, *Russian Nationalism and Ukraine: The Nationality Policy of the Volunteer Army during the Civil War* (CIUS Press, 1995); Christopher Lazarski, *The Lost Opportunity: Attempts at Unification of the Anti–Bolsheviks, 1917–1919: Moscow, Kiev, Jassy, Odessa* (University Press of America, 2008). On anti-Jewish pogroms in Ukraine during the revolution, see: Henry Abramson, *A Prayer for the Government: Ukrainians and Jews in Revolutionary Times, 1917–1920* (Cambridge University Press, 1999). On the evolution of Christian Rakovsky's attitude to the Ukrainian question, see: Pierre Broué, *Rakovsky ou la Révolution dans tous les pays* (Fayard, 1996). For the same evolution of Nestor Makhno, see: Frank Sysyn, 'Nestor Makhno and the Ukrainian Revolution', in Taras Hunczak (ed.), *The Ukraine, 1917–1921: A Study in Revolution* (Cambridge University Press, 1977), pp. 295–304. The anecdote about the fire of the world revolution comes from the diaries of Serhiy Yefremov, *Shchodennyky, 1923–1929* (1997), p. 586. Shulgin's comments on language use in Kyiv comes from V. V. Shulgin', Tri stolitsy (Sovremennik, 1991), p. 125. On the attitudes of Ukrainian youth to modern culture, see: Hryhorii Kostiuk, *Zustrichi i proshchannia: Spohady* (CIUS Press, 1987), book 1, p. 184. For the quote from Vernadsky, see: V. I. Vernadsky. *Dnevniki 1917–1921: oktiabr' 1917–yanvar' 1920* (Naukova Dumka, 1994), p. 269. For the story of Paul Wittgenstein in Kharkiv, see: Alexander Waugh, *The House of Wittgenstein: A Family at War* (Bloomsbury, 2008). For the best overview of the transformation of the Ukrainian village in the 1920s, see: Volodymyr Kalinichenko, *Selians'ke hospodarstvo Ukraïny v period nepu: Istoryko–ekonomichne doslidzhennia* (Osnova, 1997). On the national dimension of peasant uprisings against Stalinist collectivisation in Ukraine: Lynne Viola, *Peasant Rebels Under Stalin: Collectivization and the Culture of Peasant Resistance* (Oxford University Press, 1996), p. 120. On the 'Polish factor' see: Timothy Snyder, *Sketches from a Secret War: A Polish Artist's Mission to Liberate Soviet Ukraine* (Yale University Press, 2005). For a general overview of interwar Western Ukraine: John–Paul Himka, 'Western Ukraine Between the Wars', Canadian Slavonic Papers/Revue Canadienne des Slavistes, 1992, 4: 391–412. The best overview of the social roots of Ukrainian nationalism is Zenon Pelens'kii's 'Mizh dvoma konechnostiamy. Prychynok do sotsiolohiï ukraïnskoho natsional'no–vyzvolnoho revoliutsiinoho rukhu v Zakhidnii Ukraïni mizh oboma svitovymy viinamy' in *Yevhen Konovalets ta yoho doba.* (1974), pp. 502–514. The best overview of its ideology is Myroslav Shkandrij, *Ukrainian Nationalism. Politics, Ideology, and Literature, 1929–1956* (Yale University Press, 2015). I've cited István Deák from István Deák, *Essays on Hitler's Europe* (University of Nebraska Press, 2001), pp. 92–93. I tell the story of Yevgeny Khaldei based on Tatyana Tolstaya, 'Missing Persons', *New York Review of Books*, 15 January 1998 and Ernst Volland, 'Die Flagge des Sieges' in Jewgeni Chaldej, *Der bedeutende Augenblick* (Neuer Europa Verlag, 2009), pp. 112–123. Edgar Snow is quoted in: Bohdan Krawchenko, *Social Change and National Consciousness in Twentieth-Century Ukraine* (Macmillan, 1985), p. 123. Comparison of repressions in the Western and German occupation zones of the former interwar Poland and the Soviet Union as a spoiler state: Jan T. Gross, *Revolution from Abroad: The Soviet Conquest of Poland's Western Ukraine and Western Belorussia* (Princeton University Press, 1988). About Hitler and his plans for Ukraine see: Alexander Dallin, *German Rule in Russia 1941–1945: A Study of Occupation Policies* (Macmillan, 1957), p. 160–161 and *Hitler's Secret Conversations: His Private Thoughts and Plans in His Own Words, 1941–1944* – with an Introductory Essay on the Mind of Adolf Hitler by H.R. Trevor–Roper (Farrar Straus, 1953), pp. 33, 68, 577. For Djilas' memories of wartime Ukraine see: Milovan Djilas, *Conversations with Stalin* (Penguin Books, 1962), pp. 46–49.

A note regarding calendars: until February 1918, Russia utilised the Julian calendar, which was at that time thirteen days behind the Gregorian calendar in use throughout Europe. This leads to a situation in which the 1917 Revolutions, known as the February and October Revolutions, actually took place in March and November according to the new calendar. Thus the 'Great October Revolution' was celebrated on 7 November in the Soviet Union. The original dates are marked as OS (Old Style).

Interlude: A Brief History of Violence

My general inspiration in writing this text was the book: Christian Gerlach, *Extremely Violent Societies: Mass Violence in the Twentieth–Century World* (Cambridge University Press, 2010). The following works are cited in the text: Olena Betlii, 'Bil'shovytskyi teror u Kyievi u sichni–liutomu 1918 r.: zhertvy i pamiat', *Kraieznavstvo*, 2018, 3, p. 178–195; Vladyslav Verstiuk, *Makhnovshchyna; Selianskii povstanskii rukh na Ukraini* (1918–1921) Naukova Dumka, 1991); V. Serhiichuk, *Pohromy v Ukraini: 1914–1920. Vid shtuchnykh stereotypiv do hirkoi pravdy, prykhovuvanoi v radianskykh arkhivakh* (Vyd-vo imeni Oleny Telihy, 1998); Grzegorz Gauden, Lwów – kres iluzji. Opowieść o pogromie listopadowym 1918 (Universitas, 2019); Natalya Kovalyova, Seliany, pomyshchyky i derzhava: konflikty interesiv.'Ahrarna revoliutsiia v Ukraini 1920–1922 (Lira, 2016); Fedir Morhun, Stalinsko–hitlerivskyi henotsyd ukrainskoho narodu. Fakty i naslidky. second edition (Dyvosvit, 2008); Roman Vysotskyi (ed.), Patsyfikatsiia Galychyny 1930 roku. Dokumenty. Tom 1. (Vyd-va UKU, 2019); Zvi Gitelman, *A Century of Ambivalence.The Jews of Russia and the Soviet Union, 1881 to the Present* (London, 1988); Marc Jansen and Nikita Petrov, *Stalin's Loyal Executioner: People's Commissar Nikolai Ezhov, 1895–1940* (Stanford, 2002); "Arestovannye drug druga izbivali, peli i plyasali. Antologia chekistskikh isdevatel'stv nad zakiuchennymi. K 80-litiyu umanskogo dela", *Novaya Gazeta*, No. 55, 24.05, 2019, novayagazeta.ru/articles/2019/05/22/80619-arestovannye-drug-druga-izbivali-peli-i-plyasali; David Kahane, *Lvov Ghetto Diary* (Amherst, 1990); Mykola Androshchuk, "Voronii" *Zapysky povstantsia*, Litopys UPA , book 13), (Toronto–Lviv, 2011); Alexander Gogun, *Stalin's Commandos: Ukrainian Partisan Forces on the Eastern Front* (London, 2015); Oleksandr Dovzhenko, *Zacharovana Desna Opovidannia. Shchodennyk (1941–1956)* (Dnipro, 2001).

Chapter 6: Postwar Ukraine

On the distinctive characteristics of Soviet historical policy on the Holocaust in Soviet Ukraine, see: Zvi Gitelman, 'Soviet Reactions to the Holocaust, 1945–1991' in L. Dobroszycki and J. S. Gurock (eds.) *The Holocaust in the Soviet Union: Studies and Sources on the Destruction of the Jews in the Nazi-Occupied Territories of the USSR, 1941–1945*, (Routledge, 1993), pp. 3, 9–11. I quote Nikolai Nikulin from his *Vospominaniia o voine* (Izd-vo Gos. Ermitazha, 2008). Complaints about the 'khokhol yoke' at the top of the Soviet government come from Georg Miasnikov, *Stranitsy iz dnevnika (1964–1992)* (Institut natsional'nykh problem obrazovania, 2008), pp. 409, 557. Much has been written about the 'Sixties Group'. For the most recent work in English, see: Simone Attilio Bellezza, *The Shore of Expectations: A Cultural Study of the Shistdesiatnyky* (CIUS, 2019). Regarding changes in values in Soviet society, see: William M. Reisinger, Arthur H. Miller, Vicki L. Hesli, and Kristen Hill Maher, 'Political Values in Russia, Ukraine and Lithuania: Sources and Implications for Democracy', *British Journal of Political Science*, 1994, 2, pp. 183–223. On the role of the Ukrainian question in the suppression of the Prague Spring of 1968 and on Galicia and Donbas as weak links of the Soviet regime in Ukraine, see: Mark Kramer, 'Ukraine and the Soviet–Czechoslovak Crisis of 1968: New Evidence from the Ukrainian Archives', *Cold War International History Project Bulletin*, 14/15, pp 273–368. On Petro Shelest and Volodymyr Shcherbytsky, see the biographies: *Yuri Shapoval, Partiinii 'natsionalist': Paradoksy Petra Shelesta* by Yuri Shapoval (Vydavnytstvo Anetty Antonenko, 2020) and *Volodymyr Shcherbytsky. Polityk za obstavyn chasu* by Yuri Shapoval and Oleksandr Yakubets (Instityut Krytyky, 2019).

On the Chernobyl disaster, see: Serhii Plokhy, *Chernobyl: The History of a Nuclear Catastrophe* (Basic Books, 2018). About the labour movement in Donbas, see: A. M. Rusnachenko. *Probudzhennia: robitnychyi rukh na Ukraïni v 1989–1993* (KM Academia, 1995); Lewis H. Siegelbaum, Daniel J. Walkowitz, *Workers of the Donbass Speak: Survival and Identity in the New Ukraine, 1989–1992* (State University of New York Press, 1995). I borrowed the idea 'non-civil revolution' from Stephen Kotkin and Jan T. Gross, *Uncivil Society: 1989 and the Implosion of the Communist Establishment* (Modern Library, 2010). On the union of Galicia, Kyiv and Donbas as a key element in the achievement of Ukrainian independence, see: Andreas Wittkowsky, *Fünf Jahre ohne Plan: Die Ukraine 1991–96. Nationalstaatsbildung, Wirtschaft und Eliten* (Lit, 1998). Jerzy Giedroyc's letter to Czesław Miłosz is quoted from: *Nowa Europa Wschodnia*, 3–4 (2011). Konstantin Paustovsky's words are quoted from: Aleksandr Wat, *Mój wiek. Pamiętnik mówiony. Opracowanie naukowe.* T.1 (Universitas, 2011), p. 382. About the circumstances of Jerzy Gedroyc's statement see Janusz Korek, *Paradoksy paryskiej 'Kultury': ewolucja myśli politycznej w latach 1947–1980* (Almqvist & Wiksell International, 1998). Adam Michnik described his family story to me. Regarding Harvard: Oleksandr Avramchuk, *Pisząc historię narodu 'niehistorycznego'. Powstanie studiów ukraińskich i polsko–ukraiński dialog historyczny w USA (1939–1991). Ph.D. dissertation* (Warsaw, 2020). Quote from Ernest Gellner: Ernest Gellner, *Nations and Nationalism* (Wiley-Blackwell, 1983), p. 124.

Interlude: A Brief History of the Ukrainian Language

The best histories of the Ukrainian language are: George Y. Shevelov, 'Evolution of the Ukrainian Literary Language', *Rethinking Ukrainian History*, pp. 216–231; Michael Moser, *New Contributions to the History of the Ukrainian Language* (University of Alberta Press, 2016). Regarding the idea that the Russian government systematically repressed all three of the languages that developed on the Ukrainian lands – the Ukrainian recension of Church Slavonic, along with the secular Rus and Ukrainian literary languages, see Andrii Danylenko and Halyna Naienko, 'Linguistic russification in Russian Ukraine: Languages, imperial models, and policies', *Russian Linguistics*, 2019, 43 (1): 19–39. On the link between genocide and language repression see Andrea Graziosi and Frank E. Sysyn (eds.), *Genocide: the Power and Problems of a Concept* (McGill-Queen's University Press, 2022). I quote Sergey Loika's words about the Donbas airport from the article 'Zapreshchennyj efir "Ekha Moskvy"' 31 October 2014. The idea that there are no democracies with Russian as an official language comes from Tomasz Kamusella's article 'World Languages and Democracy', *Ukraïna moderna*, 28 January 2002, uamoderna.com/war/russian-and-democracy.

Instead of a Conclusion: Independent Ukraine

Regarding the emergence of an independent Ukraine as one of the three most significant European events of the twentieth century, see Zbigniew Brzezinski: 'Ultimately Ukrainian independence can only be built and sustained by the Ukrainian people themselves.' *Den'*. 31 March 1998, day.kyiv.ua/en/article/personality/zbigniew-brzezinski-ultimately-ukrainian-independence-can-only-be-built-and. For Deutsche Bank's analysis of the economic potential of the Soviet Republics see: *The Soviet Union at the Crossroads: Facts and Figures on the Soviet Republics* (Deutsche Bank, 1990). For predictions of the collapse and possible end of independent Ukraine: D Williams and R. J. Smith, 'US Intelligence Sees Economic Flight Leading to Breakup of Ukraine', *Washington Post*, 25 January 1994, p. A 7;

'The birth and possible death of a country', *The Economist*, 331, 7862 (5 July 1994). I cite Dmitrii Furman from the article, 'Ukraina i my. Natsional'noe samosoznanie i politicheskoe razvitie', *Svobodnaia mysl'*, 1995, 1, p. 70. Regarding the discussion between Russian democrats in 1991 about what to do with Ukraine: Aleksandr Tsipko 'Stalin, holodomor i druzhba narodov', *Nezavisimaia*, 16 December 2008. Regarding the theory of 'two Ukraines' and the discussion around it, in particular Roman Szporluk's thoughts on the Centre, see Szporluk 'Why Ukrainians Are Ukrainians. A Commentary on Mykola Riabchuk's "Ukraine: One State, two Countries?"', *Eurozine*, 12 September 2002. Changes in Ukrainian regionalism can be seen in: *Ukraine. Urbanization Review*, World Bank, International Bank for Reconstruction and Development, 2015. On support for the Euromaidan on social media see: 'Nova politychna real'nist' Ukraïny', see: statistika.in.ua/vk/pislyamaidan. On 2019 as a year of revolutions, see Robin Wright, 'The Story of 2019: Protests in Every Corner of the Globe', *New Yorker*, 30 December 2019. Information about Chile's protests came from the same issue. On the positive aspects of nationalism, see Anne Applebaum, 'Nationalism Is Exactly What Ukraine Needs. Democracy fails when citizens don't believe their country is worth fighting for', *The New Republic*, 13 May 2014. On Ukraine's losses after the first year of war: 'Sotsial'no-ekonomichne samopochuttia hromadian Ukraïny: pidsumky roku viiny' (February–March 2023), razumkov.org.ua/napriamky/sotsiologichni-doslidzhennia/sotsialnoekonomichne-samopochuttia-gromadian-ukrainy-pidsumky-roku-viiny-liutyi-berezen-2023r. Myla Rukhman, 'Ad na zemle: Rossiia tvorit v Ukraine ekologicheskuiu katastrofu, pervye dannye uzhasaiut, *Detali*, 27 December 2022; Thomas L. Friedman, 'Putin's War Is a Crime Against the Planet', *New York Times*, 27 September 2022. For statistics on contemporary wars, specifically the fact that 1992 had the greatest number of wars, see: Meredith Reid Sarkees and Frank Whelon Wayman, eds., *Resort to War, 1816–2007* (CQ Press, 2010). Timothy Ash's words about the dual meaning of the Ukrainian word 'volya' can be found in Timothy G. Ash, 'Ukraine in Our Future', *New York Review of Books*, 23 February 2023.

ABOUT THE AUTHOR

Yaroslav Hrytsak is a Ukrainian historian and public intellectual. Professor of the Ukrainian Catholic University and Honorary Professor of the National University of Kyiv-Mohyla Academy, Professor Hrytsak has taught at Columbia and Harvard Universities and was a guest lecturer at the Central European University in Budapest. He is the author of many history books, including several bestsellers, and is the recipient of numerous national and international awards. He has written opinion pieces for many publications including *The Times*, the *New York Times* and *Time* magazine. Sphere also publishes *A Ukrainian Christmas*, written with Nadiyka Gerbish.